THE CLICK THAT TEACHES
RIDING WITH THE CLICKER

By Alexandra Kurland

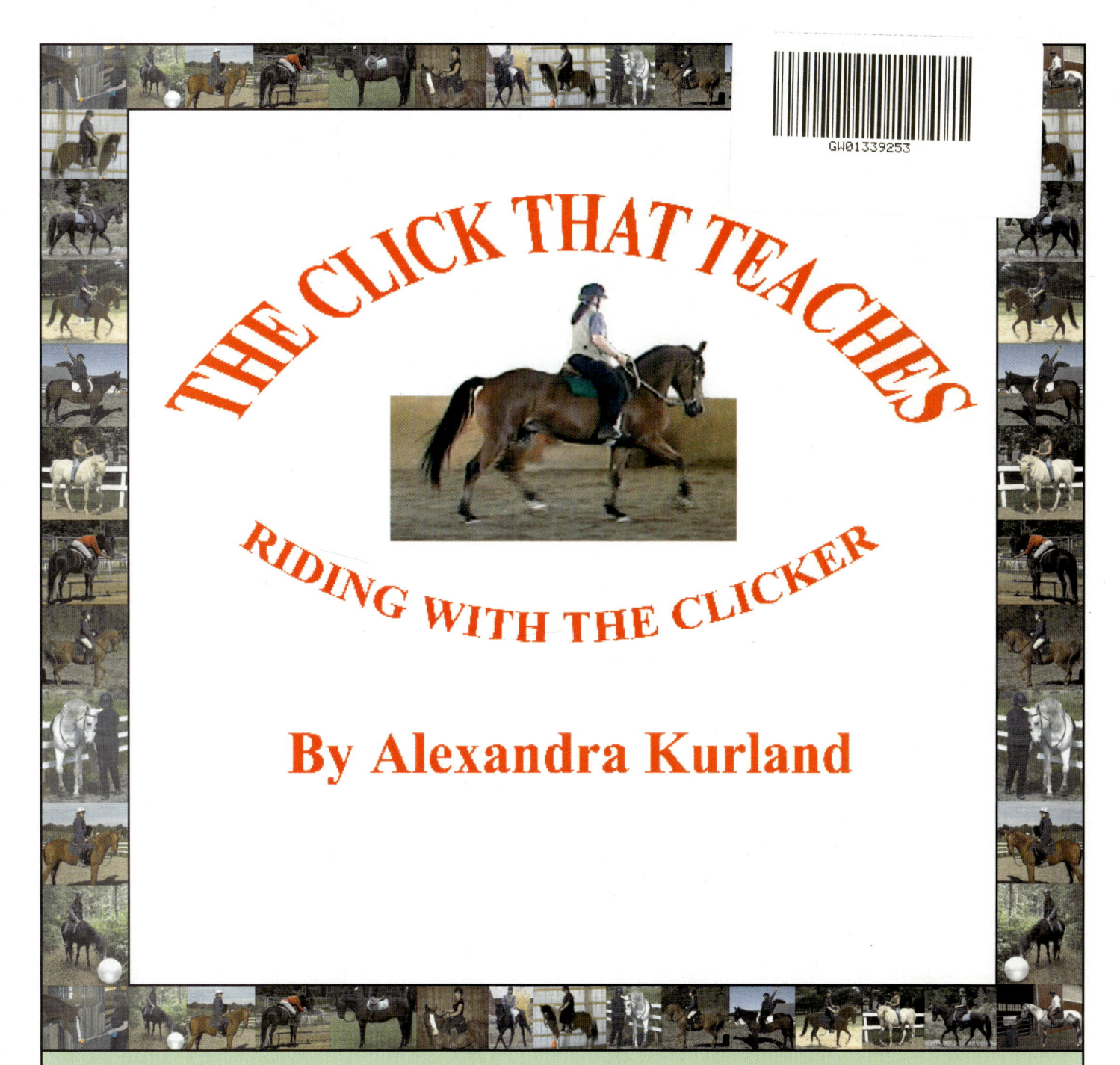

"Magic is a different horse now because of clicker training. People who "knew him when" don't even recognize him as the same horse. His face, eyes and body look different, reflecting his transformation. Magic was afraid of the world and self-protective. I was his fifth home by age seven. Clicker training transformed his mind, body and spirit. Magic is a great example of the healing power of the clicker.

The level of peace, love, joy, and communication that develops with equine clicker training is something I cherish. Sometimes Magic and I go to a place together in our hearts where laughter, joy and oneness fill us. We forget we are different species. We become two Beings sharing creativity, play, music and dance together."

Debra Olson Daniels, describing about her Tennessee walker, Magic, one of the many clicker stars you will meet in this book.

For Robin and Peregrine, my riding teachers.

Clicking With Your Horse: Riding with the Clicker
Copyright © 2005 Alexandra Kurland

All right reserved. No part of this book may be reproduced or transmitted in any form or by any means, electronic or mechanical, including photocopying, recording, or by any information storage and retrieval systems, without permission in writing from The Clicker Center LLC, with the exception of brief excerpts used in published reviews.

Alexandra Kurland and The Clicker Center, LLC shall have neither the liability nor the responsibility to any person or entity with respect to any loss or damage caused or alleged to be caused directly or indirectly by the information contained in this book, or in any of the "The Click That Teaches" books and videos.

The author has made efforts to obtain releases from all persons appearing in the photographs used in this book and from all photographers. In some cases, however, the persons and photographers identities and whereabouts were unknown. Should any names become available, they will be credited in future editions, assuming permission is granted.

Published by The Clicker Center LLC
110 Salisbury Rd.
Delmar NY 12054
theclickercenter.com

First Edition
First Printing, July 2005

ISBN 0-9704065-1-7
Printed in the United States of America

Library of Congress Control Number: 2005932411

Contents

PART 1
CLICKER TRAINING BASICS 1

The training goals of this section are to introduce you and your horse to the clicker; to establish polite manners around the food; to build good ground control using exercises that will transfer directly to riding; and to create emotional self-control in your horse.

INTRODUCTION 2

CHAPTER 1
What Is Clicker Training? 3

CHAPTER 2
Getting Started with the Clicker 7

CHAPTER 3
Foundation Lessons 13

CHAPTER 4
But What About . . . ?:
More Clicker Questions 15

CHAPTER 5
The Principles of Training 19

CHAPTER 6
Food! 29

CHAPTER 7
The Language of Operant Conditioning 33

CHAPTER 8
Manners, Manners, and More Manners 37

CHAPTER 9
Variable Reinforcement Schedules 45

CHAPTER 10
Stimulus Control: Putting Behavior on Cue 51

PART 2
BEFORE YOU RIDE 55

In this section you'll see how training works in the real world. Training a horse is not a matter of following "cook book" recipes, but of being creative and responsive to each individual. As you see how I prepared my young horse, Robin, for riding, you'll learn strategies that will help you develop a super relationship with your own horse.

CHAPTER 11
Holistic Horse Training: Developing the Physical, Mental, and Emotional Fitness of Your Horse 57

CHAPTER 12
Trick Training: Enhancing the Emotional Development of your Horse 61

CHAPTER 13
Breaking the Punishment Cycle:
Temper Tantrums and Time Outs 69

CHAPTER 14
The Time It Takes:
Building Duration Into Behavior 75

Chapter 15
First Rides 79

PART 3
RIDING WITH THE CLICKER 87

Safety, safety, safety. Safety always comes first. The lessons in this chapter give you the tools you need to stop bolting, bucking, spooking, and rearing: all the major issues that take the fun out of riding. Before you proceed very far with your riding, you want to have these lessons working well with your horse.

CHAPTER 16
Riding Basics:
Using the Clicker Under Saddle 89

Contents

CHAPTER 17
Asking Questions — 99

CHAPTER 18
Single–Rein Riding meets Dressage: — 103
Going on the Bit

CHAPTER 19
The Boxer versus the Brain Surgeon: — 111
Learning The Mechanics of Single Rein Riding

CHAPTER 20
Head Lowering: — 123
Using the "Calm Down" Cue from the Saddle

CHAPTER 21
Flipping the Hips: — 129
Power Brakes for Power Steering

PART 4 — 137
TRAINING EXERCISES FOR THE RIDER

Riding excellence is built on a foundation of body awareness. These exercises allow you to become a "centaur", exploring your horse's balance via the "t'ai chi walk".

CHAPTER 22
The Four Points on the Bottom of Your Feet — 139

CHAPTER 23
Swimming, Flying, and Flexibility — 143

CHAPTER 24
T'ai Chi, Anyone? — 147

PART 5 — 151
SINGLE-REIN RIDING AND THE BUILDING BLOCKS OF EXCELLENCE

In this section you'll learn how to transform the safety lessons of Section 3 into lateral work—the building block for advanced performance. We'll be focusing first on "how" your horse moves, then we'll combine that with "where". At the end of this section, you'll be riding patterns that are the foundation of all performance work.

CHAPTER 25
The "Why Would You Leave Me? Game: — 153
Developing Softness and Balance

CHAPTER 26
Connecting the Feet: Three-Flip-Three — 161

CHAPTER 27
Soundness, Expectations, and Problem-Solving — 169

CHAPTER 28
Collection: Hip–Shoulder–Shoulder — 173

CHAPTER 29
Gait Development — 179

CHAPTER 30
The Transition to Where: — 187
Posts, Hotwalkers, and Riding in Circles

CHAPTER 31
Putting Humpty Dumpty Together Again: — 191
Three Training Turns

PART 6 — 207
RIDING FOR PERFORMANCE

This final section shows you how to connect all the training steps to create a "one in ten million" horse. Enjoy the ride!

CHAPTER 32
Riding on Two Reins: — 209
Engagement and the 300 Peck Pigeons

CHAPTER 33
Lateral Work: Shoulder–In — 215

CHAPTER 34
Using Your Training Tools in the Real World: — 223
Riding Out with a Horse Named Fig

CHAPTER 35
Piaffe — 229

PART 1
CLICKER TRAINING BASICS

Part 1 covers clicker training fundamentals. I'll describe what clicker training is, give you a brief clicker-training history lesson and explain how to introduce clicker training to your horse.

I'll answer some of the most frequently asked questions in clicker training, and I'll show you how to structure your training around ten key training principles. You'll learn how to prepare your horse for riding by first establishing good ground control manners and a calm attitude.

MAIN LESSONS COVERED:

1.) Targeting: Introduces your horse to the clicker.

2.) Happy Faces: Click when your horse puts his ears forward. This lesson conditions a pleasant expression into your clicker foundation and makes you more aware of your horse's body language and emotions.

3.) Backing: Combines the clicker with pressure and release of pressure. Allows you to maintain safe boundaries around your space.

4.) Head Lowering: Teaches your horse to drop his head to the ground. Associates feelings of safety and calmness with the clicker – gives you a "security blanket" behavior to return to any time your horse becomes agitated.

5.) The "Pose": A beginning step towards advanced performance work.

6.) "The Growns Are Talking, Please Don't Interrupt" Lesson: teaches your horse polite manners around food – builds emotional control.

The training goals of this section are to aquaint you and your horse with the clicker; to establish polite manners around food; to build good ground control using exercises that will transfer directly to riding; and to create emotional self-control in your horse.

INTRODUCTION

Clicker–Trained Horses

Clicker-trained horses don't just walk up to mailboxes, they open them up and deliver the mail.

CLICKER HORSES

All you want your horse to do is to walk flat-footed past the mailbox at the corner of the driveway. That's all. It's a simple thing. It's the same mailbox you went past yesterday, and the day before, and the day before that. It's the same mailbox he stands next to at the corner of his paddock. All you want him to do is just walk past it calmly. Instead he has to scoot by like it's some fire-breathing dragon.

Sound familiar? This may not be your horse, but I bet you've known one just like him. Spooking isn't his only problem. He's also the most stubborn horse you've ever met. You can't get him to go down to the far end of the arena. He just slams on the brakes and refuses to move. If you try to make him, he backs twenty feet into the fence. You get so mad at him that you just want to scream!

If this is how your horse makes you feel; if you find yourself calling him names, getting mad, feeling frustrated, then read on. This may be the perfect book for you. So many of us have been trained to look at what we don't want. Our horse spooks. We react to the spook. Our horse bites at us, we punish the biting. The result is we often end up with even more of the very behavior we don't like. Clicker training changes that. It turns the world inside out. Instead of staring straight in the face of all the things you don't like about your horse, it shifts your focus onto the good things he's doing.

Once you've experienced a clicker-trained horse, you won't ever want to go back. Clicker-trained horses are bright-eyed, eager learners. They greet you with a whinny that says they can hardly wait for the day's work to begin. Lessons turn into play. Grumpiness into laughter. You can't help but smile when you are around a clicker-trained horse. They bring out the very best in people. And clicker-training helps bring out the very best in them.

CHAPTER 1
What Is Clicker Training?

In this chapter I'll introduce you to the basic concept of clicker training.

ELEVATOR SPEECHES
"So what exactly is clicker training?"

The woman standing across from me has picked up a clicker and is staring at it in a puzzled way. At her elbow are two children having a clicking contest. They are clicking the clickers as fast as they can at each other. I am sure their mother is thinking the last thing she would want in her barn is one of these infernal noise makers.

We are at the Equine Affaire™, a huge horse expo. I am at the clicker training booth, and I have about thirty seconds to give the "elevator speech" – to say something that will spark her interest and get her to ask the next question and the next. Experience has taught me what doesn't work. Telling her that clicker training traces it's origins back to marine mammal training doesn't mean anything to most horse people. They don't make the connection between a dolphin swimming in a pool of water eating fish, and the horse they are going to ride.

It also doesn't mean anything to say that clicker training uses positive reinforcement. Most people will tell you they already use positive reinforcement with their horses. Instead I want to share with her the sparkle in the horse's eye, the aliveness, the awakening of intelligence that comes with clicker training. How do I make this more than just words?

I step out around the table to the front of the booth. "Most horse training," I explain, "is based on pressure and release of pressure." I put my hand on her shoulder. She looks mildly puzzled. So I go on to explain that my hand on her shoulder is not painful, but if I left it there long enough it would become annoying. It's a mild aversive which I have introduced into her experience. If she were to take a step back, she might discover that I'd take my hand away.

The woman nods her head indicating her understanding, but she does not move. I have done this demonstration many times before, and I know this is normal. I leave my hand on her shoulder, waiting. As I go on talking about negative reinforcement, almost imperceptibly I feel her weight shift back. Instantly I remove my hand. And almost as quickly I put it back again. I continue to explain that with negative reinforcement she can get rid of the annoying stimulus by changing her behavior: in this case shifting her weight back. Again there's no initial response, then comes that tiny shift of balance. I remove my hand, and just as quickly replace it.

This time the change comes a little faster. It is a little more definite, but still it is only a small shift of weight. I go on talking about negative reinforcement. I explain that when I am taking away something she doesn't want, i.e. the pressure, I don't have a timing problem. I can remove my hand the instant I feel her weight shift so she knows exactly what she has to do to get me to remove the unwanted stimulus.

"But now suppose I do something different," I say to her as I feel

---

CLICKER TRAINING DEFINED

Clicker training refers to a new method of teaching animals using a "yes answer" signal. The signal tells your horse when he has done something right. It is immediately followed by a reward, something your horse will actively work for.

The "click" in clicker training refers to the sound made by a small plastic noisemaker similar to a child's toy cricket but designed to be much more durable.

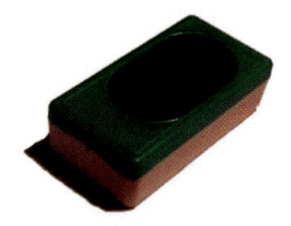

The Clicker.

The Click That Teaches: Riding With The Clicker

the expected weight shift and instantly remove my hand. "Suppose in addition to taking my hand away, I reach over here and tear off a coupon good for fifty dollars off at any booth here at the trade show." I mime the action I'm describing and hand her an imaginary coupon.

And this is the interesting part. Her face lights up. A broad smile flashes across her face. I put my hand back on her shoulder and, instead of a hesitant shift of weight, I get a full step back.

I have done this demo with hundreds of people, and this is the response you get 99% of the time. And remember, it's an *imaginary* coupon. It's not even real, and yet it still gets this response, even from the most skeptical of trade show attendees!

So in clicker training we aren't just taking away something the horse doesn't want. We're giving him something he actively wants to work for. But that raises a timing problem. The reward comes after the fact. I can't deliver that coupon at the exact moment that my training partner shifted her weight back. There's a delay. By the time I've ripped off the imaginary coupon and am handing it over to her, she's doing something else. If she were a horse, I might be giving her the coupon just as she's crowding back into my space or doing some other undesirable behavior. I have to have some way of saying, "That's the moment. That's the reason I'm handing you a goody."

The click is a bridging signal that solves this timing problem. It links the desired behavior with the reward. It makes it more likely that the animal will repeat that behavior in the future in order to get more of the good things he wants. Clicker training becomes a win-win situation for everyone involved. The horse thinks he has us trained. All he has to do is move in a certain way, and, presto!, we hand him goodies! But we know we're really the ones "in charge" because we're picking the behaviors that are being reinforced.

Okay, that's the first question answered: what is the function of the clicker? But now comes the more involved question: what do you do with it? That's what the rest of this book is going to explain. When you see how many words I've crammed into these pages, you'll see why it takes more than a thirty second "elevator speech" to describe clicker training!

CLICKER BASICS

Before I get to the specifics of horse training, let me review clicker basics. It's important to understand that there are two sides to every click: in other words, what happens before the click, and what happens after. What happens immediately before the click is a behavior the *trainer* would like to strengthen. What happens immediately after is an event the *animal* would like to strengthen, such as receiving food. The click unites these two desires.

So, behavior leads to click leads to reinforcement is for me the major defining element of clicker training. How the behavior is triggered is not part of this definition.

Behavior can be triggered in a number of different ways. It can be captured. Here's what that means: suppose your horse lies down to roll in fresh shavings. You click and shower him with treats. He discovers that lying down in your presence is a great predictor of goodies and begins to lie down more often. You've just captured a great trick behavior.

Behavior can also be shaped through successive approximation without using any prompts or lures. I think of this as the "dolphin training" model. You have a dolphin swimming in a tank. You would like the dolphin to swim through a hoop suspended in the center of the pool. Each time the dolphin points its rostrum towards the hoop, you blow a whistle and throw a fish in the water. The high-speed precision of the whistle lets you highlight the exact moment you wish to reinforce, and the dolphin very quickly catches on to the rules of this new game. From its point of view, it is learning how to "train" its humans. Any time it wants a fish all it has to do is point its nose toward the center of the tank!

That's the key to clicker training. From the animal's point of view, it thinks its in charge. This is what creates the enthusiasm and initiative you see in clicker-trained animals. Behavior is not being coerced in a do-it-or-else system. Wrong answers aren't punished, they're simply ignored. What the dolphin is learning is that turning into the center of the tank is a good thing. It produces fish. Getting fish before was a haphazard event. The dolphin could never predict when a fish would appear, but now it has its person well trained!

The handler has a dolphin that chucks down a fish and immediately turns its nose back towards the center of the tank, waiting for the next whistle. And that's when the handler begins to wait just a little longer. Looking at the hoop is no longer good enough. Now the dolphin has to swim toward it. This is what clicker trainers call shaping the behavior.

If the dolphin swims away before the trainer can blow the whistle, nothing happens. The dolphin isn't chased back to try again. It simply doesn't get a fish. It may swim around the tank ignoring its trainer, but odds are it will eventually come back to try again.

Chapter One: What Is Clicker Training?

This is all part of the learning process. Leaving, getting frustrated, quitting, having a temper tantrum, breaching, splashing your trainer from head to foot, none of these behaviors earn the dolphin any fish, but swimming toward the center of the tank does.

The trainer's task is to judge how fast he can increase the requirements—or criteria—for the animal to earn the reward. He wants the dolphin to be successful. He wants it to continue to earn reinforcements, but he also wants to get it over to the hoop.

If he expects too much too soon, the dolphin may get confused or frustrated, and the trainer will see the behavior fall apart. When this happens, he'll go back a step or two in the training and ask for less. He'll gradually rebuild the original behavior, systematically making it more complex; in this example the next step would be rewarding the dolphin for swimming through the hoop. If you've seen dolphins and whales performing at a marine mammal show, you've seen the results of this kind of progressive training.

Shaping behavior gets the animal actively involved in the training process. He isn't just waiting to be told what to do. He's expected to be an active participant in the learning process. Experimentation is encouraged, as is creativity and enthusiasm.

In the horse world we aren't used to thinking about training in this way, so a big part of clicker training is learning to deal with an enthusiastic, eager partner. Since our partner is a thousand pound animal that is both stronger and faster than we are, safety concerns must be part of clicker training. Our horses aren't dolphins in a tank; they are animals we are interacting directly with. That gives us both more safety concerns at the beginning of the process and more training options. We don't have to rely on shaping alone to trigger behaviors. We can use training "shortcuts". Two of the most useful shortcuts are targeting, and pressure and release of pressure.

Targeting introduces a powerful new tool into our training tool box. In targeting your horse orients to an object. Teach your horse to follow that object, and you can get him to walk over or past things he's afraid of. You can get him past scary objects out on the trail, over bridges and streams, and even onto trailers. You can also get him to stand still for grooming and medical procedures by having him station himself at a target. You can use targeting for foot care; for therapeutic stretches; the list goes on and on.

The other shortcut, pressure and release of pressure, is the primary training tool we use with horses: we apply pressure — the horse moves away — we release the pressure. It's a clear communication system. Safety and comfort are the motivators in this case. That's what the horse wants and that's what we are able to restore to him by removing the unwanted pressure. The catch in this system is that in order for safety to be an effective motivator, the horse has to first feel unsafe. Even light pressure becomes a threat. It comes with the understanding that if the horse doesn't respond, the pressure will increase. That's the underlying mechanism of traditional horse training.

It is certainly the case that used well negative reinforcement can control a thousand pounds of flight reaction and instinct. The clicker, however, removes the underlying threat. It transforms pressure into information. The information tells the horse how to get to his reinforcement faster. Combined with the shaping techniques of successive approximation it becomes a powerful addition to any rider's tool box.

Many people have seen good training techniques so badly misused that they are reluctant to include any negative reinforcement in their training. But with horses negative reinforcement is hard to avoid. Riding is all about pressure cues. How those cues are taught makes all the difference in the world to the horse. So, rather than throw the baby out with the bath water and avoid all forms of negative reinforcement, I prefer to learn how to use it well. For me that means in conjunction with the clicker. In a sense you could say all I am doing is sugar coating same-old-same-old by adding a click and a treat on top of the release. I would argue that from the horse's point of view this is better than no sugar coating at all. Which would you rather swallow? The bitter pill, or the one that is sugar coated? I hope that's an easy answer.

But clicker training adds more than that. It encourages people to break training down into small steps. It helps them to look at what they want their animal to do, not the unwanted behavior. It teaches them how to take the fear out of their training by transforming pressure into information only. It opens the door to other training possibilities such as targeting and shaping.

Especially in horse training, I would not want to exclude the use of pressure and release of pressure from the clicker-training tool box. It can be a valuable bridge for first-time clicker trainers. It lets them use techniques they are already familiar with. As they learn clicker basics, they'll reshape these techniques into a more horse-friendly approach.

However, I must say at the outset that you get different results depending upon how you trigger behavior. Sugar coating same-old-same-old with a click and a treat is a more humane training approach

The Click That Teaches: Riding With The Clicker

than the alternative, but used exclusively it does not result in the same kind of interactive, bright-eyed animal that shaping "dolphin style" creates. However, when that bright-eyed animal is a thousand pound horse, that may be too much enthusiasm initially for his owner to handle. So I encourage first-time clicker trainers to use a mix of training methods: shaping, targeting, pressure and release of pressure—all used in conjunction with a click and a treat to mark correct responses. Every complex behavior I train includes some elements which are shaped "dolphin style".

An easy example would be to use standard horse training techniques coupled with the clicker to teach your horse to put his front feet on a mat. You'd then use "dolphin training" to get your horse to pose on the mat with his head in a certain position and his ears forward. Choosing the means by which you trigger behavior is not part of my definition of clicker training. Rather it is the art of its execution. This book will focus on the art of clicker training horses.

MY CLICKER TRAINING ROOTS

My exploration of clicker training began in 1993. That's when I first went out to the barn with a clicker in my hand and a pocket full of treats. My thoroughbred, Peregrine, was laid up with abscesses in both front feet. I had recently learned about clicker training, and it seemed like the perfect solution to keep us both entertained during his recovery.

Peregrine was so lame he couldn't walk, but he could touch his nose to the end of a dressage whip. That simple behavior opened up the world of clicker training to us. As he became more mobile, I asked for other things, simple behaviors at first because that's all he could do, and then gradually more complex work. It was as though I was going back to the very first lessons I had taught him as a foal — basic leading and handling skills. I could almost hear him saying — "Oh, that's what you wanted! Why didn't you say so before?"

Seven weeks later he was back in full work, and I was sitting on a different horse. I had found the missing piece, the communication tool I needed to reach past all the body issues and training blocks to communicate directly with the horse I loved. Clicker training had opened a door into Peregrine's mind. Once I walked through it, there was no going back.

And once I started sharing clicker training with my riding clients, there was no going back there, either. We all recognized what we had, a way of structuring our lives with horses that brought us into harmony with them.

HOW TO USE THIS BOOK

In 1998 *Clicker Training For Your Horse*★ was published. This current book is the second half of that first clicker reference. Originally I wrote both as one text — a soup to nuts reference that would include foal handling, preparing young horses for riding, retraining problem horses, liberty and trick training, ground work, and performance training under saddle. That's a lot of ground to cover so the text was split into two books, and as often happens, instead of the second book following quickly on the heels of the first, there was a bit of a delay—a six year delay to be exact. So some of you may already be familiar with the material covered in that book, and some of you may be coming to this text without any prior clicker-training experience. This book is written for both of you.

If you need a review of clicker basics, you should begin with *Part I: Clicker Training Basics*. If you are working with a young horse that isn't yet started under saddle, or you have a horse with behavioral problems, you'll want to be certain to read *Part 2: Before You Ride*. And if you are just plain eager to get on and ride, then skip ahead to *Part 3: Riding with the Clicker*. You can always go back and read the first two sections as needed later.

For those of you who share my obsession with balance and creating beautiful horses, *Part 5: Single-Rein Riding and the Building Blocks of Excellence* shows you how to break your training down into individual elements. *Part 6: Riding for Performance* shows you how to reassemble those pieces to create a clicker superstar. And for everyone, *Part 4: Training Exercises for the Rider* gives you some easy-to-follow lessons for improving your riding skills.

One of the many images I use in my teaching is that of peeling an onion. Each layer of the onion reveals the one underneath. This book is like that. Some of you may find that you only need to go part way through the "onion" to answer your riding questions. Your previously off-the-wall horse is now settled down and ridable. The nuances of lateral flexions just don't seem relevant to what you want to do. So put the book back on the book shelf, ride, enjoy, and then take it down again at some later point and read some more. The second time through you'll see things you didn't notice before, layers you didn't understand, but that now make sense, and sound like they'd be fun to ride. Each time you read through the book, you'll find more in its pages. This book is a detailed roadmap. It is designed to be returned to over and over again. Each time you do, you'll discover treasures you didn't see before. Enjoy the journey, and have fun with your horse!

★ *Clicker Training For Your Horse,* by Alexandra Kurland; Sunshine Books, US and Ringpress books, UK

CHAPTER 2
Getting Started with the Clicker

In this chapter I'll show you how to introduce your horse to the clicker, then I'll answer some frequently asked questions.

CLICKER TRAINING FOR HORSES

In traditional training the horse is most often working to avoid unpleasant consequences. Pressure doesn't need to mean pain, but it is an initially uncomfortable stimulus which your horse can avoid by changing his behavior. Our riding aids are all based on pressure and the release of pressure. With our hands, with our seat and our legs, we say to the horse "move over; change direction; slow down; go faster." When the horse responds correctly, the pressure goes away. When he ignores us or gives us the wrong response, the pressure increases.

Using only this system of pressure and release you can certainly teach your horse to respond correctly. And you can do it humanely. The pressure can stay at a level that does not create fear or pain. However, the horse is still moving away from something he doesn't want. He's working to *avoid* pressure. In clicker training we add the extra dimension of having the horse work for things he actively desires.

So what do horses like? For most horses food belongs at the top of the list. In fact, food is such a powerful motivator that most conventional trainers will tell you to avoid it. They'll warn you that treats will create all kinds of problems. Your horse will become pushy and obnoxious. He'll mug your pockets and grab at your hands. Feed him treats, they will warn you, and you'll be ruining your horse. Their answer is to remove food entirely as a training tool.

When you take away positive rewards, what you're left with are negative motivators. This is why much of traditional training is pain based: to get performance the horse has to be coerced into it. Let's call a spade a spade. "Respond or else" lies at the heart of most traditional training methods. Even if you are a kind person with only the best interests of your horse in mind, the training methods we all use contain within them this underlying threat.

The clicker shifts this balance. The rules we set up around the clicker let us use food as a training tool. The first rule your horse needs to understand is that the only time you are going to give him treats is when he hears the click. Mugging your pockets will never get you to click. If he wants goodies, he has to offer polite behavior. Once that understanding is clearly established, the clicker lets you bring food into the larger training environment and put it to work for you.

It's important to find a couple of different things your horse enjoys, so you can vary the reinforcer. My horses love peppermints, so I reserve those for special moments. When the peppermints come out, they know they've done something particularly wonderful, and they make an extra effort the next time.

Food isn't the only reinforcer you can use. The definition of a reward is anything the *animal* finds reinforcing. If your horse goes into ecstasies of delight every time you scratch his withers, that's

FOOD

Clicker training begins by teaching emotional control. It does this by using food as it's main reward—something many horses get very excited about. The first phase of clicker training teaches your horse the rules governing the food, and in the process it creates an emotionally-solid horse. Because of the emotional control it teaches, even the most basic of clicker games serve as a great prep for riding.

What can you use for treats? Grain doled out a teaspoon at a time, carrots, breakfast cereal, chopped-up apples, sugar cubes, peppermints, animal crackers, ginger snaps, bread—really anything that your horse enjoys and that's safe for him to eat will work.

As you are choosing your treats, remember that horses have very delicate digestive systems. If you are using grain, be careful about over-feeding. Measure out your horse's daily grain ration and set aside a portion for clicker training. For some horses that will mean they will be working for their entire day's ration. In choosing alternative treats be aware that some horses are intolerant to foods with a high sugar content. Check with your vet if you have questions about what is safe to feed.

a reward you can use. Many people become too narrow in their definition of the word "treat". They think only in terms of food, but there are many other things our horses enjoy and will work for. A "treat" is a special delight or pleasure. Your first job as a clicker trainer is to discover what motivates your particular horse.

GETTING STARTED: TARGET TRAINING

I began experimenting with clicker training out of curiosity. As I said, Peregrine was laid up with abscesses in both front feet. He couldn't walk, but he could bump the end of a whip with his nose, so that was the first behavior I trained with the clicker. At the time I thought it was just a cute trick, something to do to keep us both entertained while he was on stall rest. I have since learned that not only is targeting on an object an easy way to introduce horses to the clicker, it is also a wonderfully useful tool. I use it now as the standard way I start all horses. There are a number of reasons for this:

• Targeting is a very simple behavior for the horse and the handler to understand. It's very black and white: either the horse bumped the target or he didn't.
• Even a novice horse handler can target train. Because it doesn't require a knowledge of other horse handling skills, it makes a good starting place, especially for beginners.
• It's a useful skill to have in your horse's "toolbox". Once the horse learns this behavior, you've got a great training "shortcut". Using targeting you can get a stuck horse unstuck and walking up to, past, or even on or into all kinds of fear-inducing objects, including trailers.
• It's a clean slate. Targeting is something most horses have never been asked to do. They don't have any prior experience with the behavior, so there's no confusion or frustration already associated with it.
• It's easy to control. The first part of training is getting the behavior to happen, the second is getting the behavior under stimulus control or on cue. This second phase comes more slowly than the first because the handler has to learn how to put a behavior on cue. Until you've done so, your horse may offer the behavior at times when it's not appropriate. That's why I don't encourage people to train tricks until they understand cues. (See Chapters 10 and 12.) Teaching your horse to "count" may sound like fun—that is, until you can't get him to stop pawing. Targeting is also a trick, but it's one that's easy to control. If you don't want your horse touching a target, you just take the target away.

For all of these reasons, targeting gives you a safe entry point into clicker training. I often say that if you did nothing but teach your horse to touch a target, the process would make you a better trainer overall. It's a simple behavior, but you still have to have good timing and an understanding of training principles to teach it.

(Note: if you are working with a very nervous horse, you may need to begin by "charging the clicker". That means that you click and feed, click and feed several times until it is clear that he understands the connection between the click and the treat. You can then begin linking the click to behavior.)

TARGET TRAINING: STEP-BY-STEP DIRECTIONS

Targets are easy to find: the lid off a supplement container, an empty water bottle, a dog toy — all make great targets. The silver target stick was made from an empty water bottle wrapped in duct tape. The foam target stick is a section cut off a "pool noodle". Both use old dressage whips for handles. The result: instant target sticks.

1.) Be prepared. Count out twenty carrot slices or some other easily measured treat. Put these treats in a fanny pack or coat pocket that you can reach into with ease.

2.) Put your horse in a stall with a stall guard across the door. That lets him move around freely, but it also keeps you safe. If he gets excited when you first introduce food treats, instead of scolding him you can simply step back out of range. If a stall isn't available, use a small paddock.

3.) Hold a cone or some other object up in front of your horse. Horses tend to be curious about new things. They'll sniff the cone.

4.) Click the clicker the instant your horse touches the cone.

5.) Take the target down out of sight, then reach into your pocket and hand your horse his treat. *Make sure you feed him out well away from your body.*

Chapter Two: Getting Started with the Clicker

TARGETING INSTRUCTIONS, CONTINUED

6.) Put the target back up in approximately the same location as before. Even if he's mugging you for treats, put the target back up. Do not wait for him to quit looking for goodies. This would make the game too hard and frustrating for him. You'd be introducing too many rules too fast. Instead give him something positive to do to earn goodies.

He may not notice the target at first, he'll be so interested in his treats. Be patient. He's going to bump the target eventually, even if it is just by chance. If he gets too pushy, just step back out of range. The mugging is part of the learning process, and the key is not to get distracted by it. Keep yourself safe, but let your horse experiment. He'll discover that going directly to the "vending machine" never gets him a treat. (I'll say more about how to discourage persistent mugging in Chapters 6 and 8.)

7.) When he bumps the target again, click, take the target down out of sight, and *step into his space* to give him his treat. Remember to extend your arm out away from your body to feed him. Don't offer it close in to your body. That will encourage more mugging behavior. Instead keep your hand closed over the treat until you've extended your arm out toward your horse. A good rule to follow is to click for behavior but feed him where you want his head to be. This may mean that your hand ends up pressing against his chest. Great! Your horse will end up taking a step back out of your space to get his treat. If you had to step back from him earlier to keep yourself safe, now you are telling him that he needs to move out of your way to get his treat. He's learning an all important message about space management. And you're learning how to take advantage of training opportunities.

8.) Repeat these steps until you have used up all but a couple of the treats you counted out. Save these to create an end-of-session ritual. On your last click, make a special fuss and toss the extra treats into his grain bin. That will tell him that you're delighted with him; he didn't do anything wrong to make the game end.

9.) Assess your horse's performance. Did your horse snatch the treats from your hand? That tells you you may need to focus on treat delivery in your next session. Did he get grumpy and show very little interest in the game? Perhaps you need to switch tactics and click him whenever his ears perk forward. Or was he deliberately and consistently touching the target and politely taking the treats? He's ready for you to move on to the next step.

10.) Count out another twenty treats and use the information you just gained to create the next step in your lesson plan.

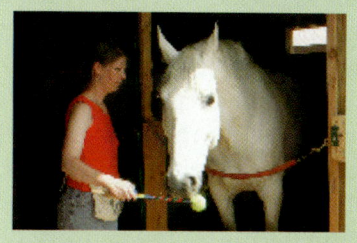

This horse is sniffing the handle of the target stick. That's close but not good enough to earn a click.

Her handler clicks the clicker as her horse nuzzles the tennis ball on the end of the dowel. The clicker is taped to the other end of the dowel making it a very easy target stick to use. Note how the stall guard creates a safe separation for horse and handler.

This horse would love to help herself to the goodies, but instead her handler controls the food delivery. She steps forward into her mare's space and extends her hand so her horse takes a step back to get her treat.

The Click That Teaches: Riding With The Clicker

CLICK THEN TREAT

Remember the order in which events need to occur. Be certain to click before you reach into your pocket for the treat. Reaching for the treat too soon dilutes the power of the clicker because horses are very aware of body movements. If you're in too much of a hurry to get to the treat, the "click" will be the premature movement of your hand, not the sound of the clicker.

Be careful to control the delivery of the treat. Don't offer it in close to your body. That will encourage more mugging behavior. Instead keep your hand closed over the treat until you've extended your arm out toward your horse. A good rule to follow is to click for behavior, but feed him where you want his head to be. You don't have to rush to get the treat to your horse, but you don't want to make him wait too long either. If you have trouble getting a treat out of your pocket, practice away from your horse until you can do so in a smooth, timely fashion.

Horses are not dogs. A dog jumping up on you and mugging you for treats is a nuisance. A horse doing the exact same behavior is a danger. But a horse is also not a zoo animal. We can't keep them behind barriers forever. The reality is we are going to be working in close to our horses, so food delivery and good manners are very important. Begin with protective contact, the barrier of a stall guard or a paddock fence. Let your horse explore, but keep yourself safe. In the next chapter I'll show you some more foundation lessons so you end up with a safe, mannerly, eager-to-play clicker-trained horse.

"LIGHT BULB" MOMENTS

Help your horse to be successful with his first clicker lesson. If he swings his head away from the target to look at something else, take advantage of that to position the target between his head and your body. He'll have to bump into it on his way back to mugging you. When he does, click, he gets a treat. As this happens again and again, he's suddenly going to realize that bumping the cone gets you, the vending machine, to work!

You can almost see the lightbulb go on. As many times as I've watched this process, it's still a magical moment when the horse realizes that he's in control, that he can make you click. All he has to do is bump the target! He's learned that the click means something good is about to happen. You've trained your first behavior with the clicker, and in the process you've shown your horse that sniffing your fingers, pulling on your coat, or bumping your arm isn't the way to earn treats. Nosing the "magic" target is the key that unlocks this vending machine!

FROM TARGETING TO TEACHING

Targeting makes a great entry point into clicker training. It's easy to understand and to control. But suppose after you've taught your horse to touch a target, you decide that clicker training just isn't your cup of tea. That's fine. You've played a fun game with your horse. You've improved your timing and observation skills, and you haven't disrupted any of his normal training. You can put your empty cider jug, or the lid off a supplement container, or whatever else you were using for a target away, and that's the end of it.

But what will probably happen instead is you will see how smart your horse is. You'll see how much fun he has playing the clicker game and, like me, you'll want to see what else you can do with it. You'll start adding it in and adding it in to your regular routine, until clicker training isn't some separate thing you do now and then with your horse but a new "language", a way to converse back and forth to let your horse know when he's doing something right.

It will become a state of mind as much as a training method. Once you get hooked, you won't be able to imagine training without the clicker.

QUESTIONS

When you first start out with clicker training, you'll have a host of question. Most of us have been so programmed to correct what we don't like that there are many aspects of clicker training that may seem very confusing. You'll be wondering if you always have to click, and how soon you can stop using food.

Those of us who have been clicker training for a while know that many of these concerns will evaporate once you actually start using the clicker, but with this first clicker lesson under your belt, you may have a number of questions swirling around in your head.

Do you have to use the clicker to be a clicker trainer?

No. Any unique, audible signal that the animal can recognize will work.

I use the mechanical clicker when I'm first introducing a horse to clicker training. I prefer that to a verbal signal because of the uniqueness of the sound. Horses are quick to notice the clicker, whereas verbal signals often get lost in the background noise of our own chatter.

Once the horse understands the basic rules of the

Chapter Two: Getting Started with the Clicker

game—i.e., that doing a behavior leads to a click leads to reward—I switch over to a tongue click. This leaves my hands free for other things. I've never had any trouble transferring the signal. The horses I've worked with have instantly made the connection. They will respond to even a faint tongue click. The more you practice, the clearer and more audible your tongue click will become.

And note: Clicks are not clucks. A cluck is a sound made from the corner of your mouth as a request for movement. A click is a much sharper noise made on the roof of your mouth with your tongue and is used as a "yes" signal. Horses have no trouble telling the difference, and once your horse has learned what the clicker means, even a clumsy, muffled tongue click will get his attention.

Why can't I just say "good"? Do I have to use a clicker?

I personally prefer the sound of a clicker or a tongue click over verbal signals. The click is a high-speed, unique signal that lets me mark very precise criteria. Verbals can do the same thing, but I prefer to use "good" and "yes" as encouragers or "keep going" signals. Think of the children's game of "Hot and Cold". "Good" says you're getting warmer, but the click is a terminal bridge. It says: "Yes! You just found the pot of gold."

You can certainly use "good" in place of the clicker, but I think you'll find that you're going to prefer tongue clicks to words. The important thing, however, is not to get hung up on what signal you use, but to understand that clicker training is really about shaping behavior in small steps with a crystal-clear "yes" signal that guides and motivates the horse through the learning process.

What happens if you have more than one clicker-trained horse in the ring at the same time? Do they get confused?

When I do lessons or workshops we routinely have four or five clicker-trained horses working together, and they all seem to sort out which click they're supposed to be responding to. What's particularly interesting is that I can be working with a client and clicking her horse from a distance, and none of the other horses will react. These are all horses that know I'm a potential vending machine, yet they also know that at that moment my click is not intended for them.

Does it matter if I ride english or western?

No. We don't all have to ride alike, or even train alike, to use the clicker. The particular style of riding you enjoy isn't important. What is important is that you understand the principles of good training (Ch. 5). These principles apply no matter what kind of saddle you put on your horse's back or what sport you engage in. Good training principles are at the heart of all good training programs.

What kinds of things can you teach with the clicker?

Anything you want. From basic manners to advanced performance, any time you need a clear "yes answer" signal the clicker can help your training.

For starters go down a checklist of basic stable manners. Does your horse lead well? Will he walk into a trailer? Does he ground tie? Will he stand quietly on cross ties? Is he good for grooming? How easy is he to saddle and bridle? Does he stand well for mounting? How is he at everyday tasks in the paddock or on the trail? Can you open gates with him? Cross trail obstacles? Ride near traffic? Does he remain calm around bicycles and other spooky objects? You can use the clicker to help you teach—or retrain—any of these basics. And you can use it to refine more advanced work as well.

I'm afraid I'm going to do it wrong. What if I accidentally teach my horse something I don't like?

You can't get it wrong.

Clicker training is the most forgiving training method there is. If you don't like what you're getting, simply reinforce the opposite response. Suppose you've spent the last couple of sessions reinforcing your horse for backing. Now that's all he wants to do. At first you were thrilled. All you had to do was look at him and he backs. That was great, except now you want him to stand still for grooming. No problem. As we'll discuss in the Chapter 5, one of the basic training principles states that for every exercise you teach there is an opposite exercise you must teach to keep things in balance (pg. 26).

If you can teach your horse to back, you can teach him to go forward. In the middle of going forward and back is standing still. The more you train, the more you'll discover that you can't get it wrong!

Do I always have to carry treats? When do you stop using the clicker?

Clicker trainers are always looking for ways to appreciate their horses. The "thank you" of the click is reinforcing to us. So rather than looking for ways to fade out the clicker, we're always on the lookout for more ways to tell our horses what a great job they

The Click That Teaches: Riding With The Clicker

are doing. Once your horse understands the clicker, it becomes a communication tool that is always with you, assisting in any situation where you need to clarify, motivate, or appreciate. For example, if you are asking an inexperienced trail horse to cross a bridge, he might at first be reluctant to step on the bridge. You could break the task down into a series of steps:

Look at the bridge: click and treat.
Take a step toward the bridge: click and treat.
Put your nose down and sniff the bridge: click and treat.
Paw the bridge: click and treat.
Take a step onto the bridge: click and treat.

You would go on reinforcing your horse for each small incremental step, building his confidence until he is able to walk comfortably across the bridge.

At the next bridge you might only need to break the process down into three or four steps, with a click and a treat for each success. At the next bridge he might walk right across, click and treat! Pretty soon he'll be so confident crossing bridges you won't even think to click him for it. He's learned the lesson well. He understands bridges, and he doesn't hesitate crossing them. Job well done!

But now suppose he slips on a bridge and scares himself. The next time you ask him to cross, he might not be so eager. This is a great time to add the clicker back in and review the earlier lesson. Going back over the steps will usually bring his confidence right back to its previous level, and he'll be crossing like a champ. At the next bridge you might click and treat just as a thank you, as a way of appreciating a job well done.

Do I have to treat every time I click?

Each and every time I click I treat. That's the bargain I've set up with my horse. The click tells my horse that he has just successfully completed a unit of behavior. He can stop and get his treat. If I want him to keep going, I'll use a "keep going signal". "Good" chanted in rhythm with his stride works great. It means: "you're on the right track; keep going and you're likely to hear the click." There's a huge potential for confusion if you use the same signal to mean "keep going", and at other times it means "yes, that's it!"

So when I click, it means a treat is coming. If the behavior was good enough to click, it was good enough to treat. But I choose what to click. At first I may be clicking and reinforcing my horse for the smallest try, but gradually I'll be asking for much more. As I develop behaviors and chain them together into larger units, my horse will have to do more and more to earn a click and a treat.

My horse paws (kicks, bites, or does some other undesirable behavior). Can I use the clicker to get him to stop?

Yes, but perhaps not in the way you mean. Clicker training is a positive training tool. It teaches the horse what to do, not what not to do. So to stop an unwanted behavior it's not enough to say you want your horse to stop pawing. Clicker training isn't punitive. You have to train for something.

You could say, "I just want my horse to do nothing," but nothing is a hard concept for your horse to grasp. You're thinking you clicked your horse because he wasn't pawing, but he thinks it was because he was pinning his ears flat. He was in fact doing something at the moment you thought you were reinforcing him for doing nothing.

You need to state in positive and very precise terms exactly what you want your horse to do. You might begin with: "I want my horse to stand quietly with both front feet on the ground." That's a good starting point. It certainly gives you a clear-cut criterion for reinforcing your horse.

Once you have both feet on the ground, you could add in some other items to your list. You could teach your horse to arch his neck like a dressage horse, or to perk his ears forward, both very desirable behaviors. Instead of crabbing at him for pawing, now you'd be reinforcing him for something useful. When he wants attention, instead of pawing, he'll arch his neck and perk his ears forward. He'll look so gorgeous, you won't be able to resist him.

You'll both be happy. He won't be ruining his feet with his annoying pawing, and you'll be showering him with extra attention because he's so beautiful. Learn to train for what you want instead of focusing on the negatives, and it will change the relationship you have with your horse.

That's enough questions for now. The best way to learn about clicker training is to try it, so let's head back out to the barn for some more clicker lessons.

CHAPTER 3
Foundation Lessons

In Chapter Two I had you put your horse in his stall or a small paddock for his first clicker lesson. I had you count out twenty treats before you began (pg. 8). During that first session I wanted you to observe your horse. How did he react to the clicker game? Did the treats get him excited? Did he get mad if they didn't come fast enough? If you missed a click or two, did he get frustrated and quit? Or did the proverbial "lightbulb" go on so he's eager for more clicker games?

Those first couple of clicker lessons will tell you a lot about your horse. When I'm working with a new horse, I watch him closely. I'm asking myself an important question: is he doing anything that makes me think I could get hurt if I went into his stall with a pocket full of treats? If the answer comes back "yes", I stay outside his stall until he understands the rules of the clicker game and can control his emotions. I'll continue to strengthen his targeting skills, and I'll add some very simple lessons that will help him understand how the clicker works—all with the safety of a barrier between us. When he's settled, I'll go into the stall with him and repeat these same lessons.

HAPPY FACES

What and why: You're going to reinforce your horse for putting his ears forward. You'll be practicing your shaping skills as you encourage a pleasant attitude in your horse.

1.) Count out twenty horse treats.

2.) Put your horse in his stall with a stall guard across the door.

3.) Watch him from a safe distance. The instant one of his ears moves forward even a little, click.

4.) Remember to click for behavior and feed for position. Reach into your pocket and take out one of the horse treats. Step in to his space to feed him just as you did in the targeting lesson. If he grabs for the treat, see Chapters 6 and 8 for a discussion of mugging and hand feeding.

5.) Repeat until you have used up your treats. Take a short break while you refill your pockets. In your next round you can focus again on "Happy Faces", or you might return to targeting.

HEAD LOWERING

You're going to use your horse's new targeting skill to get him to lower his head.

1.) Count out twenty horse treats.

2.) Put your horse in his stall with a stall guard across the door.

3.) Hold your target up in front of him. When he bumps it, click and treat.

4.) Gradually lower the target toward the ground. Click and treat each small change in height you make.

"HAPPY FACES"

As part of her preparation for riding this young horse is learning the foundation lessons of clicker training. Instead of fussing at her handler, she's practicing patience and self-control. She'll be clicked and reinforced for staying in her own space and having a beautiful, ears-forward, happy expression.

This filly is showing a wonderful understanding of the foundation lessons. Her owner has added in a mat★ which serves as a target for her filly's feet. Compare this photo to the one on page 152 to see how much she's changed in her balance after learning her clicker ground skills.

★ For more clicker ground work lessons refer to *The Click That Teaches: A Step-By-Step Guide in Pictures*, by Alexandra Kurland; The Clicker Center, NY

The Click That Teaches: Riding With The Clicker

5.) Once he is consistently tracking the target to the ground, withhold your click for a second or two so he keeps his head down for longer and longer periods. Build your duration slowly so he continues to be successful.

6.) When he is leaving his head down for three to five seconds, change the way you trigger the behavior. Take the target away, and instead put your hand on his poll. Your horse is already thinking about dropping his head so chances are he'll lower it when he feels the light pressure of your hand.

7.) Click, take your hand away and give him a treat.

This lesson shows you how easy it is to introduce pressure and release of pressure into your training. With the preparation of the target, the light poll pressure is information only, never a threat. It becomes a cue that tells your horse how to get to the correct answer faster.

BACKING

If you've been consistent in your food delivery, your horse is already backing out of your space. You've got him primed to back as you step into him. In this next exercise you're going to connect this response to a signal you give down a lead rope.

1.) Again count out twenty treats. Put a cotton lead on your horse and go into the stall with him. Slide your left hand towards the snap of the lead as you turn and walk into his shoulder.

2.) As he steps back out of your space, click and treat.

3.) Ask him to follow his target forward a step or two, click and treat.

4.) Ask him to back up again.

Note: At this point you don't want to back him into a corner where he might feel trapped by the wall. Ask just for a couple of steps, and then be certain to target him forward to the front of his stall. I'll show you in Chapter 8 how to back him through the corner.

"THE GROWN–UPS ARE TALKING, PLEASE DON'T INTERRUPT" LESSON

At this point in the process your horse may be eagerly touching targets, dropping his head, and backing from a feather-light touch. You're both having a great time, except for one thing: he's still checking out your pockets for treats. He understands part of the game, but you haven't yet explained the entire "rule book". This next exercise helps make it clear that mugging you is never the answer that produces treats.

1.) Count out twenty treats. Put a cotton lead on your horse and stand next to him in a "neutral body language" position with your arms crossed in front of you. Hold the lead about fifteen inches from the snap. If he mugs you, stay safe, but be as non-reactive as possible.

2.) The instant that he takes his nose away from your body, click and treat. Be certain to feed out away from your body *where you want his head to be.*

3.) Repeat, letting him explore so he can learn what doesn't work. Click and treat each time he moves his nose away from your body.

4.) Put him on a high rate of reinforcement. Before he can get his nose back to nuzzle your pockets, click and feed him where you want his nose to be—lined up with his shoulders.

5.) Click and feed, click and feed in rapid-fire succession, then slow down your click. He'll probably nuzzle your arm, but then you'll see him very deliberately move his nose away to the spot where he's been reinforced. The light bulb is very definitely going on!

6.) Intersperse the "grown ups are talking" game with the other clicker exercises so he understands that mugging you is not part of the game. He's learning self control. If he wants the goodies, he has to stay in his own space. Click and treat.

These simple lessons are the foundation of clicker training.

- Targeting introduces your horse to the clicker.
- "Happy Faces" makes you aware of your horse's attitude during training.
- Head lowering settles and calms your horse. It associates feelings of safety and security with the clicker.
- Backing creates respect of space.
- "The grown-ups are talking, please don't interrupt" lesson develops your horse's *self* control.

Your horse's reaction to these foundation lessons determines what you do next. For more guidance through this early process I will refer you to *The Click That Teaches: A Step-By-Step Guide in Pictures.*★ It gives you a detailed lesson plan that prepares your horse for the riding exercises in this book.

★ *The Click That Teaches: A Step-By-Step Guide in Pictures,* by Alexandra Kurland; The Clicker Center, NY

CHAPTER 4
But What About . . . ?:
More Clicker Questions

If you've tried the simple lessons in the previous chapter, you probably have more questions. So give your horse some process time while I answer some frequently asked questions.

CLICKER QUESTIONS

My horse seems to know what the clicker means, but I'm not seeing the "light" going on in his head. What do I do if he'll touch the target a couple of times but then seems to get bored?

When your horse touches the target a time or two and then wanders off or shows no other interest, he's not bored, he's stuck. He doesn't know what he's supposed to do, or he may even be feeling unsafe. Many horses who've been trained in correction-based systems will feel insecure offering behaviors because they've learned to wait to be told what to do. Perhaps in the past they've even been punished for taking the initiative and offering behaviors.

One of my earliest experiences with clicker training was helping a friend introduce her dog to the clicker. Her dog had been obedience trained using correction-based methods, so at first she just stared at me. That was the behavior the dog had learned was safe: "stare at your person until you are told what to do. If you move before you're told, you'll be corrected."

That dog had learned her lesson well. She could watch her trainer for an incredible length of time. We waited and waited, until finally she twitched an ear. Click! We reinforced that minuscule behavior. It took that dog's owner days of persistent trying to get her to interact, but it was well worth it. Her dog had been a lackluster performer before clicker training. She was obedient, all right, but timid. Now she began to express her personality and to shine at obedience trials. This change is the hallmark of clicker training. It's what has drawn so many of us to it. We love our animals and we want them to be joyful in their interactions with us.

Many of our horses have learned the same thing that the competition dogs have learned: don't offer any behavior that isn't asked for. Clicker training initially puts them into a situation that feels very unsafe for them. Touching a target may seem like an innocent easy little behavior to us, but they feel as though they've been thrown into a snake pit. If they reach out and touch the target, they're sure they're going to be punished for their curiosity. That's not the reality, but it is their expectation.

With these horses you need to be patient and understanding. Think back to your school days. Do you remember being the one kid in the whole class who didn't know the answer to the math problem? That's always when your teacher called on you. Remember the long walk up to the blackboard in front of all your classmates? Even if we haven't been there ourselves, we've all seen little kids who freeze up and can't even remember their own names. That's the same type of mental block some horses experience when

WHAT CAN YOU DO WITH THE CLICKER?

What can you train with the clicker? Anything you want. For starters go down a list of basic barn manners, then let your imagination run wild.★

★ Photos taken from *The Click That Teaches: A Step-By-Step Guide in Pictures* by Alexandra Kurland; The Clicker Center, NY.

they're first introduced to the clicker.

Some horses do take a long time to catch on to the clicker. The answer is persistence. Just keep offering your horse opportunities to use the clicker. He will catch on, and when he does it will be well worth all the effort.

Will I always have to count out my treats?

No. Once you are comfortable with the process, you'll just fill your fanny pack or your vest pockets with treats.

Counting out twenty treats in the beginning breaks the training up into small units. It gives you an opportunity to assess your horse's responses and to decide what lesson to work on next. The short breaks also give your horse valuable process time. You'll often find that he's much more responsive after he's had a chance to think through the lesson.

Counting out treats gives you a way of measuring progress. How long did the treats last? How much more does he have to do to earn the same number of treats? Keep records. Later when you're just filling your pockets, you'll still be able to approximate how many treats he's earned in a given length of time.

My horse seems as though he's really enjoying these clicker games, but is he really having fun, or does he just want the food?

At first your horse may be excited because he's found a way to turn you into a treat dispenser. For a horse, there's nothing intrinsically self-reinforcing about targeting. The first time he touched the target it was out of curiosity. He kept on touching it because he was being paid well for his action.

We operate the same way. Without the incentive of the paycheck, we would gloss over the less interesting parts of our jobs. With the clicker we can turn behaviors the horse might not otherwise enjoy into favorite games.

Backing, for example, is hard work and not something most horses enjoy doing, but reinforce it well enough, and it can take on a whole new meaning. Now it's the behavior that makes all the "bells and whistles" go off. Your horse is going to be eager to back. That's good news because a horse who is comfortable backing will be a horse that has great brakes.

When you take the fear of failure out of your lessons and reinforce instead the behaviors you want, you'll see a huge change in your horse's attitude. With many horses it almost seems as though a light goes on in their head: they can communicate with us! We're listening, and what they have to say does matter.

Clicker-trained horses really do seem to love to work. They enjoy the social interaction with their people. They enjoy getting treats, and they truly seem to enjoy the game of figuring out what behavior will unlock the vending machine next. We see this reflected in their bright eyes and their eager "Pick me, pick me!" willingness to work.

Is there ever a time when I can just click, but not treat?

There are trainers who use treatless clicks. In other words, sometimes the click means: "that was good, keep going and maybe next time I click you might get a treat." Treatless clicks keep the horse guessing. He never knows when he's actually going to get his reward. The variability can create extra effort, but it can also create frustration. One of the challenges of treatless clicks is avoiding predictable patterns. For example, if your horse notices you tend to treat after every third click, he may offer mediocre performance for the first two.

In the early stages of clicker training I experimented with treatless clicks. My conclusion was I preferred to treat after every click. Treatless clicks made me tense. I didn't like them because they didn't give me a clear basis for deciding which forms of a behavior got a click and a treat, and which just got a click. The randomness of it was stressful for me. Watching out for patterns was stressful.

With treatless clicks I had to watch my horse and at the same time monitor what I was doing. If I didn't treat the last version of the behavior, should I click and treat the current one? How was I going to remain unpredictable enough so that my horse didn't learn a pattern? If my horse just gave me something good, but I treated the last three clicks, should I not treat this one? If the behavior was all good, how could I not reinforce something that was worthy of recognition?

My conclusion: if a behavior is good enough to click, it is good enough to reinforce. But that doesn't mean that all forms of a behavior are equal. (See Chapter 9.) I'll be selectively choosing improved versions of the behavior to click, and I'll offer extras for excellence. Treating after every click makes me a better trainer. Instead of keeping track of random patterns, now I'm evaluating the behavior I just clicked. While I'm fishing around in my pockets for a suitable treat, I have plenty of time to assess my horse's performance and decide if it warrants a special jackpot. A pocket full of grain or even a single carrot can buy you a lot of training. A teaspoon of grain - one

Chapter Four: But What About . . . ?

bite of carrot is enough to keep your horse working for more. You can save his favorite treats for extra efforts. They help you to mark those special "Kodak moments". When my own horses do something I particularly like, click! the peppermints come out. They know they have just done something super that was well worth the extra effort. The result is happy horses who love to work!

Teaching my horse to touch a target was easy, but how do I know what to work on next?

Clicker training teaches you how to listen to your horse. He'll tell you what the next lesson needs to be. If he's crowding into your space, you need to work on backing. If he's spooking at shadows, he needs to live in the head-lowering lesson for a while.

In clicker training you train by priority. You look at what you want your horse *to do*, not the unwanted behavior. Then you decide what is the most important or most basic element of that behavior. That's what you train first.

For example, as a preliminary step towards ground tying, you could teach your horse to stand on a mat. Once he's standing on the mat, you can add other elements to that base behavior. In other words, you want him to stand on the mat, *and* look straight ahead, *and* put his ears forward, *and* stand square behind, *and* hold that position longer, etc. You'll keep adding elements building quality and duration until you have created the finished, polished behavior.

As you train, cues will evolve naturally out of the shaping process. Your cues will change as the behavior becomes more refined. For example, in backing you might begin by stepping dramatically into his space and gesturing him back with your hand. As he becomes more responsive, a slight wiggle of your finger will be all that's needed to send him back. (Note: these body language cues take on meaning for your horse through the training process. When you look at another trainer's work, it is always more important to understand the shaping process, than to ask what his specific cues are.)

Once you have refined a behavior and put it on cue, you can link it to other behaviors to create lengthy chains. So while clicker training begins with very basic, simple behaviors, it quickly evolves into complex tasks.

You'll learn more about cues and chaining behaviors in Chapters 10 and 12.

I understand the basic theory, but I'm having trouble coordinating my clicker with the target and the treats. I feel as though I'm all thumbs.

Whenever you are learning something new, it's a good idea to practice the mechanical skills you'll need for the task. Get a friend to help you. She'll play the part of your horse so you practice your training skills. While you are learning how to handle your equipment and deliver the treat on time, she'll be discovering what training is like from the horse's point of view.

Here are a few key elements to look for as you practise your mechanical skills.

- Keep your free hand *out of* your treat pocket until you are ready to get your treats.

- Make sure you click *before* you reach towards your treats. But *immediately* after you click, begin your treat delivery. *Any* hesitation creates a disconnect between the behavior and the reward.

- Practice transferring your clicker out of the hand that delivers the treat. You don't want to be accidentally feeding your clicker to your horse.

- Be prompt, but don't rush the food delivery. You control the pace of the lesson by controlling the treats. Think of dining out at a restaurant. Watching the waiter bring your food to the table is part of the whole experience. For your horse the reinforcing event isn't just eating the treat. It includes the treat delivery.

- Watch the timing of your click. Videotape your training sessions. If your horse is getting frustrated or he just doesn't seem to be catching on, you may see the reason on the tape. Maybe the timing of the click is off, or you're fumbling with your treat delivery. Little details can make a huge difference in training.

Refer to *The Click That Teaches* video lesson series★ for more tips on clicker mechanics.

THE TRAINING GAME

A great way to learn what clicker training is like from your horse's point of view is to play the training game. As the trainer in the game, you'll sharpen your timing and ability to spot the small tries that lead to success. And as the trainee you'll appreciate how important good timing and clear criteria are in the learning process.

Instructions for playing the game:

1.) The trainer selects a specific action for the trainee to do. This action can be anything that is physically possible, safe, and not embarrassing to the trainee. It is important to emphasize to the trainee that this is a behavior humans can do. He is not to restrict his thinking to horsey behaviors. For example: sitting in a chair, or picking up an object would be good behaviors to train. Pick simple things to start with. You want your trainee to succeed. Do not tell the trainee

---

★ *The Click That Teaches* video lesson series, by Alexandra Kurland; The Clicker Center, NY

The Click That Teaches: Riding With The Clicker

what the behavior is. It's his job to figure that out by using the information the clicks provide.

2.) To earn clicks the trainee moves about the room. The more movement the trainee offers, the more likely it is he'll be reinforced. This can include exploring different parts of the room, manipulating objects, walking specific patterns, etc.. No verbal hints are allowed. All questions from the trainee are answered with a blank stare, or a simple "I don't speak 'Horse'." The trainee can talk all he wants, and he usually does—to the great amusement of the people watching.

3.) The trainer clicks the trainee for approximations of the chosen goal. At the click the trainee needs to stop and go over to the trainer for his treat. (Treats can be a pat on the shoulder, Monopoly money, m&ms, etc.)

4.) The trainer continues to click and reward actions that bring the trainee closer to the goal behavior. A jackpot marks the final goal behavior.

One of the many things you'll learn from this game is that people and horses respond in very similar ways. They both get stuck in patterns, they repeat unreinforced behaviors, they establish superstitious links, they perform the desired behavior without having a clue that's what you want. With people you can get direct verbal feedback on their emotional states. It can actually be quite amusing listening to them talk their way through a shaping game. They get frustrated, angry, excited, eager to play the game, discouraged, bored, focused. In watching the body language of horses I would say they experience the same range of emotions.

When a horse doesn't understand what is wanted, he gets frustrated just as we do. When he's on the right track, he gets excited. A "green" animal, horse or human, doesn't know how to handle his emotions. When he's frustrated, he acts out his anger. He may quit trying or become balky. When he's successful, he gets excited and may become over-eager.

As our trainee becomes more experienced, he won't quit or get mad if something goes wrong. Instead he'll try something else. He's learning how to learn, and he's able to keep his emotions on a more even keel. He's not a "green" novice any more, but an experienced, mature partner playing an exciting game.

Another way you can play this game is simply to observe your trainee. Do not start off with any set behavior in mind that you are going to shape. Instead watch your trainee to see what he does. Capture his behavior with a click and a treat. As you reinforce specific movements, they'll become more definite, more consistently repeated. You'll be able to use this to create a completely new behavior. For example, what might have begun as a slight turn of the head to the side is now a full blown spin.

This version of the training game is much easier for the trainee. There's no set goal behavior for him to figure out so he's never "wrong". Whatever he offers initially will be reinforced. You'll be following his initiative to build a complex and often quite unexpected behavior.

It's a great way to learn more about shaping and to develop your eye for spotting the small gems that can be captured with the clicker. Collect enough gems and you'll have a treasure of a behavior.

CHAPTER 5
The Principles of Training

In the previous chapters I introduced you to the foundation lessons of clicker training. You taught your horse to touch a target. You've got him backing a few steps and dropping his head. He doesn't mug you for treats any more. As soon as he sees you, he perks his ears forward and goes into his "grown-up-are-talking" pose. It's very cute, but it's a long way from riding. That's your goal, and you aren't sure what to do next. Maybe you've got some training issues with your horse. Your friends are giving you all kinds of advice. How do you decide what training method is best to solve the problems you're having? That's the question that's answered in this chapter.

TRAINING BY PRINCIPLES NOT METHODS

We've all heard the metaphor about give a man a fish and he can eat for a day. Teach a man to fish, and he can feed himself for a lifetime. Horse training is very much like this. We haul our horses off to clinics hoping to find the magic cure for this problem and that. These can be valuable experiences, but until you understand the PRINCIPLES that govern ALL good training, you will never have a consistent program. You will always be patching up problems instead of truly fixing them. My goal with this book is to teach you how to train, not just how to band-aid problems.

One of the trainers whose work I have studied is John Lyons. During a clinic of his that I was riding in, I asked him one of those what-do-you-do-when type questions. I don't remember the specific situation I was asking about, but I do remember the answer. John didn't give me the nuts and bolts solution I was hoping for. Instead he asked me what the underlying principle would be?

I didn't get it at first. What principle? What did he mean? But it was really so simple. The training principle I needed to think about was one of the most basic: "Get the feet to move, get them to move consistently, then take them in the direction you want them to go." Even more basic than that I needed to think about this most important concept: "Go to a place in the training where you can get control." In other words keep chunking the training down until you get to a point where you CAN get the feet to move.

Of course! Once he said that, I understood how to solve the problem I was having. Not only that, but I could solve a score of others as well. Suddenly training wasn't about individual situations: what do I do when . . . . . ? It became a family of related training exercises all governed by the same underlying principles. Everything IS related to everything else.

Asking that question changed the way I thought about training. Now when I hit a sticky spot with my horses, I look first for the underlying principles that will structure my lessons. Over the years I've settled on ten key principles that form the underpinnings of everything I teach. Most are common to all good training methods, but a few are unique to clicker training. If you are scratching your head trying to come up with a solution to a problem, look first at the training principles. They will help you to unravel the puzzle and come up with a training plan that will help your horse.

BELIEF SYSTEMS

I remember years ago watching a young thoroughbred literally climb the walls of her stall to get away from her groom. He was shanking her with a chain over her nose, trying to force her to stand still while he pulled out chunks of her mane to tidy up her appearance. My trainer looked in over my shoulder and said very matter of factly that horses don't feel pain the way we do. Pulling her mane didn't really hurt her.

That was so much a part of his belief system that he couldn't see her obvious distress. Her reaction was viewed as misbehavior, not as a cry for help.

It's important to know the belief systems of the people you entrust your horses to. Belief systems color not only what we see, but the training choices we make. This trainer believed that horses were stupid and needed to be controlled with force. A corollary of this was that horses did not feel pain the way we do, therefore the use of force was acceptable.

The training methods he chose were a reflection of this underlying belief system. He was very much a product of the general horse culture of that time. Force-based training was the accepted norm. So deep was this belief system that the major horse magazines at that time even printed articles stating that horses do not experience back pain.

I didn't buy into that. My belief system has always been that horses are intelligent and deserve to be treated with respect and kindness.

Every training program is made up of three layers: the underlying belief system that governs all choices; the training principles that grow out of this belief system; and the mechanical skills and lessons that implement the training principles and belief system.

You should know what the underlying belief system is of every trainer you work with. It will effect directly the training choices that are made. My belief system leads me straight to clicker training and the ten governing principles of training described in this chapter.

The Click That Teaches: Riding With The Clicker

PRINCIPLE # 1: SAFETY ALWAYS COMES FIRST

The most important principle is SAFETY ALWAYS COMES FIRST, both for you and your horse.

It doesn't matter if someone else can ride your horse bareback and bridleless through a herd of raging buffalo. If you don't feel comfortable with an exercise, trust that nagging little voice inside you. That's your guidance system telling you that some piece of preparation is missing in your training.

That other person may have a seat like velcro. He knows he's going to stay on no matter what his horse does underneath him. You may not have that same confidence. Maybe your experiences have taught you that you fall off when your horse twists or turns too fast. If that's your belief, you're going to tighten up when your horse spooks, and that means you ARE more likely to fall off. You're right to be cautious. You should never let someone else force you or your horse into doing something you don't feel ready for.

If you've been in horses for more than five minutes, you know there are lots of different opinions about how to handle any training situation. Ask a roomful of people for advice, and you'll get a roomful of answers back. The suggestions will range from the humane to the insane, so how do you choose between them to find methods that suits you and your horse? I begin with John Lyons' three rules of training.

1.) The person can't get hurt.
2.) The horse can't get hurt.
3.) The horse must be calmer at the end of the lesson than he was at the beginning.

These are good guidelines, especially for judging the merits of a riding program. Safety for both the horse and the rider should always be the number one concern. Before embarking on any new step in the training ask yourself: if something goes wrong can either of us get hurt? If the answer comes back, maybe, you aren't ready for that step.

The good news is there is always another way to train everything. And there is always a smaller step in the training that you can focus on.

Safety also matters for our horses. "Just because you can, doesn't mean you should" is an expression I use often. Just because you can sit on your two year old, doesn't mean you should. Just because you can jump higher, spin faster, run further, doesn't mean you should. Safety and concern for our horses should always come before any other goals and desires.

A good way to integrate safety into all your horse training is to remember another Lyons' phrase:

"Train where you can, not where you can't." That means if your horse bolts with you out on the trail, school him in an arena. If he bucks you off every time you put your foot in the stirrup, begin with ground work. If he runs you over on a lead, put him in a stall with a solid wall between you.

In other words keep chunking the lesson down into smaller and smaller pieces until you find something YOU can safely ask your horse to do.

FEAR DEFINED

Fear is just common sense in disguise.

If you're afraid, it means you know there are steps missing in your training sequence. It doesn't matter what your trainer or your friends are telling you to do. If you're afraid, you need to follow a common-sense principle that says: "Go to a step in the training where you have control."

A frightened rider makes a terrible teacher, so you need to work your horse through exercises where you feel confident and comfortable. If you follow the basic principles behind clicker training, they will guide you to methods that are safe for you and your horse.

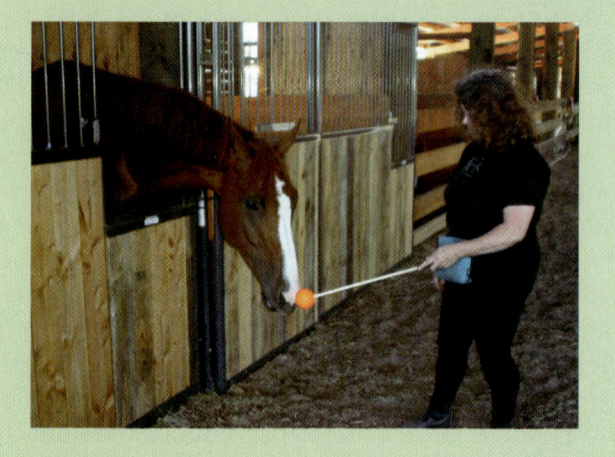

Safety often means starting with protective contact, i.e. a barrier between you and your horse. When he demonstrates that he can control himself, then and only then will you step in with him.

If you don't feel comfortable with an exercise, trust that nagging little voice inside you. That's your guidance system telling you that some piece of preparation is missing in your training.

Chapter Five: The Principles of Training

PRINCIPLE #2: SEPARATE YOUR GOALS FROM YOUR STARTING POINTS.

Never start with your goal. Put as many steps as you can think of between where your horse is now and where you would like him to be.

Goals are good things. They keep us striving for excellence. The more clearly you state your goal, the easier it is to design a lesson program. But it is important to remember that a goal is just that. It is something to strive for. IT IS NOT A STARTING POINT.

Suppose, for example, you want your horse to stand still while you pick out his feet. Starting with your goal would mean that you'd go right to work asking your horse to pick up his feet. A trainer who understands that a goal is something to achieve would find a different starting place. That trainer might begin by simply asking her horse to stand still. She understands another important principle:

You cannot ask for anything and expect to get it on a consistent basis unless you have gone through a teaching process to teach it to your horse. (John Lyons)

Your horse could stand still the very first day he was born. He didn't need you to teach him how to do it. However, if you want him to stand still WHEN you ask, EVERY TIME you ask, you need to go through a teaching process with him.

People get in trouble when they assume their horse knows more than he does. With a young horse it's easy to be patient. You expect things to be new to him. You know you have to be a teacher. But many times with older horses we make assumptions. The horse has been ridden for years, he should know how to stand still, or pick up a canter, or stop, or move off from your leg. Perhaps he does, but if YOU haven't gone through a teaching process with this horse, you can't assume he knows everything he should.

Each one of us must find a teaching process that is a match with our underlying beliefs. Do you know what your belief system is? Have you thought about it at all in relation to the training choices you make? Are your beliefs compatible with your trainer's? If not, they could be a source of conflict for both of you.

Here's another important element of this training principle:

If you encounter a problem in your training, the solution is NEVER in the layer you are working on. You need to go back to an earlier step in your training to resolve the problem. (John Lyons)

TEACHING PROCESS

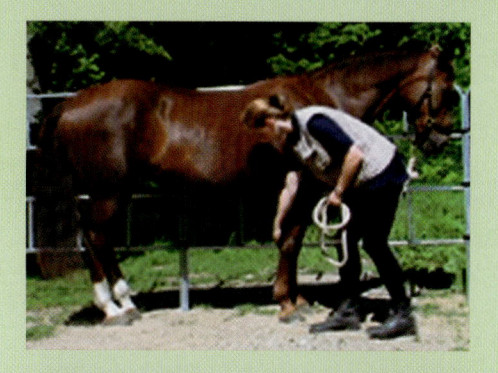

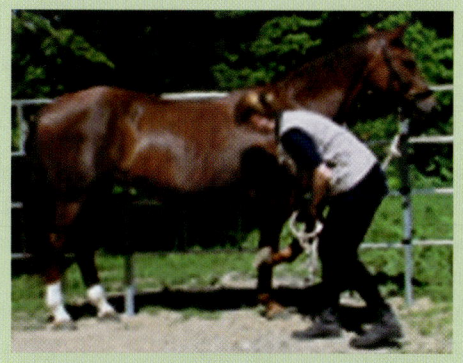

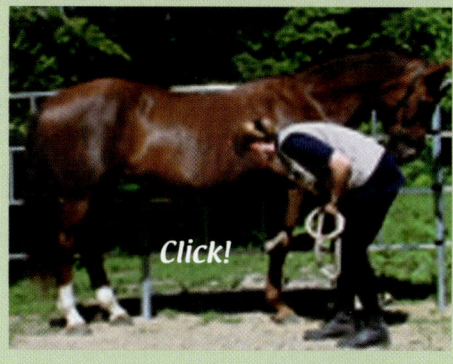

Click!

Never assume your horse knows something. This older horse is being given a review lesson in basic foot care. Her owner is being certain that she understands what is being asked of her by going through an organized teaching process.

If you haven't taught those steps, you won't be able to backtrack to resolve the problem. So, even if you bought a highly-trained horse, if you're struggling to connect with him, treat him like a youngster. Pretend that you are dealing with a yearling that knows nothing. By going all the way back to ground work and reteaching the basics, you'll develop a mutually understood set of cues. You'll know what your horse knows. You won't be making assumptions anymore.

The Click That Teaches: Riding With The Clicker

PRINCIPLE #3: TRAIN POSITIVELY

Focus on what you want your horse to do, not the unwanted behavior.

Most of us are very good at stating what we don't want. We don't want our horse dancing around when we try to get on him, or rushing his fences, or jigging out on the trail. Stating what we don't want is a beginning, but it doesn't really help us design a structured lesson plan. For that you need to state what you do want your horse to do. The clearer and more detailed you are in this, the easier it is to see the steps in your lesson plan.

For example, if you don't want your horse dancing around when you get on, what do you want? You'd like him to stand still. The principles of training lead you directly to the next question: have you taught him to stand still?

If your horse understood the lesson well enough, he would stand still. You may have taught him to stand still on a calm day when there are no other horses around and his pasture mates haven't just headed off down the trail without him. But now the wind is gusting, and your friends just left without you. You want him to stand still even under these conditions. Again, the question is: have you taught him to do this? If the answer is no, the other principles of good training will help you design your lesson, beginning with: *safety always comes first*; and *never start with your goal: put lots of steps between where your horse is now and where you want him to be.*

Learning emotional control isn't just for the horse. Learning to focus on what you want and remaining non-reactive to your horse's distracting, annoying, attention-grabbing behavior can be a real challenge. Clicker training requires a dramatic shift in thinking for many handlers.

Following the training principles in this chapter will help you learn how to think like a clicker trainer.

PRINCIPLE #4: BE A SPLITTER, NOT A LUMPER

Break each lesson down into many small steps. Teach one element of the behavior at a time.

Most of us ask for too much, too fast. We're lumpers instead of splitters. Our horse is barely comfortable being touched and we're throwing a saddle on his back. We're lumping together too many training steps into one.

Good trainers are splitters or reductionists, that is

FOCUS ON THE POSITIVE

The principle in action: This handler could react aggressively to this Icelandic stallion nudging at her arm. Instead she practices "the grown-ups are talking, please don't interrupt" lesson. She decides what she would like him to do: look straight ahead. She clicks and reinforces him for that positive behavior. She knows that the opposite of positive reinforcement is not punishment. It is no reinforcement, so she doesn't react to his attention-seeking behavior by pushing him away. Instead she waits for the good behavior she wants to reinforce.

This is what she doesn't want.

This is the polite behavior she wants to see. Click and Treat!

Chapter Five: The Principles of Training

they reduce behavior into smaller and smaller pieces. A splitter, for example, would see that the horse is nervous being handled, so before he ever thought about putting anything on his back, he'd be breaking the training down into many small steps.

Splitters are good observers of behavior. They've spent time watching the animals they will be training. They recognize all the subtle precursors leading up to the behavior they want to modify. A good splitter, for example, sees a spook coming long before it happens and inserts steps to derail it.

Before you start riding, you need to know what you're putting your bones on top of. Most of us understand that our horse is a prey animal that lives in herds and has a strong flight reaction. But do we really know what that means in terms of behavior? If you want to become a confident, secure rider, you need to learn to see behavior.

Forget about what you may have been told about herd dynamics and instead look for yourself at what your horse is *doing*!

Focus just on the behavior you can see. Don't try to figure out if he's the alpha horse in the herd, or what he's thinking. Instead look at *what* he does!

The mantra to remember is: observe without judgment. Most of us are so busy pigeon-holing our horses that we miss the details we need to be seeing. We need to forget the cliches we've been taught about horses being willful, or stubborn, or stupid, and instead learn to see behavior. Behavior means just that: what is the horse doing?

I've spent many thousands of hours watching horses, and for no other reason than I like looking at them. In watching horses I've come to appreciate the subtleties of their movement. You can see intent in a shift of weight, a change of muscle tone, a flick of an ear.

Later in training you'll use this information to help you recognize and reinforce the small tries your horse offers on the way to the larger goal behavior.

If you are new to horses, I encourage you to spend time simply watching your horse. Before you climb on his back, find out who he IS, both as an individual and as a species. How does he behave when the wind blows? When a dog comes into his paddock? When another horse spooks or kicks up its heels? Find out what is normal for your horse, and for horses in general. Remember, observe without judgment. Don't try to interpret what you are seeing—*just watch*.

Good trainers know how to see the subtleties of their horse's actions. They know what comes

SMALL STEPS

If you are new to training, practice the skill of observation. Look for subtle behaviors. Look for shifts in weight, for changes in muscle tone, for mouth activity, etc.. LITTLE THINGS CAN MEAN A LOT!

Most riders are lumpers instead of splitters. Lumpers have fewer and bigger behaviors, and the splitters have more, smaller behaviors. It's easy to spot the lumpers. They're the ones fighting with their horses and blaming them for their failure to obey.

The trainers I most admire are all splitters. In many respects these trainers are philosophically worlds apart, but the one thing I think they would all agree on is the importance of being a good splitter, of chunking training down into smaller and smaller units.

Clicker training teaches you how to be a good splitter. Every time you click you are creating a step in your training. You have to think about what it is you want to reinforce. You aren't just clicking because you thought your horse needed a treat. You are finding elements in his performance that you want to highlight. The bottom line is learn to be a good splitter, and you will be a good trainer. That's what the horses show us. You'll recognize it in their happy attitudes and outstanding performance.

Spend time just watching your horse "be a horse".

before a behavior and what comes after. They don't wait for the horse to be spooking out from under them to take action. They feel the precursors to the larger behavior in time to alter it. They never have to ride a bucking horse because they are able to stop the behavior before it ever occurs.

The Click That Teaches: Riding With The Clicker

PRINCIPLE #5: USE BABY STEPS TO PROGRESS

Raise your expectations in small increments so your horse continues to be successful and can earn reinforcement.

This principle is very much related to being a splitter instead of a lumper. One of the common mistakes people make in training is they will get a few good steps of something, and then they get greedy. Their horse gives at the poll and engages his back for two strides, and now they want it for six. Their horse touched a target a couple of times, now they want to use it to get him onto a trailer. The result is their training resembles a house of cards: it doesn't take much to knock it down. A scrap of paper blowing by, another horse trotting past, that's all the distraction it takes to topple their training.

They have fallen back into the training trap of lumping. So good splitters not only see many small steps towards a training goal, they include those steps in their training plan. Anytime their horse shows concern or his behavior deteriorates, they read that as a sign that they have moved ahead too fast. So another key rule to remember in training is: *when behavior deteriorates, go back to a previous step in the training.*

Sample Lesson:

Goal Behavior: Walk over a plastic tarp to prepare a horse for crossing water.

A lumper would spread the plastic out on the ground and begin to work directly on walking his horse across.

A splitter might see the following steps:

1.) Teach the horse to touch a target.
2.) Have the horse follow the target, forward and back.
3.) Have the horse follow the target to the ground to teach head lowering.
4.) Take the horse for a walk. Play "touch the goblins" with anything he seems concerned about. Hold the target up an inch or two in front of him. Have him touch the target, click and treat. Gradually move the target closer to the "goblin" until he is targeting directly on the scary object. Click and treat.
5.) Teach him to stand on a plywood mat.
6.) Create a "trail class" with toys for him to interact with, a beach ball to kick, a cone to retrieve, a small jump to walk over, a mailbox to open, etc..
7.) Include the plastic tarp with these other games. Use two long pieces of plastic set wide apart to form a chute for him to walk through.★ Click and treat him for walking through, then walking through calmly, at an even pace, with a relaxed expression, etc.. Let him play with the other toys as needed to relieve his anxiety.
8.) Gradually bring the far ends of the plastic together so they form the point of the V. Click and treat your horse for walking over the joined section.
9.) Gradually merge the two sheets of plastic together until they form a large rectangle. By now he will be walking confidently over the plastic. Click and jackpot!

SMALL STEPS—SAFE STEPS

The principle in action: This horse is afraid of plastic, so her handler has chunked the training down into many small steps.

She began by spreading the two sheet of plastic very far apart.

She gradually moved the far ends closer together to form a V. (Note, the cones were added to keep the plastic from gusting up in the wind.)

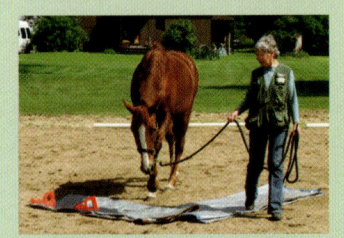

She then gradually closed the V, . . .

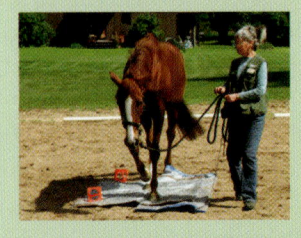

. . . until her mare was walking calmly over a solid sheet of plastic.

The mantra for this principle is: "Get behavior, get it consistently, then improve on it" - remembering always to proceed in small enough steps that you and your horse continue to be safe and successful.

★ Based on a TTEAM ground work exercise - TTEAM: the Tellington-Jones Equine Awareness Method.

Chapter Five: The Principles of Training

PRINCIPLE #6: EVENTUALLY EVERYONE WILL SIT DOWN

If you keep doing something long enough, no matter what it is, or how much you enjoy doing it, eventually you will want to change and do something else.

If you really understand this sentence, by which I mean not just the words, but the real meaning behind them, you have the keys to being a patient trainer.

If I keep you standing long enough, eventually you'll get tired and you'll want to sit down. And if I then keep you sitting, you'll eventually start to fidget and want to move again.

If your horse is stuck in cement, absolutely glued to the ground, just staring at you while you hold a cone out in front of him, that's fine. You can wait. Eventually he's going to twitch an eyebrow, shift his weight, swat at a fly. That's movement, and that's what you need to train.

If you capture those little twitches and shifts of weight with the clicker, you can encourage even more movement. You are using *shaping*, *a process where you observe a small tendency for a behavior to occur and selectively reinforce that tendency to modify it into a more complex form of the behavior.*

As a trainer you can certainly help the process along. A horse that is racing around an arena on an adrenaline high can be asked to change direction through tight turns. As he makes turn after turn, he's going to want to stop his feet. Click! he gets a treat.

The horse that is stuck to the ground in front of the trailer can be given a few extra incentives to move. You can take the slack out of his lead so he feels pressure on his face and gently tap him on his hip. Or you can put a target out just in front of his nose so he has to stretch out his neck to touch it. Both act as motivators to help get his feet in motion.

You may feel as though you are tapping on a statue, but if you truly understand that change will happen, you can be patient. You don't have to escalate and start whacking your horse, or drag him onto the trailer with pulleys and ropes. You can let the steady tap tap tap of the whip do its job. You're playing poker with your horse. He's bigger than you are. He's stronger, and he's faster, but you have an edge he doesn't. You absolutely know that eventually he will change his behavior, and you can wait.

Most of us never stay with an exercise long enough to see all the good things it can give us. We're in too much of a hurry to make things happen, to get results and to be on to the next task. Patience comes from understanding that every detail is important, and that all these little steps truly are connected to one another. Perfecting the building blocks of performance will ultimately give you top performance. As you tap tap tap your stuck horse, you are working not just on getting him on the trailer, but on his "go forward" cue in general. You're building trust. You're showing him how you operate in the world. You aren't suddenly going to lose your temper and start driving him in. You're going to be patient and help him deal with his fear. The ripple effect through all his training will be huge as you remain true to basic principles.

PATIENCE

Whatever your horse is doing, eventually he will shift and do something else. Even if it seems as though your horse is stuck in cement or has gone to sleep, eventually he will twitch a muscle, or move a foot. That's all you need to get started. Click and reinforce that tiny change. It will grow into more.

And if your horse suddenly goes into overdrive and starts racing around, that's all right, too. Eventually, he will get tired of doing that and slow down. Click and treat. With patience and an understanding of principles, you'll find the balance you're looking for.

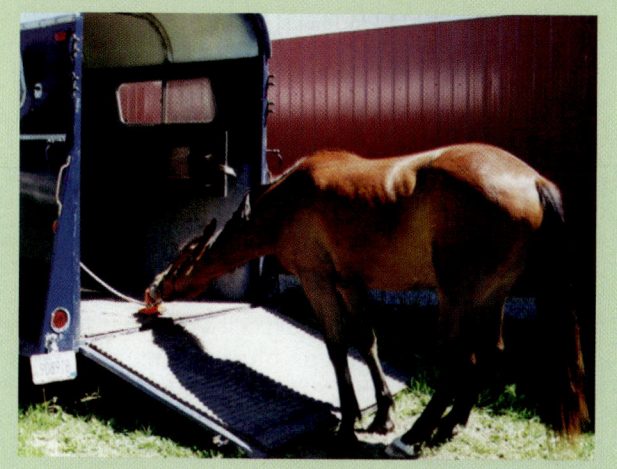

Being patient has gotten many a horse on a trailer. This horse cannot stand like this forever. Eventually his hind end is going to get tired, and he'll figure out that it's safe to take one step forward into the trailer. Click and treat. He'll be thinking his way onto the trailer instead of jumping in when he's still afraid and not yet ready for the close quarters of a trailer.

PRINCIPLE #7: KEEP THE "PENDULUM" IN BALANCE

For every exercise you teach there is an opposite exercise you must teach to keep things in balance.

If you focus on teaching your high-energy horse to stop, you may get to the point where you can't get him to move. If you then make going forward a priority, you may lose your brakes. The challenge of training is learning to keep everything in balance. If you teach head lowering to calm your horse down, you must also teach head raising, or your horse may spend the rest of his working life walking with his nose in the dirt.

You and your horse can only focus on one lesson at a time. If, in the process of learning one element in the training, you get things out of balance, don't worry. You haven't "broken" your horse. He's just showing you the next element that needs attention.

BALANCE

Balance in training is a key element. Learn to listen to your horse. He'll tell you what lessons he needs you to focus on. Resistance is your horse's way of telling you that some element of the training is out of balance. Here's the good news: if you don't notice a little resistance, don't worry, it will get bigger. Eventually, the system will be so out of balance, the lessons you need to work will become obvious.

Keep the Pendulum in Balance.

PRINCIPLE #8: PATIENCE IS JUST KNOWLEDGE IN DISGUISE

Patience comes from understanding basic principles. It comes from seeing your horse not as an adversary but as a partner.

When your horse is your partner, that changes your perceptions both of him and his training. He's no longer out to get you. He may have his jaw locked on a rein and be pulling like a freight train, but he's not doing it to spite you. He's not "stubborn", and he's not "stupid". As his partner and his teacher, you don't have to take his actions personally. That locked jaw may simply be telling you that you haven't explained yourself clearly enough. Resistance is just your horse's way of communicating that he's afraid, or he doesn't understand something, or he physically can't do it.

If an unwanted behavior persists even after a reasonable amount of training, look for physical causes. Pain is the root cause behind many behavior problems. Eliminate the pain, and you eliminate the problem.

Ask a roomful of people what they would do to solve a particular problem, and you'll get a roomful of answers back. To decide what is best for your horse, by all means listen to the advice, but remember to ask the most knowledgeable expert of all: your horse. He'll tell you if a training method is working or not. If you follow the basic guidelines of good training and observe his reactions, you'll be able to sort through all the advice you get and choose methods which suit your situation. Always remember this wonderful line: go to people for opinions, and horses for answers.

PRINCIPLE #9: PERFORMANCE IS THE PERFECTION OF BASICS.

Basics are everything. All you have to work with are a few simple building blocks: forward, back, left, right. What determines your horse's level of performance is how light and responsive he is to your requests to move in these directions.

Lightness is one of those wonderful buzz words. We all want our horse to be "light", but what actually do we mean by that? One definition would be a horse that is responsive to our cues. If that's what we mean, then we have to define just how responsive we want our horses to be. Having a horse that responds too well to our cues can be just as frustrating for some people as having one that doesn't respond well enough. Our horses are so tuned in to the subtleties of body motion that they can detect signals we don't

Chapter Five: The Principles of Training

even know we're giving. How many times have you heard somebody say: "my horse breaks into a canter before I even ask"? That horse is feeling his rider's intent. He's being a responsive, "light" horse. The problem is the rider isn't aware of the signals she's giving. I want my horses to be light, so I am always looking for the smallest clues that they are picking up from me that signal my intent. I want to craft those clues into deliberate signals so that I can make my horses even lighter still. I do this by understanding a very important concept. Lightness comes not from the signal itself, but from the "threat" of the signal.

The word "threat" doesn't seem as though it belongs in a book about clicker training, but it's important for our horses that we understand the use of this word in a training context. It doesn't mean we're suddenly going to become fierce and aggressive. It simply means we are going to follow through with our requests to the point where our intent becomes clear to the horse, and he can be successful. Soft but unclear in the long run is no kindness for the horse.

Suppose I'm standing in front of you. I want you to back, so I place my hand on your shoulder. You want to be a good "horse" so you take a step back. The pressure instantly goes away, plus you get a click and a treat – a couple of peppermints to give to your horse later.

I ask several more times in the same way. You're very responsive. Every time I touch your shoulder, you step back. That's great, but I would like you to be even lighter. So now between requests I very deliberately drop my hand down to my side. Now I have to lift my hand and reach toward your shoulder to ask you to back.

You start to notice, and before I can touch you, you're already stepping back. My "horse" is getting lighter, but I can do even better. While you're pocketing your peppermints, I'll take a step or two away from you. Now to touch your shoulder I have to walk forward, lift my arm, and reach out towards you. You know what I want, so you don't wait for me to get all the way to you. I just have to start to move, and you're backing up.

Pretty soon, I can be clear across the room, and you'll still back from my signal. Now that's a "light" horse. If you get distracted, or forgetful, I can always walk over and remind you what the pressure means by placing my hand on your shoulder. If you want to avoid the direct contact, all you have to do is back up. So it's not the direct pressure itself that makes you light, but the "threat" of it. It's up to me to observe your response. How light you become to my signal is my responsibility.

If you want a light horse, you have to give your horse the opportunity to respond to less. Lightness is your responsibility, not the horse's.

A light horse means you can ask him to back and he responds without hesitation. Ask him to shift forward, and again there's an instant change in balance. Out of those weight shifts you can build everything you want from your horse: lateral work, collection, spins, lead changes, etc.. *Performance is the perfection of basics.*

PRINCIPLE #10: THERE ARE NO LIMITS

There are no limits. Take the sum of all the other principles, and this is what you will come to.

I wrote in my first book, *Clicker Training For Your Horse*★, "If you can dream it, you can train it." That's something I very strongly believe. No matter what kind of horse you have, or what kind of difficulties you face, when you break your training down into small enough steps, you will eventually find something you can ask your horse to do. That's the beginning. It's like planting a seed. You have only to nurture that tiny step to have it grow into others.

This last principle is for me the most important. It is a lesson my horses have taught me. Peregrine's mother had neurological damage. Long before I knew anything about clicker training, she taught me the importance of these principles. I learned through her to be a superb splitter; to throw my goals out the window and to work on what needed doing today; to train in baby steps, and to focus always on the positive. When she was two, she could barely walk. Riding seemed an impossible dream, but eventually she became the horse who introduced me to the beauty of dressage. When I say there are no limits, it is because of what she taught me.

When she was giving birth, she got down against a wall and couldn't get up. Her foal was trapped in her pelvis with his head and neck jammed into a corner of the stall. She was thrashing, banging her head into the cement wall of the stall. I was alone with them in the barn, and I couldn't leave her to pull him out. Luckily we had an open intercom to the barn manager's house. Within minutes I had help. Her foal wasn't trapped long, but it was enough time to damage his back. Her foal was my Peregrine, the very first of my clicker-trained horses.

Peregrine was a dear, sweet, loving colt, who grew up with a terrible physical problem. Both of his stifles locked. The stifle is the joint that's equivalent to our knee. Imagine the ligaments in your knee locking up so you can't bend your leg. That's what happened to Peregrine. The problem with his joints originated up in his spine. His mother had a

★ *Clicker Training For Your Horse*, by Alexandra Kurland; Sunshine Books, US and Ringpress books, UK

The Click That Teaches: Riding With The Clicker

phenomenal back with wonderful lifting power, perfect for dressage, but not Peregrine. The first time I sat on him, I sang the nursery rhyme:

"London bridge is falling down, falling down, falling down"
London bridge is falling down, falling down, falling down,
My fair lady"

That will tell you what it was like to ride him. His back wasn't sore; he just had no understanding of how to engage his hips or support a rider. His locking stifles were a by-product of the way he hollowed his back. It made him an incredibly challenging horse to ride. When his joints locked, they stiffened his entire body.

Most people would have walked away from a project like this, but Peregrine was the only foal out of my beloved mare. I was determined not to give up on him. So, I went to work and learned how to unlock my horse's mind and free up his joints.

That's what brought me to clicker training. Clicker training at first was just a curiosity, something to experiment with during a stretch of time when Peregrine was laid up with abscesses in both front feet. I taught him to touch a target. I thought at first it was a cute "parlor trick", nothing more, until I saw how eager he was to play clicker games. I continued to use the clicker during his recovery. What struck me was how calm he was. He wasn't having any of those fits of pent-up thoroughbred energy I normally would have expected from him.

By the time Peregrine was well enough to ride, I was so intrigued by this new method of training that I continued to experiment with it. When I started him back under saddle, I did so with the clicker. As I clicked him for correct responses, I could almost hear him say, "Oh that's what you want! Why didn't you say so before?" But what really hooked me was something that happened as we continued to use the clicker over the next couple of months. I was going through all of Peregrine's training, reshaping everything with the clicker. That included piaffe and the beginnings of Spanish walk (the equine version of a military goose step). Peregrine's Spanish walk had never been very good. He didn't have the lifting power in his back to do it well, and his locking stifles tended to get in the way. But now I was using the clicker. When Peregrine engaged his hindquarters enough to lift his shoulders up, I clicked and jackpotted him with peppermints. Peregrine loves peppermints.

Even though it demanded the most effort from him, Spanish walk very quickly became his favorite lesson. He started offering it to me at liberty just to get me to play clicker games with him. And that's when I noticed something most remarkable. Peregrine wasn't locking in his stifles anymore. He was eight years old at that time. He'd been locking in his stifles since he was a foal. He is now twenty, and since he learned how to use his back in the Spanish walk via the clicker he has not locked in his stifles even once. That's one reason why I'm so passionate about this training. It's not about tricks or even fixing "problem" horses. It's about communication. It's about the connection it creates with your horse. With the clicker, Peregrine understood what I was asking him to do, and with that understanding came a new ability to manage his own body.

There are no limits with clicker training. Your own horses will teach you what these ten principles mean. Trust the process. It will take you to the horse of your dreams.

EVERYTHING IS EVERYTHING ELSE

There are no limits with clicker training. Your own horses will teach you what these ten principles mean. Trust the process. It will take you to the horse of your dreams.

And, there is one other very important principle that belongs on the list: *Everything is everything else*. The lessons you learn from your horses and from clicker training are just metaphors that apply to every aspect of your life.

Peregrine

CHAPTER 6
Food!

We use food in clicker training. In this chapter you'll learn why, and you'll also learn more about teaching your horse the good manners he'll need to be around you when your pockets are stuffed full of goodies.

HAND TREATS

Suppose you've been clicker training for a couple of days now. Your horse touches the target. He'll even pick it up and hand it back to you! He's SO SMART! When he sees you at the paddock gate, he comes running over to greet you. He used to be hard to catch. Now he's eager to work.

You love the changes you're seeing in him. Before you started with the clicker he was a real bully, always crowding into your space. Now he backs from the lightest touch. You can hardly wait for your next lesson so you can show your instructor all the things you've taught him.

The day you show off your clicker star he's brilliant. He fetches, he backs, he's so eager. You couldn't be more proud of him! But all your instructor sees is the one time he grabbed at your pocket.

"You see," she warns you. "You're teaching him to bite. If you keep feeding him all those treats, you're going to ruin that horse."

Before you let her burst your bubble, just remember she means well. The problem is our beliefs color what we see. Most of us have been taught that the number one rule around horses is NEVER FEED THEM BY HAND. If you do, we've been warned, your horse will become distracted. He'll get pushy, and you'll be teaching him to bite.

You could look at this from a different perspective. Instead of seeing food as a distraction you could view it as a one of the most powerful motivators in your horse's life. Control his access to food, and you can modify his behavior. That's the basic premise behind clicker training, and it's the function of the clicker. It acts as a gate keeper. It tells your horse when he can expect food, and when he can't. If you click, that means a treat is coming. In the absence of a click, your horse can nuzzle your pockets all he wants, but you aren't going to feed him. The click creates rules surrounding the food. Since we have to feed our horses anyway, we might as well use the clicker to put the food to work for us.

POSITIVE MOTIVATORS

Correction-based training asks: "What will my horse actively change his behavior to avoid?"

In contrast clicker training asks: "What will my horse actively work for?"

At the top of that list for most horses is FOOD, but that does not mean that food is the only reinforcer clicker training uses. The definition of a reinforcer is something that strengthens. If your horse spits out peppermints and turns his nose up at carrots, they are not reinforcing to HIM. If he goes into ecstasies of delight over a scratch on his withers, that's something you can use as a reinforcer. When we limit the definition of a "treat" to food, we narrow our

---

TREATS AND POLITE MANNERS

You can hand feed treats AND have a polite horse.

Temptation: a bucket full of grain.

"Is that for me?"

No. Time out. This is negative punishment. Something the horse wants is taken away.

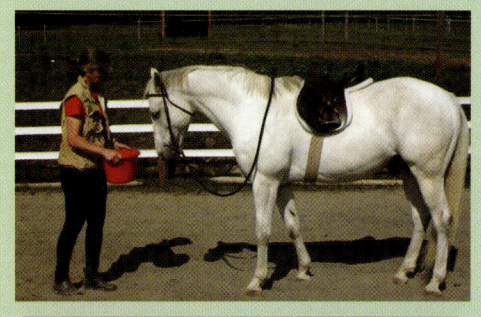

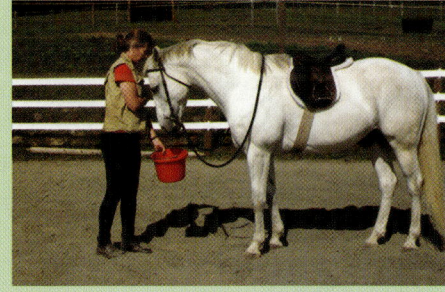

The result: "You can't get me to take that grain!" Click and treat.

Food is one of the most powerful motivators in a horse's life. The clicker gives us a way to channel it productively and use it in training.

thinking. A "treat" is a special pleasure or delight. It is up to us to find out what our horses enjoy and will work for.

Clicker training is about controlling access to resources your horse wants and will work for. How do you determine what your horse will actively work for? Mugging behavior is one good indication.

When you first get to the barn, and your horse knows he's about to go out, what is his reaction? Is he hollering for his turn to be led out? That's something he actively wants.

When you're out cleaning up his paddock, does he sidle up to you asking to be scratched? That's something he actively wants.

When you walk around with your pockets full of carrots, does he try his best to look cute so you'll feed him? That's definitely something he wants.

Mugging you doesn't have to mean biting at your clothes or nuzzling your pockets. If your horse has learned that batting his eyelashes and twisting his head upside down will get you to feed him carrots, that's the behavior you're going to see him "mugging" you with. If hollering for turnout gets reinforced, he'll holler more. If he doesn't care about going out, he won't be carrying on in anticipation of your opening the door.

Mugging behavior, whatever it is, is just the physical evidence that your horse WILL work for a particular motivator. You might be reluctant to use food because of all the negative things you've heard about horses learning to bite when they are hand fed. The question to ask in that case is what else will your horse "mug" you for with the same strong desire that he shows for food? And can you manipulate that motivator with the same ease that you can food?

Seen in this way, mugging is not a negative behavior at all, but simply the means you use to assess the power of different motivators. The function of the bridging signal is to tell the horse which behaviors will gain him access to the desired motivator. It lets you use a motivator that's as powerful as food without losing control. In a sense it's as though you've jumped from pedaling around on an old-fashioned bicycle to zooming around on a jet propelled motorcycle. That's the power you gain when you add food into the mix.

Without the gate keeping function of the bridging signal and the rules it creates, you could end up with a pushy horse. That was the lesson of the past. Instead of learning how to use food, people simply took it off the training table.

It's time to learn a different lesson. Instead of avoiding food, we should be finding ways to use it. When you harness it into your training program, you gain a very powerful tool, one it would be a shame not to use.

It's like using an old-fashioned typewriter in the age of computers. Yes, you can get the job done using outdated technology, but not nearly as well. That in a nutshell is what clicker training represents. It gives us the technology to take one of the most powerful motivators in a horse's life and put it to work for us.

Conventional trainers never learned how to do this. Without a "right answer" cue linking performance to reward, food for them was a distraction instead of a motivator. If you can't enhance performance with positive reinforcement, the alternative is to suppress behavior with pain. Historically, this was the approach people used to control horses.

If your horse is struggling with emotional control, you might want to begin clicker training with lower value treats; carrots, for example, rather than his favorite sweet feed. You'll need to experiment to find the treats that work best for your horse. Peregrine likes a mix of treats: carrot, apples, in addition to grain and his favorite peppermints. My young horse, Robin, works best if I use a hay replacement pellet. Jackpots distract him and are saved for the very end of a session.

PRAISE VERSUS FOOD

The positive and negative motivators are like the two sides of a coin. On one side are the motivators the horse will actively work to avoid. These include pain, fear, and discomfort. On the other side of the coin are motivators the horse will work for. These include comfort, security, social interactions, and, topping the list for most horses, food.

Your horse might enjoy praise and a scratch, but he'll work for food. That's a key difference. When you take food off the training table, all too often what you are left with are the motivators on the avoidance side of the coin: pain and fear. If you doubt that, go look through any tack catalog. The equipment that's being offered relies on this type of moving-away-from motivation.

Many people can see the value of the bridging signal, but they still resist the idea of using food in their training. They see the food as something separate from themselves, and they want their horse to work for them, not the goodies in their pockets. They'll click and pet, but they won't click and feed.

Jean Donaldson addresses this issue in the introduction to her book *Culture Clash*[★]. This is a dog training book, but she makes some excellent

---

[★] *Culture Clash,* by Jean Donaldson; James and Kenneth Publishers, CA

Chapter Six: Food!

points that relate directly to horse training.

She points out that in traditional dog obedience classes the trainers often believe that the primary motivation is praise. In reality, the primary motivation is often the avoidance of aversives. The dog has learned that if he is being praised that means a correction has just been avoided. I think the same is often true with horses. A dressage horse who is holding itself well is earning praise, but it is also avoiding the sharp jab of a spur. The praise does have meaning which both the dog and the horse have learned, but it may not be quite the same meaning that their well-meaning owners intended.

Praise is a conditioned response. It can mean pain has just been avoided, and it can also mean good things are coming. We often praise our animals when we are feeding them, petting them, letting them rest, etc.. The praise then becomes an indicator to the animal that the chances of it getting a primary reinforcer have just increased. If it keeps doing more of what it is doing, its owner will give it something it wants.

Many people will say that they do not want to use food with their animals because they want them working for them, not the goodies in their pocket. If praise is their main positive reinforcer, they should look carefully at what they are really doing. From the HORSE'S point of view it may be that it is really working to avoid discomfort. It sounds good to say that your horse is working for praise, but often the main motivator is discomfort.

Donaldson makes another good point in her book. Some animals do work well for praise, but for others it's not enough to motivate them in a training situation. We tend to confuse bonding activities with training, and become disappointed when our animal needs more than a "good boy" to work for us. If a rider is avoiding food and other primary reinforcers because she wants her horse to "work for her", what she is left with are aversives as motivators. Training via pain wasn't her intent, but it is often the outcome.

GRANDMOTHERS AND HORSE TRAINERS

All right, I've convinced you. You're going to use food in your training, but does that mean that your horse is going to view you as a giant vending machine? Is that what clicker training is going to reduce you to?

By no means. Think of it this way: when you were little, do you remember what it was like to have your out-of-town-grandparents come for a visit. Didn't they always bring you presents? The presents probably made you look forward to their arrival with pleasure, or did they? If your grandparents spent their entire visit criticizing the way you looked, the way you dressed, the way you behaved, you probably dreaded their arrival. You might be glad to get the present, but it didn't make you love them.

By the same token, you could feed your horse bushels of carrots, but if most of the time you're picking away at him, he's not going to look forward to your visits any more than you looked forward to your grandparents.

Instead of criticizing, maybe your grandparents spent their time telling you how wonderful you are and how much they loved you. The presents took on a very different meaning. They became linked to all the good feelings you had towards your grandparents. Yes, you loved the treats, but what you loved even more were your grandparents. That's the kind of link clicker training creates for our horses.

Clicker trainers aren't just doling out pieces of carrots, they are appreciating their horses. They aren't focusing on all the little nuisance behaviors other people worry about. They are seeing the wonderful individual that is *their* horse. With every click and treat, they are saying: "I appreciate so much the work you do for me." If you want your horse to work FOR YOU, there is no better way to do it than through clicker training.

TABLE MANNERS

In that very first target training lesson one of the things you should be looking for is how well your horse takes a treat. Does he take it gently, or does he pinch skin as he grabs for it?

Taking a slice of carrot or a bit of grain off your hand is a motor skill some horses have trouble learning. Instead of gently using their lips, they grab with their teeth. You feel as though you need to count fingers after every encounter!

If this describes your horse, put a halter on him so you can control his head. You're going to create a consistent pattern for presenting the treat, one that will remind him that he needs to have self-control —always.

Suppose you are working on "The grown-ups are talking, please don't interrupt" lesson. (See page 14.) After you click, take a hold of the side buckle of the halter with your right hand. Your horse is now limited in how far he can reach out with his mouth.

Reach into your pocket and take out his treat. If he grabs for it, restrain him with your right, and draw your left hand up to your shoulder. You've just given him a timeout. It is very important that you

The Click That Teaches: Riding With The Clicker

HAND FEEDING

Some horses have never learned how to take food from the hand. If your horse has trouble gently taking food from your hand, before you can have fun with clicker training, you need to teach him "table manners". If you feel as though your hand is being sucked up into his mouth along with the treat, your horse definitely needs this lesson.

1.) Put a halter on your horse so you have control of his head.
2.) Put him back in his stall with a stall guard across the door and review the basics of targeting.
3.) After you click, take a hold of the side buckle of the halter with your right hand. Your horse is now limited in how far he can reach out with his mouth.
4.) Offer him the treat with your left hand. If he starts to grab at you, bring your left hand up to your shoulder. You're giving him a time out. If he wants the treat, he needs to show restraint.
5.) Offer him the treat again. If he shows any self-control, let him have the goody. Otherwise withdraw it again. Repeat as many times as needed.

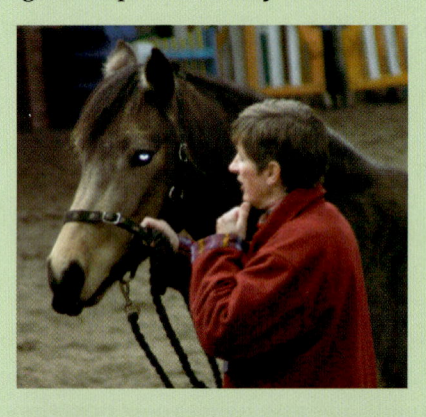

You can use the intensity of your horse's mugging behavior to judge the power of different motivators. If your horse is struggling with emotional control, you might want to begin your training with a lower value treat - carrots, for example, instead of grain.

not turn this into teasing. As soon as you feel him relax the pressure on his halter, offer him the treat again. If he grabs for it, pull your hand up to your shoulder. Repeat this as many times as needed until you feel a little improvement in his eagerness. He doesn't have to be perfect, not all at once. If you expect too much too fast, he'll get frustrated. A little improvement will quickly turn into a horse that waits for his treat.

You want your horse to get his treat. You just want him to learn that he can't lunge for it, or engulf your whole hand in his mouth. If you feel as though your hand is being sucked up into his mouth along with the treat, your horse needs this lesson.

Most horses learn very quickly that they have to show restraint to get their treat. They'll figure out how to take it gently from your open hand. This is a little bit like a toddler learning to eat with a fork. You may not think this would be a difficult skill, but some horses seem to lack the fine motor control that's needed to pluck the treat off your palm without taking your whole hand into their mouths or using their teeth.

If your horse continues to have trouble with the mechanics, be patient. Here's another tip that may help: bring your hand down from above. This removes some of the temptation to lunge forward for the goody. Keep your left hand closed over the treat. Bring it to a point that's even with his nostrils and slide your hand down his nose. Coming from above like this makes it easier for him to use his lips, instead of lunging at you with his teeth.

If your horse is generally pretty good about taking treats, but occasionally pinches skin, take a moment to assess the situation. It may be you are over-loading him: asking for too much, too fast or adding in too many distractions. His insecurity results in a too-anxious grab of the treat. The solution: ease off the demands of your lesson.

KEEP IT FUN!

Take the time in your training to pay attention to these details of food delivery and polite manners. I know the temptation is to rush through these early steps to get to riding, but clicker training is only fun if you have control of the treats.

Your horse could be doing all kinds of clever things, fetching targets, opening mailboxes, bringing you your slippers, but if in between he's grabbing at your pockets, you're not going to think much of clicker training. So spend time in the beginning to create rock-solid manners. The pay-off will be an emotionally-settled riding horse.

CHAPTER 7
The Language of Operant Conditioning

Clicker training is built on a solid bedrock of science. To use it well it's important to understand a few basic terms. It's also important to know what your motivators are and to call a spade a spade. You may think of yourself as a positive trainer, but the reality is that positive reinforcement is not the only tool you're using. You could be using negative reinforcement and even punishment and not even know it. For example, if you abruptly end a training session, your horse may feel as though you are punishing him by taking away the goodies and the social interaction. You need to understand all aspects of operant conditioning to be fully aware of the effect your actions have on others.

In this chapter we'll look in more detail at the "training shortcuts", in particular at negative reinforcement (pg. 5). I'll show you how to use it in conjunction with the clicker so that it remains a pleasant training tool for your horse.

DEFINITIONS

To understand clicker training it's useful to understand a few basic scientific terms. In training we are manipulating consequences. A good consequence makes a behavior more likely to occur again. An unpleasant consequence makes it less likely. To reinforce means to strengthen, so in positive reinforcement we are adding something the horse wants (a positive consequence). That makes the behavior more likely to occur again.

Since the addition of the reward happens after the desired behavior, timing becomes an issue. There must be a clear link between behavior and the reward in order for that reward to have any impact on the behavior. Suppose, for example, your horse has just picked up the correct canter lead for the first time. You'd like to tell him how wonderful he is. You let him canter on a few strides, then you apply pressure to his mouth to bring him down out of the canter. Once he's at the halt, you pet him and give him a bite of carrot. Your intent is to tell him how great the canter was, but from his point of view what are you really rewarding? Maybe at that moment he's got his attention riveted on the new horse that just came into the ring. So is he getting a carrot for tensing up and looking at other horses? Good deal for him, but not for you!

The clicker helps to end this confusion. It creates a link between the desired behavior and the reward that follows. It is a secondary reinforcer, that is, it is one step removed from the primary reinforcer which it predicts.

Without the clicker any time delay between the behavior and the treat weakens the connection, and you may end up reinforcing behaviors you don't want. This is why in the past trainers could not rely on positive reinforcement in their training. Without a bridging signal such as the clicker the horse was unclear why he was getting goodies and often ended up thinking he was being reinforced for something entirely different from his owner's intentions.

Another important term to understand is negative reinforcement. In negative reinforcement the horse is experiencing something

---

THE LANGUAGE OF OPERANT CONDITIONING

Reinforcer
A reinforcer by definition strengthens the behavior it is associated with. If a stimulus has no effect on the behavior, it is not reinforcing that particular behavior. Reinforcers can be either positive or negative, meaning something is either added or taken away.

In **negative reinforcement** something the horse finds unpleasant is removed. He learns to change his behavior when presented with the unpleasant stimulus, thus strengthening or making an alternative behavior more likely to occur. Our use of pressure in training is an example.

In **positive reinforcement** the animal changes its behavior and gains something it actively wants, for example, food.

Punishment
Punishment is an unpleasant or painful stimulus that stops behavior as it is occurring.

In **negative punishment** something the animal actively wants is *taken away*. Your horse pins his ears as you bring him his supper, so you turn your back on him and walk away. If he wants his food, he needs to change his behavior.

In **positive punishment** an aversive stimulus is added. Your horse bites you, you hit him. Because the behavior stops at that moment, positive punishment is reinforcing to the punisher. However, positive punishment does not necessarily stop the behavior from occurring again, and it often creates unwanted side effects. Since the unpleasant stimulus is added after the behavior, problems with timing are often an issue.

In real-world training the four aspects of operant conditioning do not occur in isolation from one another. For example, when you use negative reinforcement, you may be the good guy taking the pressure away, but you were also the bad guy who put it there in the first place. You are punishing one behavior even as you are reinforcing another.

unpleasant. By changing his behavior, he discovers that he can get that unpleasant stimulus to go away. So positive and negative reinforcement aren't judgement calls. We're not saying something is "good" or "bad". Rather it means something pleasant has been added (positive reinforcement) or something unpleasant has been subtracted (negative reinforcement) from the horse's environment.

Behavior is determined by its consequences. In negative reinforcement, when you take away something unpleasant, whatever was occurring immediately before is reinforced. If your horse tosses his head when you pick up the reins, the worst thing you can do is let go. That will simply make head tossing more likely to occur in the future. Instead if you hold onto the rein when his head is in motion, and release it the instant he is still, you will end up with a quiet head position. Add a click and a treat, and you will also have a happy horse.

TRAINING SHORTCUTS

In clicker training we train by successive approximation. We take a small tendency for the horse to perform a certain behavior and by selectively reinforcing that behavior we develop it into a more complex behavior. This is referred to as *shaping*. (See Chapter 1.)

In *pure shaping*, also know as *free shaping*, a complex behavior is developed by reinforcing small, incremental steps. The behavior is developed without luring it with food, or triggering it in any other way. When I first started clicker training, I used shaping to teach Peregrine to touch a target. Originally, I thought targeting was just an amusing trick, something to do while he was laid up. I had no idea that I was introducing him to an incredibly powerful tool that could be applied to a wide variety of training situations. The targeting I taught with shaping became a "training shortcut" which I could use to get horses onto trailers, over bridges, past scary "goblins", into wash stalls, etc..

Targeting is a shaping procedure in which the animal learns to touch, orient to, go to, or follow the movements of an arbitrarily selected object.

I could use targeting to teach Peregrine some brand new behaviors. I could turn him into a "golden retriever" and have him pick up targets, dunk basketballs, open mailboxes, even play the piano. I could take him out for walks and have him play "touch the goblin" games (pg. 24). It was all great fun, and a great way to get my horse comfortable with his environment.

While I was exploring all the things this new tool could do for me, I was also using the horse training I was already familiar with. And that's another great virtue of clicker training—it piggy backs beautifully onto other training methods. At its core, clicker training is a communication tool. It says: "yes, what you just did was what I wanted, now here's a goody for you." The clicker marks correct responses. It doesn't say anything about how that response was triggered in the first place, which brings us to another training shortcut: *molding*.

MOLDING

Molding occurs when you physically move the animal into the position you want. Molding is used extensively in horse training. When you use your reins to put your horse on the bit, you are molding him into a particular body posture. Side reins and martingales mold the horse into a set frame. The question then becomes does the horse understand the balance you are after, or has he simply agreed to be molded? Does his balance fall apart the instant that the "mold" is removed?

Shaping enhances the molding process. As you click your horse for approximating the position you want, and then release him from "the mold" by releasing all pressure, your horse will more readily allow you to mold him into the desired position.

Molding is used in conjunction with a third training shortcut: negative reinforcement or more simply put, pressure and release of pressure.

NEGATIVE REINFORCEMENT

As previously stated *negative reinforcement* is an uncomfortable or painful stimulus which the animal can avoid by changing its behavior.

Negative reinforcement is at the heart of all traditional horse training. When you add leg, when you take the slack out of the reins, when you shift your weight in the saddle to signal a change of gait, you are using negative reinforcement. Your horse feels the bump of your leg, and adds energy to his gait. That was the response you were looking for, so you immediately stop bumping with your leg. He knows he just got the right answer because adding energy got you to stop bumping his rib cage. Your legs weren't hurting him in this case. They were simply annoying.

But suppose your horse ignored you. You bumped him with your legs and instead of adding energy, he just rooted his feet in the ground. What would you do?

UNDERSTANDING PRESSURE

There are two ways that pressure can be used. In

Chapter Seven: The Language of Operant Conditioning

one, you would bump him lightly, and then, if he didn't respond, you'd increase the intensity of the pressure. If a light tap of your leg didn't work, you'd bump a little harder, then a little harder still. If that didn't work you'd add spurs, or maybe the sharp tap of a whip. Eventually, you would find a level of discomfort/pain that your horse would respond to.

This approach comes with warning labels attached. First, if you go up in tiny stair steps, tapping lightly, then gradually stepping up the amount of pressure you are using, you may actually end up desensitizing your horse. Now instead of responding to a mild stimulus, you'll have to whack him really hard before he'll listen to you. This is often the result when timid or very gentle people try to follow the advice of their horse-trainer friends. They just aren't comfortable hitting their horse, and when they try, they aren't very good at it.

If you are going to escalate the level of discomfort, you need to judge how big a jump to make so that you DO get a response promptly from your horse. Knowing how much of a stair step to jump comes from experience and a knowledge of your individual horse.

The second warning label has to do with limits. Most of us have a level of intensity beyond which we do not want to go with a horse. We have a comfort zone in which we routinely operate. We don't think twice about tapping, or even hitting a horse within this zone. However, there will be a level where we begin to feel concerned, and a level beyond which we will not go.

What these levels are depends very much upon the individual. A very gentle person might start squirming if she even has to carry a whip. Somebody else might feel very at ease tapping her horse, but would draw the line at a hard whack. While somebody else might have no problem at all hitting a horse so hard it draws welts.

When you hit a horse, and particularly if you hit a horse and it does not respond by moving away, what the horse is learning is that it can survive that level of discomfort/pain. If you then tap him harder, and then a little harder still, you may find yourself crossing over the threshold of what you're willing to do. Now you're in a bind.

Do you keep escalating until you find that level of discomfort/pain that your horse will respond to? Or do you remember that there is always another way to shape everything?

Remember the principle: *Eventually everybody will sit down.* (Pg. 25.) Another way to use pressure is to think about how the Grand Canyon was formed. A little bit of pressure applied over a long period of time can create a monumental amount of change. The same thing applies to horse training. This means that instead of escalating and running the risk of crossing over your comfort zone, you could stay at a very mild stimulus. If you gently tap your horse long enough, he will eventually shift away from the pressure. When he does, click!, he gets a treat.

In clinics when we are talking about this concept, I will have everyone stand up. They are expecting me to give them some task to do, some reason for standing.

Instead I go on talking. I'm still sitting. I'm comfortable. I watch the people begin to shift their weight, to lean on chairs. I chuckle to myself at the puzzled expressions. Everybody is wondering why they are standing. I know they want me to give them something to do. They don't think they should sit, but they are getting tired of standing. I just wait. Eventually somebody sits down. Click! I toss that person a training-game treat.

Everyone in the room has just felt one of the great truths of training: eventually everybody will sit down. If you keep doing something long enough, no matter what it is, or how much you enjoy doing it, eventually you will need to change and do something else. If I keep people sitting long enough, eventually they will want to stand up. And if I keep them moving around in a training activity, eventually they will all want to sit down.

If you KNOW this, and really understand the depth of what this means, you have the keys to being a good trainer. When you see somebody who is patient with horses, you are seeing somebody who understands this principle and knows how to apply it.

No matter how full of energy your jittery, spooky horse is, if you can get him practicing turns and moving his feet long enough, eventually he'll want to stand still. Click! He just earned himself a major jackpot.

The same principle applies to your slow-as-molasses horse, the one who would lose a foot race to a tortoise. If you sit on him long enough, eventually he will shift his weight. Click! You've got your start on building a high-energy ride. It may not seem like he did much of anything, but he just earned himself a treat.

Both of these horses can test your patience, but if you really understand that *eventually everybody sits down*, you'll be able to outlast them both. This is what I refer to as the "mosquito in the bedroom" approach to training. A little bit of pressure applied over a long period of time *will* create a desire for change.

The Click That Teaches: Riding With The Clicker

CLICKER BUILDING BLOCKS

Shaping is the backbone of clicker training. In shaping you selectively reinforce any small tendency for your horse to perform a desired action. That increases the likelihood that that action will be repeated.

❶

1.) You use shaping to teach your horse to touch a target, but then *targeting* becomes a wonderful training shortcut. 2.) It's especially useful in helping your horse overcome fear issues.

❷

3.) Pressure and release of pressure is another training shortcut. You'll use it to teach backing to establish respect of space, and . . .

❸

4.) . . . head lowering which associates feelings of calmness and security with the clicker.

❹

PRESSURE AND CLICKER TRAINING

So how do we use this in clicker training? Pressure is part of horse training. Through pressure we signal our intent to the horse. So it is not a question of whether we use pressure or not, but how we teach it to our horse. With the clicker the level of pressure never needs to escalate to the point where it is painful or fear inducing.

Instead we can break the lesson down into small steps where each correct response is marked with a click and a treat. With the clicker pressure is transformed from a threat into information the horse uses to get to his treat sooner.

In one sense you could say we are simply "sugar coating" same old same old. We are still saying "move over", "get out of my space", but we are smoothing over our demands with rewards of goodies.

If all you did with the clicker was use it to mark correct responses to traditional requests, you would have a happier horse. When you combine this with targeting and shaping, you will transform your training into something much more powerful. You'll begin this transformation with something very mundane: teaching your horse to back out of your space, a lesson you've already begun (Pg. 14) and which you'll expand on in the next Chapter.

CHAPTER 8
Manners, Manners, and More Manners

In Chapter 3 I introduced you to the foundation lessons of clicker training. In this chapter we'll look in more detail at these key lessons.

BACKING 101

When you're in close quarters with a horse, his natural response is to push into pressure. This makes sense in a herd animal. Bunching in close makes it much harder for a predator to separate out an individual and take him down. Many people will tell you your horse is being rude and showing a lack of respect when he crowds in on top of you. That's one view of the behavior. Another might be that your horse thinks he's being a polite herd member protecting you from harm. In either case, crowding in on top of you is a safety issue. It doesn't matter the cause, you need to teach your horse to back out of your space.

You began this lesson by taking advantage of the food delivery. (See Chapter 3.) Now you're going to extend the lesson to get him even more comfortable moving away from pressure.

Here's a quick review: backing evolved out of the targeting lesson. Your horse was stepping back out of your space to get to his treat, so it was easy to put a lead on him and ask him to back. All you had to do was turn in to face him as you took the slack out of the rope, and he was backing easily away from you. Click and treat.

Now I'm going to add a new detail: I want you to learn to slide your hand up the lead to take the slack out. You'll be using this skill later under saddle so it's a good habit to get into now.

To understand why this is so important try this exercise with a friend. Your partner will be your "trainer" and you'll be the "horse". Hold your end of the lead in your outstretched hands. That's your horse's "head". Your friend is going to ask you to back by turning in to face you and reaching directly for the rope just below your hands. This is how many people handle lead ropes. You'll feel how abrupt and jarring it is. No wonder horses don't like it!

Here's the contrast. Have your friend slide up the rope as she turns towards you. She may need to practice this until she can do it smoothly. Watch her balance. Does she slide up the rope using just her hands? Or does she shift her weight from her back foot to her front foot making it even easier for you to respond? (See Ch. 24.) As she slides down the rope, you'll feel how soft and clear the communication is. Unlike the first way, there's nothing jarring or abrupt about it. You can feel her coming, and you have plenty of time to adjust your own balance and take a step back.

Sliding up the lead is a key skill. When you are handling a rope, you want to say to yourself that you have all the time in the world to get up that lead. You want to get in the habit of ALWAYS sliding along it, never grabbing the lead, and certainly never shaking it abruptly. The lead is one of your primary communication tools. You want your horse to trust it completely so you need to be careful how you handle it.

BACKING: A PRESSURE-BASED LESSON

Backing uses an important rope handling skill: the t'ai chi wall.

To ask your horse to back, turn in to face him as you SLIDE your hands apart. Your left hand will go to the snap and your right hand will move towards the point of his shoulder. When you feel him even THINK about backing, - click! - release the pressure on the lead and hand him his treat.

Practice this rope handling skill with a partner.

Slide your hands apart. Note the orange duct tape markers on each person's little finger. If your "horse" is very pushy, you want to make certain to slide all way up the rope until these markers touch.

Rotate your arm. This will elevate your "horse's" head. Her energy will ricochet off your t'ai chi wall and create a shift in balance back.

The t'ai chi wall.

The Click That Teaches: Riding With The Clicker

Here's another interesting experiment. Still holding the rope in your outstretched arms tighten up your hands, your arms, your shoulders, your jaw. Now close your eyes while your friend slides her hand up the lead. Tell her when you can feel her hand on the line. Open your eyes. You may be surprised to discover that she had to slide almost all the way to the snap before you could feel her.

Close your eyes again, but this time stay soft and relaxed. Again you're going to tell her when you can feel her sliding along the lead. Open your eyes. This time her hand probably only slid an inch or two along the rope. That's quite a difference!

This is why I will be placing so much emphasis on making sure that both you and your horse are balanced and relaxed. When either one of you is tight, the communication breaks down. You can't feel each other's soft signals. You end up "shouting" at your horse by adding more pressure to the rope, and he ends up tightening to protect himself. I want you to be able to whisper with light pressure. That's so much healthier for both of you.

THE T'AI CHI WALL

Sliding down a rope brings you to a powerful leverage point, one you should know about for those times when your horse is barging into your space. Hopefully with the preparation you're doing those times will be few and far between, but it is good to know how to be solid and firm just in case you find yourself in a situation where your horse is feeling overwhelmed. I refer to this technique as the "t'ai chi wall".

Practice it first with your friend. You can break the technique down into "paint-by-numbers" steps. It helps to put duct tape markers on the key points. Put a marker on the rope about an arm's length from the snap. Put another on the edge of your left hand by your little finger. (See photos on pg. 37.) Do the same for your friend. Put a fourth marker on her shoulder. (Note: These directions are written for the left side.)

1.) Have your friend hold the snap end of the rope in her outstretched hands.
2.) Put your two hands together on the duct tape marker on the rope.
3.) Draw your hands apart sliding along the rope. Move your left hand along the rope so that the duct tape marker on your little finger touches the duct tape marker on your partner's hand holding the snap. *At the same time* move your right hand up to her shoulder so it presses against that duct tape marker. Both your hands should come to a stop at the same time, and *there should be no slack in the rope.* This is your t'ai chi wall. Test it out. If your friend tries to push into you, she'll encounter the solid wall of the rope. Just as a ball bounces back off a wall, her own energy will ricochet her back out of your space. She'll feel her balance rocked back into her heels, and she'll want to take a step back. Click!

Now try this. Slide your hands apart, but leave some slack between them in the rope. Have her try to barge through you. Before you felt solid, and the rope did the work. Now you'll find yourself getting in a shoving match: most unpleasant, and if she's stronger than you are, she'll win.

Here's another experiment: instead if touching duct tape marker to duct tape marker with your left hand, stop sliding just shy of her hands. Now have her barge forward. You have no power. She can shove her way right past you. When the duct tape markers touched, you could rock her off her feet! Why the difference? You rotated the bones in your arm. This is the power of the t'ai chi wall. The leverage you get from simply rotating your bones is amazing. It allows you to be powerful and effective without being aggressive.

The riding exercises I'll be sharing with you later in this book all depend upon an understanding of leverage and weight shifts. This ground work introduces the mechanical skills you'll be using under saddle. Learn them well here on the ground, so they can work for you later when you ride.

Repeat Steps 1 through 3, and this time notice how your arm rotates as you slide overhand down the rope and connect the duct tape markers. Feel how much that rotation grounds your balance and at the same time rocks hers back into her heels.

USING THE T'AI CHI WALL – BACKING IN A SQUARE

In Chapter 3 you asked your horse to back in a stall or small paddock. You're going to continue to work in that space, but now instead of bringing him forward away from the walls after each click, you're going to ask him to back around the perimeter of your enclosure. This will give you lots of practice sliding up your lead and using your t'ai chi wall. And it will help your horse to become more body aware. If you've never asked your horse to think about his own body in relation to tight spaces, he may feel very claustrophobic the first time you ask him to back in a stall. By showing him how he can swing his hips through a corner, you're teaching him skills that will help you later in all kinds of situations, including trailer loading.

Chapter Eight: Manners, Manners, and More Manners

BACKING IN A SQUARE

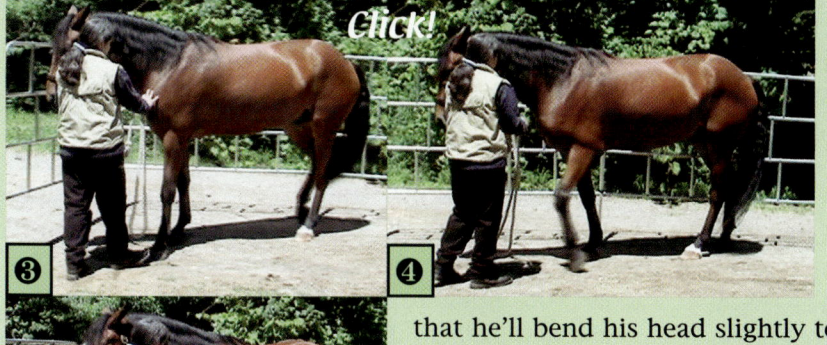

Backing through a corner★ relies on a very simple premise: two particles cannot occupy the same space. If you stand in front of your horse's near shoulder, he either has to bump you out of his space or move his head off to the side to make room for you. (1.) Since you have control of his halter, pushing you aside is not an option. That means that he'll bend his head slightly to the off side to make room for you. You'll be in front of his shoulder, not directly in front of him, but slightly off to the side. Your left hand will be steadying his halter. Your right hand will be on his shoulder asking him to back. He'll be looking off to the right at the stall wall. (2.)

This is not a comfortable position for him. He can't stay like that forever. If you doubt that, just try sitting with your head flexed to the side while you read the rest of this section. You'll find that it won't be long before you are straightening back around in your chair. That's what your horse would like to do. He'd like to straighten his head, but he can't without knocking you over. He has to find another option. All you have to do is wait for him to puzzle through this dilemma. Steady pressure is doing its job, and you just have to remember that *eventually everybody will sit down* (Pg. 25).

Eventually your horse will get tired of standing with his head bent to the side, and he'll spot the other option.

With his head turned, his hips will automatically shift (Fig. 1-3.). This is a natural response. Your hips would do the same. When you're standing, look off to one side. You'll feel your hips swing the opposite way. The more you turn your head, the further your hips will swing. With your horse's head bent more and more to the side, he will eventually notice that he has room to swing his hips over. Click! He gets a treat. (4.)

At first you'll click him for every little shift of weight back, but you'll gradually expect him to do a little bit more for each click and reinforcement. He'll have to take two steps back, then three, then four, etc. until he can back smoothly around the entire perimeter of his stall.

Note: the hand that's touching his shoulder is doing more than signaling your request for a step back. It's also monitoring his response. If your horse maneuvers through the corner by first shifting forward through his shoulder, you'll feel that as a push into your hand. He's pivoting around the stall instead of truly backing.

Once he's backing well, the next step in this process is to take him out into a larger area. You're going to use the backing skill you just learned to keep him working in a stall-sized space. If you're working with a nervous or pushy horse in a crowded arena or out on the trail where there are hazards to avoid, this is a very useful skill to have in your tool box.

In your larger work space pretend that you are still in a stall. If it helps, set out ground poles so you still have visual boundaries. Instead of letting him meander all over the arena, your goal is to back him within the boundaries of the ground poles. Use your t'ai chi wall to displace his head to the outside. That will give you control of his hips.

The swing of his hips is a very distinctive feel which you will recognize from your work in the stall. That is in fact why I recommend that you start this lesson in an enclosed space. You've learned a skill and a feel which you can apply to this more challenging environment.

BACKING IN A LARGER SPACE

★ Photos reprinted from: *The Click That Teaches: A Step-By-Step Guide in Pictures,* by Alexandra Kurland; The Clicker Center, NY

The Click That Teaches: Riding With The Clicker

"GROWN-UPS" REVISITED – GROUND TYING

In Chapter 3 I introduced you to "the grown-ups are talking, please don't interrupt" lesson. That's the beginning of ground tying: an exercise where your horse stands still without you having to hold him in place. The goal is to have him stand for longer and longer periods while you step further and further away from him.

Ground tying gives you lots of experience training by priority. What is more important to you: that he stand still or that he have his ears forward. If you click him for his ears just as he's taking a step forward, what is he going to think is the right answer? So clear criteria and timing are critical in this lesson. Which layers must be in place before you begin to reinforce the next element?

Once the first element is consistent, you can add the next layer. In effect you are asking your horse a series of questions. For example:

"Will you stand still while I feed out a coil of rope to give you more slack in the lead?"

You don't actually verbalize this question. You ask it via your actions. Your horse answers "yes" or "no" with his. If he continues to stand while you make the slight change, click, he gets his treat. If he starts to leave, there's no penalty—the opposite of positive reinforcement is no reinforcement—instead you'll slide up your lead rope to bring him back into position. If he wants his treat, he's learning that he has to use self-control to wait longer. And you're learning that you asked for a bit too much the last time. A good rule to follow in this exercise is: if you think he's going to move his feet in four seconds, click him in three. In other words increase your criteria in small steps so your horse continues to be successful. (Chapter 5, pg. 24.) When he stands consistently while you feed out a coil of rope, ask your next question: perhaps "Will you stand still while I take a step back?" Yes. Click and treat.

TRAINING BY PRIORITIES

In clicker training there is always more than one way to shape every behavior. You can teach your horse to ground tie out of "the grown-ups are talking" lesson. You can also teach it out of backing. It's useful to learn both ways.

If you've been following the exercises in this book, your horse is probably now backing from a feather-light touch. In fact as soon as he sees you, he's offering to back. He's trying to engage you in the clicker game. The only problem is he may feel more like a yo yo than a horse. He backs, you click, and before you can ask for anything else, he's backing again. He's become like an old phonograph record where the needle has gotten stuck in a groove. You've both gotten stuck in a pattern, back two or three steps, click, feed; back two or three steps, click and feed. If you don't click him after those couple of steps, he crowds right back into your space and starts mugging you for treats. It's time to put negative reinforcement to work. Remember the principle: whatever you are doing, if you do it long enough, you will want to change (pg. 25). That's what you'll be using to get your horse to back up and stay back.

Ask him to back up a couple of steps out of your space so he ends up moving to the end of your lead rope. He'll be expecting a click, but you're going to withhold it for just a second or two longer than usual. If he yo yos back into your space, ask him to back up again. Repeat this as many times as it takes for him to back up and hesitate. Click! Give him a treat.

Just as you did in "grown-ups" when you were getting him to look straight ahead instead of nuzzling your pockets, you can now begin to stretch out the duration of the hesitation. You can make it as long as you need, from just a few seconds to minutes at a time, but note, to build consistency, you must build your duration slowly. Once you've got some duration built into the behavior, you can begin to select the moment you click based on some other criteria. Ears perked forward is a good one to start with. Or you might be interested in building a square stance for a halter class. Decide what is the next most important element that will make the biggest difference now and focus your attention on that. Train by priority. You'll be building each new request on top of the underlying layers so they occur in a set sequence.

You're going to use this process later under saddle. In riding for performance there is a set order in which things need to occur to produce your horse's optimum balance. Once you've built some duration into the basic ground tying behavior, you'll see some variation in what he's doing. The elevation of his head will vary. Sometimes he'll have his ears perked forward, or he'll be standing square. Choose the criteria you want and that are most important to you, and begin to layer them into the process. If behavior deteriorates go back to your first layer and rebuild the entire structure one step at a time.

You can have it all with clicker training. But the bottom line is you have now taught the beginnings of patience to your clicker-trained horse. Instead of mugging you, he is standing quietly at the end of his lead waiting for your next request. Your pockets are full of goodies, but he's learned that the way to get

Chapter Eight: Manners, Manners, and More Manners

GROUND TYING

The result of the ground tying lesson: note how beautifully soft and round this mare's topline is. That's the result of adding in many layers of expectation, one step at a time. (See page 45 for details on shaping this lovely "pose".)

the "vending machine" to work is to offer polite attention. Being over-eager, crowding into you, bullying you, none of these tactics work, but backing up, standing still with his ears perked forward, and his attention on you, this turns you into a "vending machine". He's learned that patience is needed to play this game. He never knows exactly how long he needs to be a statue, but he is learning that if he keeps playing the game, eventually you will click and give him a treat.

Before you get too carried away teaching your horse fun tricks, you want to make certain that this piece is solidly in place. However long it takes to establish good ground manners is time well spent. With the clicker the sky truly is the limit, but for me what clicker training is first and foremost about is teaching your horse to be a good citizen. The clicker is the most powerful of all training tools. You want to learn to use it well.

HEAD LOWERING

Head lowering is another of our foundation lessons. It is one of the most important responses you can teach a horse. High-headed horses tend to be nervous horses. Get a horse to lower his head and it's almost like flicking a switch in his brain. A low-headed horse is a calm horse.

Before you add clicker tricks and advanced training to your horse's repertoire you want to be certain he understands a "calm down" cue. It's a little like being able to give a toddler a quiet time out. If your horse gets too excited playing games, you want to be able to settle him down with these well-established comfort behaviors. In my opinion, backing and head lowering are the two most important skills you can teach a horse. They are your antilock brakes and your safety-pressure valve. You want them working well, especially in emergencies.

Head lowering, like backing, can be taught in many different ways and contexts. The more different ways you teach head lowering, the better. Why? Suppose you have only taught your horse to lower his head from pressure on his poll. He responds beautifully to it. If he gets nervous while you're grooming him, you have only to reach up to his poll and his nose is on the ground. But now you're under saddle, and he's getting upset.

Reaching far enough forward to touch his poll isn't a good option. You could transfer the cue so touching him closer to his withers triggers the response. But what if he's too excited to respond? Having a second way to ask for head lowering might help you diffuse an emotional meltdown. Your horse should also respond to a signal from your rein or lead.

In Chapter 3 you taught your horse to follow a target to the ground, then you touched him on his poll. He was already thinking about head lowering so his head dropped right to the ground. Click and treat.

Once he's yielding to poll pressure, you can put a cotton lead on his halter and draw down on the rope. When he feels the slight increase in pressure from the halter, it should remind him of your hand. If he drops his head even a little, click and treat. Gradually withhold your click until he is dropping his nose all the way to the ground. You're adding the power of the clicker to a very commonly used method.

41

HEAD LOWERING AND THE T'AI CHI WALL

All of these methods are great, but now you're going to learn a fourth way that uses the t'ai chi wall to teach head lowering. This technique is especially important if you are working with nervous or aggressive horses. It creates a "demand cue" to drop the head that can override an anxious, I-need-to-be-anywhere-but-here mental state. If you find yourself in an indoor arena with the snow sliding off the roof, or out on the trail with your horse's worst nightmare coming straight at you, you'll be glad you put this lesson into your tool kit. You'll learn it first here on the ground, and later I'll show you how to transfer it to riding. Like the other exercises in this section it introduces skills you'll use later under saddle.

This lesson evolves out of the backing in a square exercise (pg. 39). When your horse swings his hips through a corner, you may have noticed that his head drops ever so slightly. You're going to take advantage of this to get him to drop his nose to the ground.

1.) Use your t'ai-chi-wall positioning to ask your horse to back in a square. This time, instead of releasing the lead as soon as he takes a step back, keep a steady pressure until you feel him drop his head even a little.

Don't worry if you miss the release the first time he softens. The drop can be so slight that it is easy to miss, but next time you'll be better prepared. You'll know what to expect. When he drops his head, you'll release the pressure completely.

2.) Slide up the lead and continue to ask him to back in a square. After a couple of repetitions of this, the drop of his head will be more definite. Click, release the lead and give him a treat. Now you'll really have his attention!

3.) Ask again, clicking and releasing each time you feel a definite drop of the head. Pretty soon he'll drop his head even before he backs up. Perfect. Click and treat.

You want to say to yourself that head lowering is not a forward moving exercise. He can stand still. He can back up. You aren't trying to bottle up his energy or force him to stand still when he's feeling nervous. He can back all he likes, but *any* forward movement from pawing to taking a step, will be ricocheted back with the t'ai chi wall.

Backing is hard work so pretty soon he'll be standing still dropping his nose to his ankles. Every time he gets nervous and shoots his head up to the rafters, you'll slide along the lead into your t'ai chi wall position. Note this means that you will be lifting *up* on the snap, not drawing it down. This is critically important. Get a highlighter and underline that last sentence. This is a skill you want to really understand.

When you are asking for head lowering, it's easy to think down. Down is the right answer for your horse, so down must be the direction that you draw the lead. But that's not going to help you under saddle. You can't draw the rein down under his chin while you ride, but you can lift up on the rein. As he raises his head, you can follow him up with steady contact. The instant he drops his head, click, release the rein and give him a treat.

"I WANT SOMETHING"

This is an important concept to understand. The lead or rein sends one of two messages to your horse. When you take the slack out of the lead, you are saying "I want something". When you release the pressure, you are saying: "Thank you, you just gave it to me."

In this lesson you started with something familiar, backing in a square. Your horse expected you to release the lead when he backed. That's what you've been doing. But in this lesson you didn't release. At first your horse might have been confused. Why wasn't this working? You always let go before? It will seem to him as though all the rules have just been thrown out the window, but that's only because he hasn't learned the entire "rule book".

When you don't release, it means he needs to keep experimenting, looking for the right answer. As soon as he gives you even a small piece of the puzzle, click, you'll let go and give him a treat.

You are teaching your horse a couple of important lessons:

• If the answer isn't the one you were expecting, don't get frustrated, just keep experimenting until you find something that works.

• When the slack goes out of the lead, your person wants something. What else is she doing that will clue you in to the right answer? Learn to read all the body language clues she's offering you.

"UP" WITH THE LEAD

When you use the t'ai chi wall to ask for head lowering, it's important that you follow through with the rotation of your arm so you end up lifting the snap up along your horse's jaw line. If it helps, put a piece of duct tape on the bottom strap of his halter. You want to lift the duct tape marker on your little finger up so it connects with this marker. That's what gives you power and transfers this lesson to riding.

Chapter Eight: Manners, Manners, and More Manners

HEAD LOWERING AND THE T'AI CHI WALL

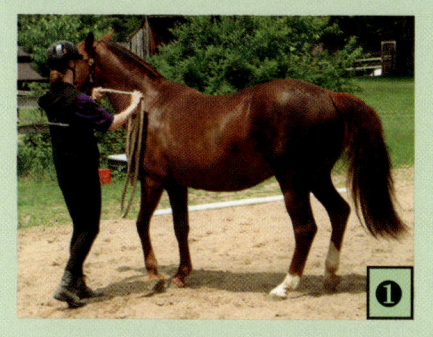

1.) The handler has taken the slack out of the lead. Note she is not trying to pull her mare's head down. Instead she is lifting the lead up into the "t'ai chi wall" power position. This will transfer later directly to riding.

2.) Head lowering is not a forward moving exercise. With her hands in this position she can keep her mare from crowding forward over her. But as her mare backs, she follows her, bending her head to the outside so she can control her hindquarters and keep her backing in a square.

3.) As soon as she feels her mare's head drop just a fraction, she releases the lead.

4.) A great result: after just a couple of repetitions her mare drops her nose to the dirt.

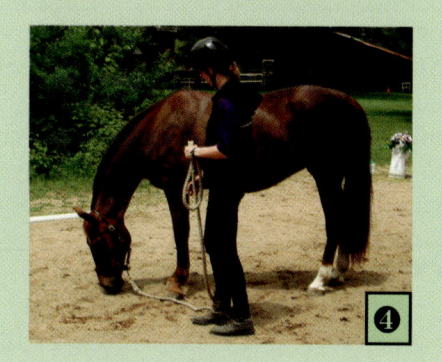

You'll be using this same lift of the rein to trigger head lowering under saddle. You'll also use the same mechanical skill to get him off his inside shoulder and to straighten him out when he over-flexes. The solid foundation you build here will serve you very well later. Refer to *The Click That Teaches: Video Lesson 3: Head Lowering*★ for more on this.

YOUR "CALM DOWN" CUE

Once your horse is consistently dropping his head as you slide up the lead towards the snap, withhold your click. You'll still be releasing him when he drops his head, but now you won't be clicking quite as soon. Your horse will probably drop his head a few inches, hover for a moment at that height, and then drop his nose even further. Click and treat the additional drop.

This raises an important point. In the beginning most people do not click enough. Their rates of reinforcement are way too low. But then they get to a point where they are clicking too much. By shutting off the behavior too soon with the click, they miss the opportunity for their horse to offer them more. The art of clicker training is knowing when to move on so you don't get stuck in a rut with your horse.

Once your horse is dropping his head down around his ankles, don't expect him to be able to leave it down there for very long. He may not feel safe in such a vulnerable position. If your horse is a nervous type, he'll go through a stage where he looks like an equine yo-yo: the head goes down from the lead; the head pops right back up; the head goes down from the lead; the head pops back up.

Why? The way a horse's eyes work, he can scan the horizon line for predators best from an elevated head position. So lowering the head is an act of trust. That's also why it works so powerfully as a "calm down" cue. On his own a horse will lower his head to graze only when he feels secure. Think about how many hours a horse spends grazing, and you'll understand the strong association head lowering has with a calm mental state.

Only now your horse is nervous. He wants his head up. But as soon as he starts to lift his head, your hand is sliding down the lead into the t'ai chi wall position. He's nervous. He'd like to leave, but all his energy gets ricocheted back. You've got his head displaced to the outside so his hips swing to the inside. He drops his head, and you let go. His head drops down to his ankles. He's not calm enough yet to leave it down. He pops his head back up, but there you are sliding down the lead again. All this going up and down is tiring. Eventually, just as he did in the ground tying exercise, he's going to hesitate at the bottom. Click and treat!

You'll gradually withhold your click, extending out the time he leaves his head all the way down. If his

★ *The Click That Teaches: Video Lesson Series,* by Alexandra Kurland; The Clicker Center, NY

43

The Click That Teaches: Riding With The Clicker

POLISHING THE BEHAVIOR

1.) A lift of the lead triggers the initial drop of the head. 2.) This Andalusian mare at first drops her head to the right. This used to be good enough, but now her handler withholds her click. 3.) Her mare pops her head back up and again encounters the "t'ai chi wall" pressure of the lead (see text). 4.) She drops her head right away. 5.) Her handler waits, and (6.) this time her mare pivots her head perfectly into a left bend. Click! and treat!

head pops back up, you'll be there to meet him with the t'ai chi wall. If he controls himself and leaves his head down, you'll click and treat. You'll build your duration slowly remembering the rule: if you think he's going to pop his head back up in five seconds, you'll click him at four.

COMFORT ZONES

The more time he spends with his head down, the calmer he'll feel. Down is associated with grazing, and sleeping, activities he'll engage in only when he feels safe. So the mental state associated with a lowered head is very much one you want as a base line in your riding.

Maybe your horse is feeling nervous because you're working him in a ring away from the rest of his friends. When he drops his head and begins to leave it down longer, those feelings of anxiety will ease just a little. The momentary relaxation feels good. The more relaxed he feels, the longer he can leave his head down. Now you're in a positive feedback loop that's going to let him leave his head down for longer and longer periods.

As he practices head lowering in different situations, at different levels of distraction, he'll learn to reach this relaxed state sooner. He'll also be building his trust in you. In essence he's saying, "I feel safe in your presence. I'm turning over the responsibility of watching for predators to you. I trust you to keep me safe." Now that's quite a statement, and one that should make you feel good about your relationship.

There's another reason he's going to leave his head down longer. You're not just using pressure and release of pressure to teach him to lower his head. You're also marking correct responses with the clicker. As he catches on, you're going to put head lowering on a differential reinforcement schedule (pg. 45). At first, you'll click and treat each time he drops his head even a little. As the behavior becomes more consistent, you'll begin to wait. You'll ask for his head to drop and then you'll pause. If he pops his head right back up again, he won't get clicked. Instead you'll ask him to drop his head again. If he leaves his head down just an instant longer, click, he gets reinforced.

That's why the clicker adds to the power of the head-lowering exercise. Your horse isn't just moving away from something mildly unpleasant. He's moving toward something he wants—the click and the treat. But to get it, he has to control his flight instincts in order to keep his head down longer. Not only does this produce goodies, it also produces feelings of relaxation and comfort.

POLISHING THE BEHAVIOR

Shaping is an important part of clicker training, but most of the time we aren't patient enough to use it. Instead we use training "shortcuts" to speed up the process. Shortcuts are fine, and they are certainly part of clicker training, but you should also shape some aspects of every behavior so you develop the full range of your horse's learning skills.

For example, with head lowering you can start by triggering the behavior via the training shortcut of pressure and release of pressure. That's what you're doing with the t'ai chi wall. Once you've got the basic behavior, the clicker becomes like an artist's paint brush, fine tuning and polishing the behavior. For example, you can withhold your click until your horse tips his head slightly to the side you're standing on (see above).

Polishing the behavior is a great way to build duration into the behavior. As you focus on making the behavior better and better, your horse will be spending more of his time with his head down. It's no longer good enough just to drop his head. Now he has to drop his head AND add the elements that create excellence. The training "shortcuts" began the behavior, but shaping will finish it.

CHAPTER 9
Variable Reinforcement Schedules

One of the most common questions people ask about clicker training is when do you stop using it. For me the clicker is a communication tool. I am not trying to eliminate it from my horse's experience, but I also don't want to get stuck having to reinforce every little instance of a behavior. To create a happy balance I use variable reinforcement schedules. In this chapter I'll explain what that means and how you use this concept in the real world of training.

SCHEDULES OF REINFORCEMENT

Schedules of reinforcement refer to the frequency with which you click and reinforce a particular behavior. In a *fixed schedule of reinforcement* the reward is offered on a predictable basis, based on the number of repetitions of a behavior. In clicker training we often begin with a fixed, one-to-one schedule, i.e. give the behavior, get a treat. Fixed schedules usually occur in the early stages of training when the horse is first learning a particular behavior.

In a *variable schedule of reinforcement* the trainer reinforces some but not all occurrences of the behavior. Variable schedules often focus on a particular aspect of the overall behavior, such as the speed with which the behavior is performed, or the quality of the movement. This is referred to as a *differential schedule of reinforcement*. Your horse must meet a certain standard of the behavior in order to get reinforced and this standard changes over time. In one sense this is still a fixed schedule of reinforcement. You have raised your standards in the response he must give you, but he will still be consistently reinforced for each correct response.

You can also reinforce a behavior unpredictably. For example, in teaching your horse to stand, you could use a *random schedule* to build duration. Your horse will never know exactly when he's going to be clicked: is it going to be three seconds or five? He doesn't know, but he'll continue to offer the behavior in the hope of getting reinforced.

In general I start with a fixed schedule. I use a one to one ratio of reinforcement to get the behavior started. Then I switch to a random schedule to build some duration into the behavior. Once I have even a few seconds of the behavior, I'll see a lot of variations. For example, if I've been working on standing still, sometimes my horse will have his ears forward, sometimes back. His head will be in different positions. Sometimes he'll be standing square; at other times he'll be very unbalanced. Once I start noticing these differences, it's time to pick the elements that will have the most impact on the overall behavior. I'll pick a behavior that is already occurring frequently enough that it is likely to occur within the range of duration I have built. At this point I'll switch to a differential schedule. For example, I'll wait for those moments when he's not only standing still, but his ears are forward. Used in this way reinforcement schedules push behavior towards excellence.

Even if you've built considerable duration into the standing still behavior, once your focus shifts to standing still and putting the ears forward, you'll click as soon as that second criterion is met.

TEACHING THE POSE

Teaching "the pose" gives you first-hand experience using variable reinforcement schedules. It also gives you an elegant first step towards upper-level performance. The task: use your hand as a target to teach your horse to pose like a fancy dressage horse.

1a and b.) Begin with your left hand out in front of your horse. Sweep your hand under your horse's chin. When he tucks his head to follow it, click and treat.

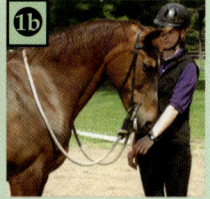

2.) For extra help hold your right hand just behind his chin. When his chin touches your hand, click and treat.

3.) Gradually lift your right hand so your horse becomes more elegant in his pose. Selectively reinforce the prettiest moments.

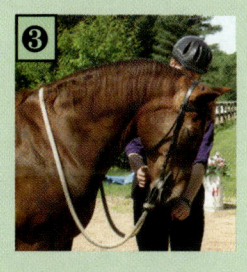

4.) Begin to fade out your targets. Reinforce your horse when he offers "the pose" on his own. Your presence will become the cue for "the pose".

The Click That Teaches: Riding With The Clicker

BUILDING QUALITY AND DURATION:

Adding "the pose" to ground work: Once this mare understood that "the pose" pleased her person and was a sure bet for lots of clicks, she started to offer it as an extra flourish in all her work. Her handler reinforced her extra effort. At first even a moment of "the pose" would earn a click and a treat.

She gradually built duration by following the "four second rule": if she thought her mare's balance might fall apart after four strides of beautiful trot, click, she reinforced her and let her stop after three.

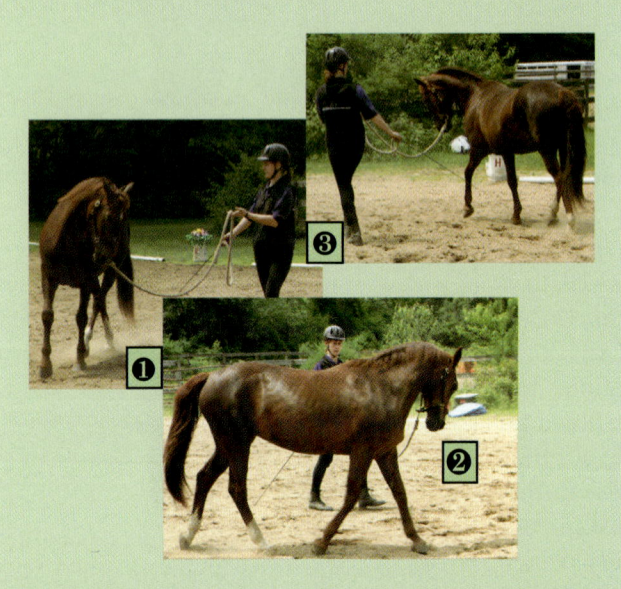

The result: this beautiful trot. Note in particular in the third photo the elevation and roundness of the topline. Note also the slack in the lead. This mare is beautifully light, wonderfully relaxed and focused. The result of good ground work is a horse that looks as though she would feel like heaven to ride.

Even if he can stand still for minutes at a time, once you've added that second element, you'll click the instant you see it. Your first criterion must still be met. His feet must remain rooted to the ground. If he puts his ears forward just as he starts to move, you won't click. Think of it like adding layers to a cake. You have to have the cake before you add the icing. Certainly you can eat the icing by itself. So, yes, you can reinforce your horse for putting his ears forward without linking it to any other behavior, but once you start layering behaviors together, you will have an order of priority. In this case, the feet must be still, then the ears get reinforced. Once you have that, you can add another criterion, such as holding his head at a certain height. You're learning to train by priority.

THE THREE ELEMENTS OF GOOD TRAINING

As you learn how to add each new element to your base behavior, you'll be practicing three skills that turn average horse handlers into great trainers. These are:

• *Good timing:* In the above example, if your horse puts his ears forward, but then moves his feet just as you click, guess what you'll get: a horse who thinks you want him to move. You get what you reinforce, so in clicker training, as in all good training, timing is everything.

• *Having clear criteria:* You have to know your priorities. What is your base behavior—what's most important to you? If your horse is nuzzling your pockets, backing out of your space is much more important than whether or not he has his ears forward. When you're clear on your priorities and you know what you're marking, it's easier to spot the subtle shifts that are a precursor to the behavior you want. This is all part of being a splitter instead of a lumper and learning to see small units of behavior (pg. 22).

• *Maintaining a high rate of reinforcement*: It may seem contradictory to tell you that you want to use a variable reinforcement schedule so that you can build duration into a behavior and at the same time tell you that you want to maintain a high rate of reinforcement. The key to sorting this out lies in understanding the first two elements. Good timing and clear criteria will guarantee a high rate of reinforcement, especially in the critical early stages of shaping a behavior. You'll spot the tiny shifts that lead toward the desired end result. Instead of waiting until your horse has everything right, you'll be clicking individual elements of the finished behavior. You'll build your expectations layer by layer so that by the

Chapter Nine: Variable Reinforcement Schedules

time you have stretched out the duration of all the combined elements your horse will be comfortable offering considerable effort for a single click. He'll know that's how the game is played, and he'll be emotionally at ease with the process.

In small increments you'll have shifted from a continuous to a variable schedule of reinforcement. In other words, with clicker training you can have your cake, plus you can pile on all the chocolate icing, maraschino cherries, and whipped cream you want. All that and you get to eat it, too!

PAYCHECKS

Clicker training has tremendous flexibility built into it. There is no one set-in-stone, right way to click. Within the clicker community there are trainers who use fixed reinforcement schedules, others who use random schedules, and others, like myself, who most often use differential schedules.

Another difference you'll see is in the meaning of the click itself. Some trainers use clicks in two ways. For them the click sometimes means: "Yes! That was the right answer, now stop and get your treat." And sometimes it means: "Yes! That was the right answer, but keep going and maybe next time you'll get a treat." In other words, the click is made to act as both a bridging signal and a keep going signal.

I prefer a different system. I have two different types of signals. I have keep going signals that mean: "You're doing great. Keep doing what you're doing, and I'll click you!" I also have separate bridging signals, and the click is the primary one. Each and every time I click it means: "Yes! That's exactly what I want. You've just earned yourself a treat."

There's no ambiguity at all in the meaning of my click. I follow every click with a reward. That's the bargain I've established with my horse. Here's an analogy that may help you understand why I've made this choice.

I live in snow country. Suppose I ask one of the neighborhood kids to shovel out my driveway after a snowstorm. In exchange, I tell him, I'll give him twenty dollars. I don't have a very long driveway, so he'll probably think this is a really good deal. Now suppose that when he gets done, I look at the driveway and say, "You did a great job! The driveway looks super." He'll feel good, but he'll still want his money. Praise is nice, but it's not what motivated him to do the work. Now imagine what would happen if I also said, "Oh, I'm a little short this week. I can't pay you this time." The next time it snows, you can bet I'll be doing my own driveway. That kid is going to have twenty good reasons not to do what I want.

THE CLICK MARKS THE END OF A UNIT OF BEHAVIOR

The click marks the end of a unit of behavior. It is always followed by a reward. That's the bargain the horses understand. It's a simple system that creates excellence. You'll keep asking for a little more and a little more to train complex sequences of behavior.

"The pose" has evolved into this beautiful carriage. At first just a step or two of this lovely trot was all that was asked for. Gradually, the horse had to stay in this balance longer.

When her rider clicks, this mare stops, knowing her treat is coming.

Stopping for a treat is a good thing. It means her rider gets to ask her again for her beautiful trot. That helps her become more solid in her understanding of the behavior. A high rate of reinforcement coupled with premium rewards means that this is one of her favorite "clicker games". Her rider can ask for what would normally be considered a highly demanding exercise, and her horse just thinks she is playing a fun game.

The Click That Teaches: Riding With The Clicker

So, as I see it, if I set up a bargain with my horse that says I'm going to pay him for work well done, that's what I need to do. That doesn't mean that I'm going to be clicking and treating every time my horse does something good. The clicker is a teaching tool. For example, I can use the clicker to teach a horse to pick up his feet for cleaning. I may start by clicking the horse when he lets me run my hand down below his knee, but I'm going to use a variable reinforcement schedule to ask for more and more cooperation.

Remember, the variable reinforcement schedule means that the horse never knows exactly when he's going to hear the click. He'll keep working, offering me more good responses, in an effort to get the vending machine to work.

Before long my foot-shy horse is going to be doing a lot more than simply letting me run my hand down his leg. He'll be picking his own foot up and holding it quietly in the air while I pick out the dirt. Pretty soon I won't click him until I've cleaned two, then three, then all four feet. And after a while I'll be able to fade the click and treat out completely as he masters that skill, but I'll be using the clicker in other areas to teach new things.

It's like saying to that kid, "Yes, I'll give you twenty dollars, and if you do a great job I might even throw in an extra tip. You can count on that, but I also want the front walk shoveled, and the snow pulled off the roof." If he quits part way, he won't get anything, but the more he gets done, the closer he gets to his reward. That keeps him going even though I'm asking for more work.

If I were to add both new tasks all at once, he might grumble and go away. But if I gradually ask for a little bit more each time, after a while it will all seem like just part of the job. If every now and then I surprise him with an extra five dollar tip, he might even offer to knock the icicles off the rain gutters. (Doesn't this sound familiar? Not only is it a lot like horse training, but isn't this what happens to most of us at work? Look back at your original job description. After a while it starts to sound as though it's referring to somebody else. You do so much more than that. The increase in your work load probably occurred so gradually that it became part of your routine before you even noticed it was happening.)

With horses a pocketful of grain or even a single carrot can buy you a lot of training. Treats are given in small amounts. A teaspoon of grain, one bite of carrot, is enough to keep your horse working for more. I vary my reinforcers. Not only does that make the training more fun and interesting for my horse, it provides him with an additional source of information. I can save his favorite treats for extra efforts to help me mark those special "Kodak moments". When my own horse does something I particularly like, click, the peppermints come out. He knows he's just done something super that was well worth the extra effort.

FADING THE CLICKER

Many people still worry that they will have to reward their horse with a treat for every little thing that he does. They want to be able to fade the food out of their training program and use the click alone to reinforce the horse. But the click is not what the horse works for. It's simply a signal that the real reward is coming. For most horses food is your currency. That's how your horse likes getting paid. Once you see what a powerful training tool it is, you won't be so eager to move away from it. But the question of treatless clicks may still come up.

As I've said, I offer a treat after every click. That's the method I prefer, but not every tiny behavior is worthy of a click. Once you get past the initial stages of teaching a new behavior, you'll be reinforcing on a variable or a differential schedule. The animal will be offering more and more behavior for the single click and treat.

Here's how it works. Imagine you've got a dolphin swimming around in a tank. It has figured out that it can make fish appear just by swimming towards a bar suspended in the water. So it swims towards the bar, only this time nothing happens. The trainer knows why. The dolphin swam under the bar and that no longer counts.

The dolphin doesn't know this, however. It just knows that swimming in the vicinity of the bar usually produces fish. The dolphin reverses course and tries again. Still nothing. This has happened before. The dolphin has learned from previous experience that it may have to swim back and forth several times before it gets a fish. It keeps offering the behavior, only now it's beginning to feel a little frustrated, or perhaps it just wants to be sure the trainer is watching. In any case, on the next attempt it jumps up over the bar and comes down with a splash on the surface of the water. The whistle blows at the peak of the jump and the dolphin gets its fish.

By withholding the click, the trainer got the behavior to vary. That's what you want. If you got carbon copies of the behavior every time it was performed, you wouldn't be able to shift the system towards excellence.

Chapter Nine: Variable Reinforcement Schedules

If, instead of swimming over the bar, the dolphin simply lost interest and quit, the trainer could back up a step or two in the sequence. That's one of the principles of good training: if behavior deteriorates, go back to a preceding step in the training.

That's also just good "horse sense", and it's one of the hallmarks of good trainers. You don't see major wrecks with experienced trainers because they've learned how to read their horses. They know when to jump ahead and ask for more, when to regroup and review the lesson, and when they can fade out the clicker entirely for that particular behavior.

VARYING YOUR REINFORCER

Varying the reinforcer is a technique that's used a lot in dog training. Sometimes the dog gets something good to eat. Sometimes he gets to chase after a toy or play a favorite game of tug. Having a large arsenal of potential reinforcers strengthens your training.

Varying the reinforcer is a lot harder with horses. You can give your horse a "yes answer" by releasing pressure. That's certainly something horses want. Relax your fingers on the reins and you're rewarding your horse. Releases are automatically built into the structure of good riding.

But with clicker training I want to do more than just take away the unpleasant things. When I first started thinking about varying my reinforcer, I was quite envious of the dog trainers. They had so many easy choices!

Stroking and scratches were already part of my standard system of rewards. Other things, like toys, aren't of much interest to most horses. In addition, it had to be something that was practical to use in a training situation, so the chance to roll in a sand pit wouldn't qualify.

That brought me back to food. Up to this point, I had used mainly grain. Small amounts for average efforts, extras for excellence. But after watching the enthusiasm dogs showed when reinforcers were varied, I started carrying other treats in my pockets. I discovered that playing a guessing game with the treats made a huge difference with the horses. It's a game they seem to enjoy, and it definitely creates added enthusiasm. When I ride, my horse certainly seems to be trying to outdo his last effort in order to earn a favorite treat.

Varying the size and quality of the reinforcer gives the horse important information. This is not random. Extra effort earns favorite treats. The clicker-wise horses I ride definitely use this information. For example, when I was teaching my youngest horse, Robin, to pick up cones, I gave him grain after each click. By withholding the click, I created variability in his behavior. Just touching the cone didn't work. He had to bump it harder to get a click and a treat. If he mouthed it, click, he got more grain. But the first time he closed his teeth around it and lifted it slightly off the ground, click, he got a peppermint! That riveted his attention. After that he knew exactly what I wanted. On the next attempt he clamped his teeth around the cone and lifted it several inches off the ground. The peppermint helped him make a quantum leap forward in his understanding of what was wanted.

RANDOM PATTERNS

Canine behaviorist Gary Wilkes advocates still another system. Wilkes produced two of the early clicker videos, *Click and Treat* and *On Target*★. He also has a third video, *The Doggie Repair Kit,* which shows how to use conditioned punishers to solve behavior problems. (See Chapter 13: "Breaking the Punishment Cycle", pg. 71.)

On his videos and at his seminars, Gary demonstrates his use of treatless clicks, meaning sometimes the click is not followed by a treat. The animal is to keep working without getting reinforced after the click. He believes very strongly in the power of unpredictability.

He has a seminar exercise in which he gives the handlers a computer-generated random schedule of reinforcement to follow. Behaviors could be: not clicked or treated, treated without clicking, clicked but not treated, clicked and treated, jackpotted, or clicked and jackpotted. Those were the choices. The computer had generated a random pattern to follow in a series of twenty trials.

Each trainer was to go through the schedule exactly as it was written on the sheet. They were asking their dogs for simple behaviors like looking around to the left or sitting down. No matter what the quality of the behavior was, the seminar participants were to do what the sheet instructed. So trial one might be click and treat; trial two, click but no treat; trial three, jackpot; trials four through six, click but no treat; trial seven, click and treat; etc. The function of the jackpot in this system was to keep the dog working through the dry spells when it was getting no clicks or treats. It encouraged the dog to keep working even when it was feeling frustrated.

Gary used the random schedule to create variability in the responses the dogs gave. He uses this technique in the early stages of shaping a new behavior. Once the behavior has started to vary, he then selectively reinforces those forms he likes best. Gary has had

★ *Click and Treat, On Target, The Doggie Repair Kit,* by Gary Wilkes; clickandtreat.com

The Click That Teaches: Riding With The Clicker

great results with his own dogs using this system. It goes against standard practice, but it works for him. He argues that until you have actually tried it you can't know what it can do for you. That to me is a powerful argument. This is how you push the edges of a system to see what it can really do for you. You have to have some people out there on the edge experimenting to keep ideas alive and growing.

So, in the true spirit of "mad scientist at work", I experimented with Gary's system. In the early stages of learning about clicker training I tried treatless clicks. My conclusion was that I preferred to treat every click.

Treatless clicks made me tense. I didn't like them because they didn't give me a clear basis for deciding which forms of a behavior got a click and treat and which just got a click. For me the randomness of it was stressful. Keeping track was stressful. Avoiding the pitfall of patterns was stressful.

With treatless clicks I had to watch my horse and at the same time monitor what I was doing. If I didn't treat the last version of the behavior, should I click and treat the next one? How was I going to remain unpredictable enough so that my horse didn't learn a pattern? If my horse just gave me something good, but I treated the last three clicks, should I not treat this one? If the behavior was all good, how could I not reinforce something that was worthy of recognition?

My conclusion was I could admire the results Gary got with his dogs. I loved his cattle dog Megan's enthusiasm and the joy with which she worked. Watching Gary and Megan together was one of the things that got me hooked on clicker training. All that said, I just wasn't comfortable with treatless clicks.

WHAT WORKS FOR ME

So what do I do instead? As noted above, I vary the standard for reinforcement and I vary the reinforcer. That makes enormous sense both to myself and to my horse. If a behavior is good enough to click, it is good enough to reinforce. But that doesn't mean that all forms of a behavior are equal. I'll be using a differential schedule of reinforcement, which means that I'll be selectively choosing improved examples of the behavior I am working on.

Varying the reinforcer removed all the stress I was feeling around the treatless click. I get to reward my horse every time I click, plus it makes me a better trainer. Instead of keeping track of random patterns, now I'm evaluating each form of the behavior I click. While I'm fishing around in my pockets for a suitable treat, I have plenty of time to assess my horse's performance and decide if the behavior warrants an extra jackpot.

When I want behavior to vary, I get that by withholding my click. I also get it through the use of negative reinforcers, which act as shortcuts in the shaping process. Gary waits for the dogs to offer behavior. With horses, pressure and release of pressure prompts them towards the responses I want.

THE CLICK ENDS BEHAVIOR

Here's something else to consider in this discussion of to treat or not after every click. It's very important to me that the horse stops when he hears a click. I don't want to create a guessing game where sometimes the click means: "Stop! You're going to get a treat." And other times it means: "That was okay, but keep going and try again." If I click, I want the brakes on, and that's something I get when I reinforce after every click.

Many of the horses I work with are owned by novice riders. The clicker lets them break their training down into very small steps. That keeps the learning process safe and fun for everyone. I want my riders to know that their horses will stop when they hear a click. That's a great confidence builder. The click ends a unit of behavior instantly, so they never have to continue on with something they don't feel safe handling.

This brings us to another drawback of using treatless clicks with horses. Yes, using treatless clicks will get behavior to vary, but it does this by creating frustration. When you're sitting on the animal you're training, that kind of frustration is something you generally want to avoid.

My training choices work for me, but that doesn't make them the only way to use clicker training. Clicker training for horses is in it's infancy. We have no idea how far we can push the envelope. Dolphin trainers began by teaching simple tricks in a tank, and now they're working dolphins out in the open ocean. That's light-years away from where they began forty years ago.

One of the exciting aspects of clicker training is that we're all learning this together and we're all making contributions to the science and the development of new techniques. This book is intended as a road map to help people get started. Experiment. Share. And above all listen to your horses. They will tell you when you are on the right track.

CHAPTER 10
Stimulus Control: Putting Behavior on Cue

In this chapter I'll explain what cues are, how you teach them to your horse, and how you establish full stimulus control, meaning your horse responds promptly to the cue each and every time it is given. I'll explain the two phases you go through in the early stages of clicker training. In the first phase you get behavior to happen. In the second phase you put the behavior on cue. The end result will be a distraction-proof, well-mannered horse.

THE TWO PHASES OF CLICKER TRAINING
There are two phases to clicker training, and indeed to all training. The first phase is the easy one. This is where you get behavior to happen. You get your horse to touch a target, or to back up, or to pick up a canter, etc. etc..

The second phase takes more work. This is where you bring the behavior under stimulus control. That means your horse backs only when you ask for it, and not at other times. Your horse only picks up a canter when you've cued it, not when he feels like it.

The degree to which someone gets control over a particular behavior depends very much on how important it is to them. To a competition dressage rider, having the canter under complete stimulus control is much more important than it is to a weekend trail rider. The trail rider might not care if his horse trots instead of canters, but the dressage rider most certainly will.

Stimulus control is an aspect of training that I think many riders do not really understand, and it's one of the reasons clicker training is so useful. I often think of clicker training as "training wheels" for riders. The structure of clicker training teaches them how to use the principles of good training. Better timing, consistency, recognizing and rewarding small tries are all things you learn via clicker training. It also helps you structure lesson plans, set clear goals, and carry a lesson plan through a complete training sequence.

Here's what I mean by that. Getting a horse to touch a target is easy, and many people might think at first that that's all there is to clicker training. You get the behavior, and you're all set, that is until their horse starts touching everything that even remotely looks like a target. That's when they begin to ask about cue control.

Getting your horse to touch a target only on cue takes much more work and understanding of training principles than simply touching the target. As you sort through this process, you will be learning a tremendous amount not just about training, but about your horse, and yourself.

WHAT IS A CUE?
A cue is a signal that tells your horse which behavior is most likely to earn reinforcement. It must be taught to the horse, and it must make sense to the horse. You may be able to point your finger at your veteran riding horse, and he'll back up twenty feet. But do the same thing with the horse you just bought a week ago, and he'll just stand there staring at you. If you haven't taught him what that signal means, it's not a cue for him to do anything.

WHAT IS A CUE?

A cue is a signal that tells the horse which behavior is most likely to earn reinforcement. A cue is a conditioned response. It must be taught to the horse, and it must make sense to the horse.

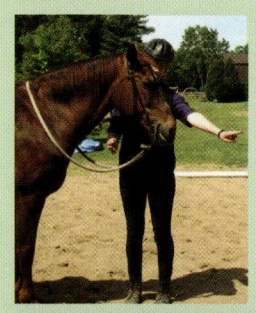

Behavior is determined by it's consequences.

Consequences can be either reinforcing or punishing. If the direct consequence of a behavior is viewed by the animal as a good thing, that behavior is likely to occur again. When you want to know why an animal repeats a particular task, look at the consequences (what comes after the behavior), not the antecedents (what comes before it).

A cue is an antecedent. It is a learned signal that tells the animal which behavior is likely to earn reinforcement. What comes *after* the behavior determines whether the behavior is likely to be repeated in the future—that is, whether the animal will respond correctly to the cue the next time it is given.

It's as easy as "ABC"
Antecedent → Behavior → Consequence

Cue → Response → Reinforcement

The result of the clicker training process: your horse responds reliably each time the cue is given.

The Click That Teaches: Riding With The Clicker

ATTACHING CUES

One of the major differences between clicker training and many command-based training systems is that in clicker training we get the behavior first before we attach cues to it. In command-based training the signal is often given at the start of training a new behavior. Think about this from the animal's perspective. If I said "Grisbak" to you, what would you do? Probably stare at me blankly. You wouldn't have a clue what I meant. But if I first shaped you to sit in a chair and then, just before I knew you were about to sit down, said "Grisbak" you'd begin to make the connection between the word and what you're doing.

As I repeat this signal each time I know you're about to sit down, and then give you a click and a treat when you do, the word will take on a specific meaning for you. Now if I say "Grisbak," instead of staring at me blankly, you'll sit in the chair because you know that doing that behavior under these circumstances will lead to a click and a treat. I'm using classical conditioning to associate the cue with the behavior.

Attaching a cue gives me the first step in developing full stimulus control, but just because you sit in the chair whenever I say "Grisbak" does not mean that I have complete control over the behavior. For that to be the case, all of the following criteria must be met :

• You respond to the cue "Grisbak" promptly each time it is presented.
• When you are with me, you do not sit in the chair in the absence of the cue.
• You do not offer some other behavior in response to the cue.
• You do not sit in the chair in response to some other cue.

Obviously getting to that point is a process that requires considerable focus and consistency on the part of the trainer. Standards may differ. I might decide that it's good enough that you sit in the chair each time I say "Grisbak" and not care if the behavior occurs at other times as well. That's a training choice. But for some particular behaviors, I might care very much that all four criteria are met.

A dressage rider, for example, would care very much that canter departs are under full stimulus control. But it might not bother her if her horse doesn't always come when called in from his paddock. But the trail rider who keeps her horse in a twenty acre field would care very much that her horse comes to her every time she calls.

GREEN LIGHTS AND EXTINCTION BURSTS

Cues are like "green lights" in that they say, "You may now do this particular behavior and you will get reinforced for it." Just as you've learned not to drive through an intersection with a traffic light until given the correct signal, your horse can learn not to offer a particular behavior until he's cued to do so.

Suppose you've taught your horse to touch a target and you've begun to associate the word "touch" with the behavior. Each time you present the cue, your horse now actively seeks out his target. But he's still touching the target in the absence of the cue. One way to establish greater control would be to present the target without the cue and then, when he touches the target expecting a click and a treat, simply do nothing.

If you try this, your horse may go through what behaviorists call an extinction burst. He knows touching the target gets reinforced. He'll bump the target harder than normal. He may even bite at it.

You can exploit this extra energy to create a new behavior. If you reinforce this mouthing, you'll turn targeting into retrieving. However, if you want to get the original behavior on cue, you must steadfastly refuse to reinforce any off-cue, target-oriented behavior. This takes patience. When you see the extinction-burst behavior diminishing, you will give your cue again and hold the target out where it's easy for your horse to find. As you repeat this cycle, sometimes saying the cue and sometimes not, but only reinforcing your horse for on-cue behavior, he'll sort through the differences.

The difficulty with this approach is that the handler must be consistent, and it can be hard to resist all the wonderful effort your horse will be making as he works his way through an extinction burst. That's when you may see the most energetic, best versions of the behavior. Suppose eventually you want your horse not just to touch a target, but also to pick it up and hand it to you. But that's for later. Right now you've got touching down pat, so you want to put that behavior on cue. As you're extinguishing off-cue behavior, your horse lifts the cone up and tosses it across the arena. Do you reinforce that wonderful effort? It's hard not to, but, if you do, you'll be undoing all your work on stimulus control for targeting.

ALTERNATIVE BEHAVIORS

Another approach for dealing with behavior that's offered off cue, one which I prefer, is to ask for an alternative behavior. Each time you see your horse about to offer a behavior off cue, you ask him to do something else instead.

Suppose, for example, I want you to spin in a tight circle, but only when I give the cue "Trenak". I've already taught you that "Grisbak" means sit in a chair. So now I shape the spin behavior and attach the "Trenak" cue to it.

You have now learned two different behaviors with two different cues that trigger them. If I see that you're about to spin off cue, I'll interrupt you by giving the cue "Grisbak". Sitting interrupts the spin. Now I can give the cue "Trenak", and in our game you'll jump up and spin around, knowing that that behavior leads to reinforcement. I've prevented you from offering the spin behavior off cue, and I've strengthened the meaning of both cues. Plus I've avoided the frustration for both of us that comes with extinction bursts.

KINESTHETIC CUES AND LIGHTNESS

We're a verbal species, so it's only natural that we should equate cues with words, but for most horses our body language is much more important than our words. We may think our horse understands what "trot" or "whoa" mean, but the horse is probably responding to a change in muscle tone and posture more than he's listening to our words. Separate the verbal cues from the physical context, and, in most cases, you'll lose the response.

The fact that our horses are so physically oriented is actually good news when it comes to establishing stimulus control. Instead of worrying about when to introduce a cue into the system, you just have to recognize that cues evolve out of the shaping process. For example, suppose you want your horse to back up. You've used pressure and release of pressure coupled with the clicker to trigger the response. You've placed your hand on the point of your horse's shoulder. When he shifts his weight back, click!, you give him a treat.

Clicker-trained horses become eager to please. They WANT to turn you into a vending machine. Your horse is learning that backing is a good thing, so now before you can even touch his chest, he's backing up! He's reading the intent of your body even before you realize you're giving him a cue. It's up to us to recognize when the actions that initially trigger a response become information for the horse. At this point we can make deliberate use of these triggers to turn them into consistent body-language cues.

WRONG ANSWERS

During the process of establishing stimulus control, the horse is going to make mistakes. That will be especially true as his repertoire expands. He'll have more behaviors he knows, more choices to make, and more potential for wrong answers. As your training progresses, you'll have to work in cycles where you keep reviewing basics so that he can keep old and new behaviors plus their cues sorted out.

When I first started working with my youngest horse, Robin, he was very easy to train because he knew very little. His choices were either "A" or "B", so it was easy for him to be successful. As the training progressed we added more elements. Now the list of behaviors he knew included "C", "D", "E", and "F". We had more pieces to play with and more choices to make. That meant that he also had more opportunities to make mistakes. The answer I wanted might be "C", meaning that was the only behavior that I'd reinforce. If he offered something else from his repertoire, it would be ignored. This is a frustrating stage for any learner. They have to discover the clues (cues) that tell them which behavior leads to reinforcement this time.

This is true for any learning system, not just clicker training. The difference between clicker training and many traditional forms of training lies in the consequences for wrong guesses. In traditional systems, the animal is often penalized for unwanted behavior. The cue becomes "poisoned". Next time the cue is given the horse doesn't know if it leads to good consequences or bad.

In clicker training wrong answers are ignored. A conflicting but desired behavior may be asked for instead. The horse is not actively punished for guessing wrong. That's part of why you see such a relaxed attitude in clicker-trained horses.

If you reward a toddler every time she guesses right, she'll be eager to play with you, but that eagerness will very quickly disappear if you start punishing her for wrong guesses. That's why I encourage people to start their horses in stalls where it is safe to let the horse experiment. The horse learns that he will not be punished for exploring and trying different strategies to get you to hand him goodies. You aren't expecting him to be a "dumb", passive animal. In clicker training we want the mind engaged. For me that's what makes clicker training so much fun, and it creates the kind of partnership that I enjoy having with my horses.

WHEN TO ATTACH A CUE

A common problem in training is trying to attach a cue too soon. Verbally telling a dog to "sit" or a horse to "canter" before we have the behavior well established makes about as much sense as telling you to "Grisbak" before you know what the word means. And there's a danger in attaching cues too early. The animal may make some unwanted associations. Suppose in learning to sit a young puppy first drops down on his stomach and rolls over on his side before sitting up. He may think "sit" means perform this whole complex sequence, beginning with a belly flop.

If he's just a pet that may not matter, but for competition obedience you've just dug yourself a training hole. Under stress animals will often revert back to the earliest form of the behavior they've learned. When it matters the most, that puppy may offer his belly-flop sit. The way out of this is to transfer the finished behavior over to a new performance cue. So the show ring version of sit would be asked for with a totally new cue.

The same concept applies to horses. "Canter" may at first mean to your horse "trot faster". You think you've cleaned this up through subsequent training, but now you're under pressure in front of a judge. You tell your horse to canter and what do you get? A bone-jarring trot. It's time to create a performance cue for your polished canter depart which is associated only with that preferred behavior. If that's what you ask for, that's what you'll get.

YOU ARE A CUE

Your very presence is a cue to your horse. What behaviors it triggers depends on your past reinforcement history together. If you're the morning feeder, it may be that just stepping into the barn creates a whole lot of raucous. Your horses might have been asleep a few minutes before, but now they're on alert, watching your every movement. Your presence is a signal that breakfast is coming!

I am a cue for Robin in an interesting way. Whenever he sees me, he arches his neck and holds himself in the elegant posture of a dressage horse. This is something I have deliberately shaped, but I no longer have to ask specifically for this behavior. My presence alone is the cue. I maintain this behavior by keeping it on a high rate of reinforcement. When I walk past Robin's stall, if he's posing, he gets clicked and reinforced. Robin knows a sure thing when he sees it. If he wants a goody and some social attention, all he has to do is pose.

I've heard many people complain that their horses are offering behaviors without being asked. What they are failing to recognize is that their very presence is a cue to their horses. Your horse is doing "something" all the time. He can't do "nothing", not and be alive. With clicker training we can pick and chose the "something" he's doing when he sees us. In effect we can say: "In the absence of any other cues asking for alternative behaviors, this is what will earn reinforcement." For Robin that's posing.

When you look at your horse, what do you want to see? The answer will tell you what you should shape as your default behavior. What behaviors do you want your presence alone to cue? When Peregrine looks at me, his ears go forward. This is not by chance, or "because he loves me". It's because I have consistently reinforced him for what I consider to be a pleasant, happy expression. When Peregrine sees me he "smiles". Stimulus control—it's a wonderful thing!

STIMULUS CONTROL – A REVIEW

Stimulus control completes the foundation of a clicker-trained horse. You started with a horse who knew nothing about how the game was played. You taught him to touch targets and that opened up a whole new world of possibilities. Targeting became a "training shortcut", but it was only step one in the process of introducing your horse to the clicker. When the target wasn't available, your horse didn't understand that your pockets were off limits, so you introduced some other "games". You taught him the "grown ups are talking, please don't interrupt" lesson. You introduced backing and head lowering. Backing taught him to move away from pressure and to stay out of your space unless invited in. With head lowering you could calm down your overly excited "toddler". Anytime your horse got distracted by something in the environment, or too wound up with the clicker games, you could give him a little quiet time by just asking him to drop his head.

Now your clicker sessions could become more complex. Instead of working just on one behavior, you could create a balance in your training, focusing for a few minutes on targeting, then switching to backing or ground tying. In the process you discovered that your horse was getting very good at reading your intent. The body language signals you used to trigger the behavior in the first place were becoming clues/cues he was using to earn his reinforcement faster. Stimulus control was evolving. Instead of an eager-beaver mugging you with behavior, you now have a polite, mannerly, easy-to-get-along-with horse. It's time to move past the foundation of clicker training and start thinking about riding.

PART 2
BEFORE YOU RIDE

Before your horse was ever ridden for that first time, somebody, either yourself or another rider, had to introduce him to the whole idea of saddles, bridles, and people on his back. In this section I'll be describing the process I went through with my own horse, Robin. I'll be showing you how to keep a young horse's training on track while you are waiting for his body to mature; how to use the clicker to solve behavioral problems; and how to prepare a horse step by step for riding.

My goal with any young horse is to develop solid emotional control so riding can be safe and fun. Whether your horse is the nervous one who wants to hide in your coat tails, or the bold adventurer who wants to be at the head of the pack, you'll find lots of answers to your training questions in this section. I'll also be showing you how to train tricks, and I'll describe what the first ride on a clicker-trained horse is like.

MAIN LESSONS COVERED:

1.) Trick Training: Fetching, bowing, lying down.

2.) Stimulus Control: Learn how to put behaviors on cue so they occur only when you ask for them.

3.) Ground Driving: Serves as a preparation for riding.

4.) "The 300 Peck Pigeon" Lesson – Breaking through the "Glass Ceiling": Build long duration into behavior, and establish greater emotional self-control in your horse.

5.) The "Pose": Trained as an alternative to punishment, the "pose" is a beginning step towards advanced performance.

6.) Relationship Building: Nature walks.

7.) First Rides: The first ride on a clicker-trained horse.

This is more than a nuts and bolts section. In this section you'll see how training works in the real world – how problems emerge and clicker solutions are found. Training a horse is not a matter of following "cook book" recipes, but of being creative and responsive to each individual. As you see how I handled issues that arose in training my young horse, Robin, you'll learn stategies that will help you resolve issues you may be having with your own horse.

The Click That Teaches: Riding With The Clicker

RELATIONSHIP BUILDING: THE FIRST STEP TOWARD RIDING

Riding success begins by building a relationship, learning who your horse is both as a species and an individual. I spent many pleasant hours wandering through the back fields and woods around the barn with my young horse Robin before I ever got on him. I gave him the time he needed to mature physically, mentally, and emotionally before I rode him.

CHAPTER 11
Holistic Horse Training: Developing the Physical, Mental, and Emotional Fitness of Your Horse

This chapter examines the elements that create physical, mental, and emotional fitness in your horse. You want to keep these three components in balance throughout your training.

WHOLE HORSE FITNESS

One thing I've learned about horse training is not to jump to conclusions too quickly. Horses are just too complex, and what we think at first glance is going on, may not be the case at all.

What do I mean by that? Here's an example: imagine you're watching a two year old gelding who is constantly crowding into his owner and barging past her on the lead. When she tries to back him, he just stiffens and refuses to move. What's going on here?

It would be easy to jump to conclusions and assume that this youngster simply has respect issues with his owner. The advice in that case would be to teach him to yield out of her space. But suppose you've watched her do that, and all it does is aggravate the problem. The more she tries try to send him back, the more he barges over the top of her. What's going on?

If the horse has a white blaze and answers to the name of Peregrine, the root cause of the problem isn't in his attitude. It's physical. The barging forward is a manifestation of the problems created by his locking stifle joints.

I cannot begin to describe what a frustrating situation Peregrine's stifles created. His joint problems intensified all the normal training issues that come up with young horses. Many youngsters go through a period where they're testing their place in their herd. Your usually sweet horse may go through a phase where he's testing you as well. That's normal, and it's often dealt with by displacing your horse out of your space. In horses that's how pecking orders are established; who moves whom is important. In training we tap into this basic herd dynamic to establish ourselves at the top of our own human-horse "pecking order".

Peregrine's stifles made that almost impossible. Whenever he stopped, his stifles would lock, causing him to shift his weight forward, which, in effect, crowded him back into my space. No matter how many times I sent him back, his stifles always got in the last word: from my point of view his brain was being sent altogether the wrong message by a body that didn't work the way it was supposed to.

Even after I learned how to manage his stifles and keep them from locking, we were left with the emotional fallout they had created. That's also normal, and it points out why physical factors must be considered in any training situation. For example, your horse may be flipping over backwards because you're using a saddle that doesn't fit. Getting a different saddle will not guarantee that the reaction will instantly go away—the sight of any saddle may send your horse racing for the next county. Until you can change his perception that saddles hurt, you won't resolve the issue.

WHOLE HORSE FITNESS

Whole horse fitness means you must look below the surface to find the answers to your training questions. Physical, mental, emotional components are inter-related and effect your horse's ability to perform.

Peregrine

Your horse's physical, mental, and emotional well-being are like interwoven threads forming a whole cloth. You can't focus solely on one element to the exclusion of the other two and expect your training to be successful. You could develop your horse's physical fitness to a peak level of performance, but if you don't also spend time teaching him how to handle adrenaline, you could find yourself sitting on an unridable powder keg. Emotional and mental fitness must go hand in hand with physical fitness.

PHYSICAL FITNESS

The physical fitness of your horse refers to more than just his level of conditioning. It also includes any injuries or conformational problems that effect his ability to perform. *Any time you encounter persistent resistance you should look for a possible underlying physical cause.*

Horses are good at hiding their injuries. They have to be. They're herd animals, members of a prey species that evolved on the open plain. If an injured horse stood out from the rest of the herd, he would be a natural target for predators. Horses, and indeed most animals, tend to hide their pain.

That means that sometimes you have to be a sensitive observer and a good detective to discover the root cause of a particular training problem. I was lucky with Peregrine. His stifles were impossible to ignore. When I say I was lucky, I mean it. There was no mistaking what his issues were. As frustrating as he was, I could always point directly at the source of all our problems—his stifles. My horse was not being "stubborn". He wasn't a "spoiled brat", and I wasn't a terrible trainer who couldn't control her horse. I might not have known what the solution was, but at least I knew what I was dealing with.

Many people aren't that lucky. Their horses suffer through years of resistance before somebody correctly identifies the physical disability that's causing their behavioral problems. These poor horses have often been labeled as "stubborn", "stupid", "lazy", and a host of other derogatory names. Go to any "problem horse" clinic and you'll find horses in pain.

Physical resistance becomes intertwined with mental and emotional resistance. Often you can't separate one from the other, and even after you've resolved the physical issues, you may still be left with layers of emotional trauma that must also be dealt with.

Physical problems are at the heart of many riding issues. They may not be as extreme or as obvious as they were with Peregrine, but they can still create training problems. This is especially true for young horses. Peregrine grew up in a body that didn't work. He spent "kindergarten" fighting with his stifles. While I was trying to teach him the ABCs of riding, he was struggling to escape joints that didn't work. What I thought I was teaching and what he was learning were often two very different things. Woven into the fabric of his physical problems were many mental issues as well.

MENTAL FITNESS

In mental fitness the question is: does your horse understand what you're asking him to do? Just because an exercise seems simple and obvious to you, doesn't mean that it's obvious to your horse. The more complex we make the training, the more potential there is for confusion.

For example, when Peregrine was three, I taught him to work at liberty around me. The first time he paired up with me I was thrilled. We were in a huge arena, and he was leading right next to me. After all the problems I'd had getting him to stay with me on a lead, I thought this was grounds for a celebration!

Then I tried to send him out away from me. Peregrine wouldn't budge from my side. The harder I pushed, the more he stuck to me. He was like a bee around a honey pot. I had spent so much time teaching him to stay that now I couldn't get him to leave!

This is a normal part of training. *For every exercise you teach there is an opposite exercise you must teach to keep things in balance.* Peregrine was showing me the truth behind this principle. What was being tested was his mental flexibility—meaning his ability to learn new things.

Here's another all too common scenario. Your horse has gotten all sweaty. You'd like to hose him off in your wash stall, but he's refusing to walk down the aisle.

"He knows better! Show him whose boss," your friends are telling you. "He's just being stubborn. If you quit now, he'll know he's won."

I'm sure every one of you reading this has heard something like this said about a horse. Maybe your friends are right, and your horse is just being stubborn. Or maybe your horse is truly afraid. Becoming more insistent isn't going to help him. Think about what that feels like from his point of view. Remember the last time you were in a riding lesson and you felt afraid to try something. Maybe your horse hadn't been ridden in a while. He felt all jittery and spooky underneath you. You were so worried about what he was going to do that you only half heard what your instructor was saying to you. You wanted to please her. You were trying really hard, but you just couldn't focus because you felt so nervous. Having your instructor yelling at you made you even stiffer.

Does this sound familiar? We do it to our horses all the time. Haven't we all at some point wanted to scream at our horse for his seeming stupidity? You feel as though you're going to explode with frustration. "Why aren't you getting this?" you want to shout. "You were doing it yesterday!"

That may well be. But maybe today he's worried about shadows on the ground that weren't there yesterday. Or maybe you're tense from a bad day at work, and that's distracting him. Whatever the reason, by giving your horse the benefit of the doubt you'll make far fewer mistakes in your training. Lets suppose your horse really is just being stubborn. Where is the harm in going back a few steps in your training to a point where you can get him to do what you want?

When you ask your horse to walk forward into the wash stall and he refuses, he's giving you a very definite "no!". He's practicing exactly what you don't want. The more he practices saying "no" to you, the better he'll get at it. You don't want saying "no" to feel normal to him. You want him to practice saying "yes" to you. That's the habit pattern you want him to form, so start with things that are easy for him.

THE LANGUAGE OF "YES"

The principles of training tell you to go to a step in the training where you can ask for something and get a "yes" answer back (Ch. 5). If that means taking your horse completely away from the wash stall while you tune up his "go forward" cue, that's what you do. You're looking for questions that give you a solid "yes" answer back.

"Will you walk forward for me in the arena?" "Yes, certainly."

"Will you walk forward for me up to the mounting block?" "Absolutely, I can do that."

Over and over again you want to set your horse up for success. That's how you establish the habit of his saying "yes" to you in any and all circumstances. "Yes, I'll walk through this gate with you." "Yes, I'll walk over this tarp." "Yes, I'll load into this trailer." "Yes, I'll go forward over this bridge; across this stream; through this narrow opening." "Yes, I'll even walk with you into the scary wash stall!"

You develop this willing, can-do attitude by being a good teacher and recognizing that it's okay to review a lesson. You aren't failing and you aren't giving up. You're simply following the principles of smart training.

Does this mean that if you follow the principles in this book your horse will never disobey? No, you could be the best teacher in the world, and your horse might still say, "Nope, it's Tuesday. I don't feel like it." That's when stubbornness is just that, and you need to focus on the emotional fitness of your horse.

EMOTIONAL FITNESS

Suppose your horse understands the lesson. You've worked him through the exercise many times and he's demonstrated that he is more than capable of consistently giving you the correct response. He's a wonderful athlete, sound, agile, full of energy. What you're asking him to do is easy stuff, but the ice is falling off the arena roof, or his best buddy just left the ring, or you just turned toward home five miles out on the trail. Your horse is disintegrating into an explosive bundle of nerves. A moment ago he was everybody's dream horse, and now he's jumping out of his own skin. You can barely sit the whirling Dervish of a temper tantrum he's throwing.

Your horse may indeed know how to do sliding stops and flying lead changes. He may be that super athlete you always dreamed of owning, but that doesn't ensure that you're going to have only smooth sailing in your training. No matter how bright and talented your horse may be, you still have to deal with his emotional development.

A "schooled" animal, horse or human, doesn't quit or feel panicky when the answer isn't obvious. He keeps trying other options because he has learned to trust the training process. Mental confusion does not create emotional anxiety the way it does in a greener student.

That for me is one of the many appeals of clicker training. It creates a "classroom" environment for the horse where you can present progressively more complex problems. The clarity of the bridging signal helps your horse to learn. It can take horses that have become so frustrated with people that they've completely shut down, and it can get them trying again. In the early stages of training you may see horses who frustrate easily, who quit, or who act out aggressively, but this behavior very quickly goes away as the horse catches on to the new game. These horses are learning emotional fitness.

EQUINE "TODDLERS"

Nowhere does the balance in physical, mental, and emotional fitness come more into play than in the training of a young horse. You could teach a weanling all the skills he'd need to be an upper-level performance horse, but if you want him to remain

The Click That Teaches: Riding With The Clicker

sound long enough to achieve your riding goals, you still have to wait for his body to mature.

He might be the most perfect yearling—polite, easy-going, sweet-tempered—but as he matures into an adolescent his behavior could undergo some dramatic changes. You have to manage his emotional development just as you do his physical and mental health.

If you currently own a horse who is going through the "terrible twos", relax. There's good news: they eventually become three! I should know. I've lived through it now with all my horses. Robin has been the latest "toddler" to test my training skills. He's a super athlete, bright, energetic, and very eager to please. Does he sound wonderful? Well, yes, he is, but all that eagerness and athletic ability has reminded me of the importance of managing a horse's emotional development.

ROBIN, MY EQUINE TODDLER

If you've read my first book, *Clicker Training for Your Horse*★, you've already met Robin. I bought him when he was twenty months old just as I was finishing up the final stages of that book. Prior to coming to me, he was growing up in a field in Canada. He was pretty typical of a lot of babies. He was halter broke, and he'd follow behind you on a lead, but beyond that he hadn't had much handling. I took advantage of his ignorance to introduce him to clicker training. (See *Clicker Training for Your Horse* for more about early work with foals and yearlings.)

When I first brought Robin home, I had a relatively clean slate to work with. With the clicker I taught him the basic handling skills every horse needs to learn. I got him used to being touched, to being groomed, and to having his feet cleaned. I taught him to lead. I introduced him to lateral work and taught him to bow and to lie down. Oops, did I say basics? Well, I guess I did get a little carried away. One of the first things that I learned about Robin was that he's a whiz kid. If he'd been a human, he would have been graduating from medical school at about age ten.

I knew that before I ever brought him home, because Robin caught onto the clicker faster than any horse I had yet met. When I first introduced him to targeting, he never missed. He figured out instantly how the game was played: "Touch the cone, get food. What else can I do for you?" That's Robin. He loves to learn, and he's incredibly quick at generalizing. In one five-minute game I knew I had found the perfect horse for me.

Of course, I wouldn't have been horse shopping at all except that my beloved Peregrine was laid up with the after effects of Potomac horse fever. Even after months of treatment, I had no guarantee that he would ever be sound again. So I went shopping. After months of looking I came home with Robin, a sixteen hand Cleveland Bay/thoroughbred cross.

And speaking of Robin, he's got the arena door open. He wants me to hurry. I'm always talking to people. He wants me to come play with him! Sound like any toddlers you know?

He's gone over to his toy box, otherwise known as a mounting block. That's where I store the plastic cones I use in training. He's picked one up and he's holding it his mouth. He's been banging the cone against the wall trying to attract my attention. He never comes into the aisle. (Actually, I shouldn't say that. He did, once, but that was only because I was taking forever to finish my chores.) He doesn't want to leave—he wants me to come play.

For Robin training is fun, and that's one of the hallmarks of clicker training. These horses WANT to work. Part of clicker training is learning how to deal with their enthusiasm. Managing Robin's eagerness has been a challenge. A large part of his early education was centered around teaching him how to handle his toddler emotions.

Toddlers can be enchanting, but they can also try your patience, especially when they tower over you. Robin has taught me many great lessons. Through him I solidified the importance of the foundation lessons of clicker training (Ch. 3). His youthful enthusiasm taught me the real value of tricks (Ch. 12). And his eagerness to learn forced me to reexamine the question of punishment and its place in training (Ch. 13). His desire to work showed me the meaning of yet another great training principle: the longer we stay with an exercise, the more we can see all the great things it can give us (Ch. 15).

At the time of this writing Robin is still at the very beginning of his under saddle work. In a sense he is the shoemaker's kid who has no shoes. My training time with him is very limited, so we don't ride very often, but even so he has opened the door to a whole new world of possibilities.

In many ways the clicker has rocketed his training far beyond other horses. He has opened the door to a whole new approach to performance work that makes upper-level collection accessible to many more horses than it has ever been before. Robin is a great teacher, and I am fortunate indeed to have him as my partner.

★ *Clicker Training For Your Horse,* by Alexandra Kurland; Sunshine Books, US and Ringpress books, UK

CHAPTER 12
Trick Training: Enhancing the Emotional Development of your Horse

In this chapter I'll show you how to turn simple targeting into a series of great tricks. Then I'll review the principles behind stimulus control as I share with you how I used trick training to prepare Robin for riding. I'll show you how you can combine different training techniques to shape complex tricks such as bowing and lying down. But I'll begin by attaching some warning labels to trick training.

TRICK TRAINING WARNING LABELS

What has trick training got to do with riding? Surprisingly quite a lot. Before working with Robin, I was a trick-training snob. Tricks might be all right for other horses, but I was a dressage rider. I was interested in serious performance training, not frivolous tricks.

How silly. Tricks are great training tools, especially for young horses. Horses need time to develop physically. Robin may have been a quick study, but he was still a very young horse with immature bones and tendons. While I was waiting for him to grow up, I taught him tricks. Horses who learn to interact with their environment and to play with toys are much harder to spook. And teaching my eager-beaver over-achiever that there were times when fetching would earn reinforcement and other times when it would not, was a great way to teach stimulus control and the emotional stability that goes along with it.

Learning to teach tricks will make you a better trainer, and it will certainly strengthen the relationship you have with your horse. To illustrate let me share a story. The other day we had two visitors in the barn. One of them glanced into the indoor arena where a horse named Crackers was working with his owner, Bob Viviano. The man did a double take and excitedly called his friend over to watch. "You've got to see this," he said. "That man's playing fetch with his horse! That's so cool. I've never seen anything like that before." And then he said the part that I really liked. "What a great relationship he has with that horse." He got it exactly right.

However, tricks come with warning labels attached. Tricks become behaviors horses like to offer. They know they get reinforced for them, so they'll start offering them any time they want attention and treats. That's the down side to trick training, and one you need to be aware of before you begin teaching them to your horse. To have good control of trick behaviors takes a tremendous mastery of training principles. You need to understand stimulus control and be able to teach your horse clear discriminations between tasks. A good trick trainer is a highly skilled horseman.

I divide all the things I teach with the clicker into two categories. The first type of behavior is governed by pressure and release of pressure. Basically that's most of horse training. This is where you establish the rules of polite behavior. You're saying things like: "This is my space; stay out of it unless I invite you in." You're also saying: "I have the right to ask you to move, and that's what I expect

TRICKS

When horses learn to play with toys, they become much harder to spook.

And teaching a young horse to lie down is a great way to prepare for riding. Long before Robin was started under saddle, he was accepting me on his back. And note: he's already adding his beautiful "pose" into this behavior.

The Click That Teaches: Riding With The Clicker

TEACHING A RETRIEVE

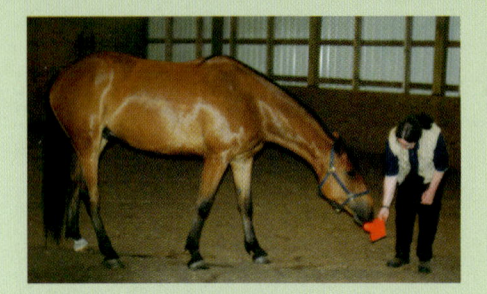

1.) Click and reinforce your horse for touching the target.

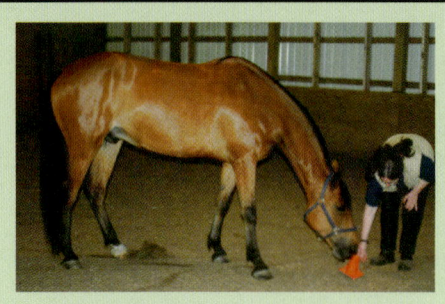

2.) Have him track the target to the ground. At first you may have to keep your hand on the target. If you take your hand away too fast, he may lose track of the target.

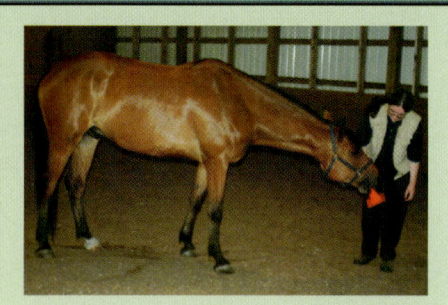

3.) Once he's eagerly mouthing the cone, withhold your click. That will encourage him to experiment. If he lifts the cone, even a little, click and give him a treat.

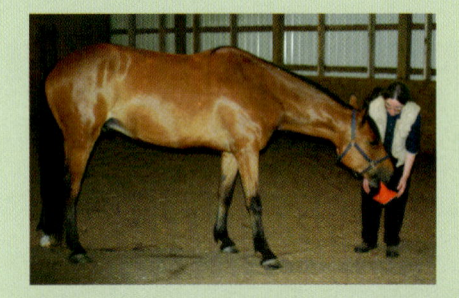

4.) It can take practice to achieve a successful hand-off of the target.

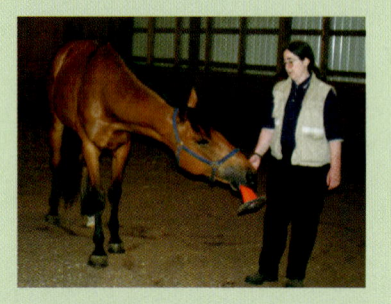

5.) When your horse is reliably handing you the target, take a step off to the side so he has to turn his head and take a step to hand you the target.

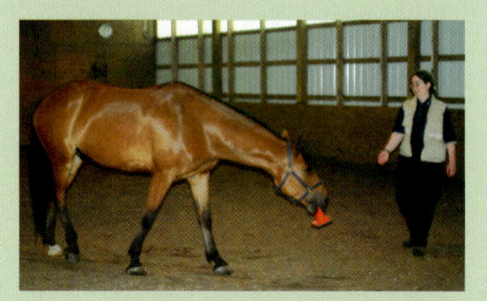

6.) Gradually lengthen out the number of steps he has to take to return the target to you. This is the beginning of your retrieve.

You'll gradually be able to move further and further away from him. As soon as he's walking a couple of steps to bring you the cone, he's ready to fetch it for you. Toss the cone a short distance away from you. He'll walk right over to the cone, pick it up and bring it back to you. Congratulations, you have just turned your horse into a golden retriever!

you to do whenever I ask." Those two rules let us move safely around a thousand-pound animal. I like clicker training because it allows me to establish those rules in a pleasant, non-confrontational way.

The other category of behavior includes most tricks. These are behaviors which I have shaped either with targets or through successive approximation. Tricks usually don't have the rules of respecting space automatically built into them, and horses can get very eager to perform them. So, while you are teaching your horse to fetch, you should also be working on basic ground manners. Initially any tricks you teach should be target-based. That way, if you don't want your horse performing his tricks, you can just take his toys away. Out of sight will be literally out of mind. If you're going to teach tricks such as "counting", you had better understand stimulus control, or your cute trick will very quickly degenerate into unasked for pawing.

RETRIEVING

Robin was my first equine retriever. I'd taught Peregrine to touch cones, but it never occurred to me to have him pick them up. Robin was my over-achiever. He not only bumped the cone, he put his whole mouth around it. "Interesting behavior," I thought, "let me click that." Robin lifted the cone a couple inches off the ground. Click and jackpot. I handed over a peppermint. For Robin that was all it took. On the next try he lifted the cone three feet up into the air, and one click later he was handing it to me! Clever horse. That was Robin. In fact that's many young horses.

Chapter Twelve: Trick Training

When you start working with youngsters, you'll discover how bright they are. When they're young, horses are amazingly eager to experiment and learn new things. The challenge is keeping up with them, which is one of the great advantages of trick training. It gives you a way to channel their playful energy into structured activities.

Retrieving will certainly help you understand reinforcement schedules and stimulus control. Here are some basic instructions to get you started:

• Use a small plastic cone, or check out your local pet supply store for suitable dog toys. Some of the triangular tug toys work great because they give your horse something easy to grab hold of.

• Have your horse track the target down to the ground. You want to be able to set the target down on the ground and have him bump it even when you aren't touching it.

• Once your horse is consistently touching the target, switch from a fixed to a variable schedule of reinforcement. Variable schedules generate variable behavior, and that's what you need to shape a retrieve. Touching the cone at first generates a click and a treat every time. But now you are going to withhold your click. He has to touch the cone more than once before you'll click.

He's learning that he has to keep on offering behavior to turn on the vending machine. If he quits after one or two tries, nothing happens, but if he goes on bumping the cone, at some point you will click and give him a treat. He's not going to be sure why some touches work and others don't. The touches will begin to vary. Sometimes he'll barely brush the cone, and other times he'll grab hard at it. He's testing the parameters.

This is what you want, because now you can pick and choose the touches you like. Once he's consistently touching the cone repeatedly, you can switch to a differential reinforcement schedule (Ch. 9). Click and give him a treat when he opens his mouth around the cone. He'll catch on fast. Pretty soon you'll see him consistently biting at the cone. When he closes his mouth around it, click, and give him a jackpot of a special goody. That will get his attention. Once he's mouthing the cone, withhold your click again. One of those times that he's grabbing at the cone, he's going to lift it off the ground. Even if it's just an inch or two, click and make a big fuss.

That's the beginning. Once you've got that, just keep shaping the lift until he's handing the cone to you.

Next you'll to want to add some distance to the trick. I've found the easiest way to do this is to shape the second half of the behavior first. That means I'm going to teach the horse to bring the cone to me. Once he's doing that, it's easy to get him to go out at a distance to pick the cone up. (See sidebar pg. 62.)

CONTROLLING TRICKS

Robin loved to retrieve. When he was first learning the behavior, if there was a cone in the arena, he'd break off whatever he was doing to fetch it. If I asked him to do something else, he'd get mad. Retrieving was a fun, easy game for him. Retrieving had always been reinforced before. If he handed me a cone, his experience had taught him that he was going to get a treat. He hadn't yet learned that these other behaviors might also be reinforced. From his point of view I was blocking him from doing something he enjoyed and which in the past had earned him goodies. He responded in the way any toddler would, he got mad!

Now that may seem like a bad thing, but it actually created a great opportunity to work on emotional control. I am always looking for safe ways to stretch the boundaries of a horse's comfort zone. That's how a horse learns to handle the inevitable distractions of the real world.

Clicker training and tricks let me work in a very safe environment on issues that plague many horses. Robin was saying in his toddler way that he wanted to retrieve. He didn't want to trot on the lunge line, or back up, or step over laterally. He wanted to retrieve the cone he had just spotted.

His emotional reaction was very much like that of the horse who is out on a trail and refusing to go down the path his rider has chosen. His rider wants to go on, but the horse wants to go back to the security of the barn. Instead of saying: "Oh, okay, whatever you'd like to do is fine with me", the horse has an emotional melt-down.

That's what was happening with Robin, except I wasn't five miles out on a trail sitting on a rearing, bucking, spinning, out-of-control horse. Instead I was in a safe arena, explaining to my horse that there were times when he could pick up a cone and be reinforced for it, and times when he couldn't. In other words, through trick training Robin was learning about emotional control. A big part of trick training involves eliminating off-cue behavior. One method for doing this is to ignore your horse and not reinforce him when he offers the behavior off cue. Many people, myself included, have trouble with this approach. When you withhold your click, your horse

The Click That Teaches: Riding With The Clicker

ELIMINATING OFF-CUE BEHAVIOR

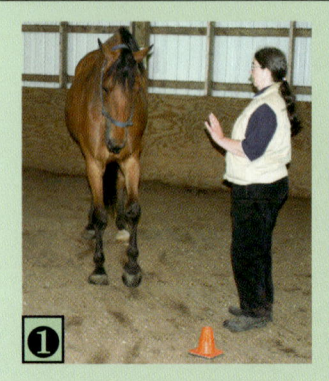

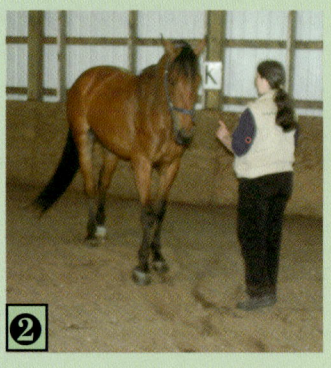

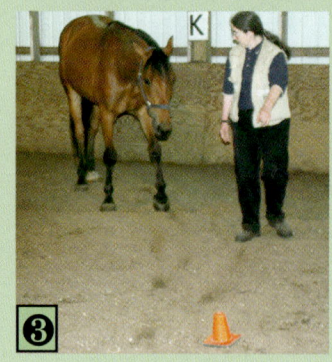

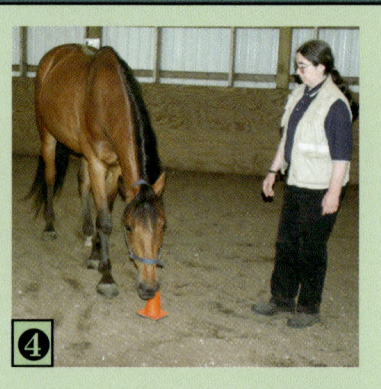

1-2.) Robin wants to retrieve the cone, a favorite game. Instead I ask him to back up, a behavior he has also been highly reinforced for. 3.) Once he has backed away, I offer him the opportunity to retrieve the cone. 4.) Retrieving will earn a click and a treat. I'm building a small chain. The opportunity to retrieve the cone reinforces Robin for backing and waiting. I am using these two incompatible behaviors to establish better stimulus control. Contrasting the two behaviors will make the significance of the cues clearer to him.

is going to try even harder to earn his reward. You'll often see the very best examples of the behavior you are training. It's a challenge not to reinforce him as he offers one good effort after another, but every time you do, you are just encouraging off-cue behavior. A way around this problem is to ask for an alternative behavior. This is the method I used with Robin. If he started to go for the cone before I gave my cue, I would ask him to back up. In other words, I was using a cue from the first category of space-controlling behaviors to keep a behavior from the second category of trick behaviors safe.

PREMACK

In simple terms the Premack principle states that you can reinforce a lower valued activity with a higher valued activity. When I taught Peregrine to retrieve, I got an important lesson in how this works. It turned out Peregrine loved to retrieve just as much as Robin did, though without all the toddler theatrics.

When Peregrine works, he gets a very wet mouth, and this presented a problem. Our arena has sand in it. If the cone tipped over after he had slobbered on it, the sand stuck to it. I didn't want him getting a lot of sand in his stomach, so I carried a towel with me to wipe the cone off. That meant we were often reaching for the cone at the same time. I'm rather attached to my fingers and I wanted to stay that way, so I needed to bring the behavior under stimulus control fast.

With Peregrine something quite unexpected emerged out of this process. Retrieving actually ended up improving his piaffe! Here's how that happened. As I was asking Peregrine to back, I started to be more particular about where he placed his feet. The backing gradually evolved into a request to square up. I rewarded each evolutionary step of the process by giving him the opportunity, i.e. the cue, to retrieve the cone. Since he loved to retrieve, he became eager to square up so the behavior got better and better.

In classical conditioning the emotional effect flows backwards. So, as I associated standing square with retrieving, all the good feelings he had when he played this favorite game were now associated with standing square. Pretty soon I could use standing square to reinforce other lessons.

That's what is so great about clicker training. You start out working on one thing, and you get so many bonuses along with it. The squaring up warmed up his back and helped him to carry himself better under saddle, so our retrieving game actually had a direct impact on the riding.

Could I have taught standing square without adding in the tricks? Absolutely, but we wouldn't have had nearly as much fun.

Targeting and retrieving form the basic skill for many other tricks. Once your horse understands the basic skill is to manipulate objects with his mouth, you can teach him to open mailboxes, dunk basketballs, blow on bicycle horns, play the piano, answer telephones, swing a jump rope, to name just a few ideas. You can even teach your horse to paint, only don't be surprised if your horse shows real artistic talent. Tricks open many windows, not least of which is the one into your horse's mind.

Chapter Twelve: Trick Training

LYING DOWN

Ever wonder how a horse lies down? Here's how it's done. First they go all wobbly at the knees. Then the front end drops down, and the hind end folds neatly to the side.

LYING DOWN, PART 1: THE LION OR THE LAMB: CHOOSING YOUR TRAINING METHOD

When I decided early on in his training that I was going to teach Robin to lie down, I wasn't sure how I was going to go about it. To get a dog to lie down is fairly simple. You ask your dog to sit, then you use a food lure to get him to stretch his nose to the ground. As soon as he plops down, click!, he gets a treat. To get a horse to lie down is far more complex. It's not a behavior they normally feel comfortable offering. Traditional methods use fatigue to force the horse down. Normally a western saddle or a sturdy surcingle is used. The trainer hobbles up the inside front leg, then draws the horse's head around to the opposite side using a long rope and the saddle horn for leverage.

The horse becomes fatigued standing on three legs and begins to collapse down onto one knee. With his head cranked to the side, the trainer can then pull him down the rest of the way. Needless to say this method can place the horse under tremendous physical and emotional stress. Even if you chunk the process down into small steps so the horse does not feel trapped, this is a hard way for the horse to learn the behavior. Collapsing down on one leg like this is not how horses naturally lie down.

Throwing a horse down is a very dominating exercise. When you take a horse's leg away and force him down, you are taking away his power. You are putting him in the most vulnerable position a prey animal can be in. You are taking him down in very much the same way a predator would. When a horse finally collapses to the ground, he is giving up.

This is precisely the reason many trainers teach lying down in this way. They do it for the same reason dog trainers use alpha rollovers. They are showing the horse who is in charge. You may just want to teach your horse a fun trick, but from his perspective, he thinks he's going to die.

That wasn't what I wanted for Robin. I've watched horses being taught to lie down in this way, and I don't like the look that comes into their eyes. There's a point in the process where they look desperate. They're exhausted, but they're afraid to go down. I wasn't going to do that to my horse, so I thought about different ways I could shape lying down.

I had one major problem. I couldn't visualize the step by step process of lying down. What does the horse actually do? I had certainly seen horses lie down, but not often enough to have a clear picture of it in my head. Without knowing the details I found myself struggling to come up with a shaping recipe.

I kept thinking about the traditional method where one leg is taken away. The truth is that's not how horses lie down. Instead they buckle at the knees. They take the muscle tone out of all four legs. There's a moment when you know the horse is going to go down because he looks all "wobbly at the knees". The front end drops first, then the hind end folds underneath the horse's body, and he shifts over onto his side. I know this now because I have watched Robin lie down many hundreds of times.

If you saw Robin's current cue to lie down,

The Click That Teaches: Riding With The Clicker

HEAD LOWERING

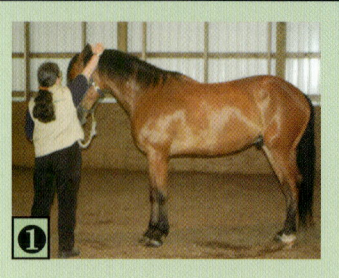

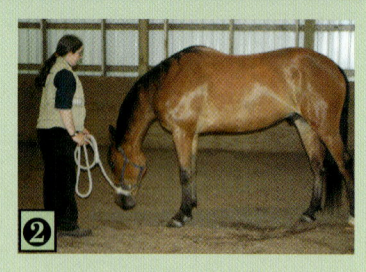

1.) I'm asking Robin to drop his head in response to the pressure of my hand resting lightly on his poll.

2.) As he drops his head, I take my hand completely away. My goal is to evolve a hand signal to cue the behavior out of this shaping process. See text.

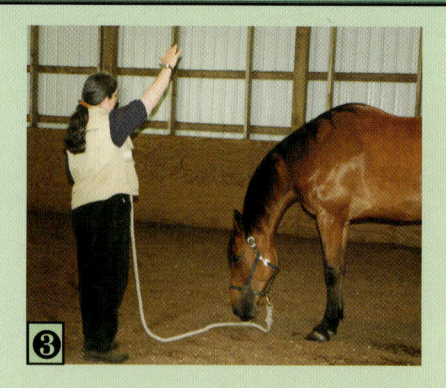

3.) The result: I can cue Robin to drop his head from a distance.

you'd probably scratch your head and wonder, now how did that ever evolve? When Robin sees me raise my hand up above my head, he'll drop his nose to the ground and begin circling, looking for a place to go down.

The one thing you can tell from this cue is that I didn't use the standard method to force Robin to lie down. I was much sneakier than that. Horses—like dogs—go through a complex ritual before they lie down. They have to circle, sniffing the ground, looking for just the right spot to drop and roll. I knew that if I could keep Robin walking around with his nose on the ground long enough, eventually he'd start to think about lying down. If I could get him to think about the behavior, I figured I could get him to do it.

Okay, circling and sniffing. That gave me two behaviors I could shape. I began by teaching Robin to drop his head on cue. (See Ch. 3: pg. 13-14.) It wasn't long before he was dropping his head to the ground whenever I placed my hand on his poll. But now I wanted a cue I could use from a distance. To teach this I borrowed a concept from John Lyons's work.

Robin had learned that he could avoid the pressure of my hand by dropping his head. What would make him even lighter and more responsive to the signal wasn't the signal itself, but the "threat" of the signal. This is an important concept to understand. You'll use it later, under saddle, to teach your horse to be feather-light to your aids.

Remember the example I cited earlier in the chapter on training principles? (See pg. 26-27.) We imagined playing a little game in which you were the horse learning to step back, and eventually just the movement of my hand toward you was enough to get you to move. You were becoming "lighter". The "threat" of the pressure was enough to change your behavior.

In training a horse, it's important to notice the tiny shifts your horse is responding to and reinforce him accordingly. You're rewarding your horse for being more attentive to you. That's what "lightness" means. If you want a light horse, you have to seize the opportunity to have him respond to less of a signal. Remember, lightness is your responsibility, not your horse's.

So how does this translate to Robin? Once I'd gotten him to drop his head from direct poll pressure, I very deliberately dropped my hand to my side between requests. Each new request started with me lifting my hand up toward him. When he responded before I could touch him, I rewarded him with a click and a treat. And once a raised hand would consistently get him to drop his head, I began stepping away from him. Eventually I could be ten to twelve feet away when I raised my hand, and he would drop his head.

Now I had the first element I needed to teach lying down. I also had a useful skill I could use out on our walks together. We've had many situations where a simple raised hand was all that was needed to get him to drop his head and relax.

The next piece of the puzzle was teaching Robin to walk in a series of small circles. I used his basic leading skills for this. Then I added in head lowering by giving my raised hand cue at the same time that he was circling. Robin responded by walking in tight little circles with his nose to the ground. That was a good start, but he still didn't seem to be thinking about lying down. Maybe those other trainers knew what they were doing when they took a horse's leg away. I needed to show Robin that down was part of what I had in mind. To do this I taught him to bow down on one knee.

Chapter Twelve: Trick Training

BOWING

I didn't use the standard method of hobbling Robin to get him to bow. Instead I used a target stick. I had him follow the target down and around to the side. At the same time I lifted his inside front leg and asked him to yield it softly back. C/R.

The key to a good bow is this drawing back of the inside leg.

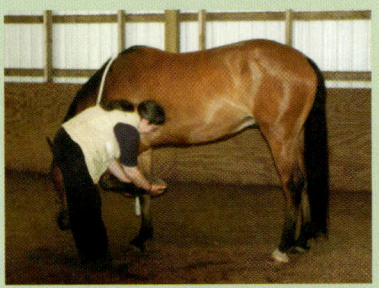

1.) Ask your horse to pick up his left front leg in the same way you would ask him to pick up his foot for routine cleaning.

2.) Fold his hoof up against his forearm. Click and reinforce him as needed until he's comfortable with this position.

You want to be certain to take all the time your horse needs with each step in this process. Some horses may be very balanced and flexible and have no problem doing what you're asking. Others may need time to develop their coordination. (Note: if your horse is arthritic, or has sore hocks or a bad back, I would forget about teaching him to bow. Even if he's willing, you may end up stressing his joints.)

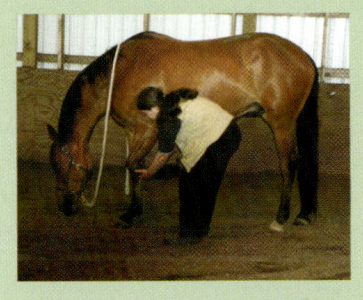

3.) Once you have your horse's leg folded up against his forearm, shift your position so you're facing forward. Again, click and reinforce each criterion shift as needed.

4.) Now suggest to your horse that he rock his knee back. Do not try to force the knee back. A suggestion is just that. Draw the leg back only as far as your horse will comfortably allow, and then wait.

5.) The instant that your horse relaxes his muscles and lets his knee release into your hands, C/R, and let go of the leg.

As your horse gets used to the balance, he'll gradually relax his leg and let you draw it further and further back. Do not rush this process. Your horse needs time to build his confidence and become comfortable with this odd new posture.

When you're rocking his knee back like this, you're really asking him to take a step back. His right front leg will remain extended out in front of him as he lets you rock his other knee back and toward the ground.

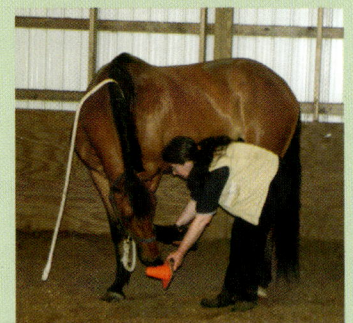

6.) The next step is to ask him to follow a target down and around to the side with his nose. This will make it easier for him to bring his bent knee to the ground.

This is an awkward position that may take some practice for the horse to get the hang of, so build this stage slowly to give him time to develop his coordination.

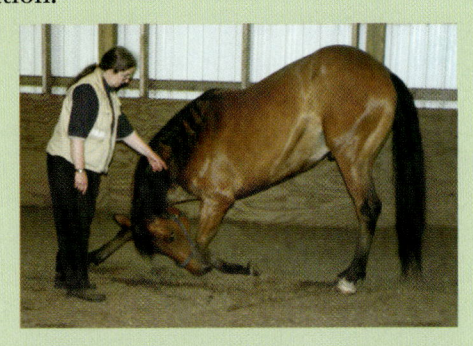

7.) Once he understands what you want, you can fade out your target. The result will be a beautiful, down on one knee bow.

That's how I did it, but there's always another way. A fellow clicker trainer took advantage of something her pony did on her own to teach the bow. This pony wasn't tall enough to reach over the fence to get to the grass growing on the other side, so instead she would get down on one knee and reach her head under the bottom board. I hate it when my horses do this. I always think they're going to ruin their manes. It bothers me so much that I failed to see what a useful behavior it could be.

The Click That Teaches: Riding With The Clicker

The pony's owner wasn't as rigid in her thinking as I was. She saw how she could use this behavior to shape a bow. She started by sitting outside the paddock and enticing her pony with a few nibbles of grass. The pony bowed down on one knee and reached her head under the bottom board. C/R. Her owner repeated this several times, then she moved to the inside of the paddock. The pony continued to bow and reach down for the handful of grass held directly under the bottom fence board. C/R. Her owner inched the pony away from the fence. She pretended to offer her a nibble of grass and her pony bowed! It was so easy. The whole shaping session had probably taken less than ten minutes.

LYING DOWN, PART 2

She also found an easy way to teach her pony to lie down. She spread some shavings out on the ground. Her pony knew exactly what to do with fresh shavings—she rolled in them. C/R. That worked for this team, but I had tried this approach with Robin early on, and it hadn't worked for us. I took advantage of several opportunities to click him for rolling, but I wasn't satisfied with the result. He was too focused on the pleasures of a good roll to pay much attention to the clicker. With Robin I got better results with a slower, more methodical method.

The point here is that there are many different ways to shape the same behavior. The approach I used with Robin is just a suggestion. You may come up with something that suits your horse even better. With clicker training you are always encouraged to be creative and to think "outside the box".

With Robin I already had the precursor behavior for lying down, i.e. circling with his nose on the ground, and now I had a graceful down-on-one-knee bow. The rest was up to him. One day, as I asked him to hold the bow for longer, I could see that he was thinking now about lying down: he kept eyeing the ground as if trying to decide what to do next. I could also tell from his expression that he couldn't figure out how to lie down from the contorted bowing position I'd gotten him into.

In traditional training, at this point you would pull the horse over. I wasn't going to do that to Robin. Quite apart from the fact that I could have injured him, it would have been a major breach of trust. But I had to seize the opportunity, so I switched tactics and went back to asking him to circle with his nose on the ground.

Now he was certainly thinking about going down. He circled, looking for just the right spot. I saw his knees begin to buckle. He was so tantalizingly close—and then he changed his mind. That spot just wasn't quite good enough. This is where you learn patience. I took him through the sequence again. Robin finally found the perfect spot and dropped to the ground.

The first time Robin went down I clicked and rushed over with a huge jackpot. He was so surprised he hopped right back up, dropped his head, circled once, and lay down again. It was as if he couldn't quite believe what had just happened, and he was checking it out!

THE END RESULT

Teaching Robin to lie down represents the way I train most of the more complex behaviors I'm after. To achieve my overall goal I break the behavior down into smaller units. I use a combination of techniques, and I look for as many different ways to shape the same thing as I can think of. Sometimes I'll simply stand back and watch while the horse experiments. I'll capture useful elements as they occur with a timely click and a treat. Sometimes I'll prompt the horse with a target. Sometimes I'll trigger the behavior using pressure and release of pressure.

This for me is the real value of clicker training: it lets me be flexible and creative. I can take a standard behavior such as backing and simply piggy-back the clicker onto existing training methods. Or I can take a non-horse behavior such as fetching and borrow shaping recipes from trainers who work with other species. I can also take a standard trick behavior such as lying down and teach it in a totally new way that avoids methods I'm not comfortable with. If I get stuck in one approach, I've always got alternatives.

Whatever I want my horse to do—from the ground or when I'm in the saddle—the clicker gives me a way of getting him there. So what were the results to this point? I had a youngster who moved like a dressage horse, fetched like a dog, and lay down like a camel. It was a little scary to think about where we were headed next!

CHAPTER 13
Breaking the Punishment Cycle: Temper Tantrums and Time Outs

In this chapter I'll define what punishment is and the problems you encounter using it in training. I'll look at alternatives to punishment, and I'll introduce you to Robin's "pose", a lesson which transformed his training.

PUNISHMENT

What most of us mean by punishment is a penalty imposed for an unwanted behavior. Whether you call it "punishment" or "correction", as soon as you introduce this kind of strategy into your training you create problems.

Penalties occur after the fact so they have built into them a timing problem. In most instances people delay too long after the unwanted behavior has occurred to impose the penalty. As a result the animal doesn't really understand what he's being punished for. But even in those cases where the trainer's timing is perfect, and the "correction" comes just a split second after the offense, the effect of punishment is unpredictable. You can never tell what the emotional fallout will be.

Behavioral scientists prefer a different definition for punishment. They take the punitive aspect out of it and define it as an unpleasant or painful stimulus that stops behavior as it is occurring. In other words, their definition is couched in terms of the effect a given action has on behavior. They also make a distinction between positive punishment—the active presentation of an aversive (something unpleasant or painful)—and negative punishment, which is the removal of something the animal wants.

Positive punishment—which is what most of us mean when we use the word—is the "bad apple" of the two because of the consequences it entails. A strong correction may indeed stop an unwanted behavior for the moment, and that sounds like a good thing, but in reality it may just lead to further problems.

First of all, because you see the behavior stop, punishment is reinforcing to the punisher—that is, the trainer. Once you start using it in your training, it can be hard to stop, even if the overall results are not what you want. Punishment is a slippery slope down which you do not want to slide.

Suppose you smack your horse for nipping at you. Your horse breaks off and stands quietly for the moment which reinforces you for your action. But that doesn't mean he may not try to nip you again in the future. What are you going to do the next time? Hit him again? It stopped the behavior the last time, so why not? But now you may have to hit him harder to get the same result. With that first whack across the shoulder your horse learned that he can survive punishment. He gets hardened to it, so the next time you may have to hit him much harder to get the same response. And the next time even harder still.

That's one of the problems with punishment: it tends to escalate. It leads you into a vicious cycle. At some point even the most hardened trainer amongst us will reach a degree of force beyond

DEFINITIONS

An excess of winter energy sent me looking for solutions from both horse training and the science of operant conditioning. Were the answers to our training issues going to be found in traditional approaches or in clicker training?

An operant behavior is determined by its consequences. Whether a behavior will increase, decrease, or stay the same is determined by what the animal perceives happens as a result of that behavior.

Here is a summary of some of the terms I'll be referring to in this chapter. Note: positive and negative do not refer to good or bad, but whether something has been added or taken away.

Punishment shuts down behavior.

Positive punishment is the active presentation of an aversive (something unpleasant or painful).

Negative punishment is the removal of something the animal wants.

Reinforcement strengthens behavior.

Positive reinforcement gives the animal something it will actively work for. Positive reinforcement introduces a timing problem. The reward comes *after* the behavior. The clicker links the behavior with the reward and solves this problem.

Negative reinforcement takes away something the animal finds unpleasant. The removal of the undesirable stimulus reinforces the behavior that immediately preceded it.

which he will not go. With this in mind, why not stop the cycle and look for alternatives before you even get started?

A second problem with punishment is that it almost always produces unwanted side effects. Your horse may indeed stop biting, but he might also become more head-shy or he might tense up and become stiff when he sees you.

So what do you do to stop unwanted behavior? If positive punishment isn't a good choice, what other alternatives are there? That's the question that working with Robin has been answering.

HERD DYNAMICS

When Robin first came to the barn as a yearling he spent his days turned out in a paddock with two older geldings. At that point he was low man on the totem pole. At dinner time when the hay nets were taken out, Robin would stand respectfully back from the two older horses. While their nets were hung up in the run-in shed, he would wait patiently outside for his. If one of the other horses wanted his hay, he'd step back without any argument.

That pattern changed as Robin turned two. Now he was in charge of the paddock. The other two horses had to wait outside while he decided who was going to eat where. Young horses need to be taught manners by their equine elders, but with Robin this wasn't happening. Instead he had renegotiated his status with his paddock mates and come out on top. Could he do the same thing with me? He was certainly going to try.

Over the next few months I experienced a decided change in his demeanor. He started crowding into my space. It wasn't a confusion in the training. He was still responsive to the lightest of cues, but he was constantly testing me to see if I would indeed make him back off. He was trying to change the structure of our little two-member "herd".

This is a normal part of the maturing process. It's not unusual for your sweet, mannerly youngster to go through a phase of totally unacceptable behavior. Sometimes the older, more dominant horses in a herd will teach your young horse manners, but you may also have to explain to your horse that these dominance-testing games just won't fly with you. That's why it's important as trainers to understand the natural ethology of the animals we are working with as well as the principles of operant conditioning.

I needed to "pin my ears" and assert myself as the lead broodmare, but Robin wasn't impressed by my gestures of assertiveness. Most horses are easy to intimidate. If you puff yourself up and swing the end of your lead rope at them, they'll jump back out of your way. Not Robin. He had never been a fearful horse. Ropes didn't scare him. I didn't scare him. He was too much at ease with me to be intimidated. I didn't want to endanger the bond we had created by making fear the reason he moved away from me. However, I still needed to tell him in no uncertain terms that he couldn't bully me.

FALLING INTO THE VICIOUS CYCLE

Over the winter our dominance issues were compounded by another problem: lack of turnout. When another horse moved into the paddock full-time, Robin lost his daytime visiting privileges. He went on the same limited turnout schedule as the other horses in his barn. This was fine for the older, working horses, but hard on a youngster. When an ice storm limited turnout to the indoor arena, Robin's normally sweet, cooperative nature took a sudden nose-dive turn for the worst.

He became a frustrated grump. It was an open question which would come first, spring or my clobbering him for his juvenile behavior. He had way too much energy to handle safely. As a rider I want that energy, but I want it channeled into work, not explosions. The solution was obvious: turn him out to burn some of it off. But the driveway and paddocks were glare ice. He was confined to barracks until the weather broke. And that meant finding training solutions to what was really a management problem.

Robin is a big horse, and all his excess energy felt menacing. I didn't like it when he crowded into me, so I responded like a traditional horse trainer. I got after him. And Robin responded like a horse. He became resentful. Yes, I could get him stepping back out of my space, but now I had another problem. He started grabbing at the lead.

And there I was, face to face with the problem with punishment. It's like a giant balloon. Squeeze the balloon in one place and the air just pushes out somewhere else. When you use punishment, you may indeed be able to stop one problem, but you'll probably create three others just as bad. I knew this, but I still couldn't resist. I did what all my years of horse training had taught me: I smacked Robin for biting at his lead. And you know what?—it just made him worse.

Robin wasn't biting because he was aggressive. He was getting mouthy because he was young and full of energy, and he was feeling frustrated. When I got after him, he became afraid. Fear made him feel insecure and that made him mouthier. What a cycle. And the crazy thing is that I knew this would happen, but I still clobbered him. How normal. I knew why he was grabbing at the lead, but there were still days when my own cabin fever kept me from being a good trainer.

It was up to me to break the cycle. Turnout alone wasn't going to resolve the issues that had come up. Now we had some very real problems that needed to be addressed. The question was how? If I wanted to keep all the things I treasured most about Robin—his enthusiasm, his eagerness to please, his obvious enjoyment of the training, his sweetness, and his intelligence—I needed to find a different way of communicating with him.

TRYING A "CONDITIONED PUNISHER"

To stop Robin's pushy, unruly behavior I first found myself experimenting with Gary Wilkes' concept of a conditioned punisher, which I'd encountered through his video, *The Doggy Repair Kit*★. Gary is a strong proponent of positive approaches to training, but he also believes that there are times when punishment is necessary. His premise is that if you're going to use punishment to stop behavior, then you need to learn to use it correctly so that it causes no harm. He advocates the use of a conditioned punisher, a signal that's been paired with an aversive, much as we pair the clicker with a reward.

The signal warns the animal that if he keeps doing what he's doing something unpleasant will happen. The aversive Gary uses is a rolled-up towel, which he throws at the dog. Punishment always creates negative side effects, and that's true even when you use a conditioned punisher. Brandish or throw the towel, and yes, your dog may stay down off the furniture, but he's also likely to slink into the other room with his tail between his legs.

Gary makes it very clear that your job is not done until the dog's tail is wagging. Conditioned punishers should be followed by conditioned reinforcers. The dog is reinforced for behaviors you want, such as lying down on his own bed instead of the sofa, or staying back from an open door instead of rushing through it, or wagging his tail at a strange dog instead of attacking it.

Punishment is certainly part of our horse culture. Ask a roomful of trainers what they would do with a horse who crowds into your space or grabs at your clothes and the most common answer you'd get back would be to smack him and "show him who's boss".

I was looking for an alternative to this answer. I had an unwanted behavior. Would a conditioned punisher help me?

To choose my conditioned punisher I borrowed an idea from cat training. The standard punisher for cats is a squirt gun. I thought the surprise value of a jet of water might be just what I needed. I filled an empty paste worming syringe with water and took Robin out for a walk. He did what I expected him to do. He crowded in on top of me. I spun around, said "No!" sharply, and squirted him square in the chest.

Robin jumped back about two feet and stood staring at me in surprise. He hadn't liked that at all! He stood back at a safe distance, eyeing me with new-found respect. I had found a way to "pin my ears" that meant something to him.

It felt great. And of course that's one of the problems with punishment. It's self-reinforcing for the trainer. I knew that, and it was certainly true in this case. It felt good to have Robin out of my space. It made me feel confident and powerful. I used the syringe once or twice more during that session, then all I had to do was begin to lift it in my hand and he'd back out of my way.

I was delighted. This was wonderful. I left the barn feeling elated. I had successfully solved yet another training problem! But the next day my euphoria turned sour. When I went in to get Robin out of the arena, he hung back away from me. Normally he would have come cantering over—it was one of the highlights of my day. Now he was hiding in the far end, and I had to walk over to get him.

"Your job isn't done until the dog's tail is wagging."

All right, I had some fence-mending to do. That was part of the process. Over the next few days I focused on reinforcing behavior I wanted, and I also evaluated my use of conditioned punishers. Robin was more respectful. He was staying back out of my space, and he did indeed seem less menacing. Those were good things. It had bought us some breathing room in the training, so I couldn't say that using the conditioned punisher at this point was entirely a bad thing. However, it changed our relationship. When I became a punisher, I stopped being a partner. I didn't like the way the training felt.

So I changed tactics. The real issues with Robin were not about herd hierarchies. I knew how to keep the pecking order clear without turning into a bully. I also knew that if I stayed consistent in my requests he would settle into his work. All this juvenile behavior that I found so annoying would go away with time.

The real issue with Robin was his eagerness and his excess energy. I was simply being overwhelmed by his enthusiasm. His mouthiness was a reflection

---

★ *The Doggy Repair Kit,* by Gary Wilkes; clickandtreat.com

of his willingness to work. He was frustrated because I couldn't keep up with him and provide him with enough play time. It was like watching a very bright child who isn't getting enough stimulation.

RETURNING TO BASIC PRINCIPLES
"Focus on what you want your horse to do, not the unwanted behavior"—now where have I read that before?

The more I focused on Robin's mouthiness, the more annoyed I became by it. Every time he grabbed at the lead I felt my own resistance rising. It didn't matter that I knew this was a stage he'd outgrow. I couldn't keep the "horse trainer" part of me from reacting.

My response to Robin was the same one I've seen so many times in the parents of toddlers. They've taken their normally well-behaved child out to a restaurant, and he's throwing a temper tantrum. They know he's not going to behave this way in another year or two, but right now it's tough not to have a knee-jerk reaction to his outrageous behavior.

So what was the answer? Traditional horse training with all its whips and swinging ropes and its "show him who's boss" attitude wasn't what Robin needed. Nor were conditioned punishers.

In case you haven't already figured this out, I'm an experimenter. My horses are my "guinea pigs". I use them to test out different ideas and training approaches. They are also the final arbiters in deciding which of the many things I try stay in the tool box. I really do subscribe to the expression: "Go to people for opinions and horses for answers."

So what do you do with a mouthy, over-eager horse?

For Robin the answer was you take a deep breath and walk away.

That was it. I gave Robin a time out. Instead of attempting to stop the behavior with corrections (positive punishment), I took away something he wanted. I used negative punishment. Clicker-trained horses love to work. They love the treats, the social attention, the fun of figuring out new tasks. When I took these abruptly away, I found a way to teach Robin patience.

TURNING "NO" INTO "YES"
I put a stall guard across his stall door and stood about six feet away. I held a whole carrot out in my hand, so it was clearly visible, and started to walk toward him.

Robin couldn't resist. He reached out toward the carrot. I closed my hand over it and whirled around on my heels, turning my back on him. I was using negative punishment, taking away something he clearly wanted in order to stop the behavior.

I counted to five and turned back to him with the carrot. Again Robin couldn't resist. As he stretched his nose out, I whisked the carrot away and turned my back on him once again. Not only did he lose the carrot, he lost all interaction with me as well. I counted to five, then turned back and started to walk towards him again.

This time he hesitated ever so slightly.

Click! I reinforced him with a bite of grain.

The exercise was taking shape. Now Robin had a choice. He could grab at the carrot and lose everything or he could control himself and earn a click and a treat. That first hesitation was a slight one. I had to be very attentive to catch it, but, instead of lunging for the carrot when I was five feet away, he waited ever so slightly. With the high-speed precision of the clicker I could capture that fraction of an inch of breathing room and grow it into self-control.

In less than five minutes I was standing in front of Robin holding the carrot directly under his nose. Instead of lunging for it, he was drawing himself back. It was almost comical watching him—he was trying so hard to avoid touching the carrot! He tucked his nose into his chest and looked for all the world like a fancy dressage horse. Click and jackpot!

I was liking this. Not only was this turning into a great lesson in self-control, it was also creating a carriage I liked. My focus had shifted from the negative don't-grab-at-the-carrot to the positive draw-yourself-up-into-your-dressage-horse pose.

Before I had been a reactive handler, responding with knee-jerk reactions to Robin's mouthiness. The result had been frustration and resentment in both of us. How predictable. When I put Robin back in his stall, I became an active handler again, and I was able to solve the problem.

If punishment creates negative side effects, clicker training creates positive ones. One of the things I

Chapter Thirteen: Breaking the Punishment Cycle

love about clicker training is you always get more good things than just the one element you think you're working on.

Robin discovered that he could get me to click by drawing his shoulders up, arching his neck, and bringing his nose in towards his chest. Initially the carrot was the signal for him to do this, but then he started offering the behavior without the carrot cue. I'd walk past his stall, and he'd strike his "dressage pose".

I spent the winter reinforcing him for looking like a grand prix horse. It became one of his favorite behaviors. If he couldn't figure out what would get me to click, he'd try his pose. He started inserting it into other exercises. In-hand he added his dressage pose as an extra flourish. He'd walk next to me with his neck arched and his shoulders lifted. He looked grand. I just loved watching him, which meant that his training sessions became even more fun for both of us.

One evening in late spring I was working him on the lunge line. He was giving me a so-so trot which I wasn't reinforcing. All of a sudden the "light bulb" went on. He'd try his "pose".

He had to add extra energy and engage his hindquarters to do it. His shoulders came up, his neck arched. He looked magnificent. His average, not-very-forward trot suddenly turned into a spectacular, knock-your-socks-off, gorgeous show. He was moving like an elegant carriage horse in full harness, except that all he was wearing was a simple halter and a lunge line. The clicker let me capture that moment. The jackpot that followed told him that something wonderful had just happened.

I put him up into the trot again, and within a couple of strides he had organized into the same magnificent movement.

His "pose" very quickly became part of the regular routine of lunging and liberty work. He began to move with an elegance that was just breath taking to watch. I've never put any side reins or martingales on him or chased him forward with lunge whips. All I've done is clicked and reinforced him for behavior he offers freely. So you never know what you're going to get when you start out with the clicker. You may think you're just solving a nuisance behavior or teaching a fun trick, but with clicker training it always turns into so much more.

Robin led the way in this, but the "pose" has now become a standard hallmark for our clicker-trained horses. It's been taught in a variety of ways, more often through targeting than timeouts. (See Ch. 9, pg 45-47.) The end result however is the same magnificent movement freely offered.

THE INFLUENCE OF THE "POSE" OVER TIME

The photo on the left appeared in my first book, *Clicker Training for your Horse**. I had just started Robin in training. He was not yet two, and he'd been with me only a couple of weeks when this photo was taken. I was pleased with his overall balance, especially in such a young horse. It was a good beginning. Many clicks and many lessons later it produced the photo on the right showing Robin as a four year old. Here Robin is trotting at liberty beside me, and you can see the influence of his "pose". This beautiful balance has become the hallmark of clicker-trained horses all over the world.

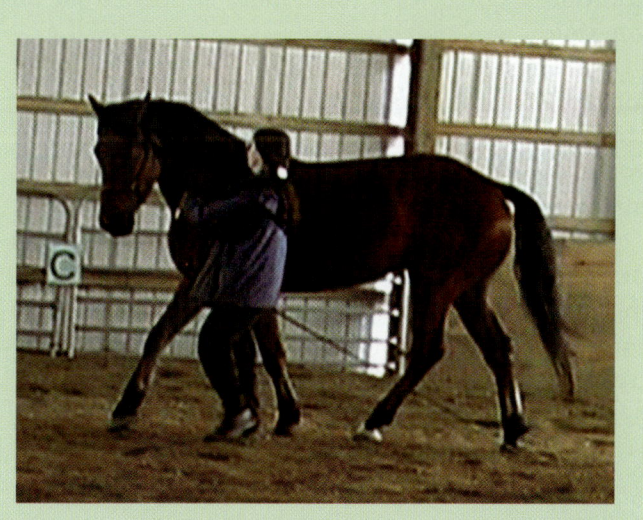

★ *Clicker Training For Your Horse,* by Alexandra Kurland; Sunshine Books, US and Ringpress books, UK

POSITIVE PROBLEM SOLVING

Robin's mouthiness was caused by a youthful excess of energy, but some horses are mouthy because they're confused or frustrated; they don't understand what you want them to do and their uncertainty and anxiety turns into mouthy behavior. Some will act as though they need a pacifier—they always seem to have something in their mouth. Others act out their frustration by snapping at you with their teeth. Becoming more aggressive with them often just makes matters worse.

What all these horses really need is for you to chunk your training down into smaller steps. If you encounter a problem in your training, the solution is never to be found in the layer you're working on.

You need to keep stepping back, stepping back, to an earlier point in the training until you find a place where you can ask your horse a question and get a "yes" answer back.

"Will you stand still when I put the saddle on your back?"

"No? Well then, what can I ask you to do that you can succeed in?"

Maybe it's as basic as: "Can I stroke my hand quickly over your shoulder while you stand still?"

If the answer to that is "yes", then click, that's where you begin.

At times it will seem as though you're going backwards by working on a very simple behavior, but it's like dropping a pebble in a pond: the ripple effect can be enormous.

Suppose you have a young horse who's just getting used to being handled. Or maybe it's an older horse who still fusses every time he's groomed. You want your vet to check your saddle fit to make sure he isn't back sore, but it's hard to do a good evaluation on a horse who won't stand still. So what do you do?

Your horse is so fidgety that his feet are never still for more than three seconds at a time—but that's all you need to get started on solving this problem. If you know he's going to move in three seconds, click him at two for standing still.

Count out twenty treats just as you did when you first introduced your horse to the clicker. You're going to use those treats to measure his progress. Each time he moves before you can click, put one of the treats into a spare pocket. When he stands still for two seconds, click and give him a treat. When you have gone through all twenty treats, count out the number you pocketed. This will give you your success rate. For example, suppose he moved off before you could click eight times out of twenty. You'll have eight treats in your pocket which means you know he was successful twelve times out of twenty. Twelve divided by twenty gives you a sixty percent success rate. When your success rate rises to eighty percent, increase your criteria. Now he has to stand for three seconds before you will click.

This is a very systematic way to track progress and to know when you can move on and increase your criterion by delaying your click just a little bit more. You're offering your horse a choice. He can fuss and fidget, but if he does, he'll miss his treat. Or he can control himself, keep his body still, and earn a click and a treat.

Trying to force your horse to stand still with restraints would only intensify his anxiety. Instead you're helping him to learn self-control. He'll be replacing his instinctive urge to flee with a positive learned response you can use throughout his training. As he learns to stand still, you can ask more difficult questions. "Can you stand still while I run my hand over your shoulder?" Yes. Click and treat.

Move your hand quickly at first—that's actually easier for a skittish horse to accept than if you moved slowly in an effort to be gentle. Pretend you're brushing a fly away. Before he has time to react, click, he's getting his treat. You can gradually slow your hand down and move it over more and more of his body. Once he's comfortable being rubbed all over with your hand, you can add some new challenges. "Can you stand still while I rub you with this cotton ball?"; "this soft brush?"; "a crinkly plastic bag?"; "this pair of clippers?"; "this needle you used to be so afraid of?"; "this saddle that always makes you fidget?"

Keep records of your progress. Anytime you get a "no" answer, back up and spend more time on the preceding step. You may even need to insert more steps. Progress may seem slow at first, but your patience will be rewarded with a horse that is eager to work. When you learn to put aside the knee-jerk reliance on punishment and the quick fix, you discover instead the rich rewards your horse has to offer.

CHAPTER 14
The Time It Takes:
Building Duration Into Behavior

In this chapter I'll describe an interesting strategy I developed for building long duration into behavior. For horses who struggle with issues of emotional control and patience, it's a key building block in their preparation for riding.

TRAINING TIME

People are in a hurry. They want to get things done fast. I know this because among the most common questions I get asked are the "how long" questions. "How long will it take to condition my horse to the clicker?" "How long will it take to start him under saddle?" "How long will it take to get him on the trailer?"

The standard answer a good trainer will give you is as long as it takes. Through experience, I have a rough idea of how long it generally takes a horse to learn a particular lesson. I've worked enough horses through their first head-lowering lessons to know approximately how much time to allot for teaching that behavior. And if I'm working on trailer loading, I know I need to leave myself a bit more time.

But I'm never in a hurry when I train. If a horse is about to figure out what I want him to do, I give him the time he needs. My goal is never to get the job done the fastest; my goal is to enjoy the process and to end up with the best possible result.

ENTHUSIASM AND 300 PECK PIGEONS

Clicker training is not without its training issues. When I talk about this at clinics, someone always ask the obvious question: what are those issues? The main one is enthusiasm. What do we do with horses who truly love to work?

People get distracted by the food issue, but the real issue is what do you do with a horse who is mugging you with behavior, who is offering you every trick he can think of to get you to play with him? We aren't used to our horses being so intent on performing for us. What do we do with our enthusiastic over-achievers? How do we help people when they're still in the stage of training where the mantra is "get behavior, get behavior, get behavior", and their horse is offering them every cute trick they've ever learned? How do we stabilize these behaviors without resorting to punishment so the end product is a polite, settled, easy-to-get-along-with horse who still loves to learn?

These and many others were the questions Robin was forcing me to examine. He was two years old, and I was juggling the demands of an over-full schedule with his need for exercise in a boarding situation where turnout was severely restricted. Over the winter the situation came to a head when we were iced in for weeks at a time and turnout was limited to the indoor arena. Robin's pent-up energy was colliding head-on with his still immature ability to control his emotions. To deal with this dilemma, I invented the "300 Peck Pigeon" game.

TRAINING TIME

How long does it take to go from this green-horse balance . . .

. . . to this beautiful trot?

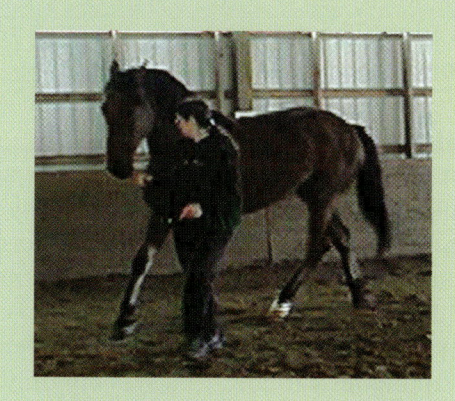

The answer is as long as it takes.

The Click That Teaches: Riding With The Clicker

The phrase "300 peck pigeon" refers to an experiment in variable reinforcement schedules I heard about a couple of years ago. A scientist was looking at how you build long duration variable schedules. She taught her pigeons to peck a bar, and by gradually extending the number of pecks they had to give her, she got her pigeons on a VR schedule of three hundred. That means that on average they had to peck the bar three hundred times before they would get reinforced.

That sounds like a tremendous amount of behavior, especially for a pigeon, but it is in fact what we want from our horses. Think about dressage riders. They want their horses on the bit throughout an entire test. In other words they want a "300-peck-pigeon" horse. This researcher found that the best way to get such long duration was to build the schedule slowly in very small increments. Most riders build their schedules too fast, and in too few steps. They jump from being delighted if their horse goes on the bit for a step or two, to expecting it as a matter of course. The result? Confusion and resistance. The solution? Build duration slowly.

BUILDING DURATION

In my own training I generally emphasize quality of movement over duration. That's not to say I don't build duration, but my focus is more on how well something is done rather than how long it is done. In this experiment I shifted my emphasis to duration. I picked a simple, very basic behavior to work with: walking next to me. That was my only expectation. I just wanted Robin to take a step forward when I did. When he took a step forward, click, I reinforced him. But in this game I increased the number of steps he had to take by one after each click. I kept count, and I walked on a large circle marching-band style, keeping a consistent, metronome pace. The only kicker in this was that if Robin grabbed at the lead rope, the count for that trial automatically reset back to zero.

Robin at this point was already a sophisticated in-hand horse. Basic leading was baby stuff for him, except that it was winter and he was so full of energy he could hardly contain himself. Robin expressed his frustration by grabbing at the lead. That was the impetus behind my experiment. I wanted to explore some non-traditional ways to eliminate this problem. My goal was for Robin to come directly out of his stall and, without any play time, go to work in a settled, focused, relaxed manner. That's a lot to ask of a young horse, and especially a high-energy horse, but that's what I wanted.

At first it was an easy game for Robin. All he had to do was walk forward one step, and click! I reinforced him. The next time he had to walk forward two steps, then three, etc., baby stuff for him, except that Robin is a very sophisticated clicker-wise horse. He was looking for the standard of behavior I was reinforcing. So as we built duration, he started experimenting. What was I reinforcing? He went into his mainstay, his "pose". He arched his neck and carried himself in a beautiful dressage-horse equilibrium. I didn't click him right away, but kept to my count. Well, that was all right. He was used to some duration in the behavior. So we'd go maybe ten steps, and I'd click him.

The next time I'd go eleven steps. The next time twelve, clicking him on that twelfth step, no matter what he was doing, so long as he wasn't grabbing at his lead. If he grabbed at his lead, the count automatically went back to zero, and I'd start again.

Robin did pretty well in the early stages of the game, but as the count started to lengthen out, he got impatient. He was posing. He was doing great. I should have clicked him by now! Robin hates being wrong. He's very bright, and he's very eager. He gets mad if he gets the wrong answer. So as my count stretched out, Robin got frustrated and grabbed at the lead. Zap! We might be one step away from a click, but the count reset to zero.

Clicker training offers us new strategies for teaching emotional control. Robin was trying to figure out what I wanted. When he tried his hardest to offer me things that previously would have earned reinforcement and that now weren't working, he became frustrated. That's very understandable. He expressed his frustration by grabbing at the lead. I didn't reprimand him for that. I simply regrouped, got him settled again, and marched off as promptly as I could.

I made a point of responding as little as possible to the unwanted behavior. If we got to our count, click, he got a treat. If he grabbed at the lead again, the count for that trial reset back to zero. So, to go, for example, a count of twenty steps, we might actually walk fifty or sixty steps. The next time we might go directly to twenty-one steps and a click. But to get to twenty-two, we might walk eighty steps or more with multiple resets depending upon how many times he grabbed at the lead.

If you are trying to sort out how to use variable reinforcement schedules, this experiment may confuse you. On the surface it would seem to conflict with the concept of randomness. A variable reinforcement schedule should be just that, variable, and yet here I am describing a very patterned exercise, the count

Chapter Fourteen: The Time It Takes

automatically increased by one after each click. Here's the key to understanding this: the pattern was set from MY perspective, but from ROBIN'S I was being the most variable and unpredictable that I had ever been.

As the count lengthened, we went through several interesting stages. First, he coupled his "pose" into the game. He'd hold it longer and longer, but when I didn't react in my usual manner to his gorgeous balance, he tried other things. At first grabbing the lead was one of the things he tried, mainly because he was frustrated that something that always worked for him, wasn't working now.

One of the advantages of this game was the counting. I could see when things happened. For example, around twenty-five he went through an extinction burst centered around the "pose". That's when he decided that the carriage I normally reinforced was not what I wanted. He gave up on looking outstandingly gorgeous and tried other things.

Twenty-five steps may not seem like very much, but remember to get to twenty-five, we first had to walk twenty-four steps, and before that twenty-three steps, etc.. To get to this point actually required considerable training time, and provided him with tremendous learning opportunities.

At forty-one it was clear he had figured out the underlying criterion: that whatever he was doing, he had to keep doing it a little longer each time. At this point Robin was experimenting with several different alternatives: posing, walking with his head at chest height, dropping his head to the dirt. I kept to my count so that all of these options were at times being reinforced. But it was clear Robin was making choices. He was testing which behavior was easiest to sustain. He started walking for longer and longer stretches with his nose in the dirt. Head lowering creates a calm attitude. I was liking his choice and decided to reinforce him for it.

By and large, you know you are ready to add the next layer to your criterion when you see it already occurring at least 80% of the time. That's what was happening with Robin. More and more, he was keeping his head down. If it popped up for any reason, within a couple of steps he had it back down again. Once I saw that happening, I knew I could target it directly with the clicker.

I hadn't started out looking for head lowering. My criterion had simply been that Robin was to walk next to me. But now I made nose to the dirt part of the criteria. If his nose was up when we made our count, I would keep walking until it dropped back down.

So we might go seventy-eight steps towards a goal of seventy-nine. If on the seventy-ninth step his nose popped up, I kept walking until it dropped back down on the eighty-fourth step, and then I'd go a step or two beyond that before clicking him. Our game had become even more interesting. I was not asking him to keep his nose down the entire time, but I would not click him until the count had been met, and his nose was to the dirt. Again, if he grabbed at the lead, the count reset to zero.

The first night we worked for a little over an hour. We ended at a count of one hundred and twenty-five steps with Robin keeping his nose to the dirt the entire time. Pretty neat.

The next night I made my goal of three hundred. That's three hundred consecutive steps where Robin kept his nose to the dirt. Very neat.

I found in my count that after about a hundred and twenty I could start jumping up in larger increments. Instead of increasing one step at a time, I jumped up in increments of ten to fifteen steps. Robin had certain sticky points. Sixty-five was one of them. At sixty-five the count kept having to be reset. It was as though Robin was saying: "I get it. I know what I'm supposed to do, but I don't want to do it that long." We got over that hurdle and had smooth sailing until we hit one hundred. That was another emotional barrier for him, as was one hundred and fifty, but after that we built to three hundred very quickly. He had the behavior, and he had accepted the idea of doing it for longer and longer periods. If I wanted a "1,000 peck pigeon", I could have gotten there with ease.

THE UNEXPECTED BONUSES OF DURATION TRAINING

In general most of us don't stay with an exercise long enough to see how much it can do for us. That's certainly true for an exercise like this. Without the example of those pigeons in mind, I would have been satisfied if Robin had gone only forty or fifty steps with his nose to the dirt, but somehow I knew getting all the way to three hundred was important for him in this case. I could not have been more right. I've said many times before, when you use positive reinforcement, you always get more good things than you expected out of a lesson. With Robin that was certainly true.

We met our goal and then some. After playing our "300-peck game" out to the end, Robin could come straight out of his stall and go right into work without any turnout or play time. I didn't have to lunge him or let him run to get his energy out. He was no longer biting at the lead rope. Instead he'd learned patience, and we had built a new default behavior he could use to calm himself: dropping his nose to the dirt. Now when he felt frustrated, he dropped his head. That's a wonderful safety valve to have in a high-energy horse.

The exercise also built a much stronger, more consistent cue for head-lowering. I hadn't been working directly on stimulus control. In fact, when Robin began offering head lowering in this situation I wasn't even asking for it. But out of the consistency of the behavior evolved a much clearer, more consistent cue for this most useful behavior.

My previous cue had become linked to bowing and lying down. Now I could get head lowering by itself without triggering those other behaviors. Since head lowering leads to calmness, this was an important development. Robin gets lots of reinforcement for brilliance. He needed the balance that head-lowering creates.

The head lowering made something else much better—respect of space. Again, this wasn't something we worked on directly, but after we'd completed the "300 peck pigeon" project, Robin became much more adept at shifting out of my space when I asked him to change sides.

That resolved another whole layer of issues and questions he had. Prior to this exercise I had always had the feeling that he was a little klutzy changing sides. It was like dancing with somebody who steps on your toes: he wasn't quite managing to maneuver his big body out of my space, and that always made him a little grumpy. But now he became much more graceful in our "dances" together.

That is, of course, the fun of training. You never know all the good things you're going to get. But I did know that stretching us both to three hundred would be good for Robin's emotional development.

Robin is an athletic horse who learns things easily. Sometimes that means too easily. He's the bright kid in class who doesn't always want to do his homework. He knows the principle, why should he bother with the details? Working on duration helped to develop his emotional maturity and mental discipline. It took us another giant step forward in his preparation for riding.

300 PECK PIGEON INSTRUCTIONS

Do you have a behavior where your horse has "trained" you to click him after just a couple of steps? I think of this as a glass ceiling. If "three steps — click" is a pattern you're locked into, it's time to use the "300 Peck Pigeon" lesson.

- Pick a simple behavior, something your horse could keep doing for longer and longer periods, such as walking on a loose lead, or standing on a mat.

- Decide what the reset behavior will be, for example grabbing at the lead, or stepping off the mat.

- Begin your count at one. One step: click and treat. One second on the mat: click and treat. Increase your count by one after each successful trial.

- If your horse grabs the lead, reset the count for that trial back to zero. For example you might be heading for a count of twelve. He grabs the lead on step seven. Get the lead back, reorganize and begin counting one, two, three steps, etc., towards a count of twelve. If he grabs the lead at five steps, reset back to zero, and begin counting toward twelve steps. When you get to twelve, click and treat. Increase the count to thirteen. Continue working toward your goal of three hundred steps.

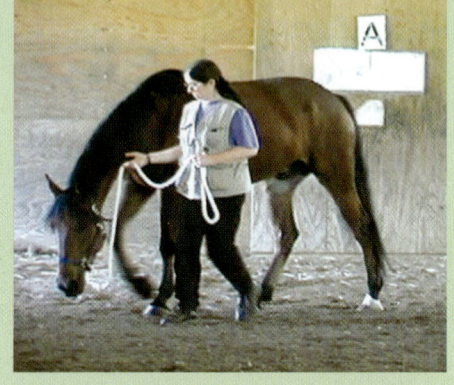

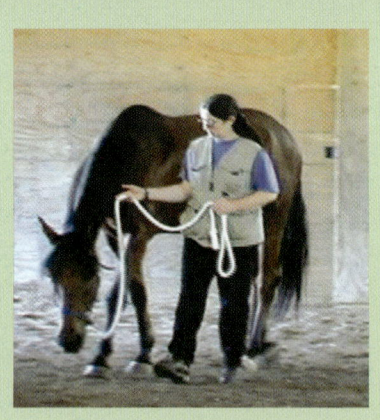

Chapter 15
First Rides

In this chapter I'll share with you Robin's very leisurely introduction into a working life. If you've been looking for the nuts and bolts of riding technique, that's what you'll be getting in this chapter, but always with a few clicker detours thrown in.

RIDING GOALS
I am never in a hurry when I train. My goal is never to get the job done the fastest. My goal is to enjoy the process and to end up with the best possible result.

My goal with Robin was to ride, but I was in no hurry. I had bought myself a huge time lag by bringing home a yearling. I was free to putz around as I call it, which is what I enjoy doing with my own horses. If Robin were part of a commercial operation, I would have left him out in a field until he was four, brought him into a round pen, spent a couple of sessions on the ground with him, and then started him under saddle.

That's not how I like to handle my own horses. Robin is my future riding horse, but he is also my pet. I'm like all the rest of you who work during the day and have horses for recreation. It doesn't matter that my work is training other people's horses and I'm around them all day. At night I still enjoy fussing over my own horses. I enjoy grooming them, and picking their stalls, and making sure they are happy. And I like doing something with them every day, even if it's as simple as going for a walk up the road, or teaching them a silly trick. I do this because I enjoy it, but it also turns out it makes good training sense. Long before Robin was old enough to ride, I was working on the skills that would make him a superior performance horse.

ITACHAN
When Robin was three I spent the summer months taking him out for long walks in the back hay fields. We formed a herd of two and went exploring. In his book, *Horse Follow Closely*★, GaWaNe Pony Boy talks about the Native American concept of leadership. The itachan is the herd's lead broodmare. It is her job to guide the herd to the best grazing, and to watch out for its welfare. The herd members trust the itachan and look to her for guidance.

I took this image with me on our walks. It's a very different idea from the Western European concept of leadership. There leadership becomes wound up with words like respect and obedience. Dominance creeps in to muddy the water, and it's all too easy to end up back at the same old, same old, showing the horse "who's the boss".

That's not what my walks with Robin were about. I turned him loose so he was free to stay with me or not, and we went exploring. Our first walk was in early June before the fields had dried up. An overgrown gully separated us from the barns and the riding arenas. We were by ourselves in thirty plus acres of open land. That's not much by many standards, but compared to the small paddocks he was normally turned out in, the space

★ *Horse Follow Closely*, by GaWaNe Pony Boy; Bow Tie™ Press, CA

RELATIONSHIP BUILDING

Relationship building is the underpinning of all good training. Robin and I spent many pleasant days exploring the fields behind the barn.

As I was learning more about how his brain worked, he was showing me that he was ready for riding.

Robin's first ride: To get Robin to walk I bent his head to the side and waited. When he took a step to rebalance himself, I released the rein, clicked and gave him a treat. The soft carriage we had developed on the ground carried over directly to riding.

seemed vast. I felt as though we had stepped back in time and were walking across the melting tundra of an ice age.

I was the itachan. Robin followed me in my search for the best grass. We would pause while he grazed, then I'd wander on a few feet. He never let me get too far ahead. I'd go five, ten feet at most and he'd trot up beside me. Click, I'd give him a treat out of my pocket. I always started off with my vest pockets stuffed full of grain, and we'd come home with them empty.

Each day we would make a circuit of the fields and the adjoining woods. Robin was fearless in the woods. He'd course ahead of me through the trees like a hunting dog. I'd lose sight of him up the trail, then he'd turn and come racing back to me, ducking under branches and between trees. Each time he returned to me, click, I'd give him a treat.

His agility took my breath away. The grace with which he maneuvered through the trees astounded me. I'd never gone out like this with a horse. I'd spent many hundreds of hours watching horses grazing in the fields, but I'd never before gone hiking with a horse at liberty. GaWaNe Pony Boy urges people to spend a day with their horse. I would say the same, only I would add go for a walk with them, as well.

I took Robin out as often as I could that summer. We became familiar with the residents in the fields. On our way out through the riding ring, we'd pass the adult killdeer trying to distract us from their chicks. I knew where to find the bobolinks balancing on the tall reeds of the marsh grass, and the hawk who regularly hunted along the edge of the field.

One day we surprised a flock of wild turkeys. I almost stepped on them we were so close. As they flew up out of the tall grass, I jumped back startled, but Robin never flinched. Good horse, I thought.

On another day we explored a new section of woods. We had to cross a wide ditch to get to it. Robin hesitated on the near side. I crossed over and held out my hand asking him to target on it. Robin jumped the ditch. C/R. After that he would cross any obstacle we encountered.

To get into one section of woods I had to lower a split rail gate. While I put the rails back, Robin usually went on ahead of me. One day I was taking longer than usual to get the rails back into place. Robin must have thought I wasn't coming. He turned back at a canter to find me and sailed over the gate. I had never before stood so close to him while he was jumping. The power of it took my breath away.

Most days we surprised deer grazing in the woods. If I stayed close to Robin, I could get within a few feet of them. I remember one day a young buck accompanied us through the trees. He walked ahead of us, keeping a steady ten foot separation between us. He seemed perfectly content to share our company.

I learned a lot about Robin from our walks. I learned how fearless and bold he is. I learned that he likes exploring as much as I do. He didn't mind that his "itachan" was never satisfied with the grass in front of us. He was willing to go wherever I took him, and he was never in a hurry to get back to the barn and the other horses. I learned he was hard to spook: deer, birds, even once somebody on a bicycle, nothing seemed to bother him. He was going to make a great riding horse.

And that's when I started to think about getting on him. It was time to head back to the arena for some "serious" work.

FIRST RIDES

I started Robin bareback in a halter and a lead rope. That wasn't my original plan. Normally, for the first ride I have the horse fully tacked up. So why was Robin different? I can't really give you a good reason, other than that's just how I felt like doing it. I didn't want to begin an intensive training program with him as a three year old. As long as he was bareback, we were still in "preschool". If he had been a slower learner, I might not have been so concerned about this, but I wanted to keep the "brakes" on his training. With Robin it was too easy to go too fast.

Of course, at first we weren't going anywhere. When you first sit on many horses, they don't move. You think: "This is great. I haven't been bucked off yet. He's not doing anything, and I'm still alive." You sit there patting your horse and congratulating yourself on what a great job you've done so far. And then you begin to think that this could get boring real fast. It's great the horse is so calm, but you need movement to train.

Robin was a non-mover. I was using a mounting block to get on. He stood perfectly while I slid on and off his back. This part of riding was easy. I'd sat on him so many times when he was lying down he wasn't the least bit concerned about me being up there. I gradually extended the time I stayed on his back, clicking and reinforcing him for each small increment in time. So now I could sit on his back and enjoy a "trail ride", so long as I wasn't interested in going anywhere!

To create movement I took slack out of the lead rope. Robin responded by turning his head to the side. I dropped the lead out of my hand. The release of the pressure was a signal to him that he had just done something I wanted. I lifted the rein again. He turned his head a little further. Again I released the rein. I repeated this several more times until the turning of his head caused him to take a step. C/R.

I was wearing my usual fishing vest with the pockets stuffed full of goodies, grain in the left hand side; carrots, peppermints, molasses cookies, and sugar cubes on the right. After I clicked, I leaned forward to give him a piece of carrot. I wasn't too sure what the shift of position would do to him. He was craning his neck around trying to reach my hand. I've seen some horses become frightened by this kind of extreme shift in balance, but Robin wasn't bothered by it at all.

LEG AIDS VERSUS REIN CUES

You might be wondering why I didn't just bump him with my legs to get him to move. I've found with greenies, leg doesn't mean anything to them. They either goose away from it, which isn't what you want, or they just stiffen and plant themselves even more to the ground. The rein works much better to get them started. Once they're accustomed to carrying a rider, you can introduce leg aids.

If you are riding an older horse who has stalled out, you can do the same thing to get the feet moving again. It becomes a waiting game. Maybe your horse has gone as far as he's going to out on the trail. He wants to go home, and he knows the direction you're heading will just take him further away from the barn. You've got his nose pointed in the right direction, but he won't budge. You could sit there kicking him with your legs, but the chances are you're going to get tired long before he gives in. If you quit before he moves, you've just taught him to ignore you. Next time you'll have to kick even longer because he'll be convinced you're going to quit. You may not have enough strength in your body to outlast him.

An alternative is to take the slack out of the rein so that he has to bend his neck to one side. Now you just wait. (See Part 3 for instructions on this technique.) He may fall asleep on the rein, but that's all right. You're sitting down. You're comfortable. It doesn't take much energy to keep that rein anchored against the saddle. His neck is bent to the side which means eventually his muscles are going to start to ache.

He's in a bind. He can't straighten out because of the rein. He may try to pull the rein out of your hand, but you've got it solidly anchored with your hand pressed against the saddle. His other alternative is to bend his head even more and take a step to the side, C/R. You have movement! That's all you need to get your horse's feet unglued and down the trail.

That's how I got Robin to take his first steps. Our first "ride" was a tiny circle to the left. I slid off at the end of it. We had just completed our first "trail ride", and it was a total success.

TEMPER TANTRUMS

I rode him perhaps a dozen times in all through the fall. I took him outside a couple of times and rode him in the back field where he was turned out. I let him graze and walk, and graze some more. In the arena he offered me beautiful lateral work. I jackpotted him with a peppermint, and Robin bowed.

Robin's bow is the full down on one knee, head around to the side bow. His whole front end suddenly went out from under me as he dropped to the ground. It was like teetering on the edge of a cliff with nothing to hold onto. I clicked just to get him to come up. And that's when I decided it was time to bring bowing under full stimulus control (Ch. 10).

Robin loves to bow. When he was three, he would go out by himself in the arena and bow. I don't know why he latched onto this particular behavior more than any of the others he'd learned, but it was certainly one of his favorite games.

If I tried to discourage bowing by asking for something else, he would get mad. Robin didn't want to do any of the other easier activities I was asking for. He didn't want to back up or go sideways. He wanted to bow. Here was yet another great opportunity to work on emotional control.

The one method I was not going to use to control the bowing was positive punishment. That would only have succeeded in creating resentment and a sullen attitude. What I wanted to do instead was ask for other behaviors and make those just as reinforcing for him. The reality was that Robin wanted to bow so much that initially he regarded not being able to bow as punishing. It didn't matter that he was being reinforced for other behaviors. He wanted to bow. It truly was like having a toddler who has his heart so set on doing one thing that he refuses to be enticed by anything else. You're offering him chocolate cake, but he only wants ice cream, and he's going to throw a temper tantrum until gets it.

Robin had the equine version of a temper tantrum. He got grumpy, frustrated, mad, resentful. And then he figured it out. There are times when bowing is a good thing and will get reinforced, and other times when it won't. As soon as he got over being mad, he started to enjoy the other options I was giving him.

STUCK ACCELERATOR PEDALS

Robin's training was going well. He was sorting

through the emotional ups and downs of stimulus control. He was developing well physically. I just had one more major hurdle in his ground work to sort through before he'd be ready to ride again: his accelerator pedal was stuck. When I first bought Robin, he followed beautifully. Wherever I wanted to go, he'd tag along behind me. But if I asked him to move forward from behind, he was clueless how to respond. A gentle tap on his hip rooted him to the ground in a trembling panic of confusion. Someone, somewhere had poisoned that cue big time!

Since those early days, Robin had learned a lot about pressure. By breaking my requests down into very small steps I had taught him to yield his hips over and had gotten him moving well from a "go forward" cue on his hip. He learned to lunge around me, and we had the beginnings of lateral work and liberty training, all within the first couple of weeks we were together. (See *Clicker Training For Your Horse*★, and *The Click That Teaches: A Step-By-Step Guide in Pictures*★★.) Everything was smooth sailing until Robin discovered his "pose" and began to add it into the rest of his work. Now, all of a sudden, the "go forward" cue was colliding with the "pick yourself up and soften back to me" cue. Robin didn't know what to do with the conflict, so he stalled out.

PUSH ON YOUR NOSE

Robin's confusion was a natural result of collection. When a horse collects, he is stepping forward actively from behind. At the same time he is softening his front end, and rounding his topline. In essence you are saying to the horse: "leave, but don't leave." The challenge for all riders working in collection is maintaining the forward energy. This is most clearly illustrated with a simple demonstration. You'll need a friend for this, someone who is used to your weird horse experiments. Don't give this person any hints about what you are going to do. You want to see what her natural reaction is.

You are going to press your finger against her nose. Keep a steady pressure. She may stiffen at first, then she'll probably take a step back. That's normal. Continue to press your finger against her nose. She may take another step or two back, but eventually she's going to nod her head slightly, that is, she'll give at the poll. Release the pressure.

She's just shown you the progression in which horses naturally respond to pressure from a bit. They will first change leg speed (in this case your friend backed up) before they will give at the poll. A well-trained horse gives at the poll before it changes leg speed. The natural response to rein pressure is reversed which maintains the forward energy in the gaits. This is fundamentally important in the training of an upper-level performance horse.

Think about some of the dressage horses you may have seen who are very stiff in their gaits. This is the opposite of what the rider is trying to create, but this individual may not understand this progression. She wants her horse to round his topline by giving at the poll. She puts pressure on the reins, which the horse does eventually respond to by softening his poll, but first he backs off the energy he's putting into his gaits. The more the rider works to get him "in a frame", the stiffer, and less dynamic the horse becomes.

You'll see a similar problem arising in upward transitions. As the rider asks for an increase in leg speed, the horse will first stiffen and go above the bit. He'll be pulling through his upward transitions. To the rider it will feel as though the horse is rushing forward. The normal response is to pull back and block the horse's upward transition even as the rider is driving the horse forward. This just compounds the problem. Instead of learning how to balance himself through the upward transitions, the horse begins to pull harder. The result is the rider often ends up resorting to stronger and stronger bits in an effort to control leg speed.

THE CHALLENGE OF COLLECTION

Reversing the natural order of changing leg speed before softening the poll is the challenge every rider faces who asks a horse to go on the bit. You want your horse to soften and yield at the poll as he engages his hip angle. I hope you have dog-eared this page. You will want to refer back to this concept many times as you work through the exercises in the riding section. It is one of the major training issues that makes the difference between a ride that flows and one that looks stiff and forced.

Robin was still sorting through this stage. He understood how to give, but he sometimes got stuck going forward. In a sense he was colliding with his own front end. In the instant that he was changing gaits into an upward transition, he was also softening back to me. The combined effect would stall out his feet. We were both getting frustrated. In-hand Robin was confused. I would touch his hip asking him to move forward from behind. He understood that, but at the same time he also felt light pressure on the lead which he responded to not just by yielding to me, but also by adding in his "pose". He was so tuned-in and sensitive, the lightest shift of the lead would trigger this response. He didn't yet

★ *Clicker Training For Your Horse,* by Alexandra Kurland; Sunshine Books, US and Ringpress books, UK
★★ *The Click That Teaches: A Step-By-Step Guide in Pictures*, by Alexandra Kurland; The Clicker Center, NY

Chapter Fifteen: First Rides

REVERSING NATURAL ORDERS

❶ ❷ ❸ ❹

People show the same tendency that horses do. Pushing on someone's nose can seem like a silly thing to do, until you think about the pressure a horse feels from a halter or bit. In this demo our volunteer stiffened, inverted her "topline", and took a step back (1-3.) before she thought about giving at the poll (4.). This mirrors the horse's reaction. Horses will naturally go "above the bit", and change leg speed before they will give at the poll.

understand how he could step forward from behind and simultaneously soften to me in the front end. The conflict made him grab for the lead rope just as he picked up a trot. That was a pattern that I wanted to eliminate before I started riding him again.

GROUND DRIVING
I decided to try a new approach to explain what I wanted and that was to ground drive him. Ground driving is an exercise where you attach two long leads to your horse and walk behind him as though you are driving him. It is part of the preparation for a carriage horse, and it can also be used to help balance the gaits and as a prep for riding.

I drew on my TT.E.A.M.★ background for his introduction to ground driving. When you first start hooking lines up to your horse, you don't want to make assumptions about what he's comfortable with and what will scare him. Instead you need to break the process down into small steps.

This was Robin's first experience with girths, so I took care not to skip steps here. I was pretty sure he wouldn't be bothered by the surcingle I was using, but it's always better to be safe than sorry. As a preliminary step, I swung a lead rope over his back and drew it back to me under his belly. I now had a full loop around him just where the girth would be. If Robin had objected, I could have loosened the rope instantly, or even released it all together. But he had no problem with it even when we went for a walk around the arena. I moved on to the actual surcingle. Robin did what I expected him to do. He turned around to sniff at the surcingle. He wasn't afraid of this thing around his middle. He just wasn't sure how he was supposed to interact with it. Was this one of the touch games, or was he supposed to do something else?

Once I put his feet to work, he very quickly lost interest in the surcingle. The next step was adding the drive lines. These I put on him one at a time. The first line went through the ring on the surcingle and attached to the near side of his halter.

I stepped back at an angle away from hip. I could bump his side with the rope, but I was not directly behind him. I kept myself safely out of kicking range, just in case the rope spooked him. That went fine, so I attached the second line.

Robin had no problem accepting the lines against his body, but he was confused when I asked him to follow the feel of the ropes instead of me. He wanted to turn back to me. The requests from the drive lines contradicted what he thought he should do.

GET THE FEET TO MOVE
Most of the time when Robin becomes confused, he stalls out. That's what he did now. My normally light-as-silk horse became very heavy in my hand and glued himself to the ground. Get the feet to move; get them to move consistently; then take them in the direction you want them to go. That's the principle I needed. The problem was, Robin's feet weren't moving. Rather than cue him to move with a whip, I used pressure on the drive lines. I took the slack out of the inside line only and waited. The line was attached to a flat nylon halter, not a bridle. Robin's response was to turn his head. The turn of the head

★ TT.E.A.M.: The Tellington-Jones Equine Awareness Method

earned him a release of the line, not a click. As soon as I released, I took the slack out again and waited.

Basically Robin was having to stand with his head turned to the side. That gets tiring pretty fast, so he started to look for alternatives. He couldn't straighten out his neck because of the pressure from the line, so instead he tried stepping to the side. C/R.

This segment was repeated many times, until a light touch of the line created movement. Since I was behind him, and I'd previously shaped him to back up following a target behind him, he began offering a behavior he already knew: he backed up.

The principle is: *get the feet to move*. It doesn't say anything yet about direction, so I reinforced the backing. Backing showed me the next step I would need to shape - shift your weight forward. And that created the third step - walk on. I triggered forward movement by placing my hand on Robin's hip. He'd back up into my hand, then shift forward - click!. I then withheld the click until he walked forward a couple of steps. Those three pieces created a gorgeous collected start.

I didn't teach this all in one session. It was a process that I stretched out over several days. I broke each training session up into five minute segments. In the first five minutes we played fetch, a favorite game of his. Then I put a surcingle on him and hooked up the drive lines. I followed a principle of training that says to train only one element at a time. In our first five minute driving session I worked only on getting movement. Each time he shifted his weight back, click, he got reinforced.

After five minutes I took the surcingle off, and we played with another new behavior: kick ball. After a few minutes of play time, I put the ball away and did another round with the drive lines. I continued alternating between these two activities: five minutes for ground driving, five minutes for kick ball.

The fun of this method is watching the progress your horse makes from one segment to the next. When you take the time to solidify each step, the horse truly understands what you want him to do.

Robin made this very clear to me with a surprise offering one night. As usual he stood perfectly while I put the surcingle on, but before I could hook up the lines, he shifted his weight back and walked off in a collected start. I suppose I could have corrected him for not standing still, but instead I recognized just how light he had become. We worked the entire driving session without lines attached. He turned, stopped, started, trotted. He did everything I had taught him with the lines. I could walk behind him down the center of the arena changing rein, and he would change the bend just as if the lines were attached.

Why did this method produce such extraordinary results? Consider for a moment just the process of tacking Robin up with the surcingle and drive lines. In a normal training session I would have tacked him up once, worked him for a period of time, become satisfied with the result and put him away. In that session he would have had one experience practicing good tacking-up skills. Over the course of ten days that would give him a total of ten such experiences.

By chunking my training down into smaller units, in just one evening Robin probably got tacked up over ten times. At the end of ten days that would add up to over one hundred experiences being tacked up.

Which horse is going to know more about saddling, the one trained in a traditional manner, or my clicker-trained horse?

This is an important concept to understand. Under saddle you'll be asking your own horse to repeat small units of behavior. The process is the same. By offering your horse more learning opportunities you stack the deck in your favor that he'll end up truly understanding what you want.

SADDLES AND BRIDLES

For Robin this system solved the problem of the stuck accelerator pedal. He was telling me that it was time to think about riding again. I put a saddle on him and turned him loose in the arena. He posed and followed me around, totally unconcerned with this new piece of equipment. Preparation. That's the key to avoiding wrecks. A few minutes later I was sitting on him, riding around the arena. He was wonderful! All our ground preparation combined with those few times I had sat on him bareback were paying dividends now. He walked around the arena adding in his "Robin pose" and looking beautiful. I still had him in a halter and lead rope. That had been okay before, but my sense now was we were ready for a bridle. It was time for Robin to leave kindergarten and go to school.

The first time I bridled Robin I simply held the bit out in front of him. He did the rest. He opened his mouth around it, and I lifted the head stall up over his ears. It was so easy, I almost forgot he'd never done it before. But then Robin acted like any young horse who has a bit in his mouth for the first time: he gaped his mouth open and tried to spit it out. It was all so normal. I put him to work, and after a couple of minutes he basically forgot he had it in his mouth.

RIDING FROM THE GROUND

Over the next few sessions I "rode" him from the

Chapter Fifteen: First Rides

ground. I walked beside him at his shoulder and asked for the same turns and stops I would be looking for under saddle. This was just another "systems check" before I climbed aboard.

From the ground I asked for forward motion by pressing my curled finger tips against his side. This mimicked the leg cues I would be using later under saddle. As soon as he moved off, the cue released. I don't want to ride with my legs glued to his side, so I wanted to be certain to train us both to "starter button" signals. We started off to the left along the track with the reins resting on his neck. That's important. I wanted to know that he could just walk along quietly without my having to tighten up on the reins. If I had to grab him to keep him from rushing off, he wasn't ready to ride.

Confidence is a product of preparation and experience. I had certainly done my preparation, but clicker training had created a level of engagement and sensitivity in Robin that was not the norm for an unstarted horse. I was taking my time because I was exploring uncharted territory for both of us.

A GROUND RIDING CHECKLIST

Just as a pilot inspects an airplane before takeoff, I had my own pre-ride checklist for Robin.

Do the brakes work? I asked for a halt by lifting the rein slightly off his neck. He came to a soft, collected halt. C/R.

Can I turn him? I slid my hand down the inside rein so it became an opening rein. Robin followed the feel and circled off the rail. C/R.

Can I bring him back to the rail? Yes, with a flourish. The circle turned into a lateral flexion. He stepped forward and over, forward and over, lifting into his outside shoulder so he reunited with the track in shoulder-in. C/R.

Will he take a diagonal? As I came around the corner, I slid my left hand down the rein again. Robin softened and followed the feel of the opening rein off the track. A slight lifting of the rein kept him from over-rotating onto his inside shoulder. He shifted into a lateral flexion and floated across the diagonal. C/R.

Can I change rein? Midway across the diagonal I asked for a halt. C/R. I changed sides to the right. I had to remind myself to use my finger tips against his side to ask for movement. If I didn't use the signal here on the ground, I couldn't expect him to understand a leg cue under saddle. It took a lot of focus and concentration to remember all these little details. If I were training a trail horse, I might not have been so particular, but someday I want to teach Robin to piaffe. These details mattered for

RIDING FROM THE GROUND

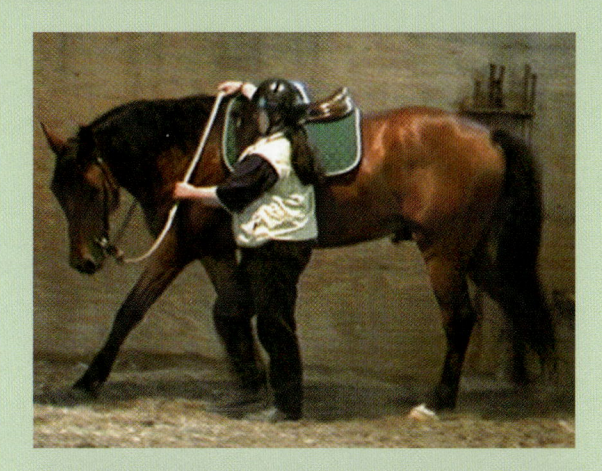

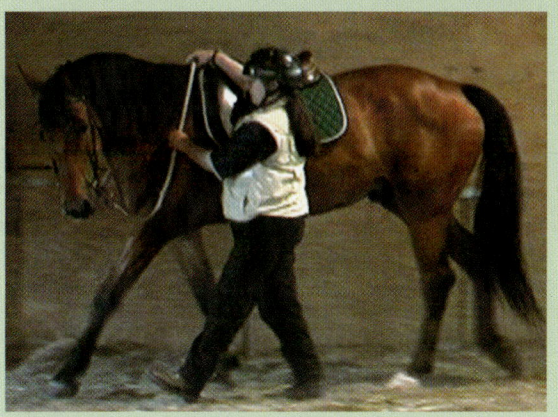

Note how Robin's balance shifts as the two of us come into perfect unison in our strides. Think about how this will transfer to working in harmony under saddle.

both of us. This ground work was as much for my benefit as it was for his. Consistency is important, and that's my job, not his. *He'll be consistent when I am.* Robin felt stiffer in his jaw on the right rein. To the left he floated in my hand and felt like heaven. To the right his left hind wasn't stepping up underneath his body, and that interfered with the feel. I asked him to circle and waited for him to adjust his balance. C/R. I worked the right side until it began to match the smoothness of the left. Again I focused on my own hands. I stroked down the rein easing all the tension out of my fingers. Robin responded with a delicious feel. He was so light on his feet, there was no weight in the rein. I loved looking at the arc of his neck, and feeling the power coming from his engaged hind end. It was this power that reminded me to be thorough in my preparations.

The Click That Teaches: Riding With The Clicker

ROBIN UNDER SADDLE

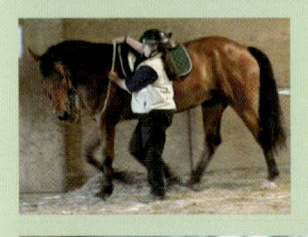

Note the similarity in Robin's topline in these two photos. They illustrate powerfully the connection between ground work and riding.

I went through the same check list on the right side that I had on the left.

Can I ask Robin to halt. Yes. C/R.

Can I turn him. Yes. C/R.

Can I take a diagonal and change rein? Yes. C/R.

Is there anything here that would get us into trouble if I were riding him? Well, he did stiffen at the far end of the arena. It's dusk and the deer are coming up into the back paddocks. I felt myself holding the rein a little too tightly, but he softened to the feel and walked on. Not bad, but we could both do better.

What will he do in the trot? Let's find out. I put Robin on a circle in the walk. I could feel him thinking about the trot. I touched his sides with my right hand, signaling my intent for a change of leg speed. Robin reverted to one of his old habits. He tossed his head which created a sudden pressure in my hand. He was surprised by the feel and surged forward, throwing his weight forward and up against the bit. I stabilized my hand which brought him back around me and settled him into a beautiful trot. He offered me his "pose" as he collected into a "magazine-cover" trot. C/R.

He was almost ready, but I had found a hole in the training which I needed to take a little time to fill in. The riding could wait for another day while I sorted this out. I was in no hurry. Each piece we explore makes the whole so much more enjoyable.

TRAINING

And so it goes. That's training. It's like exploring a giant mansion. Each new room you enter reveals a storehouse of treasures. You could rush through the house, running from room to room, but you'd miss so much. I prefer to linger in each room to examine the treasures that each one holds. What I find sometimes are doorways into parts of the mansion others have overlooked. I have no set time table with Robin. Each segment of his training is like a chapter in a book. I'm in no rush to get to the end. I want to enjoy every page.

I started this book with Robin because I wanted to show you how I use the clicker with my own horses. Training is not linear. You follow this thread and that. You read an article on ground driving that sparks your interest, and for the next few days that's what you focus on. Your horse comes in with a cut, and you suddenly discover that you forgot to introduce him to hoses. Oops! No time like the present for filling in that gap. You have a stretch of bad weather, and you can't get your horse out of the barn. He's totally bored, so you teach him "silly tricks". And then you discover your "silly tricks" will get your horse onto the trailer. Good deal. You decide to go riding with your neighbor. His horse freaks at some cows, and now your horse is convinced those things that moo are fire-breathing dragons. Sigh. Time to review the calm-down cue.

That's training. In fact that's life. Things go wrong, and things go right. You figure out one piece, and something else comes up. I wouldn't have it any other way. I don't need to "fix" everything at once. Robin isn't a horse I'm going to have for a few months or even a few years. He's with me for the long haul.

Training happens fast, and it happens slow. You could say it took Robin just a matter of minutes to accept a saddle and bridle, or you could say it took two years. Both answers are correct, and neither answer matters. When I'm with my horses, I'm not watching a clock, I'm enjoying their company.

Time is our ally. Whatever twists and turns the training takes, whatever interruptions get in our way, whatever new puzzles there are to solve, whatever the seasons bring, we always have time to enjoy each other's company. Clicker training is about appreciation. With each click that is what you are sharing with your horse, and there is always time to enjoy a job well done.

PART 3
RIDING WITH THE CLICKER

This section is your riding "toolbox". I'll be gathering in riding "tools" and showing you how each one works. It's like building a house. Before you can begin, you need to know what a hammer is and how to use it. So in this section I'll be looking at individual skills that are the "tools" you'll use to build the complex patterns of your horse's training "house".

Safety always comes first, so this section will be concentrating on simple exercises that give you lots of control. You'll be learning how to keep your horse from bolting, bucking, rearing, spooking — in other words, how to prevent all the big, nasty things that take the fun out of riding.

I'll begin by introducing you to the basics of riding with the clicker. Then I'll show you how to deal with spooking by breaking your lesson down into one of two criteria, "where" or "how".

I'll teach you how to ask your horse to lower his head and calm down when he gets upset, and I'll show you how to disengage his hips to develop great brakes. This section will give you a safe horse to ride. In the later sections I'll show you how to use these lessons to create a feels-like-heaven ride.

MAIN LESSONS COVERED:

1.) The Figure-Eight Lesson: Cures "Far-End-of-Ring-Itis".

2.) Head Lowering: Builds a calm attitude into your riding foundation.

3.) "Flipping the Hips": Takes the "runaway freight train" power out of your horse's hind end. Stops bolting and spooking. Gives you power brakes and an entry lesson into advanced performance work.

Safety, safety, safety — safety always comes first. The lessons in this chapter give you the tools you need to stop bolting, bucking, spooking, and rearing: all the major issues that take the fun out of riding. Before you proceed very far with your riding, you want to have these lessons working well with your horse.

The Click That Teaches: Riding With The Clicker

RIDING WITH THE CLICKER

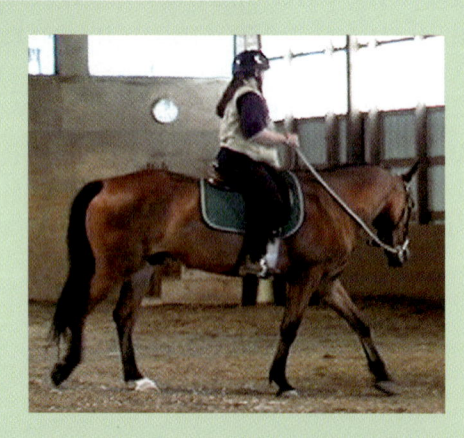

Safety and emotional control come first, but along with that come beauty and grace, the hallmarks of a clicker-trained horse.

CHAPTER 16
Riding Basics: Using the Clicker Under Saddle

In this chapter I'll be introducing you to the basics of riding with the clicker. I'll begin by answering that most frequently asked of all questions: how do you deliver a treat from the saddle? I'll show you how to stop spooking and get control of your horse by piggy backing the clicker onto a simple figure-eight pattern. This lesson will show you how to break your training down into small steps so you can find the "clickable moment".

MISSION IMPOSSIBLE

So, finally, after a mere 89 pages, we're actually going to ride! I have to tell you I really wasn't sure how I was going to tackle the riding section. The questions it posed seemed so intimidating. How could I talk about riding in a way that would be meaningful to everyone reading this book, beginners and experts alike? How much detail should I go into? What should I say about dressage, and how much should I talk about my own riding? After all, what I do is hardly the norm. Much of the time when I'm schooling, I'm riding with a single rein. While John Lyons, Pat Parelli, and other trainers like them have gone a long way towards popularizing this kind of training, it is still far from the norm, at least not in my neck of the woods.

I'm a dressage rider, but about the only thing that tells you is that I prefer training a horse to simply riding out on a hack. What I mean by dressage is probably very different from the images most people have of it. Even when I talk to other dressage riders, I often find that we are coming from very different systems of training. How could I speak to our common interests and goals without becoming mired down in the differences? And how could I talk about dressage in a way that wouldn't exclude the rest of the riding community?

I had another dilemma. I needed to talk about work that was not my own. I didn't originate single-rein riding. I just use it. Single-rein riding has become so integrated into everything else that I do, I can't imagine talking about riding without including at least some mention of it.

Once I started down that path, I knew I'd have to go the whole way and give a detailed description of the technique. I couldn't tell you how to incorporate the clicker into this kind of training without first explaining what it is. That meant I had to begin with basic theory. I would need to explain that riding for me is not just going from point A to point B. It is a form of communication. I would need to show you how to build the communication out of pressure and release of pressure. I would need to explain what a give is, and how that lets you carry on a "conversation" with your horse.

This was a huge block of material to tackle, and I really wasn't sure how to do it. Finally, I just gave in and started writing. I wrote over eighty pages of text before I came up for air. Once I began, it became like Topsy in the nursery rhyme. The material just kept growing. This is the product of all that, organized into smaller, more digestible units. I hope I have given credit where credit is due. Much of what I am presenting I learned from other people, and their

RIDING WITH THE CLICKER

How do you like to ride? Whether it be bareback, or under saddle, English, or Western, there is a place for the clicker in your training.

The Click That Teaches: Riding With The Clicker

FEEDING FROM THE SADDLE

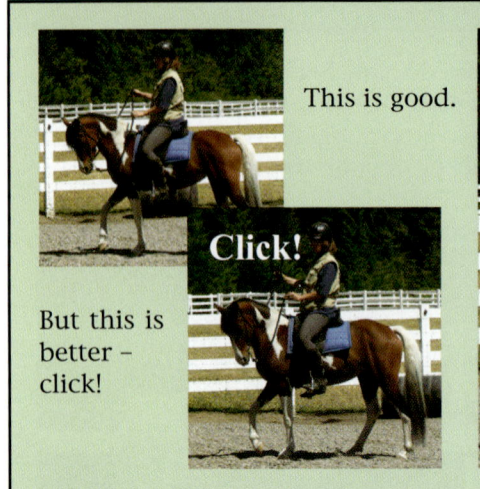

This is good.

But this is better – click!

This young horse has just been started under saddle. This is only her fifth ride. She has just been clicked for elevating her topline.

She knows a treat is coming, so she stops and waits patiently while her rider gets a treat from her pocket.

She takes the treat politely from her rider's hand. A couple of clicks later and she was bending her neck to help her rider out.

work is well worth investigating separately. People like Bettina Drummond, John Lyons, Sally Swift, Mary Wanless, Pat Parelli, Clinton Anderson and Linda Tellington-Jones have all made major contributions to the horse world. I have incorporated their work into the material I am presenting.

I also want to give credit and thanks to the horses. They were my best teachers. What I learned from them goes beyond anything I can put into words. Podaisky took the best title of them all for his book: "My Horses, My Teachers." Ultimately, whatever we learn about riding, the credit must all go to them.

RIDING WITH THE CLICKER

Riding with the clicker is easy. You just get on and ride. If you like what your horse is doing, you click and reinforce it. I know, you want details, and that's what the following chapters are going to give you, but let's start out simple.

Most of you are probably already riding your horses. When you ride, it's easy to find things to reinforce. Suppose your horse normally shoots off like a rocket the instant you put your foot in the stirrup, but today he stands still for three seconds. Click, and give him a treat. Before you know it, he'll be standing rock solid on a consistent basis. Or suppose, instead of spinning and bolting for home, your horse faces the stream bank. Click and give him a treat. When he stretches his nose towards the water, C/R. When he takes a step towards it, C/R.

Okay, that's fine, you're saying. I get that part, but how do I give him a treat? That's the question I get asked most often about riding with the clicker.

People just can't visualize feeding a horse from the saddle. It seems awkward mechanically, and it goes against everything they've ever been taught about not letting a horse eat with a bit in its mouth.

First, let me assure you that horses have no trouble eating with a bit. Anyone who has ever gone on a trail ride knows this. Horses are perfectly capable of snacking their way along the entire trail. If they can eat mouthfuls of grass and leaves, they can certainly manage a sliver of carrot or a tablespoon of grain. And unlike all that grass they're snitching, small clicker treats aren't going to get wadded up in the bit.

Next is the question of delivery. When I ride, I wear a fishing vest. Some of my clients use fanny packs or builder's aprons. We stuff the pockets full of treats. One client's goody pouch must weigh about five pounds when she starts out. She's got pieces of carrots and apples, sugar cubes, peppermints, molasses horse cookies, and her horse's current favorite, ginger snaps, all stuffed into her pouch. At the end of the ride it's usually empty.

She and her horse are working on piaffe. When he gives her a good step or two, she clicks with her tongue. None of my riders use the actual clicker when riding. They want their hands free for the reins, so they've trained their horses to recognize tongue clicks.

When her horse hears the click, he stops. As she's reaching into her pouch for a treat, she's assessing his performance. Was it good enough for a peppermint? Absolutely. Was it spectacular? Did he give her an extra degree of lift that hasn't been there before? Yes. Well then, he gets a molasses cookie and a ginger snap. To give him his treat she leans forward across his neck. He's an experienced clicker horse, so he's already got his head bent to the side. He takes his treat gently from her fingers. She lets him chew it for a moment while she strokes his neck and tells him how wonderful he is. Standing still is also part of his reward. While he's eating, he's resting. Piaffe is physically demanding. The little breaks in the work keep him fresher. When she's ready, she organizes the reins and asks for a few more steps.

That's how you use the clicker on a clicker-wise horse, but the first time you try it from the saddle, your horse may not react so smoothly. You'll click, and you'll see your horse's ears airplane around in surprise. The click marks the end of unit of behavior, so he may slam on the brakes and start looking around for his treat. He won't know how to get to the goodies, so help him out. Draw his head around to the side with the rein and hand him his treat. Remember to reward him on the side to which he was bent. If you were working on the left rein, feed him from the left.

Occasionally, instead of stopping, you'll get a horse who backs up trying to get to you. He knows a treat is coming. He heard the click, but he just can't figure out how to get to the vending machine. When this happens, just sit quietly and wait for the horse to stop. Backing is hard work, so he isn't going to keep going very long. When he quits, reach down and give him his treat. Within two or three clicks the backing behavior will go away. The horse will learn fast that all he has to do is stop moving and the vending machine will reach out to him.

Some horses don't seem to notice the click at all. If your horse doesn't flick his ears or show any other signs that he heard your click, that probably means he doesn't really understand the clicker yet. You need to go back and do more ground work with him. Once you think he's really caught on to the game, you can try again.

Your horse may need an extra training step inserted to help him make the connection between ground work and riding. Have a friend give you a "pony ride". Get on your horse, but let your friend lead the two of you around. Your friend is going to ask your horse for some of the same work you've taught him from the ground. When he responds correctly, she'll click him and give him a treat. Repeat this a few times, gradually transferring the job of clicking and treating over to you.

Occasionally you'll get a horse that keeps walking after he has heard the click. You can tell by his ears that he knows what the click means, but he doesn't realize that it's okay to stop. This horse has been so programmed not to change gaits that he can't stop for the click. In this case just use your active riding aids to bring your horse to a halt so he can get his treat. Again, it won't take him long to catch on.

WHY STOPPING IS A GOOD THING

This raises another issue many riders have with the clicker, at least initially. They see stopping as a bad thing. It may be all right on the ground, but under saddle they've been taught that horses shouldn't be allowed to break gait. Stopping to get a treat goes against everything they've learned.

This issue comes up most frequently when riders are thinking about the canter. Suppose you got interested in the clicker primarily because your horse has trouble picking up his leads. You've taught your horse to touch a cone, and you've done some preliminary ground work on backing. He clearly understands the clicker. You want to get right to work on your main problem, so you saddle him up and head out for a ride. The first couple of times you ask him to canter he picks up the wrong lead, but on the corner he finally gets it right. You click him, his ears airplane around, and he slams on the brakes. You weren't prepared for such a sudden stop so you end up wrapped around his ears.

At this point you're probably thinking, "This is no good. Once he's cantering, I want him to keep going. If he keeps stopping, how is he ever going to learn to stay in the canter?"

You're forgetting the discussion of reinforcement schedules in Chapter 9. Think about how you've taught other things with the clicker. The very first time you asked your horse to back up, weren't you satisfied if he just shifted his weight back even a little? That shift in weight very quickly became a full step back, and then two or three steps, until finally you could back him any distance you wanted.

You're going to work the same way under saddle. When you ask your horse to pick up the correct lead, you're focusing on one element: the transition. Staying in the canter is another criterion. The rules of shaping tell us to focus on one element at a time.

Once your horse is consistently picking up the correct lead, you can withhold the click for a stride or two. If he goes back to a trot before you can click, that just means he's just given you another opportunity to work on transitions. Ask him to canter again. The more you practice transitions, the better he'll get at them. When he finally gives you those extra couple of strides you were looking for, click, let him stop and give him his treat. He'll quickly learn that if he wants to get reinforced, he has to stay in the canter longer and longer. The stopping to get his treat just lets you practice picking up the canter again. Think of it this way — after ten days which horse is going to have the better canter departs: the horse who was asked to canter three times in an evening for a total over ten days of thirty departs, or your clicker-trained horse who stops to get his treat but practices twenty departs in an evening for a total over ten days of two hundred canter departs? Easy answer. Once you've built some duration at the canter, you can begin to layer your priorities (pg. 17). You can add other criteria, such as head elevation, correct bend, and changes of speed or direction.

For more on the value gained from these small steps each click creates refer back to the section on teaching Robin to ground drive (pg. 83-84).

LESSON PLANS
The key to using the clicker under saddle is to break down every exercise into tiny steps. The steps you put in will vary with each horse, and will depend very much on your riding background and level of experience. But as always, in developing a plan, you will look first at basic principles (Chapter 5). They will remind you to break your training down into small, achievable steps so your horse can be successful and the training remains safe.

Lesson plans develop out of positive goals. When you state your goals clearly, it's easy to see all the small steps your horse needs in order to be successful. The more specific you are the better. Suppose your horse spooks at the "goblins" hiding at the far end of your arena. Just saying you want your horse to ride around the arena without spooking isn't enough. Instead you need to describe in detail what you want him TO DO.

"I want my horse to walk down the fence line with his head at or below the height of his withers, correctly bent, and relaxed in his body." Right now your horse may be so nervous his nose never comes down out of the rafters, and his body feels like a coiled spring about to explode. The contrast between where he is and where you want him to be makes it easy to develop a plan of action.

As you spell out in detail what you want from your horse, the next question becomes does he know how to do this? If the answer is no, then you need to design a lesson plan that will teach him the skills he needs.

You'll design a lesson plan for every element your horse doesn't understand, until the real horse you're riding matches the ideal horse of your goals.

TRAIN ONE CRITERION AT A TIME
Begin your lesson plan by dividing riding into two main categories: "where" and "how".

"Where" refers to geography. "I want to ride my horse down to the far end of the arena."

"How" refers to the carriage of the horse. "I want my horse to be soft, correctly bent, and engaged."

In shaping you train one criteria at a time. That means you need to begin your goal setting by choosing which one of these two main categories you want to focus on. You could meet your first criterion "where", and not have your second, "how".

You might be able to get your horse to go all the way around the arena, but he might have his nose up in the air the whole time. Or you could have him nice and round, but not be able to get him anywhere near the far end. The goal is to have both; location and carriage. To get there you need to pick one to work on first.

Most riders tend to focus first on "where". They want to ride around their entire arena, or past the scary rock out on the trail. In our example, your horse is saying there are ghosts hiding at the far end of the arena. Anytime you start to head into the far corner his head shoots up into the rafters. His shoulders stiffen. His back hollows. His feet feel as though they are stuck in cement.

Even if this doesn't actually describe your horse, I'm sure you've seen horses like this, so let's suppose for the moment that this really does describe your horse. You'd love to have your horse stay all soft and round, but your primary goal is one of geography. You don't care what he looks like. You just want him to stay on the track all the way around the ring. Right now he spooks twenty feet across the arena every time you get anywhere near the far end.

If that doesn't feel safe to ride, you could shift your focus and say: "All right, I don't care where you go. You can stay right here where you feel safe, but I want you to drop your nose. I want you to bend correctly. I want you on the bit." When you say all that, you've shifted your focus to "how".

Can you get both? Of course. That's what a dressage test, or a hunter course, or a reining pattern is all about — having a horse moving beautifully and correctly through a prescribed pattern. So how do you get there? Let's take our spooky horse example and focus first on geography. We'll look first at how you could solve this problem without the clicker, and then we'll see what the clicker would add to the training.

Chapter Sixteen: Riding Basics

Let's suppose half way down the long side of the arena, your horse starts to suck back and counter-bend. He's saying: "You have to be crazy! I'm not going down there!" Maybe he really is afraid of the corner, or maybe he's just gotten into the habit of spooking as a way to distract his rider.

SPOOKING VERSUS STARTLING

I differentiate between spooking and being startled. Anyone can be startled. We've all been there. You're concentrating deeply on something and your best friend walks up behind you and says "Hi!". You nearly jump out of your skin. A startle is not a spook.

Even the best trained horse can be startled, and even the best trained horse can be genuinely afraid of something. You can get your horse used to blowing tarps, tractors, bicycles, and all the other usual things in his environment, but the world is full of strange encounters you can't prepare for.

One of my clients told me the story of her chance meeting with a porcupine. She had her horse out on a narrow trail, the kind with steep banks on either side where you absolutely can't turn around. The porcupine waddled down the bank, right between her horse's legs! Another told me about her brief encounter with two bear cubs. They came racing up the trail towards her. How are you going to practice getting your horse used to these things? You can't, but a well-trained horse will know how to listen to your directions even when he's afraid.

Spooking is different. Spooking has its origins in fear, but it quickly turns into something else. Think about this scenario. You're focused on getting your horse to soften onto the bit. He doesn't understand what you want. He's gotten stiff, which makes it even harder for him to listen to you. He's going down the long side of the arena with his nose cranked up in the air, resisting your hand. He's so focused on the rein that he doesn't see the jacket someone just tossed over the top rail of the fence. Suddenly he catches sight of it out of the corner of his eye and jumps three feet to the side. The sudden change of direction unbalances you, and you release the rein.

What did your horse just learn? Jumping sideways is a great way to get you out of his mouth. He jumped that first time because he was startled. Now he may begin jumping whenever the work gets hard. The emotions he was feeling become the cue to jump sideways. He's not being "stubborn". He isn't "testing" you. He has simply learned that when he feels pressured, jumping sideways gets you to let go. I've ridden lots of horses who were like this. Spooking was a learned response, no longer prompted directly by fear.

"WHERE" VERSUS "HOW"

Where: The rider focuses on riding from point "a" to point "b".

How: The rider focuses on how the horse carries itself. Where the horse goes is less important.

You could ride for a lifetime focusing on geography and never experience the pleasure of a horse that is carrying itself well. "How" will eventually give you control of the feet, i.e. geography. When both criteria are met, you can get from point "a" to point "b" on a beautifully moving horse.

Spooking can also be thought of as a balance issue. Watch any group of horses schooling in a ring and you'll see what I mean. It's the horse who is sucked back, counter-bent, falling on his front end who spooks, not the balanced, forward-moving, correctly engaged horse. Body position has a direct impact on the horse's mental state. You can make a fearful horse feel much bolder just by changing the way he carries himself. The same thing also applies to riders. Change your posture, and you'll change the emotions you're feeling.

The age-old cure for spooking is to ride your horse strongly forward, using your seat and legs to keep him from ducking out. If he tries to spook and spin, you counter by driving him vigorously forward, adding a crop or spurs as needed. This is a straightforward, effective means of eliminating a potentially dangerous problem. One of the main reasons people send horses off for training is so that they can have a bold, confident rider teach their horse to go forward no matter what.

These confident riders don't get unseated when their horse ducks sideways. They're able to stick to a horse like glue and drive him forward through any and all evasions. Whenever the horse tries to bolt away to the part of the arena where he feels comfortable, the trainer knows how to chase him forward onto a big circle that takes him right back to the far end. The trainer keeps bringing him back through the corner the horse finds so intimidating until gradually he begins to settle.

"That's fine for some people," you may be saying, "but I can't afford to send my horse off for training, and I'm afraid to ride down at that end. I know I can't stay on if he spooks, and I don't have anyone else who can ride him for me. What am I supposed to do?"

CRASHING THROUGH BRICK WALLS VERSUS GOING AROUND THEM

There are two ways to solve any problem: directly and indirectly. This book is about indirect solutions. Think of it like riding a horse up to a brick wall: you can either try to ride right over the wall, or you can find a way to go around it.

If the wall is only an inch or so high, most of us would be able to get over it. We could solve the problem directly. But suppose it's a two foot wall. That may not sound very high to a lot of you, but that's enough to eliminate quite a few horses and riders. They'd have to find another way to get to the other side. A three foot wall will eliminate even more people. At four feet even more, and so on until eventually everyone will have to find another way around. There will always be a few people who will try to force their horse over every wall no matter the height. They have the attitude that all problems have to be met head on. Eventually with that kind of mind set, they're going to have a wreck.

Good trainers recognize which problems they can solve directly and which ones they need to chunk down. The person who starts finding alternate routes around tiny problems may actually end up with a better trained horse than the person who deals with everything directly. The first person will have created a flexible attitude both in himself and in his horse. He'll have a partner who trusts him and will work hard for him. The second person may be the kind of trainer who's gotten stuck in a rut. He does everything the same way every time, no matter what the individual needs of a particular horse may be. He hasn't learned how to be flexible, so is it any wonder he often clashes with his horses?

FEAR

When you go around the "wall", you are remembering that safety always come first. If you don't feel comfortable riding through a particular exercise, there's probably a good reason. Just because someone else can do it doesn't mean a thing. They haven't had your experiences, nor you their's. And it isn't always that they're a better rider and know they can stick to a horse no matter what. Sometimes it's the beginners who take the most risks. If you're an experienced rider, you know what I mean by this. You've probably seen beginners doing things that make you shudder. The old expression, ignorance is bliss, certainly applies when it comes to horses.

If you don't feel safe in a given situation, trust your common sense. Fear is something good trainers pay attention to. If you're afraid, that's just your guidance system telling you to chunk your lesson down. Making it easier for both you and your horse is the mark of a smart trainer. You want to set your horse up to be successful. You don't want to put yourself in a situation where either you or your horse feels over-matched and afraid.

A seat like velcro is a great thing to have, but you can still be a good trainer even if you feel a little uncertain in the saddle. It just means you have to be more creative and think your way through problems. You're going to take your horse around the "brick walls" instead of trying to muscle your way over them. You aren't going to force him into situations where his only option is to explode. This approach, over time will give you the skills and confidence you'll need to help your horse through just about any situation the two of you will encounter.

"WHERE": RIDING PAST THE HORSE-EATING GOBLINS

So what do you do with your spooking horse? Right now he threatens to rear or bolt any time you get within twenty feet of the far end. So start in his comfort zone, down by the gate. Pick a point you'd like to ride to at the far end of the ring. Your

Chapter Sixteen: Riding Basics

goal is to have your horse standing quietly at that spot. To get there you'll begin by riding a figure-eight pattern in the near end.

The figure eight is going to have a very particular orientation in the arena. The two loops of the pattern will lie to the left and right, joined together by a straight line down the center of the arena. That means that as your horse changes from one loop of the pattern to the other, he'll be walking towards the goblins at the far end.

• Start him on the rail. For these directions you'll begin on the right rein. Turn him up the center line so you're walking straight towards the far end.

• Before he has a chance to tense up and refuse to go forward, turn him to the left and circle back towards the rail.

• Come around on a left circle and take the center line again. You'll be riding a figure-eight pattern with a straight line connecting the two halves. (Note: you don't have to be in a ring to use this exercise. Any time your horse is afraid to go forward, you can set up this pattern.)

At first your figure eight may be squashed into the near end of the arena and look more like a flattened road kill than two round circles. Don't worry about that now. Just keep your horse's feet moving and keep him turning. As he starts to relax, he'll let you take him a little deeper into the arena. When he does, offer him a chance to stop. As he walks up the center line so he's facing the goblins at the far end, ask him to halt. Just relax into the halt, the way you would at the end of a long ride. If you feel as though you have to really pull back, he's telling you he's not yet ready to stop. Don't force it. Give up on the halt, and instead ride him forward into the next loop of the figure eight. The more he walks and turns, the more he's going to listen to your offer to stop.

The principle here is: *if you do anything long enough, eventually you'll want a change* (pg. 25).

No matter how energized your horse feels at the beginning, if he keeps moving, eventually he's going to want to rest. Understand this principle and you have the keys to patience and persistence. Even the most bouncing-off-the-walls, high-energy horse is eventually going to relax and start listening.

The more you ask your horse to practice turning in figure eights, the more he's going to want just to stand still. As his feet slow down, he'll start to notice that your seat is saying, "It's okay. You don't have to go anywhere." He'll come to a stop. So now you have him standing calmly, facing the far end. Let him rest for a few seconds and then start again.

Can you see all the places in this lesson where you could click and give him a treat? Click when he turns up the center line and faces the goblins; when he relaxes; when he takes a breath; when he stops.

As you repeat the pattern your figure eight will shift position. You'll be able to go deeper and deeper into the arena, until finally your horse will walk on a loose rein right to the spot you picked out. You've succeeded in changing his perception of the far end. It's no longer the scary zone. It's the place where he gets to rest and relax. You've used two motivators to

THE FIGURE-EIGHT PATTERN

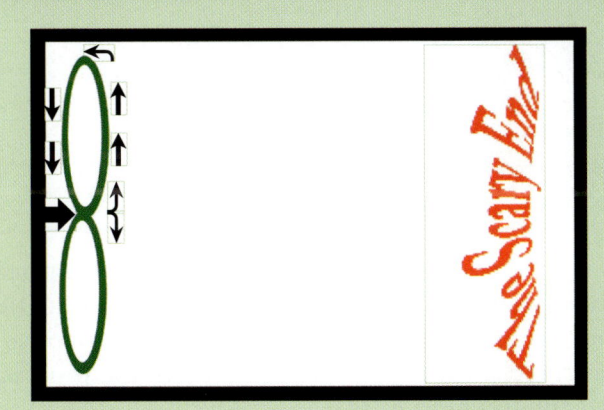

1.) The "squashed road kill" portion of this exercise. Your figure eight will be jammed down in your horse's comfort zone—far away from the "goblins" at the far end. Note how you will be turning up the center of the arena so your horse will be facing the far end as he changes loops of the figure eight.

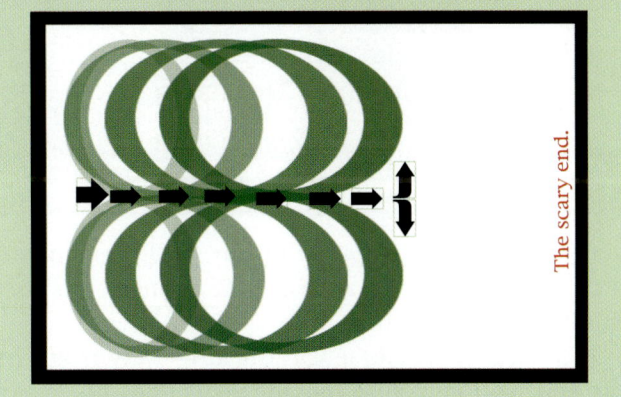

2.) Midway through the lesson the pattern is looking more like a well-formed figure. At this point the horse will be walking confidently down the center line on a loose rein. The rider continues to turn to the left and right until the horse is marching right up to the "goblins".

The Click That Teaches: Riding With The Clicker

RIDING THE FIGURE EIGHT PATTERN

1.) Begin at a distance from the "goblin". Set up the figure eight where your horse is comfortable, then gradually move closer to the scary end.

2.) As your horse turns down the center of the figure eight, click and give him a treat. Your goal is to be able to walk right up to the "goblin" on a loose rein.

3.) The end result: the horse walks right up to the tarp on a loose rein. Click and treat!

accomplish the first part of your goal. Remember, a motivator is simply a reason to change. The first motivator was fatigue.

As long as your horse was ducking away from the far end, you kept him moving. This does not mean you ran him into a lather. This entire exercise can be done at the walk, and your horse may never break a sweat, but he's still going to get tired of all that turning. I've used this exercise with very fit hundred-mile endurance horses; it can take a while, but eventually even they want to stop.

The far end becomes the comfort zone, the place where your horse gets to relax and drop his head. He gets to stand still and rest. That's your other motivator, the chance to relax. Fatigue began the process, and comfort ends it.

So now you have him standing at the far end. You haven't gotten into a wreck. He hasn't been rearing or bolting sideways. You've just been practicing turning, and you're both getting good at it. He's following your seat more than he ever did before. You know he really will turn when you ask. As an added bonus, you just think halt and its there. You're feeling more confident. All those changes of direction have created a more secure seat in you. You're becoming a better rider, and all you've done is walk figure eights.

By using the figure eight pattern, you've tuned up his steering wheel and his brakes. You've shown him how to approach something that frightens him, and how to leave it. Take your time, and don't try to force him into the far end before he's ready. Think about it. Turning your back on something that scares you can be even more terrifying than walking up to it.

You see that when people force their horses to walk up to trail obstacles. Yes, they can get the horse to put his nose on the mailbox, but then what? As soon as the horse has his hindquarters turned to it, he's bolting back to his safety zone. Working in a figure eight gives your horse lots of experience approaching and leaving the scary object. He'll see it from all different angles. By the time he's up close to it, it won't be bothering him any more. You are teaching him an alternative to flight: one you will use again and again throughout his training.

ADDING THE CLICKER
The figure-eight pattern is a standard horse training exercise, one many of you will already be familiar with. You can certainly ride it without using the clicker and get good results, but adding the clicker makes this lesson even more effective. Not only will your horse settle faster, you'll be able to couple "how" he carries himself with "where" he goes.

Begin by picking the criterion you're going to click and reward. At first you might decide to click your horse just for turning up the center line. The clicker marks the end of a unit of behavior. Your horse is going to stop for his treat. When he does, he'll be facing the dreaded far end. The whole time he's getting his treat he's also looking at the ghosts he's been spooking at. He's learning that ghosts are good things. Look at their hiding places and you get treats.

So now you'll ask your horse to go a little further into the ring. At first you'll click him just for walking a step or two up the center line. Then you'll gradually extend the distance he has to go. If he turns on his own before you can click, he's missed his chance for a goody. Ride him back onto your figure-eight pattern. If he wants his treat, he has to control his fear and stay on the path you're riding.

As his comfort zone expands, you'll layer in a second criterion. Now as he walks up the center line, pick the moments to click him when his ears are at or below his withers — a sign that he's relaxed. If he walks up the center line with his head up as if he's expecting

trouble, you'll just keep riding the figure eight. You're offering him a clear choice. You can stay all tense and nervous. That's fine. We'll just keep working on turning. Or you can relax your muscles. If you relax, all kinds of good things will happen. You'll get clicked. You'll get to stand still. And you'll get a treat.

You aren't forcing him into the far end. You aren't telling him he's "just being stupid, there's nothing down there to be afraid of." Fear is fear. It's not up to you to tell your horse how he should feel. You are simply setting up a situation in which you can both stay safe, and he can make some choices. If he wants the vending machine to work, he has to control his fear. He has to stop fretting over something that's half a ring away and pay attention to what you're asking him to do. The result is going to be a horse who not only walks boldly up the center line, but who carries himself beautifully and is more responsive to you.

"HOW"
In describing the figure-eight pattern I said nothing about how you rode, what kind of bit you used, how you asked for a turn. I simply set you a task: ride a figure-eight pattern and find as many reasons as you can to click and reinforce your horse. The result will be a horse who walks right up to the "goblins" on a loose rein. Pretty neat! This exercise shows you how to piggy back the clicker onto a standard riding pattern. You could stop reading at this point, and with just that piece you could easily incorporate the clicker into your riding.

But thumb through the pictures in this book. You'll see that for me riding isn't simply about getting from point A to point B. It's about beautiful horses: horses who are sound in their bodies and happy in their spirits — horses who feel like heaven to ride. In other words, "how" a horse carries himself is just as important as "where" he goes.

To teach "how" requires an attention to detail that many riders have never been taught. For example in the figure-eight lesson, you could say: "If you don't want to go down to the far end, that's fine with me. You can work wherever you like, just so long as you meet my other criteria. To start with I want you to relax your jaw."

You'll still be riding a figure eight, but now your focus will be much more on how your horse feels under you rather than where he is in the arena. You're going to train by priority (see page 17). As your horse relaxes his jaw, other things will follow. His head will drop. The muscles in his neck will relax. You'll be able to yield his hips over. You'll

The Click That Teaches: Riding With The Clicker

RIDING PAST 'GOBLINS"

This Tennessee walker used to spook and bolt. His rider is using the figure-eight lesson to take him past the jacket.

At first he gave it a wide berth. He flicks an ear in its direction and changes bend to avoid getting too close.

His rider has stayed focused on "how" her horse carries himself. He's still a little tense and giving the jacket a look as he goes by.

"Touch the Goblin" (pg. 24) helps him become more comfortable with the jacket.

be able to move his front end over to make a larger figure eight. As his body relaxes, his brain will relax. He'll forget about ghosts and scary corners. Now you can ride him right down to the far end of the arena past all the goblins. You focused on "how", and "where" just happened.

At this point you may be thinking to yourself: "I know how to ride a figure eight. I understand riding for "where", but I'm not so sure about asking my horse to soften his jaw, or what it means to yield his hips over. How do I separate out softening his jaw when there is so much else going on, and how is that going to get him down to the far end?

That's what this book is about—getting to the far end and beyond—on a horse that feels like heaven to ride. Here's an analogy that may help: imagine you've just moved into a house that needs major renovation. Before you unpack your furniture, you've got some remodelling to do. You may need to tear down some walls to get the job done right, but the end result is going to be a stunning house.

That in essence is the process I'm describing here. In the next couple of chapters we'll look at the "blueprint" of what you're building. Then I'll give you some tools to work with: head lowering (Ch. 20) and flipping the hips (Ch. 21). In Part 4 we'll "remodel" your balance with some very simple Feldenkrais and T'ai chi exercises. Then in Part 5 we'll look at the internal structure of your "house": the foundation, the wiring, the plumbing — all the pieces you don't see that make a "house" comfortable and safe to live in. In Part 6 we'll frame the "house" with exercises that tie the whole process together. From there you can "decorate" in whatever style suits your fancy.

Before you begin this process take some pictures of your horse. You're going to love the before and afters!

Success! He rides beautifully past the jacket.

CHAPTER 17
Asking Questions

Are you ready to begin remodeling your "house"? In this chapter we'll look at the fundamental tools you'll be using. We'll be looking at the motivators, both positive and negative, we use in riding. You'll see how pressure becomes cues. Combine these with the clicker, and you can carry on a complex "conversation" with your horse.

MOTIVATING YOUR HORSE TO LEARN

The conventional methods we use to train horses rely to one degree or another on the horse's desire to avoid pain. The horse learns what our signals mean and performs the behaviors we connect them to in order to avoid correction. The horse learns to stop when his rider shifts her weight. If he doesn't, he'll feel an increase of pressure from the bit.

This is not to say that traditional trainers are cruel people; it's just that with very few exceptions, they've accepted "correction"—the infliction of some degree of discomfort—as a training tool. And horses certainly can be motivated to learn what our signals mean in order to avoid unpleasant consequences. They can also be motivated to perform in order to gain pleasure. That's the alternative the clicker offers them. Come to a stop when I settle into the saddle, and click, I'll give you a treat.

So the question isn't whether or not our horses can learn, but how we decide to teach them. You can dig a spur into your horse's side. If you give him enough pain when he's standing still, and immediately stop spurring him when he moves, he will very quickly learn to respond to a light touch of your leg. You are using his desire to avoid pain to teach him to be a responsive, obedient riding horse.

Thanks to clicker training you can change that picture for your horse. You will still be using negative reinforcement. We might as well call a spade a spade. Pressure is the basic tool you'll use in riding, but that doesn't mean you're being harsh, any more than using positive reinforcement means you're being permissive.

Pressure doesn't necessarily mean pain. Even very light pressure applied over a long enough period of time can get a horse to move. Once you have movement, you can shape the rest with positive reinforcement: "Move this way, and I click you; that way and the pressure continues."

The difference between clicker training and more traditional approaches isn't so much in the signals we use, but in the way we teach the horse what those signals mean. Follow an incorrect response to pressure with punishment, and the horse may well become sour and resentful. Instead pair a correct response to pressure with the clicker, and the horse becomes a willing partner.

Both methods may end up with the same set of signals. Both will say to the horse "move away from my leg, respond to the pressure of my rein." The difference comes in how the horse learned what those signals mean. As I've said before, clicker training isn't about learning to ride differently. It's not about putting a dressage saddle on your horse instead of a western stock saddle. You

ANIMAL INTELLIGENCE

Much of traditional horse training is based on an underlying belief that horses are stupid. In this view horses have to be trained with pain. You can only get them to listen to you if you make yourself more terrible than all the goblins and predators they are trying to avoid.

Our belief systems color what we see. If you believe horses are stupid, what you will see are stupid horses. In contrast, if you believe horses are intelligent animals, that's what you'll find. The horses I work with are all wonderfully bright animals who love to learn. Viewing them like that makes training a lot more fun for me.

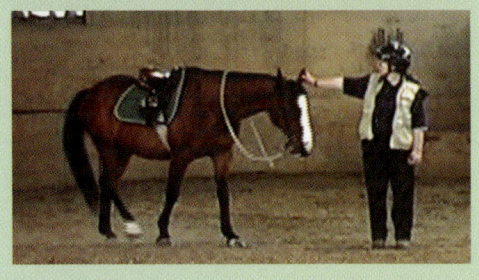

For example, Peregrine has learned the names for different parts of his body. When I ask for his ear, he walks over to me and puts his ear in my hand. Note how he is walking to me, orienting his ear toward my outstretched hand.

This simple targeting exercise turns our post-ride walks into a fun game. For an ear-shy horse the same exercise could be a life saver.

don't have to change your boots, or wear a different hat. Clicker training is about teaching. It's a way to achieve your goals, whatever they may be, whatever style you ride.

THE TWO–WAY STREET

Once you get in the saddle, you're going to be doing more than simply sitting on your horse, you're going to be communicating with him—and that means a dialogue—listening as well as talking. You're going beyond "I command—you obey."

With pressure gently applied (negative reinforcement) and the help of the clicker (positive reinforcement), you're going to develop a language that lets you ask your horse simple yes/no questions. That's how computers work. Just think of all the incredible things we can do with computers, and at the heart of it all is a simple binary on/off language. In our language, your horse will be able to ask questions of you as well. So with both of you communicating back and forth, you ought to be able to do some pretty fancy riding.

ASKING QUESTIONS

What do I mean when I say your horse can ask questions? Let's consider a green horse who still thinks pressure is something you resist against. When you take the slack out of the reins, he isn't going to be thinking he's got choices. He's just going to stick his nose up in the air and pull.

If you stabilize your hand when he resists, and instantly release if he even thinks about softening in the direction you want, he'll quickly learn what works. Resisting up against the rein leads to more pressure, but dropping his head gets you to let go. And it also produces a click and a treat. Good deal.

So now your horse thinks he has things figured out. Any time he feels your hand on the rein, if he drops his head, click you'll give him a treat. Life is good. Except he's about to learn that life isn't that simple. Pressure on the rein doesn't always mean down. That just happened to be the correct response for that first series of requests.

Pressure on the rein really means: "I want something." You can want all kinds of things: a step back; a turn to the side; even a lift of the head. It is the release that indicates a correct response has been found. So what turns this from a trial and error guessing game on the part of your horse into real communication? Cues. Through the training process your horse will learn to read your intent, the subtle signals you can't help but give as you focus on different requests. And you in turn will become more aware of those signals so you can use them more deliberately and with greater clarity. That is the process that turns average riders into great trainers.

So next you'll take the slack out of the rein, only now the answer you're looking for isn't down. It might be "soften your jaw to the left." Your horse is going to be convinced that the right answer is down. It was the right answer the last ten times. It must be the right answer now. He tries to drop his head, but you keep your hand stabilized against the saddle so he can't pull it out of your hand.

"Stupid human!" your horse is thinking. "Why is she making this so difficult?" As he fusses against the rein, he'll accidentally move in the direction you want. Click, release the rein and give him a treat.

Over the next few trials he'll learn that there are two possible answers. And over time instead of fussing at you for being a "stupid human", he'll learn to ask questions. Through his actions he'll be saying: *"You have your hand on the rein. You must want something. Do you want me to lower my head? No, your hand is still on the rein. How about moving to the right? No, that isn't it either. You still haven't softened the rein. How about to the left? Yes. That's what you wanted. You just released the rein."*

By trial and error your horse found the right answer. Give him a few more training sessions, and he'll be using the clues/cues you're providing. *"Your hand is on the rein. What can I do for you? Let me check a few things. What are your legs doing? How are you sitting? Generally when you sit like that you want me to lower my head and turn to the left. Is that right? Yes, you just let go."*

The cues you'll be using in this "conversation" are changes in pressure. If he feels an added light pressure from your inner thigh muscle, that becomes a signal to move. Pushing into pressure creates more pressure. That's a wrong answer. Shifting away from pressure releases pressure: right answer. Your horse asks: *"Do you want me here? No, now I feel more pressure. How about here? Yes, that releases pressure."*

A horse who isn't fully conversant in the language feels the pressure and just keeps pushing against it. With his swishing tail and pinned ears, he's saying: ***"That was the right answer the last three times! This has to be the right answer NOW. Let go of that rein! Stop bugging me with your leg. I KNOW what I'm doing!"***

This horse isn't asking questions, or looking for other options. He knows what's right, even if you don't. He's simply barging through your hand and ignoring your other signals. He's learned one pattern, and he isn't interested in looking for other answers. Sound familiar?

This is where many people get stuck in their

Chapter Seventeen: Asking Questions

training, and they start thinking that they're doing something wrong. They worry about their position. "If I were just a better rider," they lament, and they start wiggling around trying to fix things. The truth is, it isn't their position that's the problem. In fact, there is no problem. This is just a normal part of the learning process. You're asking for more complexity. You're beginning to differentiate between subtle cues. You're combining responses into complex patterns, and your horse is still stuck in his first response. He's not paying any attention to your signals. He's not asking questions, or looking for other answers. He's just saying: *"I picked up a canter the last three times we were in this corner. You must want me to pick up a canter now!"*

This happens to people, as well. You see it when they play the training game (pg. 17). They'll circle around and around in the same pattern, even though they aren't getting reinforced for it. They've stopped experimenting. They aren't asking: "Do you want me to do this? What if I try this?" Those are the kinds of questions an animal or human asks who has learned how to play the training game. They know how to look for other options, and how to ask questions through non-verbal experimentation. It is this experimentation that creates excellence. If jumping is good, what about jumping higher? Jackpot!

LISTENING FOR RESPONSES

A big part of riding is understanding that this conversation is going on. That means understanding that a conversation is a two way street. It isn't enough simply to take a firmer feel on a rein, or to nudge your horse a little harder in his sides. You want an answer. You're expecting a response. You are offering your horse suggestions to follow. Learning to listen for his response is part of the process. This goes beyond the basics of learning how to sit his gaits. Riding at its best is about communication.

You may have been in a riding lesson where your instructor kept telling you to soften your hands. Your instructor wasn't hammering away at this point simply because she wanted you to be nice to your horse. She was doing it because she wanted you to communicate with him. There's a huge difference. Being nice is a lovely ideal, but it doesn't always help your horse. Nice riders can get their mounts just as confused and frustrated as harsh riders. When you have a rider who communicates clearly, what you see is a happy horse.

TEACHING CUES

A key difference between clicker training and more traditional training approaches is the order in which cues are taught. In traditional methods the cue is often given before the behavior is even present. Imagine if I told you to "lum". What are you going to do? The word has no meaning. How can you respond to it? If I increase the pressure when you don't respond, I've "poisoned the cue" right from the start Now the first association with that cue will be one of confusion and worry. We do this all the time to horses. We put them on a lunge line and verbally tell them to "Canter!". We know what the word means. The answer is clear to us, but not to the horse. When he doesn't respond, we whip him forward chanting: "Canter! Canter!" If the horse thinks anything, it's probably that "canter" means trot as fast as you can without falling on your face.

Clicker training follows a different order. First you get the behavior happening consistently, then you add a cue. The cue at first will have no meaning to your horse, but after you have paired it with the behavior over a number of trials, the cue will trigger the desired behavior (Ch. 10).

NATURAL AND ARTIFICIAL CUES

Depending upon how you've shaped a behavior, cues will emerge in different ways. You can have primary or "natural" cues, and secondary or "artificial" ones. For example, you can teach your horse to back by gently tapping his legs with a whip. The whip will become a signal to your horse. If your timing is good, you'll find that soon you don't actually have to touch your horse. All you have to do is wave the whip towards him, almost like a conductor's baton, and he'll back up. Waving the whip is a natural signal that emerges out of the way the behavior was triggered in the first place.

Once the horse is backing consistently, you can transfer your signal to a verbal cue. You could say "lum" just before you give your whip signal. If you repeat that several times, and then fade out the whip signal, the word "lum" by itself will get him to back.

The whip tapping was the primary or natural cue. It's what prompted the behavior in the first place. The word "lum", meaning "back up", is an artificial or secondary cue that you have taught your horse through association by linking it to the first cue.

Cues emerge as a natural part of training. The key is to be aware of them as they develop so you can make use of them. Good trainers are quick to pick up on the signals a horse is paying attention to. These are most often physical gestures (or, in the saddle, weight shifts). By becoming aware of the clues you're presenting you can turn these into cues to prompt specific behaviors.

The Click That Teaches: Riding With The Clicker

CUES

When people first start thinking about clicker training, they often think the click triggers specific behaviors. They are giving it a job it doesn't have. They are confusing the click with cues, signals that have a very different function.

A cue comes at the beginning of a sequence. It acts like a green light telling the horse which behavior is likely to earn reinforcement.

The click comes later in the sequence. It's the "yes answer" signal that tells the horse he did the right thing and he's going to get his treat.

Think of it like a sentence:

The cue ➡ the behavior ➡ the click ➡ the treat.

That's the order of a finished sequence. The cue triggers the behavior. The click signals the successful completion of a unit of the behavior and is followed by a reinforcing treat. However, that is not the order in which these signals are taught.

A teaching sequence would look like this:

The behavior ➡ the click ➡ the treat.

Horses are experts at reading body language. They will be looking for hints that tell them what behavior is likely to get reinforced. These hints become cues that trigger specific responses. The trainer's job is to spot these cues and make deliberate use of them. These are "natural" or primary cues because they evolved out of the shaping process. They are generally body language cues involving weight shifts or hand gestures. So now you have the original sentence:

The cue ➡ the behavior ➡ the click ➡ the treat.

Transferring Cues: You can easily change to a new cue. Here's the sequence:

New cue followed immediately by the original cue ➡ behavior ➡ click ➡ treat.

After several repetitions of this, fade out the old cue. Now you have:

New cue ➡ behavior ➡ click ➡ treat.

This is a secondary or "unnatural" cue. It was taught using classical conditioning. In classical conditioning the emotional effect travels backwards. That means that the emotional state associated with the reward will also become associated with the cue. Using food and other positive reinforcements in training creates strong positive emotional connections with the cue. The cue itself can become reinforcing and be used to build complex chains of behavior. But be aware, you can poison your cue by inserting negative consequences for wrong responses. A poisoned cue will break down chains and create performance anxiety.

BUILDING A VOCABULARY

An exercise I recommend to all my riders involves experimenting with their own movements. Begin by standing in front of a mirror. See if you can move just your right shoulder, or just your right hip, nothing else. When I first tried this, I found it was easy to move my left shoulder alone but not my right. Instead of just my right shoulder moving my whole right side would turn. That's not uncommon. It just took a little practice, and some Alexander sessions, to give me the control I was looking for. (The Alexander Method has helped many riders find better balance. See Sally Swift's *Centered Riding*★ for more information on this.)

Next I did the same thing while riding. My aim was to see what response, if any, I got from each individual movement. The challenge was to observe without judgment. I wasn't after a particular response, so it didn't matter what happened. I wanted to see what my horse thought I was asking for. I was making a catalog of reactions that I could use later when I really did want a specific response.

The first time I tried this was with Peregrine's mother. I remember being absolutely bowled over by how little I had to do to get a huge response from her. I'd ridden for years thinking I needed the full strength of my arms and upper body to stop a horse. Now I discovered that just a tiny shift in my shoulder joint was all I needed to bring a thousand pound horse to a screeching halt. The more I played with this exercise, the more in tune I became to the subtle signals my horse was listening to. If I got strong, I blocked her ability to listen to me. It was like trying to have a normal conversation with a radio blasting hard rock in the background. You have to shout to be heard. I don't know about you, but when I shout, I begin to sound harsh.

The same thing happens in riding. The stronger I got, the more rigid I became, and the "louder" I had to make my signals to get a response. But when I took the time to listen to my horse I found I could whisper my aids. The more I did, the more aware I became of the subtle cues she was listening to. Our conversations changed, and my riding became much softer and more enjoyable for both of us.

Recognizing cues as they emerge is an important part of training. The more I think about riding as communication, the easier it becomes to spot cues as they emerge and to put them to use in a variety of combinations. The exchange becomes a two way street. With this in place we can build everything else. We can build a relationship based on trust, and communication based on understanding.

★ *Centered Riding*, by Sally Swift; Trafalgar Square, VT

Chapter Eighteen: Single-Rein Riding Meets Dressage

CHAPTER 18
Single-Rein Riding Meets Dressage: Going on the Bit

Horses who learn to use their bodies well stay sounder longer. That's the bottom line goal of this entire book. If you love your horse and want to have him around for a long time as your riding partner, you want him to learn how to carry you in balance. This chapter will take you a few steps closer to that goal. I'll introduce you to the basic theory behind single-rein riding, and I'll describe in detail what it means for a horse to go "on the bit".

SINGLE-REIN RIDING

So far I've been dancing around the whole issue of how to ride. I don't want to exclude anyone in this discussion of clickers. I don't want you to think you have to change your riding style to apply the principles. No one has to take up dressage in order to use the clicker. On the other hand, I want to *include* everybody. In Chapter 16 on riding basics I talked about softening a horse to the bit, getting him to bend correctly, connecting the rein to his feet, etc.. To do this I used a standard riding exercise: the figure-eight pattern (pg. 94-98). Without changing anything about your basic riding style, you could successfully use this lesson. On a very frightened horse it might take three or four hours to get to the far end of the arena, but at the end of that time, he'll be better balanced and more connected to you, and you'll definitely be a better rider. So without making any fundamental changes in how you ride, this basic lesson can shift your relationship.

Now I'd like to take you another huge step towards creating a "feels-like-heaven-to-ride" horse by introducing you to single-rein riding. Let me begin with some background. Like most riders I started out in a normal two-rein system. I had some good training along the way and learned how to communicate clear signals down the reins. When I first encountered single-rein riding through John Lyons' work, I was puzzling my way through the early stages of lateral work. At that first clinic I saw Lyons take a stiff, nose-in-the-air, frightened horse and within the space of thirty minutes get her to drop her head to the ground, soften her entire body, and glide smoothly over in her first steps of lateral work. He did this by riding entirely on one rein. He never picked up his outside rein.

I was impressed, but puzzled. I didn't understand what he was doing, and my first reaction was: "that may be how they get sidepass on a western horse, but that's not what we're after in a dressage horse. We want engagement. We want suspension. Shoulder-in is totally different." How silly.

Anyway, I went home and experimented with the pieces from the clinic that I did understand. I worked through his ground exercises, and I loved them. Here were the building blocks, the alphabet, if you will, for the more complex exercises I was struggling to understand. I went back for more, and in the process I learned to ride on a single rein.

TAKING THE TWO-BY-FOUR OUT OF YOUR HORSE

Why a single rein?

The instant you pick up two reins, you're setting yourself up to

---

EQUIPMENT FOR SINGLE-REIN RIDING

The basic equipment for single-rein riding:

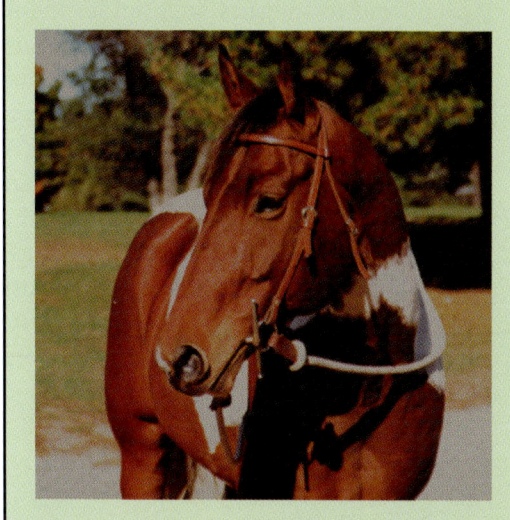

The ideal bit is either a full cheek or D ring snaffle: the bars on the mouthpiece keep the bit from sliding through the horse's mouth, and they also distribute the pressure the horse feels against the corner of his mouth over a wider area. Used properly, these are very mild bits. The single-rein exercises will show you how to turn them into clear communication tools. (Note: the rope reins are more for the rider than the horse. Once you get used to their soft feel, you'll never want to go back to leather.)

Also note: you don't need a noseband. If your horse opens his mouth, we read that as communication and try to figure out what he needs. Forcing the mouth closed with a noseband is like squeezing a balloon. You may eliminate the mouth opening behavior, but the resistance will turn up somewhere else. Learning to listen to your horse's needs is part of good riding.

be leaned on. As Lyons puts it, it's a great way to turn a horse into a two-by-four. You've probably ridden enough stiff horses to know what that feels like. If not, try this little experiment:

Stand with your feet apart and one arm raised straight out to the side at shoulder height. Now have a friend push on your out-stretched hand. Lock your elbow and resist him. Even if he's quite a bit stronger than you are, you'll find that you can. You can probably stand there for quite a while. You'll feel all the pressure going through your arm and down into your opposite foot. The more he pushes, the more he'll just root your foot into the ground.

Now bend your elbow and try to resist the push. You won't be able to hold out for very long. Why? When your arm was locked in a straight position, your friend was pushing against your skeleton. You didn't have to use your muscles to resist him. In the second case, with your elbow bent, you've given up that advantage. Now you have to rely almost solely on your arm muscles to resist the push. You may be able to hold out for a minute or two, but not for much longer before your arm will give way.

When you take hold of two reins on an unschooled horse, he can line up his skeleton just as you did in our experiment. He can stiffen his jaw, stiffen his neck, and make his whole body rigid. Pull all you like, it won't matter. Your arms may ache from the strain, but he won't be tired at all. You're using muscle to try to hold onto him, and he's resisting with his whole skeleton. If you're twenty miles out from home when he starts pulling, you'd better be prepared for the workout of a lifetime.

You could try to solve the problem by switching to a more severe bit. Or you could use leverage devices that give you more of a mechanical advantage. You could lunge him in side reins, or ride him in draw reins. He'll learn to drop his head, but he might also learn to lean down into his shoulders and go behind the bit. The danger with this is that you can lose your connection to his feet. It's like driving a car that's leaking brake fluid. Eventually you'll press down on the pedal and nothing will happen—not a good deal in a car and certainly not when you're on a horse.

An alternative is to put him back in a simple snaffle bit, take off all the martingales, and learn single-rein riding instead. You'll be asking your horse to bend to the side. In the above experiment bending meant you had to use muscle. You couldn't just stiffen and resist. The same thing happens when you get your horse to bend. He loses the mechanical advantage stiffening the spine gave him. Get a horse to bend his neck by riding on just one rein and you can take the "two-by-four" out of him.

My goal isn't just to keep a horse from pulling on me. I want my horse to look and feel beautiful. I want a horse who stays sound in his body over a long lifetime of work. I want a horse who is fun to ride; who makes me smile and laugh. I want a horse that feels like heaven to ride; who floats over the ground on a magic carpet ride. I want a horse who responds to the lightest touch of my aids, who is quick and athletic and willing to work. I want a horse who looks happy, whose steps are lively, and whose attitude is bright. To get all that I need to teach my horse to go on the bit, and to do that correctly I need to flex him laterally.

What does all this mean? In this chapter I'll talk about what "on the bit" means and why it is useful. In the next chapter I'll talk about the mechanics of single-rein riding and lateral flexions. I'll begin by defining three terms: above the bit, behind the bit, and on the bit. You can feel all three in your own body by mimicking what the horse does in his.

ABOVE THE BIT

Above the bit is easy because it's the most natural both for horses and people. A horse who is above the bit has hollowed his back. His pelvis is tipped down and back, so his hocks are positioned out behind him. His head is raised, which shortens the top of his neck and stretches the bottom. His muscle development reflects his carriage. Horses who habitually travel like this develop what's called a ewe neck: the muscles on the underside of the neck are the most prominent. The middle of their backs will look sunken. Often these horses are troubled by sore backs and hind end problems. (Refer to Photo 1 on pg. 105.)

ON THE BIT

When a horse is on the bit, his hind legs are engaged, meaning they step more deeply under his body. He uses his abdominal muscles to rotate the back of his pelvis forward and down, with the result that his back lifts. That in turn releases the base of his neck and lifts his withers. You see the characteristic rounding of the neck, with the plane of the horse's face coming into vertical. (Photo 2 on pg. 105.)

BEHIND THE BIT

A horse who is behind the bit has gone past the vertical. His nose is tucking in toward his chest. He's over-bent. His poll will often be lower than his withers. Yes, he's round, but he's also pulling down into his shoulders and his hocks are no longer engaged beneath him. (Photo 3 on pg 105.)

Chapter Eighteen: Single-Rein Riding Meets Dressage

ABOVE, BEHIND, AND ON THE BIT

This horse was startled by something in the bushes. She's giving a great demo of going above the bit. She has stiffened her neck, raised her head and hollowed her back. Note the bulge in the underside of her neck. If she made a habit of carrying herself like this, she would develop what is referred to as a ewe neck.

Even though this filly is little, she looks big because she is on the bit. Her back has rounded, and she's lifting from the base of her neck. Note how her nose is perpendicular to the ground. All this gives her a lovely spring to her step. She is learning to carry herself with grace and elegance.

A moment before this photo was taken this horse was carrying himself beautifully, but now he's gone behind the bit. He's over-bent. His nose is pulled in towards his chest. He's leaning down onto his shoulders so he'll feel heavy to his rider. Note how his hind end seems to be trailing out behind him.

THE PROBLEM WITH DOING WHAT COMES NATURALLY

Being above the bit is the most natural carriage for the horse and for one very simple reason: that's the best way for him to see motion along the horizon line. That's why a horse will lift his head when he's concerned. He's checking for predators.

A horse may feel most in control emotionally when he's above the bit, but mechanically it's the worst way for him to carry a rider. A horse is constructed like a giant suspension bridge. When you ride, you're sitting in the middle of that bridge, right in the weakest part. That's why some people believe that riding—any riding at all—is ultimately bad for horses.

That's certainly true if you're riding badly. Sit in the hollow of the back of an above-the-bit horse and all you're doing is making the dip bigger. Gradually, as the back sinks, the vertebrae will begin to rub against each other, sometimes causing severe pain.

Natural riding sounds great until you stop and think about what that really means. Horses naturally go above the bit, and they naturally counter-balance to stop and turn. Watch your horse move next time he's turned out in his paddock. Watch him race the length of his field and come charging into a corner. How does he stop? Nice and square? Of course not. How does he turn? Correctly bent? I don't think so.

To stop he throws his head up and slams on the brakes. To turn he swings his head one way and his shoulders the other. As he runs, he twists and turns to make it harder for a predator to cling to his back. He counter-balances into turns to keep from falling. That may be great for a rodeo horse, but not for a saddle horse. How many times have you watched your favorite riding horse when he's out racing around with his pasture mates and thought "Yikes. And I ride that horse!" For me the goal isn't to be able to ride horses naturally. My goal is to teach my horses to carry me in balance.

CHOOSING "UNNATURAL" RIDING

When a horse is on the bit his back is lifting up. That means he can support his rider. His spine will stay relaxed and healthy; his joints soft and elastic. He'll learn how to flex his body both laterally—that is, bending to the side—and dorso-ventrally—rounding his topline. When he goes through a corner, he'll be upright and correctly bent. He won't be dropping away from the rider.

Instead they'll both have a feeling of flowing together. His stops won't jar the rider out of the saddle. He'll come into his halts square and even, and his back will stay soft. Overall he'll be easier to ride, and that means it will be easier for the rider to relax and follow his movements.

Mechanically it may be easier for a horse to be on the bit, but emotionally it's something he has to learn to be comfortable with. When you put a horse on the bit you're limiting his sight lines. He can't see the horizon, and for many horses that's an unnerving

The Click That Teaches: Riding With The Clicker

THE "NATURAL" VERSUS THE "UNNATURAL" HORSE

The "natural" horse.

The "unnatural" horse.

experience. They can get used to the physical feel of it much faster than they can adjust to the uncertainty of not being able to scan for predators. That's why some of your more reactive horses resist going on the bit. It isn't that they physically can't, or that they don't understand what you want. They just don't feel safe with their heads in that position.

ZEN RIDING: LEARNING TO LET GO

You need to ease most horses into the on-the-bit posture gradually. If a horse is particularly anxious, forcing him to hold himself on the bit by putting him in lunging rigs or riding him with a martingale may only make him more resistant. Instead, ask him to go on the bit for just a stride or two, then release the rein completely. As soon as you let go, his head will pop back up. He'll go right back to his above-the-bit head carriage.

Letting go goes against human nature. We want to hold on to what we've created. Suppose you just spent five minutes getting your horse to relax his back long enough for him to go on the bit. The last thing you want to do is let go of him. You'll want to hold on to savor the feeling. The problem is, if you hold on, all that lovely softness will stiffen into resistance. To get a horse on the bit consistently, you have to let go.

So you let go and the horse pops his head right back up in the air. Great! He's given you an opportunity to ask again. He may resist for a few strides, but eventually he'll relax enough to respond to you. He'll soften his poll, round his topline, and drop his head onto the vertical. When you feel the softening in your hand, you'll again instantly let go. What you are saying to your horse is: "It's all right. You can trust me. You can relax your guard for a moment and go on the bit because I won't make you stay there very long. You'll be able to check the horizon again in another stride or two."

Put together enough of these sequences and you'll begin to notice that it becomes easier and easier to get your horse on the bit. You're working on all three elements of the horse: physical, mental, and emotional (Ch. 11). Through all these repetitions, he's learning how to go on the bit from any position he happens to be in, and he's doing it whenever you ask. He's learning what you want, and he's beginning to feel comfortable letting down his guard. You haven't just put him on the bit once and held him there. By letting go each time he responds to you, you've given him hundreds of experiences to learn from. So now, when you ask him to go on the bit, it happens almost instantaneously. That means you can string together a whole series of requests so the overall effect is he keeps himself on the bit.

ADDING THE CLICKER

Sometimes you'll find your horse will respond to you right away. Other times he'll be distracted, or he'll be out of balance physically, so it will take him longer to get himself organized. His behavior will vary. Perfect. That gives you an opportunity to use the clicker.

You want him on the bit. You pick up your reins and signal him through your seat and legs. He ignores you for four strides because he's busy looking at your friend's horse. Finally he relaxes and gives

106

Chapter Eighteen: Single-Rein Riding Meets Dressage

COMPARABLE PARTS

We don't always need a judge or a riding instructor to tell us what's right. Our horses are really the ones we should be consulting. This quarter horse is telling us exactly what he thinks of his rider's position. As his rider demonstrates three different postures, he's giving us his candid opinion of each one.

The rider has deliberately hollowed her back and "come above the bit". The horse has responded by doing the same. His unhappy expression tells us what he thinks of his rider's position. Note his upright head carriage and hollow back matches his rider's. His whole body is bracing against his stiff hind legs. His hip and stifle joints look as though they're being driven into the ground.

Now our rider has gone "behind the bit". She's roached her back and rounded her shoulders so her head drops towards her chest. Her horse doesn't like this any better than when she was "above the bit". He's got his ears pinned back and his overall sour expression tells us what he thinks of his rider's new position.

The rider has adjusted her position to bring her more "on to the bit", and her horse has responded immediately. He's softened his back and relaxed his jaw, giving a much rounder look to his topline. As his rider learns to relax and line her skeleton up even more, his topline will undergo another transformation and he'll look even softer, but this is a good beginning for both of them.

to you. You release the reins. His head pops back up and you start another cycle. This time he answers you right away. Click! The message is "Soften to me right away and you get a goody. Let yourself be distracted, and yes, I'll release the rein when you finally soften to me, but you'll have missed your opportunity to get a treat."

With the clicker motivating him, your horse won't be fighting the bit. He'll be offering you softness. He'll forget about imagined predators lurking in the bushes and become much more interested in pleasing you.

HUMAN EQUIVALENTS

Horses follow our suggestions. Think about the matches you see. Don't you see relaxed riders producing relaxed horses, and stiff riders sitting on stiff horses? When I'm giving a position lesson, I often leave the horse in his stall, and focus first on the rider. The horse just complicates the picture. Put a crooked rider on a crooked horse, and how do you sort out who is responsible for which piece of the puzzle?

Too often the rider takes all the blame. "What am I doing wrong?" is a common lament during lessons. "What am I doing to make my horse so crooked?" Maybe nothing. Maybe you're sitting on a saddle with a twisted tree or uneven stuffing. Maybe you're sitting on a horse with a dropped right shoulder that throws you off balance. You won't know which piece of the puzzle is yours to fix until you explore your own postural alignment.

Riders can also be above, on, or behind the bit. To find out which tendency you have, stand opposite a mirror with your feet a hip's width apart. Pretend you're riding a horse and your legs are straddled around his barrel. Now look at yourself. Are your knees locked? Is your back hollow? What is the orientation of your pelvis? Is it tipped forward? Are your shoulders tight, and your chin up so that the back of your neck is shortened? Congratulations. You're normal! And you're also above the bit.

Now as you stand there on the ground, look down at your navel. Don't just glance down with your eyes. Roll your head and shoulders forward so you're really looking down. Again, congratulations! You have done exactly what most horses do when they're ridden on steady contact. You are now behind the bit. Your back is "roached", your hocks are still out behind you, and you're "falling on your forehand", but not to worry, at least you aren't pulling on your "rider's" hands.

Going behind the bit is a common result for horses who are ridden on steady contact rather than pressure and release. If I mold a horse into a set position and hold him there, sooner or later he's going to start to lean. This is the problem with side reins and martingales. You have to be a very skilled trainer to keep the horse from leaning down onto his shoulders and getting over-bent.

Leaning is a natural response to support. And it's not just horses who succumb to the temptation. Next time you're at a horse show watch the people.

At the start of the day you'll see the spectators standing around looking bright and attentive. Watch a little longer, and you'll see most of them will have found a fence to lean up against. The next time you're riding and your horse starts to lean on your hands, remind yourself that you're not going to get mad at him for something you yourself do.

To go on the bit you have to find the balance between your horse hollowing above the bit and overflexing behind the bit. (Refer back to the photos on page 105.) It's like swinging a pendulum. You want to find the point where the pendulum finds the center but still has movement. The minute the pendulum stops moving, the whole system becomes rigid. So the pendulum has to oscillate around this perfect balance point. You want a slight, almost imperceptible bob of the head of the horse, and that's why riding on a release is so important. Another way you can think of it is to imagine a ballet dancer going on point. To stay up and in balance, she has to move. The instant she becomes stiff she'll collapse. Add a partner, and the ballerina can either accompany him lightly or look like dead weight in his arms.

GOOD POSTURE—SOUND HORSES

Take a steady, unyielding contact with your horse, and he'll give you a steady pull back (above the bit), or he'll lean (behind the bit), or he'll stiffen and compress his spine. If he does the latter, he may look like he's on the bit, but he'll lack elasticity in his stride. **Compress a horse enough and you'll damage his spine. Even a little compression, if done long enough, will lame a horse.** Compression creates resistance, and resistance creates pain. Horses who carry themselves and work on a release feel lighter and softer in their bodies. Their gaits are freer and easier to ride, and they stay sounder longer.

★ *The Natural Rider,* by Mary Wanless; Summit Books, NY

To get a sense of this, hold your hands out in front of you with your elbows bent at your sides. Make a tight fist. Next pull down your shoulders and tighten all your neck and arm muscles. Now lift your arms. Observe how high you can lift them, and how they feel. If you're like most people, you'll feel restricted in your movement.

Now release all that tension. Shake out your arms so that they're nice and loose, and repeat the exercise, only this time keep everything relaxed. You'll probably notice a big difference both in your range of movement and in the feeling of ease with which you can move.

Imagine what it would be like if you were a horse being asked to work day after day, especially on hard footing. Suppose you were that first horse, all tight and stiff in your body. Can't you feel what a pounding your joints would take?

Your rider is going to feel it, too. Your trot is going to jar her with every step. Is it any surprise that you both finish the ride with sore backs? The other, more relaxed horse doesn't feel the pounding. His joints are free and he's able to give his rider a smooth, magic-carpet ride.

When you hold yourself rigidly on the bit, you tighten your jaw and your shoulders. You shorten your neck and pull it into your shoulders. All that affects the ease of your movement. You can feel this just sitting in your chair. Look down slightly at your navel and hold yourself rigidly in that position. Stay there while you continue to read this section. After a few minutes you'll begin to feel the tightening in your neck as your muscles fatigue. When you're in this position, you'll also discover that it's hard to concentrate. You'll get to the end of this paragraph and you won't be sure what you've just read.

That's what your horse feels when he's ridden on a steady contact with no softening. Only he also has to move. He has to walk, trot, and canter, and he has to concentrate on his rider's signals. He has to travel laterally, or jump, or turn and spin, all this with his head and neck rigidly compressing his spine. The stress of this shows up as arthritic hocks and sore backs. The solution is for his rider to learn to let go.

GETTING YOURSELF "ON THE BIT"

I've said all this and I still haven't really given you the human equivalent for being on the bit. The easiest way to experience this is to try an exercise derived from Mary Wanless's *The Natural Rider.*★ Lie down on the floor, on your back with your knees bent and your feet flat. Check out the position of your pelvis and your back. Do you have a hollow in the small of your back, or can you feel the floor?

Chapter Eighteen: Single–Rein Riding Meets Dressage

Since most people start out above the bit, you'll probably feel a small gap between the floor and the small of your back—that's the equivalent of a hollow back for a horse. To get rid of this gap you're going to do a pelvic tilt. If you know how to do sit ups, you already know how this feels. Rotate your pelvis, using your abdominal muscles to draw the front of your pelvis up. That will bring your back solidly in contact with the floor—the equivalent of a rounded back for a horse. This rotation is the key element that will release your whole spine.

If you're not sure you're doing this right, release the rotation of your pelvis. Go back to your original pattern and let the contrast guide you. Really exaggerate the hollow in the small of your back. What does this do to your hips? To your thighs? Really exaggerate the hollow, so you can feel the effect. You'll feel your thighs drawing up towards your body.

If this is how you ride, what will this do to your ability to keep your feet in the stirrups? Imagine yourself riding a horse that pulls. If you pull back against him, that's just going to make you tighten your shoulders and arch your back even more. Sound familiar? No wonder your horse can pop you out of the saddle. You aren't grounded.

If you're an above-the-bit, hollow-backed rider, do you see why you tend to get stiff? You have to grip and brace your body to stay in the saddle, and that's a bad deal for both you and your horse.

PUSHING DOWN WITH YOUR SEAT

So suppose you decide to take a few lessons to work on your position. Your instructor sees that your horse isn't really engaged, so she tells you to push with your seat. What are you going to do? Push down towards the ground, of course.

Try this out while you're lying on the floor. Push your pelvis down towards your feet as if you're trying to push yourself down deeper into the saddle. You'll feel the small of your back pressing against the floor. Great, you think, I've solved that problem. I'm not above the bit any more. But wait. Check out your thighs. Aren't they still shortening and coming up towards your torso? Again if you're not sure, release that pattern. Go back to what is normal for you, and then repeat the exercise. Let the contrast show you what each of these patterns does for you.

Pushing down may flatten your back, but it isn't going to help you develop a secure seat. And if you're pushing down, what's happening to your horse's back? At first it may come up. Horses tend to push into pressure, but you're not making it easy for him. Think about it. You're asking him to lift up against someone who is pushing down. Gravity is

> **MECHANICS**
>
> Being "on the bit" is more than just a matter of looking pretty. For a rider this is the most stable position she can be in. You can easily test how you're sitting by asking a friend to try to pull you out of the saddle.
>
> The rider has deliberately arched her back so she's "above the bit".
>
> With her back in this position, her partner can easily pull her forward out of the saddle. If her horse were to pull suddenly on the reins, she'd pop forward just like this.

working in your favor, not his. It's no wonder many horses develop sore muscles from riding. Once your horse's back is sore, he's going to be reluctant to engage. Instead of rounding up, he's going to hollow his back away from you. Here's a scary suggestion. Take a look at your horse's back after you've ridden. He'll tell you how you've been using your seat.

So the real answer to the question of how to develop a secure seat isn't pushing down but rotating your pelvis as I described earlier: in other words, do a pelvic tilt.

The Click That Teaches: Riding With The Clicker

MECHANICS

Structure does matter. Real power comes from the alignment of your bones. Without that you have to depend upon your muscles to keep you in the saddle.

Backstroking as though she's swimming helps this rider to realign her bones. (See Ch. 23: Swimming, Flying, and Flexibility, pg. 143.)

Note the change in her back. Compare this to the photos on the previous page.

Here's the test: with her pelvis rotated, she's more "on the bit". When her partner pulls on her, she stays solidly in the saddle.

CENTERING AND GROUNDING

When you do a pelvic tilt, you'll feel your thighs lengthen and draw away from your pelvis. You'll feel your hips open and lift. This is the basis for a secure, grounded seat. You may also feel your shoulders relax, and the back of your neck lengthen, all from the rotation of your hips. These are linked responses that you can make stronger by noticing them.

When we talk about being "on the bit", whether it's a horse or a human, it's easy to get distracted by head position. This exercise shows you that it's the rotation of the pelvis that's important. That's really what it means when people talk about riding a horse from "back to front", instead of vice-versa. It's easy to get a horse to arch its neck, but unless the hindquarters also engage to lift the back and release the topline, the horse won't truly be on the bit.

Having a horse go on the bit not only makes him look pretty, it gives the rider more control and softer gaits to ride. You'll be able to hear the difference. Horses who are out of balance will sound heavy. "Thundering hooves" describes them well. Horses that are on the bit float over the ground. You'll barely hear them. Think about the difference that makes to the concussion their joints experience.

It makes sense that we should want our horses to carry themselves well, but why should we be concerned about our own posture? The next time you're riding, try this little experiment. You'll need a friend to help you. At the halt, hollow your back. Now have your friend pull on your hand. She won't need much strength to pop you right out of the saddle.

That's what your horse does to you when he jerks on the reins and you fly forward. In anticipation of that happening, you may stiffen up even more, but that only makes it easier for your horse to pop you out of the saddle. (See the photos on page 109.)

Change the rotation of your pelvis so your hips open and your thighs lengthen, just as they did when you were lying on the floor. Now have your friend pull on your hand. What happens? Isn't that amazing! She can't pull you forward anymore. You'll feel as though you're rooted in the saddle. Now if your horse pulls on you, you won't go flying forward. And you won't be pulling back either, trying to use the reins like a set of handlebars to steady yourself in the saddle. You can be as steady and stable as a post rooted in the ground. That's exactly what you need for single-rein riding.

When a horse picks up speed, it's normal for the rider to be thrown backwards against the motion of the horse. Tie a "crash dummy" to a horse's back, and you'll see this in action. The dummy's shoulders will be thrown back, and you'll see it assume an all too familiar posture.

If you ride like this, you can't let go. You're dependent on the reins for your balance. Mary Wanless refers to this as the horse becoming a motorboat for a rider who has turned into a water skier. Neither one can let go of the other without losing their balance. That's a bad deal for both of them. As you'll see in the next chapter single-rein riding breaks this cycle and teaches riders how to have an independent, balanced seat.

CHAPTER 19
The Boxer versus the Brain Surgeon:
Learning The Mechanics of Single-Rein Riding

In this chapter I'll be defining lateral flexions. I'll show you how they evolve out of a simple softening of the jaw, and how they relate to the engagement needed for upper-level performance. Then I'll take you through the nuts and bolts details of how to ride with a single rein.

LATERAL FLEXIONS

"All right! All right!" you're exclaiming. "Enough already. You've convinced me. Having my horse on the bit is a good thing. But how do I get him there?"

You begin by getting him to bend to the side. Remember our "two-by-four"? We have to take that out of the horse. Did you ever put together any wooden models as a child? Maybe you were building an airplane out of balsa wood. Do you remember how you had to soak the wood to soften it? Once it was soft, you could bend it easily without snapping it.

A horse can be straight and stiff, or straight and soft. How do you transform the first horse into the later?—Through lateral flexions. You get the horse to bend to the left and to bend to the right, then you combine the two to create straight, soft and engaged. Sound simple? It is, but sometimes the simplest ideas need the most explaining, so here goes:

When you're asking your horse to jump, or to head down a trail, or any other performance-oriented task, you want his nose lined up with his tail. In other words, the performance zone of the horse lines his body up on a straight twelve-to-six-o'clock line. The problem with this, as you saw in the previous chapter is that with his body lined up in a straight line, your horse can easily become very stiff. If you draw back on both reins, instead of using muscles to resist you, he can line up his skeleton to brace against your pull. The mechanical advantage is all his.

To resolve this you're going to get him to bend. A stiff horse will first lock his jaw and resist any suggestion to soften. When he finally does bend, he may keep his jaw locked and simply bend his neck to the side. This first-approximation lateral bend will help you out at first. With a bend in his neck you can use your inside rein to leverage his hind end into a tight turn to create an emergency one-rein stop. That's good news if your horse has the tendency to bolt into the next county. The problem is that a little neck bend will very quickly turn into too much. The horse will overflex. He'll lean down onto his inside shoulder and bend his nose around to the rider's knee. Instead of creating a balanced horse, this kind of flexion just strips the control of the feet away from the rider.

The solution is to straighten out the horse's neck and begin again, this time making sure that the horse releases his jaw and the rest of his body in a set sequence. The result will be a correct bend that engages his entire body. In this case a lateral flexion means the horse steps deeply up under his body with his inside hind leg. His abdominal muscles are working to lift his back. As he steps under from behind, the upward release of his stifle joint is exactly

LATERAL FLEXIONS

From stiff...

... to soft via lateral flexions. (Refer back to the photo on page 105.)

The Click That Teaches: Riding With The Clicker

in time with a softening of his jaw and poll. This allows the long muscle of his neck to relax creating a slight bend. His shoulders and hips line up like a well-formed drill team to match the curve so his entire body feels level and balanced.

As the work progresses the engagement of the hind end and the release of the jaw and poll will result in a softening of the base of his neck. This will allow him to lift his withers and elevate his poll. His shoulders will become very light and mobile. At this point you have created the engagement needed for advanced collection. Your single-rein riding has done its job, and it's time to move from lateral flexions back to straightness, only now your horse will be soft, incredibly responsive and a true joy to ride. That's the process in a nutshell. It will just take the rest of the book to show you how to achieve it.

LINING UP THE DRILL TEAM

Take a look at the figures in the side panel and the opposite page. The clock shows the working zones for lateral flexions. The horse's nose should stay between 12 and 9 o'clock on the left and 12 and 3 o'clock on the right. When a horse is engaged and looking straight ahead he is working in the "performance zone". This is where we want to end up on our schooled horses, but to get there we have to flex them to the side.

Now divide the clock into zones that line up with the clock lines:

In Zone 1 (between 11 and 12) the horse's head is bent slightly to the side. This is the zone where it is easiest to teach your horse to soften his jaw in preparation for a lateral flexion.

Zone 2 is between 10 and 11 o'clock. Here the horse softens the long muscle of his neck in response to the rein.

In Zone 3 between 9 and 10 o'clock the horse learns to lift from the base of his neck. This in turn lifts his withers and elevates his poll into the lovely arc we so admire in top performance horses.

In Zone 4 the horse has bent past 9 o'clock. He's taken his nose too far to the side. Instead of lifting he's now leaning down onto his inside shoulder. This zone can be used to get an emergency one rein stop, but it does not lead to engagement.

Leaning is easier than lifting, so most horses will experiment with this option before they discover how good it feels to engage. When a horse becomes over-bent, the rider needs to lift the rein up so it presses against the horse's neck. The pressure of the rein will encourage the horse to straighten out his neck. This acts like a "reset button". It's like pressing the rewind button on a VCR. You are in essence saying to the horse: "Bending your neck so far around was not the answer I was looking for. Straighten out and try again." If the horse over-flexes a second time, you'll use the "reset button" again. You'll repeat this pattern until the horse stabilizes in the zone you're working in. In this manner you'll build lateral flexions that create great balance and soundness in your horse.

An easy way to create these lateral flexions is to activate just one rein at a time. It's a little like riding in a halter and a lead rope: but you still have access to both reins should you need them. Why a single rein? When you pick up both reins, your horse can stiffen into them. Throw one away and the remaining rein will bend the horse.

On a very stiff horse, you may not see the horse bend right away. He may be so used to pulling that he just throws his nose up in the air and resists. That's perfect. With only one rein opposing him, he can't line up his skeleton. He has to use his muscles to resist, and that means he's going to get tired. Eventually he's going to have to let go, and that in turn gives you a chance to establish (*go to pg. 114.*)

TEACHING ZONES

Imagine you are looking down at your horse from above. If he's looking straight ahead, the line his crest forms would point to twelve o'clock. Now imagine a second, horizontal 9 to 3 o'clock line that intersects with this first line at the base of his neck. The two lines form a right angle triangle. This is the zone you want your horse to work in.

The clock shows the working zone for lateral flexions. The horse's nose should stay between 12 to 9 o'clock on the left, or 12 to 3 o'clock on the right.

Chapter Nineteen: The Boxer Versus The Brain Surgeon

THE WORKING ZONES OF THE HORSE

Straight is your goal, but not straight and stiff. To get to the goal of straight, soft, and engaged, you'll first use lateral flexions. You're going to end up back at 12 o'clock, but you'll get there by first teaching your horse to flex laterally. The key to the success of this exercise is to teach your horse to lift from the base of his neck, by working in zones 1-3, rather than leaning down through his shoulders in zone 4.

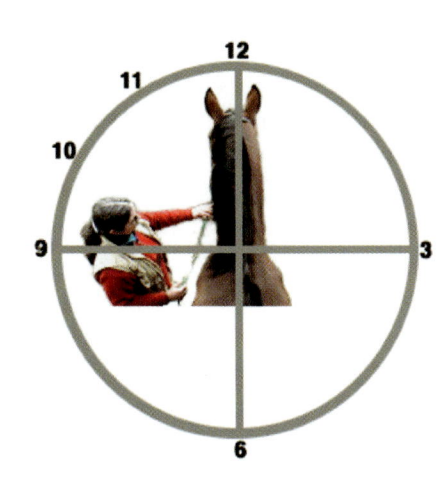

Zone 1: Between 11 and 12. This is the zone where it is easiest to teach your horse to soften his jaw in preparation for a lateral flexion.

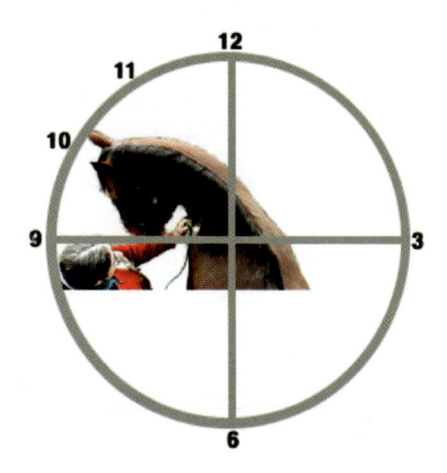

Zone 3: Between 9 and 10. This is the zone where you teach your horse how to lift from the base of his neck. This in turn lifts his withers and elevates his poll into the lovely arc we so admire in top performance horses.

Zone 2: Between 10 and 11. This is the zone where you teach your horse to soften and yield the long muscle of his neck.

Zone 4: Past 9 o'clock. Here the horse has gone too far and instead of lifting will be leaning. This zone is good for teaching emergency stops, but not engagement.

The Zones of the Horse: Showing the working zones for teaching engagement.★

★ Reprinted from: *The Click That Teaches: A Step-By-Step Guide in Pictures,* by Alexandra Kurland; The Clicker Center, NY

113

The Click That Teaches: Riding With The Clicker

THE HORSE'S RESPONSE TO PRESSURE

There are three ways that a horse can respond to a rein. He can: resist against it; passively it follow; or actively give to it.

1.) This rider was demonstrating some poor riding techniques for the camera. Her horse responded by resisting against the rein. Note the tension in both of them.

2.) The rider has pulled her horse's head around to her knee. Her horse has followed the take of the rein. He's flexing, but note the twist in his neck. He's been pulled out of balance.

3.) Here the rider has taken the slack out of the rein, but she doesn't pull her horse's head to the side. 4.) Instead she waits for him to move his own head to put the slack back into the rein. Note: he's bending without twisting as he steps up into a lateral flexion (Ch. 26).

Even though he's shown here demonstrating what not to do, this Connemara cross is one of our clicker superstars. Gelded late, Lucky used to be an aggressive, dangerous horse to ride. Single-rein riding gave his rider more than just the control she needed to be safe. Perfected the same lessons turned him into a stunningly beautiful horse.

that you will let go of him. You're going to say to him, "If you give me what I want, a soft rein, I'll give you what you want, my hand out of your mouth."

That's a bargain your horse will eventually be all too willing to agree to. But first he may have to go through a process of resisting your hand. Other people have taken hold of him, and they haven't let go. He doesn't yet know that you're not just like them.

FOLLOWING VERSUS GIVING

There are three ways that a horse can respond to a rein: he can resist against it; he can follow it passively; or he can give to it. Obviously we don't want the first choice, but what about the other two? Basically, these are two very different responses, and we want the horse to learn to do both.

When a horse follows the rein, he's following a suggestion. Suppose you pick up your left rein and draw your hand down to your knee. If your horse answers by bending his head around to the side, he's following the feel of the rein. He's learned to go where you take him. Teaching him to follow that kind of feel is an easy way to ride and a good beginning place.

Getting your horse to "give" requires another level of learning on both your parts. To teach your horse to give, you take the slack out of the rein and then you stabilize your hand. You pretend you're a post. You don't pull him to the side the way you did when you moved your hand to your knee. Your goal is not to move your horse's head. You want to put only enough pressure on the corner of his mouth so that he knows you're there, but not so much that you pull him to you.

This is an important distinction and one that relates back to the previous chapter's discussion about soundness. Following may give you control, but it does not necessarily create good balance. (Refer to the side panel.)

When your horse gives to you, what you have given to him is the time he needs to find his own balance. It's up to your horse to figure out what you want. At first he may simply ignore you. He feels your hand on the rein, but he'll try to wait you out. He'll lean against the rein. When that doesn't work, he'll walk in small circles like a dog chasing it's tail.

Remember our discussion of *where* versus *how*? (Ch. 16) Don't worry about where he goes. Just focus on keeping a steady feel on the rein. Remember, if your horse does anything long enough, eventually he'll want to change. Patient trainers know that once the horse moves away from the behavior he's stuck in, you can begin to shape him towards the desired goal.

Chapter Nineteen: The Boxer Versus The Brain Surgeon

SINGLE-REIN RIDING

This rider is asking for a simple softening of the jaw. 1.) She begins by picking up the buckle with her left hand and sliding down the inside rein with her right. 2.) As she takes the slack out by stabilizing her inside hand against the front of the saddle, her horse at first responds by cocking his ear back to her. She has his attention. Note the rotation of her arm. This lets her lock the rein into a very stable position as she waits patiently for her horse to give to her. She's aligning her bones and letting them do the work instead of relying on muscle to keep her hand still. Sliding down the rein helps her find this powerful rotation that includes her shoulder and helps anchor her seat in the saddle. 3.) Her horse has moved his own head in response to the pressure. Click! To complete the sequence, she'll release the rein and touch down to his neck with her buckle hand.

BE WARY OF SHORTCUTS

Most traditional training methods are really designed to circumvent the waiting period. We get impatient, so we put stronger bits on the horse or we bring out our martingales. We use whips and spurs to try to provoke reactions instead of waiting for them to happen.

Shortcuts can be great. When I drive, I have a few favorite shortcuts that always work for me. I've also encountered some so-called shortcuts that have taken me miles out of my way. Some have even run into dead ends or have taken me over dangerous roads.

A horse who's turned into a two-by-four has had one too many shortcuts used on him. You need to go back and redo his training in a slow, methodical way.

You're going to be patient with your horse and wait for him to respond. You're not going to try to provoke reactions by dragging his head around to the side. You don't need to. You know eventually he'll get tired of resisting. Armed with that knowledge you can outlast him.

When your horse gets tired of wandering around on a small circle, maybe he'll start to pull on the rein again to see if he can force you to let go. You'll just stabilize your hand against the saddle, matching whatever pressure he puts on you, but not pulling. Pulling only gets you into a tug-of-war. Keep your hand steady. If he thinks that no matter how hard he pulls he can't jerk the rein away, he'll quit trying. He'll either go back to ignoring you—until he remembers that didn't get him anywhere, or he'll try something very unnatural—he'll give to the pressure. He'll move his head around to the side. Bingo! The instant he does, you're going to let go of the rein. Does he know what he just did? Probably not. Maybe he gave because at that moment he was facing away from the barn, and he wanted to turn his head to see who was coming out the door. That's the real reason he moved his nose. He wasn't thinking about you at all, but that doesn't matter. Pick up the rein again, take the slack out, and repeat the whole thing. When you've done this five or six thousand times, he'll know what you want.

Five or six thousand times! That sounds like work! That sounds boring.

Actually, it's anything but. You're going to see some truly amazing changes in your horse as you go through this process. It won't be long before you'll be wondering why anyone would ever ride on two reins! You're going to feel your horse responding to you the instant you pick up the rein. His jaw is going to soften, his neck is going to relax. You'll begin to feel his back come up, and his hocks come underneath him. He's going to bend and turn easily. In fact, you'll probably go through a stage where that's all he'll do. You'll get the most gorgeous circles you've ever ridden, but you may not be able to walk a straight line any more!

Don't worry about that. Straight will come back as you connect up both sides of your horse to this system. In the meantime just enjoy how light your horse feels now that you have him flexing. As his head and neck soften, you'll be able to connect up his feet. It's as though you're untangling a marionette. A stiff horse is like a puppet with its strings all tied up in knots. Pull on a string, and nothing happens. But, once you start sorting them out, you can pick up a string, and the puppet will

115

The Click That Teaches: Riding With The Clicker

DUCT TAPE POINTS

The "Duct Tape" Markers*: Each spot marks a particular direction you would like your horse to move. By focusing on individual spots instead of the whole horse, the handler becomes clearer and more consistent in her requests.

Jaw: moves left and right for softness.

Poll: down for calmness.

Chest: back for respect of space.

Withers: to the left or right away from the handler. The withers move the shoulders over into lateral steps.

Upper hip spot: to the left or right away from the handler: "disengages" the hind end to prepare for lateral work.

Lower hip spot: "go forward" cue spot.

Each "duct tape" marker can move: up and down, left and right, forward and back. For example, my "three-headed" Robin is illustrating the different directions his head can move. Change one of these directions and you change the entire look of the horse.

lift the corresponding foot. That's what it's going to feel like with your horse. You'll pick up the rein, and his feet will move in the direction you intended. He won't be locking you out with a stiff neck and shoulder.

TALKING DOWN THE REIN

Picking up the rein and holding onto it gives me a way of saying to the horse, "I want something."

That's all the rein is saying. And it's one of only two messages I need to send to create a totally responsive horse. I'm not saying slow down, or turn, or back up. I'm just saying: "I want something." I'm not hauling on the rein to get my horse to stop; I'm not pulling it to the side to get him to turn; and I'm certainly not jerking on it to punish him. I want my horse to trust my hands, so I never want to send harsh messages down the rein. I'm simply taking a hold of it so my horse feels pressure.

It's up to my horse to figure out the rest. He does this by learning to ask a series of questions. Remember our discussion about communication? (See Ch. 17.) It's up to my horse to notice that I'm there, and to respond by softening to pressure.

Picture the following: I've picked up the left rein in anticipation of my horse bending smoothly around my left leg. I want him to soften his left side in order to line his nose up on the arc of a correct bend. Right now he's got his nose tipped too far in the opposite direction. I'm going to take the slack out of the rein so he can feel pressure on the corner of his mouth, but I'm not going to pull him to the side.

If he resists me with ten pounds of pressure, I'll match his ten pounds, but I won't add any more beyond that. I don't want to drag him to the left. I want him to learn to bring his own head around. That means that I'm going to stabilize my hand on the saddle so I know I'm not pulling on him. I'm going to wait until he gives to me.

If he ignores me completely, I can add more pressure to the rein, but I never want to add so much that I pull his head toward me. As soon as I feel him soften to the rein, I'm going to release it, and that means I'm going to open my hand and COMPLETELY let go.

Now my rein has said the second thing I need to say to create a totally responsive horse: "That's right." With those two pieces of information: "I want something" and "That's right" I can shape any behavior I want.

UNTANGLING THE STRINGS

If you had a badly tangled marionette, you wouldn't try to unknot all the strings at once. You'd pick one string at a time to free up. We're going to do the same thing with the horse. To understand this better, let's look at one element of the total picture of putting a horse on the bit: head position.

A horse has six possible directions he can move his head (or any other part of his body). We can divide

★ Photo reprinted from: *The Click That Teaches: A Step-By-Step Guide in Pictures,* by Alexandra Kurland; The Clicker Center, NY

Chapter Nineteen: The Boxer Versus The Brain Surgeon

PICKING UP THE SINGLE REIN

There are many different techniques for picking up a single-rein. These riders are illustrating two methods that are similar in many ways, but they use very different images to describe them. Both work, but they create a very different response in their horses. (See text.)

1.-3.) This rider is using the image of a knife to help her find the right position for the rein. To bring her horse's head to the side she reaches for the rein as though she were picking up a butcher knife. She "stabs" herself in the thigh. Then she pulls the "knife" out and "stabs" herself in the abdomen to ask his hips to yield to the side. If her horse did not respond to this degree of pressure, she would pull the "knife" out again and "stab" herself in her opposite shoulder. Mechanically this image works. It will rotate your arm giving you tremendous leverage. However, it's just not a match with the spirit of clicker training. I prefer a different image.

4.-5.) In the second series, the rider brings her arm up as though she were cradling a kitten. This also produces the desired rotation of her arm, but it keeps her body softer and produces a softer, more balanced response in her horse. However, it is useful to experience the "knife" image to understand how much power you can produce with the leverage should it be needed.

these into three sets:
- to the right or left,
- up or down,
- in toward his chest or out away from his body.

Think of it as though you're determining the position of a star ship. Define these three sets of coordinates, and you've identified the location of the ship. On a trained horse I want to be able to set each one of these parameters. Change any one, and I change the entire look and feel of the horse.

The principles of good training remind us to train one criterion at a time. Your horse will tell you which direction you need to focus on first. If his nose is up in the rafters, head lowering is going to be your starting point (see Ch. 20). If he's shuffling along with his nose to the ground, tripping over his own front feet, *up* would be a good direction to begin with. And if he's traveling with his nose cranked to the outside, you might want to start with left and right.

PICKING UP A SINGLE REIN

Okay, all this makes sense, but how does it work? How do you pick up a single rein? I learned single-rein riding from John Lyons. At the first clinic I attended he instructed the riders to pick up the inside rein, bring our hand to the saddle, and then draw the rein through our anchored hand with our free hand as though we were scraping mud off a garden hose. That works, but since that early presentation, Lyons has refined his technique and the images he uses to describe it many times. The one constant that remains is the importance of stabilizing the inside hand. He stresses this over and over again throughout all of his teaching.

Pat Parelli is another advocate of single-rein riding, and he has a simple image that works well. You hold the center of the reins in one hand (where the buckle would be on a set of English reins). You reach forward with your other hand and take a hold of the rein as though you were grabbing a butcher's knife. Then you bring your hand to your leg as though you were stabbing your thigh. To disengage your horse's hips through a tight turn you pull the knife out of your thigh and stab it into your navel.

Mechanically this works, but this image just isn't a match for me. I like the function of it, but I just can't go around all day advising my clients to stab themselves, even if it is just a visualization!

When I have them flip their horses' hips around in a tight turn, I tell them to bring their hand up to their body as though they were cradling a kitten. This keeps the wrist soft even on a horse who is pulling hard. (See the photos on pg. 117.)

The important thing to remember with all of these images is what it is you are trying to do:

1.) *Become a tortoise.*

You want to pick the rein up slowly. You don't want to grab it, and you never want to jerk on your horse's mouth. Remember, you only want to send positive messages down that rein. You are **never** going to use it to manhandle or punish your horse—ever. Picking the rein up slowly gives your horse time to soften and respond even before you've anchored your hand. That's really what you're after. You want your horse to be so light that he's responding to you even before you've touched the rein. He feels you start to reach for the rein, and he's already organizing his body.

It's easy to rush through this step on badly trained horses. They aren't soft. Their first response to the rein is to stiffen and stick their heads up in the air. The idea that someday they're going to respond easily to the lightest touch of the rein is so different from what they're doing now that you can't even imagine it. They almost force you to grab the rein because they're pulling back so hard on you. But if you fall into that trap with your horse, you'll never give him a chance to be truly soft. Slow and steady are certainly good principles to apply here.

2.) *Learn to be a telephone pole.*

You want to bring the hand holding the rein to a stable reference point. If it's up in the air, you could be pulling back on your horse and you wouldn't even know it. You need to anchor your hand down on the saddle. That way you'll know it's not moving. Anchoring doesn't mean you have to lock it down in a death grip. If your horse is only resisting with half a pound of pressure, you can rest your hand lightly on the saddle with a soft, relaxed wrist. (See side panel.)

If your horse pulls on the rein with forty pounds of pressure, you may need to do more than simply rest your hand on the saddle. You may need to cup your other hand over it to keep the rein from being dragged forward. On a committed puller, one who has really learned how to use his whole topline to unseat the rider, I'll anchor my hands on either side of the pommel. That way the horse ends up pulling on the saddle instead of on me. With a Western saddle you can anchor your hand behind the horn to give you the same leverage.

Why is anchoring the hand so important? Why do you need to have a reference point even on a light horse? If your hand is moving even a little, your horse will go on trying to tug the reins away from you. You need to be like a post. He has to believe that the rein is anchored fast to something as solid as a telephone pole. No matter how hard he tries, he's not going to be able to pull away. If your hand

YOUR HAND IS A POST

If your inside hand is up in the air, you have no stable reference points. You could be pulling back on your horse and not even know it.

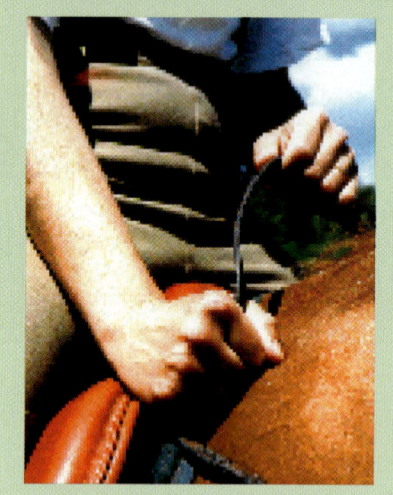

1.) This rider is using the saddle as a reference point. Note how she has closed all her fingers around the rein, including her little finger. As a test, I'm pulling hard on the rein, but her hand is not moving. It acts like a solid post. This is what she wants her horse to believe the rein is attached to.

As her "horse" gets lighter and stops pulling, she'll soften her wrist. Instead of anchoring her hand flat against his neck, she'll rotate her wrist so just her little finger rests against the saddle.

2.) If your horse is pulling so hard that you can't keep your hand steady, try cupping one hand over the other. Locking your hand over your little finger makes it hard for your horse to pull the rein away.

Chapter Nineteen: The Boxer Versus The Brain Surgeon

bounces around, he's going to go on resisting. If your horse continues to pull on a single rein, it's because you aren't anchoring your hand.

3.) Be a brain surgeon instead of a boxer.

The third thing you want to think about is the difference between gross motor control and fine motor control. What this comes down to is how you want to ride your horse—like a boxer with gross motor control, or like a brain surgeon fine motor control? If you've made it this far into the book, you already know what I would answer, and it doesn't involve putting on padded gloves.

It's easy to get heavy-handed with a horse that pulls. You have to anchor your hand so much that it's hard not to make a tight fist. To stabilize the rein you may have already gotten into the habit of locking your hand down on the saddle. The problem with this is it creates a broken line in your arm. Your wrist will bend at a right angle to your elbow, making your whole arm tight, and this in turn affects your whole posture. (See side panel.) That may get you through the first few steps of lightening up a horse, but eventually it's going to limit the quality of your riding.

Gross motor skills:

When you grab the rein with your whole hand, you end up using gross motor control, which tightens up your whole body.

Practice makes perfect: Here's an exercise that doesn't involve your horse that will help you develop fine motor control:

Set your saddle on a sturdy saddle rack. If you don't have one, a wooden sawhorse will do. Use thick saddle pads to widen it out, and to protect the underside of your saddle. Now sit in your saddle. Have a friend hold the bridle for you, or you could just hang it in front of you on a doorknob. You'll do this exercise both to the left and to the right, but I'll describe it for just the right side.

The first question is what length of rein do you want? Rein length tells the horse what balance you want him in. Pick up a long rein, and he can stretch his topline way out; shorten the rein, and he has to engage more.

Either way, you want to be able to pick up the rein so that when you bring your hand to the saddle you've taken all the slack out. The tension on the rein is your motivator.

The pressure your horse feels on the corner of his mouth is the reason he's going to respond to you. You don't want to take so much rein that you end up pulling his head around to the side. Nor do you want to leave the rein so loose that he forgets you're there.

Let's imagine that to do this on "Trigger", our saddle-rack horse, you're going to reach down to pick up the right rein about ten inches from the midpoint or buckle of the reins. Try that. You can do it just sitting in a chair by reaching forward to pick up an imaginary rein. But you'll find that when you reach down that far, your shoulders come forward.

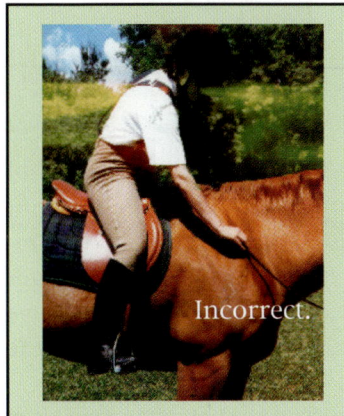

Incorrect rein pick–up:

If you reach too far forward to pick up the rein, your shoulders will come forward and pop you out of the saddle.

That isn't safe, so instead you're going to use your free left hand to help out your right. Hold the center buckle of the reins in your left hand and lift it straight up off the saddle. This will bring the reins closer to your right hand, so now you can easily reach eight inches down from the buckle without leaning forward.

Correct rein pick–up:

Use your free, outside hand to help you pick up the rein. Lift the rein up at the buckle with your free hand. This will keep your seat in the saddle. Now you can easily reach the length rein you want without popping forward out of the saddle. You're going to use fine motor control to pick up the rein.

119

The Click That Teaches: Riding With The Clicker

FINE MOTOR–CONTROL SKILLS

Pick up the reins as if you were picking up a flute. Begin with just your thumb and index finger. Finger by finger cover up each of the "air" holes.

From this position you can close your hand lightly around the rein, and rotate your arm so your hand rests lightly, but solidly against the saddle.

Take a hold of the rein with just your thumb and index finger. Pretend you're holding a flute and put your other fingers over imaginary air holes one finger after the other. Then hold the rein in your finger tips and feel how easily and lightly you can move your wrist around. What you're experiencing is the feel of a light horse.

You don't even need reins to experience this. Just imagine yourself picking them up. Bring your thumb and index finger together as though you're catching hold of a feather, then finger by finger pick up your flute. It's a lovely feeling. Wouldn't it be wonderful if your horse were that light? He can be with a little practice. Once you have the rein on your finger tips, you can roll your fingers around so you'll be holding it loosely in your whole hand.

In her book *Centered Riding*★, Sally Swift uses the image of holding a little bird in your hand. Your hand is closed around the rein, but it's held lightly, just as you might hold a bird softly in your hand without either crushing it or letting it go.

If your horse pulls hard, you can always close your hand on the rein, but you also have the option of staying light. In both cases you'll have a smooth line from your wrist to your elbow, which in turn will open both your shoulders and your hips. You'll be anchored in your seat and soft in your body.

Most of my clients have ridden "Trigger" at one time or another. It's a great opportunity to work on position. One thing I almost always zero in on is the angle of their wrists. Most people tend to have a broken line at the wrist. This in turn pinches their elbows to their sides. Try it yourself. Hold your hand so you have a slight backward bend to your wrist and feel the pressure of your elbows against your sides. Now ease your wrist into a slight curve, and you'll feel that tension from your elbows ease.

It took me a long time to recognize what I was seeing and to come up with the remedy for it. What I was looking at were right-handed people. They needed to learn how to let their wrists curve gracefully upward into a soft release the way a left-handed person would. (And from this paragraph I bet you can tell which hand I write with!)

Remember when we talked about the rotation of your pelvis (Ch. 18). When you hollowed your back and got tight, your friend could jerk you out of the saddle. When you rotated your pelvis so your hip joint opened, even if she pulled hard, you stayed anchored in the saddle.

When you make a hard fist like a boxer, you aren't grounded, either. You have to try to hold the rein steady with your arm muscles. As you learn to use fine motor control, your whole body will become part of the structure that anchors your hand. That means you can stay soft and relaxed even when your horse is pulling hard.

4. Pick the rein up slowly, but pick it up completely.
When you pick the rein up lightly, you still want to pick it up completely. Think of it like shaking hands with someone. A good firm hand shake feels great. A mushy, barely-wants-to-touch-you hand shake feels terrible. It's a horrible sensation, and one you don't want to give your horse. Light does not mean absent. Pick up the rein slowly, but pick it up completely.

Put ALL your fingers around the rein, and yes, that even means your little finger. When you leave it off the rein, your horse can still pull the rein forward. Put your little finger all the way around the rein. It will stabilize your entire wrist.

You can test this for yourself. Pick up your rein as I've described, but leave your little finger off the rein. Now have a friend pull on the rein. She'll probably pop you right out of the saddle!

Now pick up the rein, this time completing the process by wrapping your little finger around the rein. Note how this rotates your wrist. Now have your friend pull on the rein. You'll probably find that you're rooted to the saddle! Big difference. You're working less and you're a lot more solid. Why? The rotation of your wrist didn't just end there. Note the difference in the position of your elbow; the

★ *Centered Riding,* by Sally Swift; Trafalgar Square, VT

Chapter Nineteen: The Boxer Versus The Brain Surgeon

SLIDE TO YOUR POINT OF CONTACT

Remember all the steps in this process. Each one is important and will create a more responsive horse. Train the details in well at the beginning to get great results later.

1.) Pick up the buckle. This tells your horse to get ready, you are about to ask for something. It connects your hand to his hips.

2.) Bring your inside hand up to the "buckle".

3.) Slide your hand down to take the slack out of the rein.

Note this is an experienced rider. She has learned how to stabilize her hand so she no longer needs the reference point of the saddle. As soon as her horse softens to the rein, she'll release the rein with her left hand and touch down to her horse's neck with her right.

openness of your shoulder. Feel how that connects you into your hip. All that just from remembering to include your little finger on the rein!

What I see very often are riders who hesitate. They pick up the rein and, part way to their anchor point, they hover in uncertainty. It's almost as though they're waiting for the horse to tell them what to do next. These riders need to take charge. If your horse responds before you can get your hand to the saddle, that's great. By all means let go, but otherwise take your hand directly to the saddle.

Once you pick up the rein, make a commitment to it. It's your horse's job to respond to you, so you need to be clear in your directions.

5. Let go.

Your left hand anchors the rein and waits for your horse to respond. When he does, let go. That doesn't mean you take your hand forward and set the rein down. Let go means LET GO. You open your hand and release the rein. That's your horse's instantaneous "yes" answer cue. Think of the children's game "Hot Potato". When the horse gives to you, you want that rein to become like a hot potato. You can't get it out of your hand fast enough.

Letting go is a scary thought for many riders. They feel as though they're dangling over the edge of a cliff, and you just told them to let go of their only safety line. They can't do it. If that's how you feel, if the idea of letting go of your horse sounds insane, and you get a sick feeling in the pit of your stomach just thinking about it, remember, you're going to pick the rein up again. You're going to pick it up the instant after you let go, not three or four strides later, but as soon as it leaves your hand.

Use the saddle rack exercise to practice picking up the reins until you can do it smoothly with either hand. When you can do it without thinking about it, you're ready to ride your horse.

A beautiful moment: this rider is showing excellent form as she asks for her horse to yield her hips. Her lifted, buckle hand is alive with energy. Her inside hand has lifted to the perfect height to connect with her horse's inside hip. She has created a post-like intent even as she is staying soft in her joints.

The Click That Teaches: Riding With The Clicker

GIVING TO THE BIT: A TRAINING SEQUENCE

1.) This teenage rider is doing an excellent job waiting for her horse to soften his jaw. She has her right hand stabilized on the front of her saddle and she's waiting for him to give. Note how her horse has stiffened his whole body against the pressure. His head is up. His back is hollow. This is the reaction to pressure his rider wants to change.

2.) It took a few strides, but her horse has softened to the rein. Compare this to the first photo. Note how round and soft her horse now looks. He's stepping deep under his body with his inside hind leg. He's connecting to his rider. This is the result the rider wants. Her job now is to release the inside rein completely and to touch down to her horse's neck with her lifted buckle hand.

As she repeats this pattern through many repetitions, her horse will get softer and softer to the rein.

3-8.) Here's what part of this sequence looked like. It took a couple of steps and patience on the part of the rider, but her horse found the right answer and softened to her hand. Click and treat.

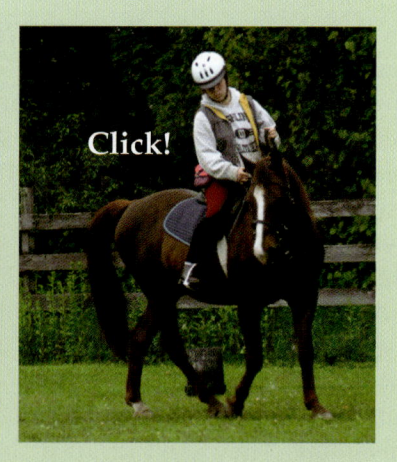

Click!

122

CHAPTER 20
Head Lowering:
Using the "Calm Down" Cue from the Saddle

Okay, you've read through the previous chapters. You understand why softening a horse via lateral flexions is important, and you've practiced the mechanics of single-rein riding. But what do you do with all of this? How is it going to help you ride your horse?

The beauty of single-rein riding is that the lessons that give you safety and control are the same lessons you'll use to create the balance for upper-level performance. The main difference between a green horse and an experienced performance horse is how well each responds to your requests. The green horse is distracted by the "movie" that's going on around him. The performance horse is in the habit of saying "yes" to you. His focus is on you. So how do you get from green to performance horse?

In this chapter I'll describe the head-lowering lesson. Head lowering builds calmness and emotional stability into the foundation of your training. Before you add speed or adrenaline into your training, you want this calm-down "security blanket" solidly in place. And if you're going to ask for collection, you definitely need this lesson. Remember the phrase: for every exercise you teach there is an opposite exercise you must teach to keep things in balance. That's one of the fundamental principles. If you're going to ask your horse to round and shorten his topline, you need to be able to have him stretch and lengthen it as well. The head lowering lesson keeps your horse from compressing his spine, or over-flexing laterally.

SAFETY FIRST

Before I can talk about performance issues, I first have to deal with any safety concerns your horse may present. Let's imagine the following scenario describes your horse. You've just moved to an indoor arena for the winter. Your horse has been great all summer riding out on trails, but here in the arena with all the added activity he's coming unglued. He's forgotten everything you've ever taught him. He's stiff as a post. He spooks at every little noise. He jigs at the trot. He shies off the walls, and to top it off he's started kicking at the other horses. He's even bucked a couple of times, and, when you tried to take him down to the far end, he threatened to rear. Riding on two reins is enough of a challenge. The thought of letting go and riding on one scares you to death. So where do you begin?

The principles of training say safety always comes first. If you don't feel safe riding this horse, then ground work is the answer. The basic training principles (Ch. 5) will give you a starting place for your lessons: *Go to a place in the training where you can ask for something and get a "yes" answer back.* You need to find a simple behavior you can ask for consistently. One of the first things I would want to teach this horse would be to drop his nose to the dirt. Head lowering gives me a "calm-down cue".

Another principle of good training is: *Train where you can, not where you can't.* If you're an experienced rider, you may feel perfectly confident working your horse in the arena. You can ride him

SAFETY FIRST

Safety always comes first. Before you ride out in the open, first make sure you can safely ride in a paddock or small arena.

This beautiful Tennessee Walker used to bolt out on the trail. His rider used the exercises described in these chapters to settle him emotionally and to teach him better balance. For fun she also taught him many tricks, including pushing a beach ball. She used his targeting and trick training skills out on the trail in a game she calls: "Bravery in the Wilderness".

The Click That Teaches: Riding With The Clicker

through the figure–eight pattern described in Chapter 16 to get him settled. Even if he panics and tries to bolt off, you know you can keep things safe and help him through the lesson. If that's the case, that's where you'll begin. But, if you aren't sure you can manage him, you need to find a different, easier starting place. If you and your horse can't handle the commotion of a busy arena, begin where you both can be successful. That may even mean getting off and taking your horse back to his stall or a small paddock for a review of ground work. No step is ever too simple to take. (See Chapters 3 and 8.)

HEAD LOWERING★

Head lowering begins with a review of backing in a square (pg. 38-39). Remember how you displaced your horse's head to the off side to turn his hips? As your horse swings his hips to the inside, he'll have a tendency to drop his head ever so slightly. Click, and release the rein. Backing is hard work, so your horse will very quickly figure out that all he has to do is stand still and drop his head.

You want your horse to be very comfortable with this exercise. It's not enough that he drops his head for an instant or two. You want him to be able to drop his head and leave it down, even when there are distractions. (See Chapters 9 and 14 for duration.)

You also want to duplicate from the ground what your horse will be experiencing once you're up in the saddle. Under saddle you have two things you can do to communicate via your reins. You can put pressure on the rein, and you can release it. The pressure gives your horse a reason to change his behavior, but it's the release that tells him what you want. (See Chapters 17, and 19.) If you add pressure when his head is up, and release it the instant he drops his head, he'll very quickly figure out that down is good.

Even though you're on the ground you'll still be using the mechanics of single–rein riding. (Note: The directions I'll be giving are for the left side. You'll want to repeat this lesson on the right.) Your right hand will act as your lifting buckle hand, helping you to find the right rein length. Your left hand will slide down the rein towards your horse's mouth. As you slide, you'll rotate your arm into the stable "t'ai chi wall" position. (See Chapters 8 and 19.)

Even though you are on the ground, you're "riding" your horse. When you get into the saddle, you aren't going to be able to pull his head down. You want him to respond to an increase in pressure by doing something very unnatural. You want him to drop his head. What would be far more normal would be for him to fling his head up. That's why nervous, panicked horses rear. They respond to the extra pressure they feel by going up. That's the reaction you're going to reverse with this exercise. The first step is finding the right rein length. If you end up with slack between your hands, you won't have the leverage you'll need to handle an anxious or pushy horse. Here's the lesson:

HEAD LOWERING IN-HAND

1.) Practice finding your t'ai chi wall.

Here the handler ended up with too much slack between her hands. On a pushy horse this would not give her the control she needs.

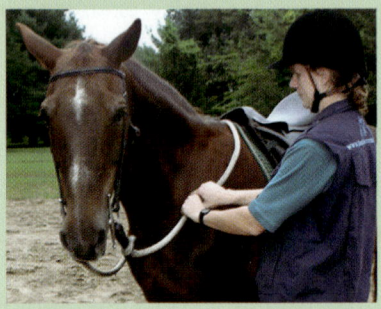

2.) To get the right connection between your hands, begin by putting both hands together on the rein.

Touch the base of your horse's neck with both hands. Treat this as *your* target spot.

3.) Slide your hands apart. Slide your right hand to your horse's withers; your left to the jaw.

It can help to put duct tape markers on these target spots. Note how the rein is lifted up. You aren't trying to pull your horse's head down.

4.) If he walks forward, slide your left hand up the inside rein until it is close to the bit, and at the same time turn to face the point of his shoulder.

★ Refer also to: *The Click That Teaches: Video Lesson 3: Head Lowering: Your Calm–Down Cue*, by Alexandra Kurland; The Clicker center, NY. This two hour video covers in detail the lessons described here.

Chapter Twenty: Head Lowering

The lift of your left hand combined with your body language creates a solid t'ai chi wall. This should get him to take a step or two back. Note: he can back all he wants. The only direction you aren't going to allow in this exercise is forward. Use your "backing in a stall" skills to control his hips so he doesn't get trapped in a corner (Ch. 8).

As long as his head is up, keep a steady contact on your horse's mouth. He may throw his head even further up or try to curl in a circle around you. In this latter case move both your hands up so they rest firmly against his neck. Lifting your hands up will result in a firmer feel on his mouth. To relieve the pressure, he'll straighten out his neck. Do not release yet. Straightening the neck is a good thing, but it's not what you're looking for.

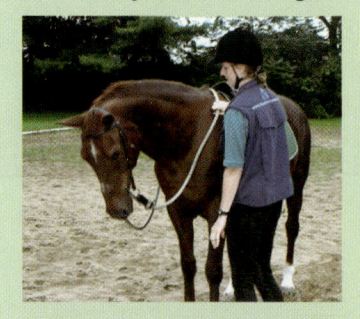

5.) Keep a steady feel on the rein. The instant your horse even *thinks* about dropping his head, release the rein. Click and reinforce him. Repeat steps 2-5.

6.) Your horse may surprise you by dropping his nose all the way to the dirt.

A clear drop of the head is definitely worth a click and a treat. When he's able to drop his head promptly and leave it down for an extended period even in a distracting environment, he's ready to ride.

HEAD LOWERING UNDER SADDLE

At this point, get on your horse and begin working on the behavior from the saddle.

1.) Let him walk a few steps forward, then pick up one rein and take all the slack out. Note how similar this looks to Fig. 4 on the previous page.

Note: your horse will quickly learn that dropping his head is much easier than all that backing. Instead of taking a step back, he'll go straight to the right answer: dropping his head. But remember: head lowering is NOT a forward moving exercise. If he creeps forward at all, you must FIRST ask him to back BEFORE you allow him to drop his head. This is a vital piece. If you let him just plunge his nose to the ground when he feels your hand on the lead, you will not be addressing his pushiness, and you will not get the connection to his hips that this lesson creates. I really should put this entire paragraph in caps, it is that important. So read it, go out to the barn, work with your horse, come back inside and read it again. The more you explore this lesson, the more you will understand the significance of the phrase: head lowering is not a forward-moving lesson.

2.) The lifted inside rein creates a wall. This horse will quickly discover that straightening the neck is a better option than over-flexing or walking forward.

3.) Again, the instant your horse even thinks about dropping his head, release the pressure on the reins.

4.) The result we're after: head lowering to the ground.

See the next page for more detailed instructions.

125

The Click That Teaches: Riding With The Clicker

On the previous two pages you could see the connection between the ground work and riding. Here are more detailed riding instructions that will help you understand this foundation lesson.

To begin the head lowering lesson let your horse walk forward a few steps. Then pick up the buckle with your outside hand as you slide your inside hand down the rein. Keep shortening the inside rein until he yields his hips to the side and stops his feet.

Do not release the rein. The continued pressure says to your horse: "I want something"—something beyond the halt he's given you. Your horse may respond to the pressure in a number of different ways:

1.) He may throw his head up. That's a natural response, especially if your horse is nervous or "green". If up is his response, continue to keep a steady, solid feel on his mouth by lifting the rein. The higher his head goes, the more solid your hand should feel to him — not because you're pulling on him, but because he's pulling on you. Your hand should feel like a post to him (Ch. 19). Up increases pressure. Down releases it, and earns a click and a treat.

2.) Your horse may try to walk forward. Remember this mantra and keep repeating it to yourself: *head lowering is not a forward moving exercise.* Shorten the rein and keep adding pressure until your horse yields his hip and stops his feet. **Do not** release the rein.

At this point your horse's head will be bent around to the side because you had to shorten the rein to get his hips to yield. Lift both your hands up with a steady contact so the rein presses against his neck. Do not try to push his neck over. Instead wait for him to straighten out his own neck and take a step back. You're using the backing in a square skills you taught him on the ground (Ch. 8).

You will not release the rein simply for straightening out the neck. Remember you're looking for head lowering. As your horse straightens out his neck, you'll lower your inside hand back down to it's original position, but now you'll have more pressure on the rein. This pressure was added when he was bending his neck. You had to shorten the rein to keep a steady feel of his mouth. Now that he's straightened out, the shorter rein exerts more pressure on the corner of his mouth. You've just given him more of a reason to change his behavior. He may try to lift his head or walk forward again. As many times as he tries, stay patient and counter each move with your "t'ai chi wall" mechanics. He's learning that bending his neck doesn't work. Nor does going higher. The only option left is dropping his nose down, and yes! that gets you out of his mouth. Down may not be natural, but your horse has just discovered that it

HEAD LOWERING

1.) Something has startled this mare. She's raised her head prepared to spook.

2.) As she encounters the rein, her head goes up even more. Her rider has kept a steady feel on the rein.

3.) To get this horse to stop, the rider had to establish a solid contact on the rein. Her horse is now standing with her neck bent around to the side.

4.) Head lowering is not a forward moving exercise. The continued pressure encourages her horse to straighten out her neck and take a step back. The instant her horse offers to drop her head, her rider will release the rein.

works! Give him a click and a treat.

ELEVATORS AND YO-YOS

You're still a long way from your final goal—having your horse's nose all the way down. Pick up the rein and ask again. Horses lower their heads in stages. Your horse probably won't drop his nose to the ground all in one smooth step, though with your earlier ground preparation he may surprise you.

Most likely your horse will start by dropping his nose an inch or two at a time. At first he'll keep it above the point of his shoulder. Every time he drops his nose, release the rein, then pick it up and ask again. Click and treat the definite drops of his head.

You'll pick up and release, pick up and release, and finally he'll drop his nose past this point. It's a little like bending a coat hanger. Bend it enough and suddenly the wire will be soft enough to break in two. So the key to this exercise is persistence. You don't

Chapter Twenty: Head Lowering

get your horse's head down lower by pulling harder on the rein. You get it to drop lower by asking for head lowering over and over again.

Once your horse is lowering his nose below the point of his shoulder, you're going to change tactics. Instead of picking up the rein as soon as you let go, you're going to wait. A sequence will look like this: you'll pick up the rein and take the slack out; as soon as he drops his head, release the rein; wait.

It's a little like pushing the "down" button on an elevator. Once the elevator is moving, you don't continue to press the button. You let go and the elevator goes down by itself. Except in this elevator you don't know what floor you're going to land on. You might drop only one or two floors, meaning your horse dropped his nose only an inch or two. Or you could drop all the way down to the lobby. That means your horse's nose is now down around his ankles. You don't know which it's going to be when you release that rein, so you have to be patient. At this point, if you pick the rein up again too soon, you'll block his response. He may drop down a couple of inches only, pause, and then drop another foot or more as he releases the tension in his neck and back. When you get a definite drop like this, be sure to mark it with the clicker.

As long as his head is down, leave him alone. Let him just stand there for as long as he likes, but the instant his head **starts** to come up, pick up the rein and ask him to lower his head again. This does not mean that you wait until his head goes all the way back up to its original height before you pick up the rein. It means **as soon as** he begins to lift his head you will begin another sequence. If his nose dropped down to twelve inches from the ground, you'll be back in his mouth at twelve and one quarter inches. The sooner you begin the process of picking up the rein, the faster he will learn what you want. The longer you leave him with his nose up in the air, the longer this lesson will take. This is an exercise in focus for the rider. Learn this concept well here, and all the exercises that follow will be much easier.

Your horse will drop his nose from the point of his shoulder to down around his knees fairly promptly. It's like a big stair step that he's taking. Then he'll plateau off again. You'll pick up the rein and his nose will drop down to knee height, but no lower. You've probably heard of glass ceilings. Well, this is a glass floor. Again the solution is persistence. Keep picking up the rein and asking him to drop his head. Eventually he'll drop his nose consistently below his knees. Click and treat. You'll get another stair step of improvement. He'll drop down around his ankles. Again highlight this with a click and a treat.

At this point your horse is going to resemble an equine yo-yo. His head will drop down, then it will pop right back up. You've already experienced this stage in training when you taught him head lowering in-hand. You understand that he has to get comfortable leaving his head down. Now every time his head pops up, you'll ask him again to lower it. When he hesitates at the bottom, click, you'll reinforce staying down. You'll use the clicker to mark longer and longer duration until he is relaxed and leaving his head down for extended periods.

This is where most people quit with this exercise. It's certainly where I used to stop. My horse's head was down and he felt relaxed, but he was still a critical step away from having learned the "demand cue". I first experienced the difference at a John Lyons clinic. I was riding a client's horse, an Arabian named Whizzy. At that stage in his life, Whizzy was a total wiggle worm. He could twist himself into a pretzel faster than any horse I have ever known. He was also round as a barrel. You had to be a champion log roller to keep the saddle in the middle of his back. If you didn't have good balance, you didn't stay on. Whizzy needed the head lowering exercise

HEAD LOWERING – THE RESULT

5.) An excellent result. Click . . .

6.) . . . and treat.

127

The Click That Teaches: Riding With The Clicker

to straighten out all the kinks and twists he put into his body. He also needed it to straighten out the emotional turmoil these contortions had created.

On the last day of the clinic, Lyons had us spend the afternoon on head lowering. Whizzy was one of the first to drop his nose down to his ankles, but there he plateaued out. This is where I learned the next, critical step of this exercise. To get the nose all the way down to the dirt, you have to change tactics one more time. As the horse begins to raise his head, you're not simply going to take the slack out of the rein. You're going to add extra pressure. The natural response from the horse will be to raise his head even further.

He may take his head all the way up, right back to the rafters where he began. You're going to follow him, adding pressure as he goes up. As soon as he thinks about dropping, release the rein. His nose will drop back down to his ankles. Wait. As soon as his head begins to go up, repeat this process, adding pressure as he goes up.

This process fills in each little stair step of head lowering. Think of our elevator metaphor. When you first started out, the elevator dropped from the twentieth to the tenth floor (from the rafters to the point of your horse's shoulder). It essentially skipped all the floors in between. Then it dropped from the tenth floor to the fifth floor (from the point of his shoulder to his knees), again skipping the floors in between. Finally it dropped from the fifth floor to the lobby—but you're trying to get to the basement.

To get to the basement you have to go all the way back up and begin again. In the process, the elevator is going to stop on each and every floor of your skyscraper. Once it has, you'll be able to get it all the way down to the basement. Once you've completed this whole process, you'll be able to add pressure to the rein and your horse will actively try to pull his head down. This is your "I need you to do this for me now" cue to calm down. The more upset he is, the more pressure you can add, and his head will drop. This is your safety valve. Your horse won't react to pressure by feeling trapped and panicky. Even under extreme distractions he'll drop his nose to the dirt.

As you work through this stage, you'll feel a release through your horse's back that surpasses anything you have ever felt before. You'll feel him relax deeply through his entire body into a calm mental state that goes far beyond the simple act of head lowering. You will also be able to place your horse's head at any height you need for performance. By filling in each stair step from the highest to the lowest elevation, you gain an ability to fine tune his carriage beyond anything you had before.

The "demand cue" is just that: a demand cue. You get to this final result by adding pressure as your horse raises his head. This is one of the very few times in all the exercises that I will be sharing with you that you will do more than just match the pressure your horse gives you. Adding pressure at this stage in the process is what reverses his natural response. At first he'll raise his head up, then he'll drop it down. Once he's made the switch, he'll respond to any extra pressure on the rein by trying to pull his head down.

"Wait!" you may be thinking. "Are you saying you're *teaching* my horse to pull on the rein? That's the opposite of what I want." That's exactly right. You are teaching him to pull, and yes, you do want him to be light. Oddly enough, this is the first step towards achieving that goal.

The pull down is going to give you more than just the demand cue to calm down. It's also going to provide you with the leverage you need to open up the next layer of your horse's training: disengaging the hips. You'll learn about that in the next chapter. For now, if he pulls, know he's right on track. However, if he creeps forward, remind him that head lowering is not a forward moving exercise. Have him take a step back. He'll be trying to drop his head, but stay firm on the rein until he connects with his hips and takes a step back. Only then will you allow him to drop his nose down.

Once your horse understands the exercise at the halt, you're going to ask him to walk and drop his head at the same time. You'll go through all the stages you went through at the halt until he's walking along with his nose dribbling in the dirt. At this point a certain percentage of horses are going to lie down.

Do you remember how I shaped Robin to lie down? I got him to circle with his nose to the ground and after a while he started to think about lying down. That's what may happen now with your horse. He'll be walking along with his nose to the ground and he'll start to think, "Why am I down here? There's no grass to eat in this arena, so why does my person keep insisting that I put my nose down here? I guess she wants me to lie down." And that's what he'll do.

It's okay. You can let him. Horses won't roll all the way over with a saddle on. As your horse goes down, kick your feet out of the stirrups. Watch to see which direction his withers tip. Then, as he sinks to the ground, step off in the direction of the withers. Congratulations! You have just found an easy way to teach your horse to lie down!

Chapter Twenty-One: Flipping The Hips

CHAPTER 21
Flipping the Hips: Power Brakes for Power Steering

Head lowering creates calmness. Now you need to get some brakes. With those two pieces in place you'll be ready to send your horse forward and have some fun. In this chapter I'll show you how you can take the steamroller power out of your horse's hind end. The result will be a mechanical skill that will keep you safe when your horse is having an emotional meltdown. And perfected it will develop into the collection needed for advanced performance.

"GIVING" REVISITED

Head lowering is a good exercise for learning what a "give" is all about because it's very clear that you cannot pull your horse's head down from the saddle. He has to drop it on his own. You can increase your motivator—i.e., pressure on the rein—but ultimately he's the one who's going to move his head, not you. When you're asking your horse to turn to the left or the right, you can certainly use a rein to pull him around to the side, but that's not what a give is.

John Lyons defines a give as: "the body part you are focused on comes alive with energy and moves in the direction you want." Each part of this definition is important. To know whether your horse is giving, you have to know the following.

1.) The body part you want to respond to you. A horse can "give" with any part of his body—his head, his shoulder, the base of his neck, etc.

2.) The direction you want that body part to move. Remember, each spot on the horse's body can move in one of six directions: up/down, left/right, forward/back (Ch. 19: pg. 116). To know whether your horse is pulling or giving, you have to know the direction you want that spot to move. Neutral is not a give. If you pick up the rein and the horse just hangs there on the other end of the rope, that is not what you're after. A give is having the spot you're focused on come alive with energy and move in the direction you want. In the case of head lowering you could focus on his ears. That was the spot, and the direction was down.

A give has a definite feel that you'll learn to recognize as you take your horse through this next exercise and the others in this book.

DISENGAGING THE HINDQUARTERS

A horse's hindquarters can act like a giant steam roller pushing the rest of the horse in front of it. Anyone who has ridden has probably experienced this sensation. Suppose you're sitting on a horse who wants to bolt off. You've got his nose cranked around to your knee. His front end can't go anywhere, but his body is going around in tiny little circles. His back end is "running away" with his front end. It just keeps shoving everything in front of it forward or to the side. So how do you get those haunches to stop? You take the power out of them: you disengage them.

Try a little experiment to understand what this means. Stand square with your feet a comfortable hip's width apart and your arm outstretched to the side. Now have a friend try to knock you over by pushing on your hand. Lock your elbow. That will line up

DISENGAGING THE HIPS

This horse is twisting his nose to the side rather than yielding his hips. If he overflexes much further, his rider will lose control of his hindquarters. To prevent this she needs to use her "t'ai chi wall" mechanics to disengage his inside hip.

The human "equivalent":
(1.) With her legs spread apart our human "horse" (on the right) can easily resist being pushed over by the other person.

(2.) As soon as she crosses her feet, she can easily be knocked over.

The horse "equivalent": disengaging the hips.

129

The Click That Teaches: Riding With The Clicker

your skeleton, so it will take considerable effort on his part to knock you off your feet.

Now cross one leg in front of the other and have him try again. This time it will be easy for him to knock you over. By crossing your legs, you "disengaged your hindquarters". You've made yourself more vulnerable to attack.

As a prey animal, horses do not want to do this. They want to keep their legs squarely under them. When you disengage their haunches by getting their inside hind foot to step across the line of their body, you're taking away their ability to resist pressure. Disengage the hips and you can stop a runaway horse, even out of a full gallop, but this is not something a horse is going to give to you on his own, not without a little added incentive.

A ROCK AND A HARD PLACE

In conventional training the incentive is pressure. In effect the horse is given two choices. He can disengage his hindquarters which makes him feel vulnerable. Or he can endure increasing pressure from the swing of a rope or the crack of a whip. When his fear of the whip exceeds his reluctance to give up his power, he'll step over.

In clicker training we give the horse a different choice. We say to the horse: "I know you don't want to feel vulnerable. I understand that, but I need you to disengage your hips for all the same reasons every other trainer needs it. Disengaging your hips stops bolting. It stops spooking, and bucking, and all the other things that take the fun out of riding. Disengaging your hips gives me brakes, and it opens the door to lateral flexions which are the gateway to collection. So I need you to step over for me. I'm going to use steady pressure to suggest to you what I want, and, when you shift your weight even a little, — click —I'll take the pressure away AND I'll give you a treat. Disengaging the hindquarters will become just another behavior, one you're eager to perform for me."

THE FIRST STEP

You've already disengaged your horse's hip in the head–lowering exercise. When you kept adding pressure to the rein until your horse stopped, you were disengaging his hips. With his feet at a standstill, you taught him to drop his nose to the dirt (pgs. 124-128). Now you're going to put him back in motion. You're going to ask him to walk forward by lifting the buckle of the reins forward and up off his neck while you simultaneously bump him with your legs and add energy to your seat. He should respond to these cues by walking forward.

Let him walk a few steps, then slide your inside hand down the rein, and, *as you do*, turn back to look at his inside hip.

1.) To ask for the hips, slide down and lift the inside rein as you look back at the inside hip. This rider is showing good form. Note how upright she remains in her torso. She has only turned as much as she comfortably can without collapsing through her ribs.

In photo #2 she's leaning down, collapsing through the ribs. She can still get her horse to yield her hips, but the more balanced, upright position is safer and will help her horse find her own good balance faster.

CAROUSEL HORSE

Turn only as much as you comfortably can without distorting your upright position. Think of yourself as a carousel horse with a pole running down your central axis. You want to turn by rotating around this pole, not by twisting or collapsing through your ribs.

Try this experiment. Stand with your feet a hip width apart. Turn first by collapsing and twisting through your rib cage. Next turn by rotating around your carousel horse central pole. Which way did your knees move more? In the carousel horse turn your knees become part of the turn. Which one will be clearer to your horse?—The carousel horse turn.

INTENT

How does your horse know the difference between a request for head lowering versus hip flipping? At first he won't. He'll probably feel confused and frustrated. Remember Robin's early learning stages, how frustrated he got when answers he was sure were right didn't bring reinforcement? (Ch. 12, pg. 63.) This is a normal part of the training process. Your horse will be thinking: "Down worked before. Why isn't it working now? Why does my rider let go of the rein sometimes, but not all the time?" It may take quite a few trials before your horse notices what he is doing with his hips and is able to repeat it deliberately. That's just step one of this process. Next he has to

Chapter Twenty-One: Flipping The Hips

DISENGAGING THE HIPS

This is Tibra, the Icelandic filly featured in *Clicker Training For Your Horse*★. In that first book she was just a foal. Now she's all grown up and learning the fundamentals of riding. Here she's at a clinic, riding in a distracting arena. Her owner has asked her to walk forward on a relaxed, loose rein. Tibra has started to rush forward, so her rider slides down her left rein (1.), lifts her left hand up to create a leverage effect (2.), that swings Tibra's hips around (3.), taking the steam roller energy out of Tibra's hindquarters (4.) and bringing her to a halt 5.). Even though her ribs are twisted down a little too much through the turn (see page 130), this still worked.

to learn the difference between when you are asking for head lowering, and when you want him to disengage his hips. "When you think different, you are different" is the motto for this stage. When you are thinking about head lowering, your body responds in one way. When you want the hips to disengage, your attention changes, and your body feels different to your horse.

FADING SIGNALS
Initially to get your point across to your horse, you'll make the differences in your body position very big and obvious. When you want him to disengage his hip, you'll actually look back at his inside hip. But don't worry, that's not how you're going to ride forevermore. As your horse tunes in to what you want, he'll start responding to less. You'll just begin to turn, and he'll already be stepping under with his inside hind leg. Pretty soon all you have to do is think about his hip, and he'll be responding to you.

This ability to fade a signal is an important concept in training. Once a given signal is learned, the size of that signal can be diminished. As long as the animal can perceive it, he can still understand and respond to it. Think about traffic lights. We all know what the red signal means. You could make the red light quite a bit smaller and we'd still understand its meaning and respond. However, if you made it too small, eventually drivers wouldn't be able to see it in time to stop. The goal in performance training is to create a communication system between the horse and the rider that's as subtle as possible while still being clear. An observer should see the effect of the cues, but not the cues themselves.

Once your horse is responding to your cues to disengage his hips, you can fade them down to meet that goal, but in the beginning you have to make them big and obvious. This answers a question many people have about training on a single rein, and about training in general. They ask: "How can I use this in the show ring? I can't ride with my hands all over the place. I'll never win."

These riders have been taught to carry their hands in a "four-inch box" — i.e., four inches above the withers, four inches apart, and four inches in front of the saddle. If you're riding a well-schooled horse, that may be correct for competition, but this is a training process. To connect up all the different parts of your horse, you have to go outside this box. Remember, one of the first principles of training is never start with your goal (pg. 21). You're going to end up in the "four-inch box", but you're going to take a circuitous route to get there.

When you are focused on your horse's hip, you're looking back at his hip. Your body will feel different to him. These differences in your position are clues/cues you want him to notice. They are information that will get him to his goal sooner. He wants two things: he wants you to let go of his mouth; and he wants a click and a treat. Once he figures out that all he has to do is step over with his hip every time he feels your weight shift in a particular way, he will begin to offer that response more consistently. This is how riding mechanics are transformed into a communication system.

POINTS OF CONTACT
To ask for the hip you're going to lift your buckle

★ *Clicker Training For Your Horse,* by Alexandra Kurland; Sunshine Books, US and Ringpress books, UK

The Click That Teaches: Riding With The Clicker

hand up while you slide down your inside rein. The lifting of your buckle hand will help your inside hand find a length of rein that connects you to your horse's mouth. At that point you're going to lift your inside hand up towards the midline of your body. This changes the leverage effect of your rein. When your hand was low, your point of contact was with the mouth. Now when you lift your hand, you'll have a major impact on his hip.

In single-rein riding, each of your horse's body parts has a different leverage point. Find that point, and you can have a major impact on that area. This is referred to as a point of contact. For the mouth, the point of contact is down lower: when you ask for a give of the jaw, you anchor your hand down against the saddle. But when you want his hip to move you raise your hand higher—if need be all the way up to your sternum.

As your horse tunes in more and more to the subtleties of the system, these different leverage points will move closer and closer together until eventually your hands will be in a "normal" riding position. You'll have faded down your signal to the point where only you and your horse are aware of the tiny shifts you're making. But in the beginning stages you need to differentiate one request from another by exaggerating your body movements. By making your signals big and clear enough you help your horse learn what it is you want.

CLICKER CLARITY

The clicker adds clarity to this process. It highlights and marks correct moments. That makes it easier for your horse to discover exactly what he was doing that got you to let go of the rein. And it changes the very nature of the exercise. Your horse isn't working solely to avoid a negative consequence, i.e., the pressure from the rein. And he isn't having to choose between the proverbial "rock and a hard place".

Initially, getting a horse to disengage his hindquarters may seem like a very dominating, "show him who's boss" exercise. Remember, at first it makes a horse feel more vulnerable. From this perspective it might seem as though this exercise doesn't belong in the clicker repertoire, but it's essential for riding safety and upper-level performance. We need to teach this to our horses, but we need to do it in a way that is emotionally and physically acceptable.

With the clicker we can have all the benefits that hip flips have to offer, but the horse will be at ease organizing his own body. When you take away the defensiveness and guardedness that traditional methods may arouse, you can reach a much deeper level of relaxation. The horse who's learning through fear will eventually submit to his rider, but his submission will be reflected in his attitude and performance. If you want brilliance in your riding partner, you need to give him positive reasons for working for you.

RIDING IN TRAFFIC

So far you've established two responses: head lowering and disengaging the hips. These are two critically important safety valves for your horse. Head lowering keeps his emotional engine from boiling over, and disengaging the hips gives you brakes. These two pieces make your horse a lot safer to ride. Now that you have these basic controls in place you can go out into that busy arena you couldn't handle before and begin to school your horse.

If your horse starts to act up, all you have to do is ask for head lowering, and your "nervous Nelly" will be transformed into "quiet old Nell". Traffic isn't a problem, either. You can ride anywhere you want in the arena without having to worry about what the other horses are doing. Any time your horse starts to veer into another horse you can just pick up the rein, disengage his hips, and head off in the opposite direction. The other people can school any way they want. You'll never interfere with their ride. Except for dodging an obstacle or two, it will be as though you and your horse are the only ones in the arena.

That's the theory. Now for the practice. The first time you see yourself about to collide with another horse and rider you're going to feel like grabbing up both reins. That's a natural response. As you get used to riding on a single rein, you'll be able to resist the urge to drag your own horse off. Instead you'll pick up the inside rein, stabilize it against your body for a hip flip, **and at the same time you'll urge him forward with your legs.** The added energy will spin him away from the other horses. Congratulations! You just took an important step toward developing a high-energy performance horse. You didn't correct him by pulling back on the reins. You rode him forward—meaning not necessarily straight, but with energy—right past the problem.

By the way, did you dog-ear the corner of this page?

You should (unless, of course, you've borrowed someone else's book, and even then maybe you should). It's all too easy to miss the significance of this particular exercise, but that last paragraph just told you how to control a runaway horse, a barn-sour horse, a buddy-dependent horse, a spooking horse, and a just plain stiff-doesn't-want-to-pay-attention-

Chapter Twenty-One: Flipping The Hips

to–you horse. It also gave you the underpinnings for lateral work, collected starts and stops, roll-backs, spins, pirouettes, and eventually even fun stuff like piaffe and passage. Hmm, that's pretty important. Let's take another look.

FLUENCY

You're riding on a single rein. Let's begin with the left rein. You're asking your horse to walk along quietly with his head low. You're remembering the principles of training which say train one criteria at a time. That means you don't really care where he goes, so long as he keeps his head down. The only problem is that you happen to be riding with three other people, and your horse is dragging you over to his buddies. One of them is a known kicker. Every time you get within twenty feet of that horse you feel yourself tense up.

So what is it you should do? For starters, resist doing what is natural. Don't grab up both reins and drag your horse away. Instead, you're going to use the hip-flip exercise you and your horse have been practicing. The difference is that now you're going to ask your horse for the response in a more distracting environment. You're working on fluency. It's not enough that your horse respond to you in a quiet arena when all is well. You also want him to understand and respond to your cues in a busy arena, in a new environment, at feeding time, when a new horse arrives, at a show, etc..

This is your opportunity to begin that process. Use your buckle hand to lift the reins to you. Slide down the inside rein until you have connected with your horse's mouth. Lift your inside hand and press it against the mid-line of your body as you look back over your inside shoulder. As you do this, bump him forward with your legs.

The combined action of the turn in your body and the extra energy will flip your horse around. It's just like a judo throw. You just tossed a thousand-pound horse over your shoulder. Pretty neat. His hindquarters were acting like a steam roller shoving past your hand. You put an end to that by simply pivoting him around his own body. He's no longer headed toward the other horse. You've taken an important step in teaching your horse to follow the subtle suggestions of your body. He's going to learn that when he feels you turn, he should turn. When he feels you thinking about stepping sideways, he should step sideways.

(Note: if this doesn't work as I've described, it means you didn't find the right rein length. Next time, slide your inside hand a little further down the rein before you lift up. The flip of the hip should

FLIPPING THE HIPS

This is Robin demonstrating the re-balancing effect of the hip flip:

1.) He's leaning down onto his forehand so I've slid my inside hand down the rein.

2.) Ground work has made him very responsive. A slight lift of my inside hand is all I need to connect to his hips.

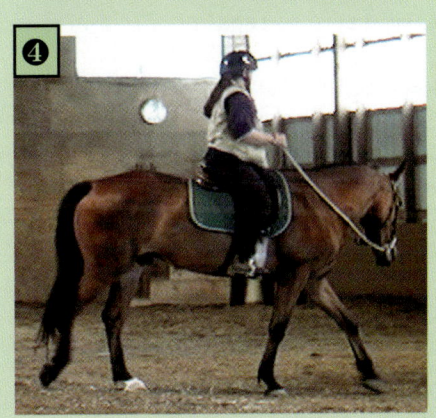

3.) As I think about Robin's inside hip, that shifts my weight, and Robin responds by stepping further underneath his body with his inside hind leg.

4.) After a hip flip, I feel Robin's hips supporting me more evenly, and his balance is more level overall.

133

The Click That Teaches: Riding With The Clicker

happen within one stride—which it will if you have the right rein length.)

Once you have mastered the mechanics of this lesson, the other horses won't be a problem interfering with your ride. You'll see them as an opportunity, helping you with your training. Every time your horse tries to drag you over to them, he's just giving you another chance to teach him to listen to you instead.

Traffic isn't the only problem you can solve with the hip-flip. This exercise is also the beginning step you need for riding patterns, in other words, for connecting "how" to "where" (Ch. 16). Suppose you want to ride in a specific area out in your field, but your horse has other ideas. Every time you come near the barn, he starts to lean out through his outside shoulder and drag you towards it. Flip the hips, and head him back the other way.

Repeat this a couple dozen times and your horse will stop trying to drag you off through his outside shoulder. You'll be creating more than just good manners. You'll also be building the foundation for high-performance sports. This may sound like a lot from one simple exercise, but learn to flip the hips, and you'll be amazed at the changes in your horse.

WALKING IT THROUGH

Suppose you read this through and you think it all makes sense, but you still can't quite visualize what you're supposed to do. Get off your horse and walk

RIDING PATTERNS

This young Arab and her rider are in the early stages of learning how to ride on a single rein. Her rider has built a ring about the size of a round pen to ride in, but her mare has other ideas. She'd rather go back to the barn.

1.) At the start of this sequence she was heading out of the ring back to the barn, but her rider remembered to lift her inside rein to regain control of direction.

2.-3.) Instead of continuing back to the barn, her horse has "flipped her hips" and is following her nose back on to the circle. As her rider releases the rein, the mare's head drops and she steps softly into the bend. Notice the slack in the reins as she returns to the ring.

4.) Riding is like learning how to walk on a balance beam. As the rider reaches for the rein again, her horse over-compensates in her balance and 5.) drops her weight onto her inside shoulder. So first she was bowing out and leaving the circle. Now she's falling in and collapsing into the center.

5.-6.) Her rider is ready for her. She stabilizes her hand, and she sends her horse forward with both legs.

6.) The mare isn't back on the rim of the circle yet, but she's much better balanced through her shoulders. Her rider is going to remember that geography isn't of primary importance at this stage. What matters more is that her horse learns to soften and give to pressure. Once she responds consistently, they'll be able to ride perfect circles.

7.) As they approach the side that's closest to the barn where her mare ran out before, they are much better connected. It's not a perfect circle yet, but with a little more schooling it will be.

Chapter Twenty-One: Flipping The Hips

through the exercise. Remember how you used to play horse when you were a little kid? Well, now you're going to be both the horse and the rider.

Pretend you've got the reins. Pick up your imaginary inside rein just as you would if you were riding. Go through all the steps, including lifting the buckle up with your outside hand. Look back over your inside shoulder. You'll feel how that simple action flips your hips around. Repeat this a couple of times until you really understand the dynamics of the exercise.

Pretend you're a horse dragging your rider off across the arena. Lean into your outside shoulder, just as your horse does. Now pick up the imaginary inside rein and look back over your inside shoulder. You'll discover that you (the horse) really want to turn. It's a much easier choice than falling sideways over the outside shoulder.

I walk through everything I teach my horses. It's a habit I started years ago when I was trying to figure out lateral work. Shoulder-in was a total mystery to me. (We'll get to that in Ch. 32.) I didn't understand what correct bends were, or why they were important. I was confused. My horse was confused. My usual riding space was a five acre field. Without a fence line to act as a reference point, the lateral work seemed especially mysterious.

My solution was to walk through the exercises I was trying to ride. In the process, I discovered that what you do on the ground is exactly what you need to do under saddle. If I'm working on something new, something my body doesn't yet have a pattern for, I walk it first. That way when I think about the exercise, I'll have a response already programmed in.

It's like walking a jump course before you ride it. The good riders aren't just memorizing the pattern, they're visualizing how they're going to ride every stride. They feel the flow of the course as they walk it. In their minds they ride the turns, they adjust the stride length, they set up their distances, all while their horse is still back in the barn munching on hay.

RIDING IN THE REAL WORLD

Hip-flips aren't simply for ring riding. The hip-flip can keep you safe and in control out in the real world. To give you a sense of how this works, let me introduce you to Barley, a horse who came with some very real safety issues.

Barley was a thoroughbred gelding somewhere in his late teens. His previous owner was a novice rider who wanted a calm, steady horse. That was not Barley. He certainly could be very well-mannered, but when he got nervous he became explosive. Whirling, bolting, and a twisting rodeo buck were all part of his repertoire. His previous owner had gotten scared one too many times and decided she had to find him a new home.

Barley got lucky. He was taken on by a rider who loved working with difficult horses. In one of our sessions together we took Barley out to the arena. It was a fair distance away from the barn, down a long gravel road.

Just getting to and from the arena was a lesson in itself. Riding away from the barn presented one type of problem. Barley hated leaving his pasture mates. His resistance manifested itself as a lack of energy. He felt as though his feet were stuck in cement. He was reluctant, but not explosive. Coming home was where his rider expected the real problems to surface. When she rode him out on the trails, Barley was always in a rush to get home. He didn't want to go back at her pace. The conflict often coiled him into knots of tension that could erupt into bucking.

In the arena we worked on the building-block skills that Barley's owner would need to stay safe in situations like that. He had obviously had some good schooling mixed in with some bad experiences. He understood how to go on the bit. He was a very beautiful horse in a ring situation where he felt comfortable. If the arena had been just around the corner from the barn, we wouldn't have had any problems. We could have given him a good training session and put him away on a positive note. The problem was, it wasn't. We had that long hike back to the barn.

On this particular day, Barley's owner decided to ride back to the barn. For the first hundred yards or so, Barley kept a steady pace on a loose rein. But as we got closer to the barn, he started to rush. It's a familiar situation that most trail riders have encountered.

I called out to his rider to flip his hips. As she slid down the rein, Barley exploded sideways in protest. He was not going to be turned away from the barn. His jittering steps headed them toward a ditch filled with a tangle of shrubs and barbed wire.

"Flip the hips! Flip the hips!" I shouted against the wind.

Because we had schooled together in the ring, his rider knew perfectly well what this meant. She also had the seat and riding experience to handle the intensity of the situation. If she hadn't, we would never have tackled this step at this point. We would have spent more time and inserted more steps into the training. So if you're thinking as you read this, "I couldn't ride a horse like this," the good news is

The Click That Teaches: Riding With The Clicker

you don't have to. You can always break your lesson down into smaller, more manageable steps.

Barley's owner understood how to use hip flips to reschool behavior problems. As Barley tried to dislodge his rider into the bushes, she lifted her left inside rein and added pressure. She used Barley's own energy and resistance to create a judo toss. His hips swung around, so he was heading back into the center of the road instead of into the ditch. His rider released the left rein and instantly picked up the right. She swung his hips around in a move, counter-move dance. He was now facing me and heading away from the barn. He took a step in my direction. Click!

The click halted him instantly, and he waited calmly while I walked up to him and gave him a treat. The click had snapped him back into thinking mode and settled his emotions.

In a situation like this, it's a real advantage having someone on the ground who can reinforce the horse. The rider can stay in position ready for any sudden moves the horse might make. It also gives the horse something to focus on other than the distant barn. Treats happen when you look *away* from the barn and your pasture mates.

I instructed his rider to walk Barley past me and then, when she was ready, to turn him back toward the barn. I didn't want him just wheeling around the instant they were in motion.

Barley walked a couple steps beyond my position, turned in an acceptable manner, but then started to rush as soon as he was headed for home. His rider lifted the left rein to flip the hips. At which point Barley flung his head up against the pressure of the left rein and started to leap sideways. "Take the hip!" I shouted. His rider added pressure, and Barley swung around to face me.

"Ride him forward to me," I called to her. His rider tried, but Barley balked and tried to spin out to the other side. His rider slid her hand down the right rein and lifted it up in one smooth movement, which spun Barley around until he was again facing me. This time when she asked him to walk toward me, he did. *Click.* He got a treat.

Barley was learning an important lesson. He was discovering that the world didn't end when he turned away from the barn. Furthermore, all the intimidating tactics that had worked so well to frighten and dislodge his previous riders weren't going to work with his new owner. Leaping sideways, dragging his rider into ditches, bolting, even bucking, were all stopped by the single-rein hip flip.

He was also learning that every time he settled and walked away from the barn, click, he got to stand still for a moment and eat a bite of carrot. This is how you combine single-rein riding with the clicker and apply it to real world riding. If you have to deal with "reform-school" behavior, the combination will keep you safe while you deal with toddler temper tantrums. And once your horse is convinced that these tactics don't work, you'll have a training tool in place to assist in the next lesson: the "Why would you leave me?" game (Ch. 25).

But before we move on to that lesson, I'll show you some exercises for the rider which will make it much easier for you to communicate clear intent to your horse.

PART 4
TRAINING EXERCISES FOR THE RIDER

In this section I'll share with you some of my favorite riding-awareness exercises. These are all things you can do on your own without an instructor guiding you through them. Not only will they improve your own balance and flexibility, they will help you understand the balance shifts you are asking your horse to make through the single-rein riding.

MAIN LESSONS COVERED:

1.) "The Four Points on the Bottom of your Feet": A body awareness exercise that helps you become more centered and grounded.

2.) "Swimming" and "Flying Lessons": These exercises free up the rider's shoulders.

3.) "Hip Flexions": Lessons to free up the rider's hips.

4.) The "T'ai Chi Walk": Creates engaged balance – allows you to experience in your own body the balance shifts you will be asking of your horse in the exercises covered in Parts 5 and 6.

Riding excellence is built on a foundation of body awareness. These exercises allow you to become a "centaur", so you can explore your horse's balance via the "t'ai chi walk".

The Click That Teaches: Riding With The Clicker

TRAINING EXERCISES FOR THE RIDER

T'ai chi balance for both horse and handler creates equine beauty on the ground and under saddle.

TRAINING EXERCISES FOR THE RIDER

138

CHAPTER 22
The Four Points on the Bottom of Your Feet

In this chapter I'll share with you an exercise called "The Four Points on the Bottom of your Feet". It will increase your flexibility, improve your balance, and make you more internally aware of the range of movement you have in your joints.

RIDING AWARENESS

By now you know that for me riding is more than simply kicking a horse to make it go and pulling on the reins to make it stop. And riding is also more than ambling down the trail looking at the trees, as pleasant as that can be. For me, riding is about partnership, and what I am looking for is something beyond the ordinary. I don't want just another ho-hum performance from my horse. I want excellence. That means I have some training to do with my horse, and it also means I have some work to do with me.

In the previous section I talked about taking the two-by-four out of the horse. Now it's time to do the same for the rider. It isn't just that a stiff rider has a harder time following the horse's motion. We've talked about riding as a kinesthetic language, a way of communicating with the horse via your body. A stiff rider is missing out on all the richness and variation that this language has to offer. It's as though he's speaking in a dull monotone instead of in a voice rich in nuance and feeling. What I call "riding in a state of excellence" means learning to come alive within your body. The exercises in this section will help you towards that goal.

"The four points on the bottom of your feet" is a Feldenkrais lesson I learned many years ago at a TT.E.A.M. clinic★. Because we're talking about how you use your body, reading this chapter isn't enough. You have to do the exercise. I suggest you make an audio tape of this lesson so you can practice it on your own. Each time you go through it you'll discover new subtleties of movement you weren't aware of before.

When you make your audio tape practice toning: that means drawing your words out in a long, slow cadence. You'll find your breathing changes when you tone. Instead of being up in your chest, you'll be breathing down in your center. Notice also the change in how you feel when you use toning. It's hard to be tense and tone at the same time. Remember this the next time you want your horse to settle, or you are feeling nervous or angry around him. Stretch out your vowel sounds: "eeeasy" instead of just "easy." "Aaand whooooah" instead of just "whoa!" You'll see your relationship with your horse change once you start using toning.

As you read through this next section, practice toning. You'll notice the rhythm of the words works like a meditation to help you find a state of excellence with your balance.

THE FOUR POINTS ON THE BOTTOM OF YOUR FEET

Stand comfortably with your feet a hip's width apart. Begin by simply observing how you feel. Observe without judgment. Observe the ease with which you are standing. Observe any tension in your body. Feel your feet underneath you. Do you feel grounded? Do

★ TT.E.A.M.: The Tellington-Jones Equine Awareness Method

THE FOUR POINTS ON THE BOTTOM OF YOUR FEET

These riders were good sports at a clinic to let me take photos of the before and after of the "Four Points on the Bottom of the Feet" exercise.

1.) Before: most of us don't give much thought to how we stand, but all the time we are standing out of balance, we are strengthening muscle patterns that work against good riding.

2.) After: The "Four Points" exercise made these riders more aware of their balance. This body awareness is part of riding excellence. On the ground or under saddle, the enhanced awareness of balance and flexibility affects a horse's performance.

The result: equine magnificence.

you feel balanced? Or do you feel stiff and tight? Do a general body check, but don't try to change anything just yet. For now you're simply making observations to use for comparison later.

You're going to begin by focusing on one foot at a time. You'll start with your right foot. You're going to keep your foot flat on the floor while you roll gently around on the four points on the bottom of that foot: the inside heel, outside heel, outside toe, inside toe.

Follow the points counter-clockwise. Let yourself circle around the entire surface of the foot. How big is your circle? Observe without judgment. Just keep flowing around the four points—inside heel, outside heel, outside toe, inside toe. Maybe you feel very tense and uncertain. That's okay. Just make a tiny circle. Be easy with this. Just do what's comfortable.

Maybe you're flowing through a big circle, feeling yourself rolling from the inside of your foot to the outside and forward up to your toes. Feel the rhythm of the motion. Is it smooth and easy throughout, or do you rush past certain points? Do you feel stable and balanced, or uncertain and stiff?

Observe the shape of the circle. Is it round and symmetrical, or is it an oval? Is it centered over your foot or angled off to the side? Slow the circle down so you can feel each point. Feel your whole body flowing from inside heel to outside heel, to outside toe, to inside toe, and back again to the inside heel.

Feel your ankle following the four points on the bottom of your foot. Feel your calf and your knee following the motion and the shift in weight. What shape is the figure your knee makes? What size is it? Feel your hip flowing over to the right, and forward, and back toward the center in a smooth circular path. Is it as easy to go forward as it is to go back? Can you feel the four points under you?

Let your ribs and your shoulders and your head follow the four points. Then go on down your left side. Follow the four points on the bottom of your right foot as you let its motion flow through your shoulders and your ribs. Feel your left hip, left thigh, and left knee, then your left ankle and your left foot, all softly responding as you rotate through the four points on the bottom of that foot.

Go back up your left side. Feel your ankle, your knee, your hip, all softly rotating. Feel your shoulders and your head, feel your right hip and your right knee, your right ankle. Feel the size of the circle. Feel how free and easy it's become. Feel the four points on the bottom of your right foot. Let yourself circle gently around and then come softly to center. Stand quietly. Take a deep breath and feel the ground under your feet. Feel the ease in your body, the sense of freedom in your joints.

Now change and circle clockwise, still focusing on your right foot. Go from the outside heel to the inside heel to the inside toe to the outside toe. Feel the whole surface of your foot as you gently rotate around the four points. Feel the shape of the circle. Take a moment to get used to this new direction. Is it as easy for you as the other? Which way does your body circle with the greatest ease?

Feel the circles going up through your ankle, up through your knee and your hips. Feel the circle as your shoulder follows the four points on the bottom of your foot. Feel your head softly turning in rhythm with the motion. Feel your left shoulder and your left hip following the motion. Feel it like the circle of a clock: six o'clock, nine, then twelve and three. Feel your knees following the motion. Feel your ankles. Feel both feet softly following the four points on the bottom of your right foot.

Come softly to center. Take a deep breath and again feel the ground under your feet. Do you feel as though you are rooted to the spot? Enjoy the ease and the sense of comfort that's washing over you.

Repeat this whole pattern, only this time begin by focusing on your left foot. Circle first clockwise from the inside to the outside. Feel the ground under your left foot; feel the circles going up into your ankles, your knees, your hips. Feel the circles flowing up through your shoulders and your head. Does your left side circle as freely and easily as your right? Are the circles bigger or smaller, faster or slower? Where is it easy to turn, where is it harder? Remember, observe without judgment. If you feel any strain, make the circles smaller or come to the center and rest.

From your still place of rest, change the direction of the circles. Follow the four points from the outside heel to the inside heel, forward, up and across your toes, and then back to your heels. Let your weight flow easily. Feel the circles spiraling easily up through your whole body. Feel the ground under both your feet. Feel the ease and comfort within your joints. Feel your breath, deep and relaxed.

Come to a soft, easy stop. Let your arms hang freely at your sides while you enjoy your deep, relaxed breathing. Feel how grounded you are. Your feet may feel as though they've grown roots down into the floor. You feel relaxed, peaceful, at ease.

Now begin to rock from the outside of your right foot to the outside of your left foot. Let yourself sink down on the outside of your left foot, then send yourself up over the center of both feet and down

Chapter Twenty-Two: The Four Points on the Bottom of your Feet

into your right foot. Send yourself back, up over the center, and down into the left. Let your whole body rock from side to side.

Remember as a child playing with a toy slinky, Remember what it felt like to have the coils roll from one hand to the other. That's how your body will feel as you let your weight sink into one foot. Like the coils of a slinky, you'll send your weight from foot to foot.

Feel your left knee soften and bend as you sink onto the outside of your left foot. Feel your hip and your shoulder rest easily down onto your foot. Feel your foot send your weight up and over, and feel your right knee soften and give as it passes that weight easily onto the outside of your right foot. Continue to rock from side to side, feeling the ease and grace of the movement. Then come up over the center of both feet and come gently to rest.

Again pause to enjoy the feeling of ease in your body. How do you feel compared with the last time you rested? How do you feel compared with how you started? Much more relaxed and grounded? Much more aware of even the tiniest movement in your joints?

Now begin again. This time you're going to rock forward into your toes and then back onto your heels, keeping your feet flat on the ground the whole time. Begin by letting yourself sink down into your heels. Do you feel as though you're falling backwards? If so, remember to bend your knees and let your hips and shoulders follow the movement down.

Rise up over the center of your feet, and then bend your knees again and let yourself sink forward onto your toes. Rise up again over your center, and drop down into your heels. Let your hips and knees help you.

Rise up over your center by carrying your hips forward. Sink down over your toes. Rise up over your center, and sink back down into your heels. Flow from your heels up through your center and down into your toes. Feel your whole body becoming part of the movement as you flow up through your center and back into your heels.

Now just do part of the cycle. Rise up over the center of your feet, letting your hips carry the motion forward and up. Then sink back down into your heels, letting your knees give and your pelvis sink. Rise up, sink down. Rise up through your hips, sink down through your knees. Rise up, sink down.

This should feel familiar to you, especially if you ride in the English style. What are you doing? Aren't you posting? Rise up through your hips, letting your knees open. Sink down into your heels, letting your knees give and your pelvis sink. Now add your arms. Hold imaginary reins lightly in your hands and continue to post through your pelvis. Observe how steady your hands are. You need to have quiet hands to communicate clear messages to your horse. Now you do.

(You can post another way, of course, simply pogo-sticking up and down through your knees alone. Try doing it this way, for contrast. Just move up down, up down, without shifting your weight through the four points on the bottom of your feet. Your pelvis won't need to move at all, and it's really easy, except your hands will also be moving up and down. That's no good if you want to use the reins for real communication with your horse.)

Go back to the other pattern. Find it again in your body. Let your knees give and your pelvis drop as you sink your weight into your heels. Let your hips travel forward and up as you rise up over the center of your feet. Find the rhythm of the motion. Feel the thrust forward of your hips as you rise to the top of your post. Feel the soft settling down of your weight as you sink into your heels. And most of all, observe the stability of your hands.

If you've been a very stiff rider, you may only feel pieces of this the first few times you go through this exercise. That's normal. One of the greatest challenges in developing a good seat is learning to use your hips and back to follow the horse's motion. The release of the hips is the key.

Review this exercise many times. When you find yourself waiting in line at the grocery store, let yourself softly revolve around the four points. You can make tiny circles so no one will notice, but you'll feel huge changes happening in your joints. The smaller and softer you make the circles, the more you'll have to focus on the movement and the more finely tuned it will become. Keep a journal of your riding over the next few weeks as you practice this exercise. I think you'll be amazed at how much improvement you see in your horse's gaits and overall responsiveness.

The Click That Teaches: Riding With The Clicker

T'AI CHI EXCELLENCE

The "Four Points on the Bottom of your Feet" exercise gives the rider greater structural stability. This rider can take a "substantial leg" meaning all her weight is balanced over one foot, and yet she's very grounded and balanced. She can help her horse find her own self-balance. Think of a ballet dancer on point supported by her partner. That's the relationship this rider has with her beautiful horse. (I have to share a little of this mare's history. She belonged originally to drug addicts who beat and starved her. When her current owner, Julie Jacobs, rescued her, Aimee was so weak she could barely walk out of the barn yard. Now she is the picture of equine grace and beauty.)

CHAPTER 23
Swimming, Flying, and Flexibility

In this chapter we'll borrow some exercises from the swimming pool to free up your shoulders and hips. They will help you become more grounded in the saddle.

LUNGE LINE LESSONS

Several years ago I was working with a wonderful group of riders who met once a month for a clinic. One of these ladies owned an elderly ex-polo pony who was a super lunge-line horse. When the group met at her barn, we always borrowed him for position lessons. What we discovered was that as long as the person being lunged didn't have reins, her seat was wonderful. She'd be relaxed and soft and able to follow the motion of the horse with ease. However, the minute any of these riders picked up the reins everything changed. They became stiff and tense. That was true even of the more experienced riders.

What was it the reins were doing? Why was there such a drastic change? Even when they just picked up a loose rein, their bodies stiffened. We started to look in detail at what was going on, and we made an interesting discovery. These riders all picked up their reins overhand—that is, they reached forward and picked them up with their knuckles facing towards the sky.

This created a gross-motor-control grab of the rein that's very normal and very stiffening. Try it the next time you ride, and you'll see what it does. As you reach forward for the rein, your shoulders comes forward. It may just be a slight movement, but it's often enough to tip you past your center, ahead of the balance point of your pelvis. This in turn makes you counter-balance through your thighs, so just the simple act of picking up the reins can cause you to stiffen up.

In our group we solved the problem with a few easy swimming lessons. Swimming lessons? I know what you're thinking: now she's really gone off the deep end (no pun intended!). First she has me clicking my horse, then she talks about zen and "letting go", and now I'm supposed to go swimming! How is that going to help my riding? Try the following exercise and you'll see.

THE BACKSTROKE

Swimming is one of my favorite lunge-line exercises. I use most of the strokes, including the breast stroke and the freestyle, but my favorite is the backstroke. It's like the various windmill exercises many riding teachers have their clients do on the lunge line, but it adds in two important elements: the muscle tone of your body and your breath.

With your horse at the walk, imagine that you're doing the backstroke in a beautiful pool. The water is supporting you, holding you up, but you have to put tone into your back to stay up on the surface. The water is warm, and you're relaxed, enjoying your swim. Now start to breathe in rhythm with your stroke. Breathe deep into your center, and swing one arm up over your head and down behind you. Really stroke it through the air just as though you were pushing it through water.

SWIMMING

Swimming is one of my favorite lunge-line exercises. Pretending that you're backstroking does a lot more than just free up your shoulders. As you think about supporting your back enough to float, your breathing will change, and your entire position will improve.

The Click That Teaches: Riding With The Clicker

THE BACKSTROKE

One of the biggest benefits of the backstroke is the way it helps a rider's hands. Many riders stiffen when they pick up the reins. They reach for them overhand, which pulls their shoulders forward and makes them grip with their thighs to catch their balance. This rider is practicing picking up her reins from the backstroke. As her arm drops down behind her torso, it opens up her collarbone and draws her shoulder back.

As she reaches for the rein out of the backstroke, her shoulders stay open and back. She doesn't have to grip with her thighs to maintain her balance, so she doesn't stiffen up as she picks up the reins.

A great result: with her body relaxed and better aligned, she can stay in the saddle, even when she's pulled on.

Now swing your other arm up over your head and down behind you. One arm, then the other; one arm, then the other. As your horse walks forward, you'll feel yourself coming into rhythm with his stride. If he had a pokey walk before, you'll feel it become more lively. He's enjoying the rhythm and the freedom of movement your swimming lesson is creating.

Continue to follow the swing of the backstroke. As your shoulders free up, you'll feel your seat get deeper. Now you're ready to pick up your reins. Let's start with your right arm. As it swings back behind you, notice how your elbow drops and your shoulder opens. Notice how that helps to lift your hips.

As you swing your arm back to it's furthest point, your elbow will straighten. When your hand comes forward, your elbow bends and you're ready to begin another swing up over your head. Instead, you're going to pretend that you're scooping up the right rein. As your hand comes forward, imagine you're just softly picking up the rein and come to a still place with your hand in riding position. Now do the same thing with your left hand. Repeat this several times until it feels easy and natural.

Now try actually picking up the reins using your backstroke. When my riders did it this way, they discovered that their seats stayed deep and relaxed, and the reins felt incredibly light. What was most striking was how different each of them looked to the rest of us. Suddenly I had a group of tall, elegant riders, and all we'd done was gone for a swim!

FLYING

A similar exercise, one that I especially like because it's so quick and easy to do, involves a different kind of shoulder rotation. I call it flying, and you can do this either mounted or standing, or even seated in your chair as you read through this section.

(One word of caution: if you've never done this kind of warm-up exercise on your horse, proceed slowly. Some horses will spook when they first see your arms swinging out to the side. If that's the case, start with a small movement out to the side with just one arm, and before your horse has a chance to jump, click him for standing still. If you use the clicker to ease him into the exercise, it usually takes only a few minutes before you can move your arms any way you want, and even a horse that was skittish at first will be rock solid.)

Begin your flying lesson with your arms at your side, elbows bent, hands held up ninety degrees in front of you, very much as though you're holding the reins. Keep your elbows at your side and swing your hands as far apart as is easy and comfortable for you. This is just to check of your range of motion. You're going to use it later for comparison. (See the photos on the facing page.)

Now straighten your elbows and lift your arms up and out to the side at shoulder height. Start with your thumbs pointing straight up, then rotate your arm so they point behind you. Then point them back up. Rotate your arms again, this time so your thumbs point forward, then down, and finally back under and around behind you. (This is the fun one, but be careful not to strain your shoulder.) Rotate back so your thumbs point down,

144

Chapter Twenty-Three: Swimming, Flying, and Flexibility

then forward, then up.

With your thumbs still pointing straight up, drop your elbows back down to your side. Bring your hands forward in front of you, as if you were holding the reins. Now move your hands again as wide apart as you can with your elbows at your side. Most people will find that loosening up their shoulders has increased their range of motion in their lower arms and hands dramatically. This is a great exercise to do any time you need to gain greater freedom in your arms or shoulders.

Another fun exercise is just to imagine that you are moving your arms. Go through the entire sequence, then check your range of motion again. You may be surprised at how much further you can extend your arms. You've just discovered the power of visualization! Use it to improve your riding.

LOOSENING YOUR HIPS

Here's a similar exercise for loosening up the hips. Try it first at the halt, one leg at a time. (Refer to the photos on the next page.)

Reach back behind you, grab your foot by the ankle, and draw your leg up behind you. Don't try to force your leg back too far—do only what's comfortable. Hold it there for a couple of seconds, and then, without letting go, rotate your leg out to the side. Again, go only as far as feels comfortable. With practice, most people will eventually be able to bring their legs almost ninety degrees around to the side. For now, though, even if you can rotate your leg only an inch or two, that's a good start.

Try to keep your seat down in the saddle while you do this. Don't let yourself pitch forward. Now release your leg and let it just hang down free. Compare it to your other leg. You'll probably feel a huge difference. The inside of your thigh will fall more evenly against the saddle. You won't be sitting on the back of your thigh in a "chair seat". Your leg will feel longer, your foot will be more grounded under you, and your seat will be deeper.

Repeat this with your other leg. When you first get on your horse, do this a couple of times on each side. You'll start to notice a huge difference in the stability of your seat.

The key to this exercise is to keep your seat down in the saddle and let your thigh swing down and back so it ends up underneath your hip. This is a good exercise for riders who tend to grip with their thighs. It's something you can do between lessons or when you don't have someone with you to check your leg position. But remember, do only what is comfortable. Don't twist or force your joints into something you aren't ready for.

FLYING LESSONS

1.) This rider has a stiff right shoulder. She begins this exercise with a pre-flight check. With her elbows at her side she swings her hands out to the side to check her range of motion.

2.) Next she lifts her arms up and out to the side so her thumbs are pointing straight up.

3.) She rotates her shoulders so her thumbs point behind her. Then she points her thumbs back up.

4.) Next she rotates her arms so her thumbs point forward, down, and then back behind her.

5.) She ends this part of the exercise by rotating her arms so her thumbs point down, forward, and then up. With her thumbs still pointing straight up, she drops her elbows back down to her side.

6.) She again swings her hands as far apart as she can with her elbows at her side. Compare this to her original range of motion.

The Click That Teaches: Riding With The Clicker

HIP FLEXIONS FOR THE RIDER

1.) Try this at the halt. Reach back behind you and grab your foot by the ankle. Draw your leg up behind you. Do only what is comfortable. Just as with any stretching exercise, over time you'll be able to do more.

❶

2.) Hold your foot behind you for a couple of seconds and then rotate your leg around to the side. Again, do only what feels comfortable. When you let go, compare your "before and after" leg position. Most riders notice a huge improvement in the way their inner thighs rest against the saddle.

❷

Another simple hip-loosening exercise can be done with a saddle stand. Put your saddle up on the stand. (Of course you'll have made sure that the stand is sturdy enough to support your weight, and that it's well enough padded to protect your saddle.) Sit in rider's position. Begin with the shoulder and hip exercises described above to warm up your joints. Now just click your heels together under the "belly" of the horse, like Dorothy in "The Wizard of Oz" or a Russian cossack dancer in mid-leap. This means you'll have to swing your legs out and a bit back so your heels can meet under the saddle.

What these last two exercises will create for you is tremendous freedom in your hip joints and a much greater range of motion in your legs. Instead of gluing your legs to your horse's sides, you'll be able to brush back and touch him with a foot. If you've been using your hand on his ribs to ask him to shift over when you're on the ground, you'll be able to mimic that same light touch with your leg from the saddle.

Once you've mastered the gross movements that loosen up your hips and legs, you can slow them down and refine them. Instead of swinging your leg forcefully back, see how slow and how small you can make the movement. Feel the lift through your hip and the accompanying rotation through your ankle. Now you have the makings of a secret code. Your horse will feel it, but everyone watching will be left wondering what special aids you're using.

LEG POSITION

3.) It's easy for even very experienced riders to lose track of their position. Video and photos are a great way to review your position. This rider was surprised how far ahead of her hips and shoulders her feet were.

❸

4.) It may seem funny to be sitting on a saddle stand instead of a horse, but it's a great way to work on position. The rider can focus on her seat without having to factor in her horse's balance. This photo was taken after the hip flexion exercise. Note the dramatic change in her leg position. The line shows how much more underneath her hip her foot now is.

❹

CHAPTER 24
T'ai Chi, Anyone?

In this chapter I'll share with you some basic warm-up exercises for t'ai chi. They will teach you how to become more grounded while still remaining very soft and flexible. They are a great preparation both for ground work and for riding.

T'AI CHI

T'ai chi, one of the Chinese martial arts, is made up of a series of movements that were originally designed as training for combat but have become stylized into flowing sequences that many people use to keep themselves physically fit and tuned in to their bodies. There's a parallel here with dressage, which began as training for war horses and became stylized into patterns of movements that are useful for many other reasons.

Just as dressage is good for horses, t'ai chi is an excellent source of centering exercises for riders. It gets you moving through all the joints of your body. It helps you develop balance and flexibility. It teaches you engagement, and it gives you the human equivalents for much of the "collected" work we ask of our horses.

To study t'ai chi in depth you need to find a good teacher, one who understands how to teach movement. What I'm going to share with you here are just a few warm-up exercises that I've found very helpful for riders.

EMBRACING AN ENERGY BALL

At the core of t'ai chi movements is a grounded, very stable posture called, appropriately enough, the "horse rider's stance."

Stand with your feet a hip's width apart, knees bent, hips soft and relaxed, shoulders over your hips, arms relaxed at your side. Pretend you're sitting, straddling your horse's back. Remember what you learned from the previous exercises about keeping your body loose, then bring your hands up in front of you as though you're holding a giant beachball, or, better yet, a delicate soap bubble.

Now, with your tongue resting on the roof of your mouth, breathe in through your nose. Breathe deep into your diaphragm. Let your breath melt down through you and out through your hands so the imaginary soap bubble floats up and expands. Breathe out, a long, relaxing breath. Then breathe in, letting the soap bubble expand and grow. As you relax, you'll begin to feel a tingling in your fingers. You won't have to imagine the bubble anymore. You'll feel as though you have a giant ball of energy held between your hands.

Let the ball float in front of you. Follow it with your hands as you flow around the four points on the bottom of your feet. Your arms will be following a soft circular motion as you keep the ball balanced between your hands. Follow the ball wherever it goes. Follow it down to the ground and up over your head. Draw it back down in front of you and then turn your palms face out and push it away. Catch it. Turn your palms in towards your body and draw the bubble of energy back to you. When you feel totally centered and relaxed, bring the energy ball in towards your center and let your hands

T'AI CHI BASICS

This rider is keeping the grounding she learned from the "four points on the bottom of her feet" exercise as she follows an imaginary energy ball.

The Click That Teaches: Riding With The Clicker

FINDING YOUR SUBSTANTIAL LEG

This rider's balance is very secure. She's able to stand with ease on one leg. This is the beginning point for the "t'ai chi walk". The goal is to be able to shift your weight from one foot to the other with no loss of balance. (See below.)

rest against your abdomen, one hand over the other, thumb in your navel. Breathe deeply, in and out, enjoying your breath.

FINDING YOUR SUBSTANTIAL LEG

Now let your arms relax at your side. Shift your weight entirely over to your left leg and stand just on that foot. If your balance is shaky, support yourself with a hand on a chair or a nearby wall. In the beginning, most people balance by stiffening their leg. That's not what we want. Let your knee have a slight bend to it and keep your hip soft. Bounce gently up and down to make sure you aren't getting rigid. Now, still with that nice soft bounce, swing your free leg forward and back.

Switch legs. Shift your weight over onto your right leg. Bend your right knee and bounce. Most people will find a big difference from one side to the other in their ability to balance. Let your good side teach your wobbly side. If you feel really unstable, spend some more time with the "four points on the bottom of your feet" exercise until you achieve more balance.

On either side, your supporting leg is called your substantial leg. To feel truly balanced you need to learn how to lower your hip joint and engage your pelvis around this position.

THE "T'AI CHI" WALK

Once you feel fairly balanced on either leg, you're ready for some movement.

• Start again by standing just on your right leg.
• Now bend your right knee, so your torso is lower to the ground. This allows you to swing your left leg forward to prepare for the next step.
• Set your left heel down on the ground, but keep all your weight balanced over your right foot. You are preparing a platform before you commit your weight to it.
• Roll out over the four points on the bottom of your feet so your left foot is now flat on the ground. Your weight will still be back over your right foot.
• Bend your left knee forward so it lines up over your toes.
• Shift all your weight forward onto this foot. This now becomes your substantial leg.

THE T'AI CHI WALK

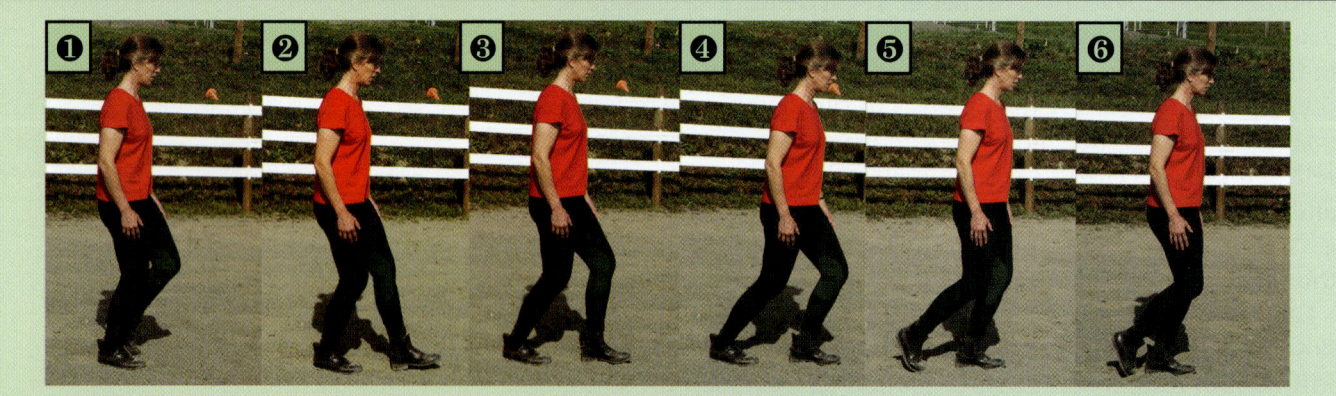

This rider is demonstrating how she can shift her weight from one foot to the other while remaining in balance throughout the sequence.

1.) She begins by standing on one foot. 2.) She swings her left leg forward so she can set her heel down, but she keeps her weight supported on her right foot. 3.) She rolls her left foot down onto the ground, preparing the platform before committing all her weight to it. 4.) She lines her left knee up over her toes, and (5.) shifts her weight out over her left foot. At the same time she rolls up onto the toes of her right foot. All her weight is on her left foot. 6.) Her left foot is now her new substantial leg.

Chapter Twenty-Four: T'ai Chi Anyone?

THE T'AI CHI WALK CONTINUED

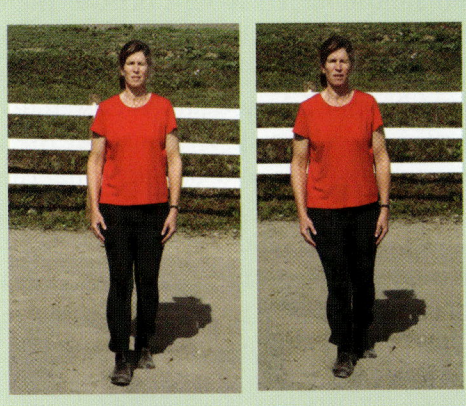

Note how in this case the rider has let herself lean out to the side to transfer her weight from one foot to the other. If she leans like this under saddle, her horse will have a tendency to lean as well.

No, this isn't Scottish line dancing, but the "t'ai chi walk" an important ground exercise for exploring balance. See the text for detailed instructions.

As you study this series of photos, you'll see a direct parallel with the work we've been asking of the horses. Panel two matches the same position that your horse would be in if you were asking him to yield his hips. The rider's head is bent to the side, her weight is off her left inside leg. If she were to pick up imaginary reins—lifting the buckle with her right hand and sliding down the rein with her left—it would be very easy for her to take "her horse's hips" around.

In the third photo in the sequence she would be releasing the rein to begin a new sequence of requests. Once you have the steps of the t'ai chi walk, you can add imaginary reins and become a "centaur". This allows you to tease apart the lessons you're going to be presenting to your horse. You'll understand better the balance shifts you're asking for. Your own mechanics will be well in hand before you ever get on your horse.

• Take all your weight onto that foot and let your right leg swing free.
• Bounce on your left leg to check to make sure you're staying relaxed in your joints. Now bend your left knee so your torso lowers.
• Swing your right leg forward.
• Set your heel down on the ground, but again do not yet shift your weight forward. Take the time to prepare the platform before stepping out on it.
• Roll out over the four points on the bottom of your feet so your right foot is now flat on the ground.
• Bend your left knee forward so it lines up over your toes. Shift all your weight forward onto this foot. Your right leg is now your substantial leg.

You've now completed one full cycle. Continue shifting your weight from one "substantial" leg to the other, and pay attention to the flow of motion from hip to hip. At any point in this cycle you should be able to "freeze frame" and be perfectly balanced. Since you never transfer your weight before preparing the next step, you are always supported in your balance. You can transfer your weight from one foot to the other without ever having to catch your balance.

This is what I want my horses to learn, as well. A green horse falls through his balance. He's heavy on his forehand. Within each stride there's a moment when he has to catch his balance or fall. He may end up rushing or using the reins for support. I want this horse to learn how to engage his hind end so he can support his weight. Instead of falling through his shoulders, he'll move with t'ai chi elegance and grace.

149

So far you've just walked in a straight line. Now you're going to practice turning in balance. This time as you prepare to swing your free leg forward, rotate your hips. Line them up with the new direction of travel. Set your heel down and continue as before to prepare a supporting platform for the next step.

This is an important exercise, and one you should return to many times. Each time you do, you'll make new discoveries about how your own body works, and you'll be able to relate these balance shifts to your riding. They will certainly help you understand the advanced exercises in the next two parts of this book.

BECOMING A CENTAUR

When I was first learning lateral work, I was totally confused. Which way were my shoulders supposed to go? What was I supposed to do with my hips. I would watch other riders in their lessons and try to mirror in my own body what the rider was supposed to be doing. Whatever the instructor was saying I figured would apply to me at some point or other. So I explored what it felt like to lean too far forward, too far back; to collapse through my ribs; or too sit too heavy on one side or the other.

What effect would all this have on my horse? And how did my horse's balance effect me? These were important questions because I was riding Peregrine's mother. With her neurological problems she couldn't compensate for me. Any loss of balance on my part was magnified ten fold in her. I became as a result super-sensitive to balance. I was boarding my horses at the time at a small farm. The barn was a converted dairy, one of those wonderful old nineteenth century barns with massive hand-hewn beams and lofts that made you feel as though you were standing in the belly of a sailing ship.

At night I used to go up into one of the large storage bays and walk the lessons I was learning. I remember one night I was walking circles, trying to figure out where my weight should be in the saddle. I was using the t'ai chi walk, slowly revolving around a small circle.

"What would happen," I asked myself, "if I dropped my inside shoulder?" I let my ribs collapse and kept circling. This was an "observe without judgement" exercise. I had no idea what the outcome was going to be. I had changed one element. The rest was up to the forces of the circle.

With my shoulder dropped I could feel my hips leaving the circle. I immediately recognized the pattern. This is what happens to horses when they lean onto their inside shoulder: they lose the engagement of their hind end. Their hips drift to the outside, and the rider ends up chasing body parts to try to maintain a round circle.

"What would happen," I thought, "if I lifted my inside shoulder?" I took the collapse out of my ribs and felt my hips coming back into balance underneath me.

I felt like a centaur. I could imagine myself as the rider or the horse, or as both. I could ask questions by changing one element in my balance and observing the effect it had.

What happens to the horse if . . .?

Why does the horse lean in this particular way?

Whatever the questions, I could walk the pattern and understand it better. Later that evening when I rode, I asked the same question of my horse. What happens if I, the rider, drop my inside shoulder? Wouldn't you know it, my horse's hips drifted off the circle. I knew the correction. I'd worked it out earlier in my t'ai chi walk. I lifted my inside shoulder by lifting through my rib cage. She came back into balance underneath me. Pretty neat!

I started walking all the riding questions I had. I worked out shoulder-in and haunches-in. I resolved a major glitch I had in the canter. (Yes, I know it sounds silly, but if you're reading this book, you're as horse crazy as I am. And let's face it, we all played "horse" as kids. Now I'm just using that game to help my riding.)

I continue to walk the exercises I ride. There is no end to the learning, especially now that I am working with horses I do not know. The "four points on the bottom of your feet", and the "t'ai chi walk" are my reference points. I know what feels balanced to me. When I walk a horse's pattern, I can understand better the difficulties the rider is having, and quite often we can use the discoveries we make to track a balance issue to an underlying physical cause.

So becoming a "centaur" is an important element in this training. I would urge you to walk any of the exercises in this book that you don't understand. At every layer of your training, walk the lessons. You will learn so much from the process. These next sections of the book will take you deeper into single-rein riding and into advanced performance. There may be times when your head is feeling like mush. "Enough already!" you may be shouting. "What is she talking about?" That's a good place to put the book down, warm up with a little "four points", find your substantial-leg balance, and become a centaur.

PART 5

SINGLE–REIN RIDING AND THE BUILDING BLOCKS OF EXCELLENCE

In this section you'll learn how to transform the safety lessons of Section 3 into lateral work—the building block for advanced performance.

We'll be focusing first on "how" your horse moves, then we'll combine that with "where". At the end of this section, you'll be riding patterns that are the foundation of all performance work.

> MAIN LESSONS COVERED:
>
> 1.) The "Why Would You Leave Me?" Game: Connects your horse's jaw and feet to the rein – gets your horse riding in sync with you.
>
> 2.) The "I Know An Old Lady Who Swallowed A Fly" Lesson: Creates a softening of your horse's head, neck, and shoulder. This is a critical lesson for maintaining soundness as you build performance.
>
> 3.) Three–Flip–Three: Builds on the preceding exercise: connects the softening of the front end to the hips. This lesson builds the foundation for lateral flexions: the building blocks of performance.
>
> 4.) Move–Counter Move: Gives you control of lateral flexions.
>
> 5.) Hip–Shoulder–Shoulder: Creates a soft reinback – the beginning of collected stops.
>
> 6.) Collected Gaits: Gives you a collected start, a collected stop, with a collected middle in between to build gorgeous, feels-like-heaven collected gaits.
>
> 7.) The "300 Hundred Peck Pigeon" Lesson Under Saddle: Allows you to ride freely forward on the buckle with your horse maintaining a balanced, steady gait.
>
> 8.) The "Hotwalker" Lesson: Creates perfect circles.
>
> 9.) Sinle-Rein School Figures: Rollbacks, half turns, half-turns-in reverse, plus diagonals, reverse arc circles and broken lines. These exercises connect the lateral flexions to the geography of a riding arena. Now you can have beautiful carriage, plus a functional "steering wheel".

The Click That Teaches: Riding With The Clicker

SINGLE–REIN RIDING AND THE BUILDING BLOCKS OF EXCELLENCE

Every lesson is connected to every other lesson, and each makes the rest stronger.

Clicker training is for all types of horses, all breeds, all ages. In this book alone the following breeds are represented: thoroughbreds, Arabs, quarter horses, paints, Anglo-Arabs, Morgans, Tennessee walkers, appaloosas, Dutch warmbloods, Missouri fox trotters, Friesians, and Icelandics, plus Cleveland bay, Andalusian, Connemara and draft crosses. This filly represents three great breeds. She's a quarter horse, Arab, Welsh pony cross. She may be little, but she can still do great things. Her owner, Debra Olson-Daniels, has given her a solid foundation of clicker ground work. (See Part 1.) Now she's ready to ride. These photos show her fifth ride. Like Robin, June Bug has transferred the ground work easily to riding. She's had less than thirty minutes of total riding time, and already she looks gorgeous. She's relaxed, happy, enjoying her very grown-up job. She's also learning to keep both herself and her rider in balance. On a horse of this size that's particularly important if she is to stay sound over the long haul carrying adult riders. (Refer back to page 13 to see how much this filly's balance has changed as she's mastered each of the foundation lessons.)

152

CHAPTER 25
The "Why Would You Leave Me?" Game: Developing Softness and Balance

Imagine you're exploring a house. You've been in all the rooms. You thought you knew what was in each one, but now you're standing back in the simplest room of all, just a small entryway without any fancy furniture, and you see it—you see the doorway you didn't notice before. You can peek through the key hole into a room you thought you'd explored, only now you see treasures, wonderful treasures, but the door is locked. How do you get through? This chapter contains the key that lets you into that room — and all the rooms beyond it. It is one of the most important chapters in this book.

THE "WHY WOULD YOU LEAVE ME?" LESSON

Remember "Nervous Nelly"? He's the horse we started with (pg. 123). The horse who fell apart when you brought him to an indoor arena for the winter. The head-lowering and the hip-flip lessons put an end to the spooking and bucking. He's a lot more manageable, but he still wants to be anywhere but with you. His focus is with his buddies, out the door, on the cat, anywhere and everywhere but on his job. Before you even think about getting on, you're going to play the "Why would you leave me?" game.

It helps to set out a circle of cones. They will serve as reference points for you so you'll know when his energy is steering you off course. If you don't have cones, any markers will do. Empty laundry detergent bottles work great, as do the mats you used in his early clicker training lessons (pg. 13). Walk with your horse around the cones. As soon as you are on course, let go *completely* of the reins.

The instant he starts to leave the path, take a hold of the inside rein with your buckle hand. This will start to swing him back towards you. Slide down the rein toward his mouth with your inside hand as you continue to walk your circle. Imagine there's a box directly in front of you. You want him to put his nose in the box.

As soon as he brings his nose back towards you, release the rein completely. In the time it takes to say "Why would you leave me?" you can usually get this whole sequence completed. As soon as you let go, he'll probably leave again. Repeat the whole process.

Keep marching around your circle. You'll see to what degree you let him drag you around by how hard it is to stay on course. This may be as much about you learning to be a good post as it is about your horse learning to stay with you. At some point he's going to bring head back to you, and, instead of leaving, he's going to keep his nose in the box. Click and treat!

Repeat this until you have three clicks on one side, then change direction and begin again. Get to three clicks and change sides again. Pretty soon he'll be staying with you all the time. You'll get three clicks, one right after the other. Perfect. Now begin to lengthen out the number of strides he has to stay with you before you click. You can turn this into a "300-peck-pigeon" game (pg. 75). Eventually you'll be able to walk the entire circle with your horse staying consistently at your side. You won't have to touch the rein. Wherever you go, he'll be right by your side. All the

NOSE IN THE BOX

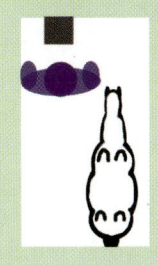

This the way many people want their horses to lead, behind them as though they were on a narrow trail. I certainly want my horses to be able to walk behind me, but I also want them to know how to add energy to their walk so they are in front of me, not behind. In other words, I want my horses to be "ahead of the rider's leg".

Step One: Level with the handler. Set out a circle of cones. Put a bridle on your horse. Use your "t'ai chi walk" (pg. 148) to establish a steady rhythm around the cones. Imagine there is a box floating directly in front of you. You want your horse's nose to be level with the box. If it falls behind or drifts away from the circle, reach out with the hand that's closest to your horse (the right in this example). That's your buckle hand. Take a hold of the rein, then slide down toward the bit with your inside hand. Bring his nose level with the box, then let go completely of the rein with both hands. Repeat as needed until he keeps his nose level with the box. C/R.

Step Two: Lateral flexions. Now use the rein to place his nose in the box. Release the rein as soon as his nose is in the box. Click and treat when he is able to keep his nose there on his own. He'll be stepping laterally out of your way as you walk forward around the circle.

distractions in the arena will have disappeared. There will just be the two of you moving together as partners. If you keep working this exercise, you'll be able to develop lateral work at liberty, but more on that later. For now you're going to get on and ride this same exercise. Under saddle you're going to use your single-rein riding skills to ride the same "Why would you leave me?" lesson you were just walking. You can ride around your cone circle or you can forget about geography and just let him wander around the arena. Both approaches work. But first you might want to practice the lesson with a friend.

"WHY WOULD YOU LEAVE ME?" GAMES

You'll be the "rider"; your friend will be the "horse". Here are a couple of different games that will help you with your riding:

• Standing directly behind her, place your index fingers on her ribs. Your fingers are the rider's "legs". Now go for a ride. If she's like "Nervous Nelly" she's going to have her own plans about where she wants to go. You'll feel times when she's directly lined up between your hands and you're both heading in the same direction, and other times when she's definitely running through you to head off on her own agenda.

Get feedback from your horse. Some of you may be too tight. You're holding your breath, so your body feels rigid and your signals aren't clear. Others may feel too soft, too absent. There's no clear intent coming from your signals. Review the riding awareness exercises in Part 4. They will help you with this exercise.

• Play the "Why would you leave me?" game with your friend. Walk side by side. Any time she starts to wander off, reach out and take a hold of her hand. Wait for her to move towards you. Release her hand. If she follows you, continue walking. If she doesn't, take her hand again. Note: this is a "set it up and wait" game. Do not pull her to you. Or better yet, pull her to you just to see what that's like. She may indeed follow you, but you'll see how unbalanced she is by the pull. So next time wait for her to give to you. Release her hand and then immediately pick it up again until she is walking with you. Can you get her to follow you around the arena? What about around the circle of cones?

Be both the horse and the rider in these games. When you're the horse, try walking with your eyes closed. Imagine you are your own horse. What would you do? Are you "Nervous Nell" dragging your rider off to see the other horses? Or are you the horse standing with his feet in cement refusing to move? You'll gain a lot of insight into your horse with these awareness exercises. You may experience some "ah ha!" moments that help you understand why he responds the way he does.

RIDING THE "WHY WOULD YOU LEAVE ME?" LESSON

So now you're finally on your horse. You're riding him on the buckle and he's wandering off to the far end of the arena where the hay is stacked. Pick up the buckle with your right hand. Slide down the rein with your left and stabilize it against the saddle. All you want him to do is bring his nose to the side. That's the "why would you leave me?" response that you're looking for. If he resists, the tension on the line will bring his feet onto a small circle. Wait for his jaw to soften and give to the side. Release the rein completely. If he's riding with you, leave him alone. But chances are he'll veer right back in pursuit of his own interests. Slide down the rein and ask again.

If at any point in this he breaks from a walk into a trot, or spooks, slide down the rein, connect with the corner of his mouth, lift the rein and take his hips around (Ch. 21). Add enough pressure to the rein to stop his feet and drop his head (Ch. 20). The mantra for head lowering was: this is not a forward moving exercise. The mantra for this game is: *this is a walking only exercise.* Later you can do this same lesson at the trot and the canter, but it's important for now that your horse stays in the walk.

That means that if he stalls out along the fenceline, bump him forward with your legs. If his feet are truly stuck in cement, slide down the rein and displace his head off to the side just as you would with a green horse (pg. 81) until his feet are in motion again. Then leave him alone as long as he's with you. The instant he goes off course slide down your inside rein and ask for his nose to come back to you.

How will you know when he's off course? Relate what you're feeling to the games you just played. When he's on the same course you are, you'll feel him evenly between your legs. Each time you release the rein and he stays with you, click and give him a treat. When you have three clicks in a row on one side, change rein. Get three clicks in a row on the other rein. Again remember, if he stiffens up and barges through your rein, slide down and take his hips around. Until he is soft and responsive to the rein on both sides, this is a *walking only* exercise.

Keep track of your count. Later you're going to be riding patterned exercises where counting matters, so this is a good skill to learn now before I add in more elements. When you can get three clicks one right after the other, begin to lengthen out the number of strides he stays with you before you click.

Chapter Twenty-Five: The "Why Would You Leave Me?" Game

DEVELOPING AN UPPER-LEVEL PERFORMANCE HORSE

As you stretch out the number of strides your horse stays with you before you click, you'll discover that your previously "Nervous Nelly" is becoming fun to ride. He's no longer jumping out of his skin at every little sound. If something does startle him, you can instantly get him to stop and drop his head. When he's settled, you can go on, and now he actually feels as though he's connected to you. You're riding together having a real conversation. You can add distractions. You can ride in different locations. The tools you're building keep you safe and keep him focused on you. There's just one problem: he's still crooked.

Does this sound familiar? When you ride, are you constantly readjusting your saddle? Does it always seem to slip over to one side so you never feel as though your horse's hindquarters are truly underneath you? On a circle does your horse go with his head bent to the outside and his weight falling onto his inside shoulder? Is it hard for him to pick up his true canter leads? That's the stage our "Nervous Nelly" horse is in. In this section we're going to address all of these problems and more by applying a very simple mantra to the lesson you've just started: **the longer you stay with a lesson, the more good things you will discover it gives you.**

In this case the lesson is going to be a very simple one. You're going to pick up the rein and wait for his jaw to give. This is what you've been doing in the "Why would you leave me?" game, only now you're going to pick up the reins not just a few dozen times, but many hundreds. The end result will be a horse who is soft as butter and ready for lateral work. That's it. That's all you're going to do. It's very simple. In fact it's so simple, it takes some explaining and that's what the rest of this chapter is about. What you do with this softening once you've got it will be explained later.

BENDING REVISITED: AVOIDING THE CONTACT TRAP

You already started this lesson in the "Why would you leave me?" game. Now we're going to see where it can take you. Here's a scenario by way of review. Let's suppose you're working your horse to the left in your arena. You're making progress with the "Why would you leave me?" game. He stays with you most of the time, but when you get near the gate, he still tends to veer off. So you slide down the rein and stabilize your hand. He tips his nose back to the inside. You know you're supposed to let go at this point, but you also know that every time you do, he just drags

LATERAL WORK

1.) Stay with an exercise long enough and all kinds of wonderful things emerge. The "Why would you leave me?" game evolves into lateral flexions. Lateral flexions prepare the horse's balance for upper-level performance.

2-3.) With just five short rides under her belt, this filly is well on her way to becoming a clicker superstar. Single-rein riding has given her rider so much more than just the control she needs to be safe. It is also turning this filly into a stunningly beautiful horse. Note how much her balance changes between photos 2 and 3 as she picks herself up via the single-rein lateral flexions.

2.) At first she's all strung out and on her forehand. She's calm. She's relaxed. All good things, but there's no energy in her walk.

3.) Now she has picked herself up. Note how she has lifted through the base of her neck creating a rounder balance overall. Lateral flexions are the key to this shift in balance.

4.) Photo #2 has been superimposed over photo #3. The two riders overlap exactly. You can see how much she has picked herself up, and how much longer her strides are when she engages her hindend. She's a small horse so it's important that she carry herself well.

you right back toward the gate. You so don't want to let go. No one is watching. Your horse won't tell! You hang onto that rein until you are well past the gate.

What you've just done is perfectly normal. You've fallen into the contact trap. A rider who thinks like this becomes trapped in a pattern where she can never let go. When she does, her horse's balance falls apart, so she ends up holding on longer and longer. Sound familiar? This is what many people call "riding on contact", and the problem with that is it tends to make both horses and riders stiff and reliant on the reins for balance. There is another solution to this dilemma, and that's to let go completely and then ask for the bend again right away. — Get a response, let go, ask again. — It's like bending a coat hanger.

Repeat this a couple hundred times, and, even without any help from the clicker, your horse will stop leaning on you for support. He'll have to find his own balance because he can't depend on you to hold him up. He'll also discover that it's easier just to leave his head bent slightly to the side rather than lugging it back to the right each time you release. Now he'll be staying flexed all on his own. You don't have to hold him in that position. All you had to do was keep releasing him every time he was right.

That's the theory behind the "Why would you leave me?" game. If you're persistent, your horse will stay with you for longer and longer stretches without your having to hang onto him. And now that he's staying longer, something else interesting is happening. He's getting softer, and he's more balanced. The saddle is staying more in the center of his back. All you've been doing is asking for his jaw to soften to you, and all these other things have been happening. All you've done is ask for a couple of hundred gives of the jaw.

REPETITION

I know for a great many people when I say a couple of hundred repetitions their ears instantly flap shut. More than a couple of repetitions of an exercise and they're thinking — boring —, but that's because they have the image of an assembly line. An assembly line turns out thousands of exact duplicates of a given item. That could not be further from what is happening here. Each release of the rein is a piece of information for the horse. He's processing and learning from that information and changing his behavior as a result. He's not only learning to bend and give to pressure; he's also learning how to learn.

The mantra truly is: stay with an exercise long enough to see all the good things it can give you.

Here is the key that unlocks that door I described at the beginning of the chapter. You're going to ask your horse to soften his jaw not once, but hundreds of times. Think of it like bending a coat hanger. The more you bend it, the softer it gets. Each time another layer softens and releases along with the jaw, it unlocks another door. Your horse lets you a little further into his "house". You connect the rein a little deeper until every muscle, every joint is in balance and moving with you. The centaur you imagined in Chapter 24 is now the centaur you are riding.

SOFTNESS: BRINGING THE STATUE TO LIFE

Do you remember the children's stories you read when you were little where a magic spell would breathe life into a stone statue? Imagine a statue of a horse coming to life. First the very tip of his nose would start to wiggle and move. Then the stone would melt away from his head and neck. He'd be able to bend his neck and then shake his shoulders. As the stone dropped away from the rest of his body, he'd come alive. He'd toss his head and race about, shaking the last bit of stiffness out of his joints. That's the change you feel with single-rein riding. The entire horse seems to come alive with energy.

First you pick up the rein and focus just on softening the jaw. As you do, your horse's head and neck will free up. You won't be asking for this directly. It's just something that evolves as the jaw softens. In order to soften his jaw consistently, your horse has to line his hips up under his body and stop leaning through his shoulders. He has to soften his neck and release his poll. If his head is too high, he has to lower it; too low, raise it. And remember, this doesn't happen because you're pulling his head up or down. It happens simply because you've taken the slack out of the rein to say "I want something." And the "something" you want is for his jaw to soften. That's all.

DEVELOPING "FEEL"

Many riders worry they won't be able to tell when their horse has softened to them. Maybe they're just beginning, and they think they need years of experience to develop "feel". That's a belief system you don't have to buy into. When a horse stops leaning on the rein and gives, even a novice rider will feel it.

Try this experiment. Hold onto one end of a lead rope and have a friend hold the other. Hold your end steady. Don't let your hand move. Your friend is going to alternate between taking the slack out of the rope and releasing it again. Your job is simply to tell her what she's doing. You can see her hand moving, so this part of the experiment is easy. Now close your eyes, so you have only the feel down the rope to guide you. How many times did you get right? If you're like most people, probably all of them. Feel isn't hard unless you're convinced that it's going to be.

LET THE FORCE BE WITH YOU
As your horse softens his whole body consistently into the bend, you'll be able to connect his feet to the rein. Now you can ask him to soften his jaw and bend to the left, and at the same time you can think, "I'd like you to step over a little to the right."★

Your horse is in the habit of listening to your body. When he feels your hand on the rein, he'll soften his jaw, and he'll also be asking "What else do you want?" (pg. 100). Your body will be giving him the clues he needs to find the answer.

At this point you're probably thinking, "I have no idea what she's talking about. What am I supposed to be doing to get my horse to step sideways?"

When riders ask me this, I tell them all they have to do is think about the horse's shoulders moving over. They hate that answer. They think I'm holding out on them. There's got to be some major thing they're supposed to be doing with their hands or their seat or their legs, and I'm not telling them. They want aids! They want a formula! And I'm spouting some zen stuff about just dream it and it will happen—sort of like the mantra "Let the Force be with you" in Star Wars. And that's really exactly what it is.

I'm not talking here about some spiritual transformation but a simple physical fact. Remember how you taught your horse the difference between head lowering and a hip-flip? The motivator was the same in both instances, pressure on the rein, but the additional clues he tuned in to were the shifts in your position. After a while, all you had to do was think about moving his hips over and he'd respond (pg. 130-132). Horses are so sensitive that they can feel the difference your thoughts make in your body. You can't think about going sideways without the thought causing changes in your body. It's up to your horse to notice those changes and to make the appropriate responses to them.

If you get into the heavy-duty "trying" mode, you'll just get stiff and your horse may respond by becoming resistant. If you can get him to step sideways at all, it'll be by dragging or pushing him over. We want the opposite. Get your horse to soften to you, then think about where you'd like him to take his feet. Imagine your own feet walking in that direction, and your horse will float over with you. Use your center. This is a term borrowed from Chinese martial arts. It is one of the building blocks Sally Swift talks about in her book, *Centered Riding*★★. These exercises will help you energize your center so you ride with invisible signals. Everything will feel light and easy. Just a thought will turn your horse. I talked about becoming a centaur in the last chapter. As you ride these exercises that is exactly how you will feel.

TRANSLATING WORDS INTO ACTIONS
Building the "centaur" connection via single-rein riding is such an easy way to learn to ride. I keep thinking of all those lessons where an instructor was trying to explain in minute detail what I was supposed to be doing with my body. Even when I could remember it all, I couldn't always manage to put the words into action.

Words make very poor translations for movement. Just try explaining to a friend what you do with your back when you ride, and you'll see what I mean.

To understand the process behind single-rein riding try this little experiment: Look up from this book. Go ahead, try it. . . . No, I didn't say move your head. I just said look up, but I'll bet most of you did more than just move your eyes. That's exactly right.

Now look over your right shoulder. See what I mean? You didn't just glance over. You moved your head, your neck, your shoulders, and maybe even your ribs and your hips. You didn't have to think about it, and I didn't have to spell out in detail each little shift of your body. The sequence of movements came naturally. I just had to ask you to look over your shoulder, and your body automatically did the rest.

When you're in the saddle and you think about turning to the right, your body responds to your thought. If your horse can feel the change, the possibility exists for him to respond to it. Since he can feel a fly landing on his back, he can certainly feel you shifting in the saddle.

Perceiving a signal isn't enough. He also has to understand what it means (pg. 131). Maybe you've been very inconsistent in your riding. Perhaps your balance isn't very stable, or you weren't very clear yourself about what you wanted. Your horse has learned to tune out all the extra movement he feels—by now it's become like static on a radio. Your job as a rider is to teach him which of those many shifts mean something he should pay attention to.

You do that by becoming more consistent in your requests. Picking up the rein means you're asking your horse for something. Where you hold the rein and how you shift your body are signals that tell him what that something is. Your horse won't be consistent in his responses until you're consistent—and persistent—with your requests. If you pick up

---
★ This lesson is also in *The Click That Teaches: Video Lesson 4: Stimulus Control*, by Alexandra Kurland; The Clicker Center, NY
★★ *Centered Riding*, by Sally Swift; Trafalgar Square, VT

The Click That Teaches: Riding With The Clicker

the rein to ask for something, make sure you get at least an approximation of the response you're after before you release that rein. If you're asking for a turn and your horse just keeps barreling straight ahead, don't release the rein just because the moment has passed where you needed the turn. If you do, you'll be digging yourself a training hole.

Every time you release the rein without getting at least some piece of the response you're after, you're teaching your horse to ignore you. The deeper the hole, the longer he'll resist against the rein. He'll be convinced that he doesn't have to change. Your hand on the rein means nothing. It's just static down the line, and sooner or later you will let go.

I see so many riders fall into this trap. Perhaps the horse is leaning onto his inside shoulder through the corners of the ring. The rider has been told to use inside leg to move her horse over. Her horse feels her leg pressing against his side, but he just ignores it. The rider is beginning to doubt herself. Her horse isn't responding. In fact he's getting worse! She must be doing something wrong. She lets go of the rein before she makes an even bigger mess.

The reality is that this is the worst thing she could have done. Now she's going to have to deal with an extinction burst of mammoth proportions. Her horse meekly isn't going to stop pulling on the rein. He knows what works, and he'll be fully committed to sticking with it. The next time she picks up the rein he'll be even more determined to hold out for what he wants to do.

Often it's the nicest people who dig the deepest holes for themselves and their horses. They want to be kind; they want to be fair. They don't want to upset their horses, so they let go just when they should be insisting. All too often the result is that their sweet horse becomes confused and frustrated. The extinction bursts become dangerous to ride, and the horse has to be "straightened out" by a professional trainer.

Don't let this happen to your horse. Follow the principles of good training (Ch. 5). Ride where you can, not where you can't. Train in small steps, so that every time you pick up the rein you know you can get a "yes answer" from your horse. If your horse is dragging you off through his shoulders, you don't have to get a complete 180 degree turn to be successful. If you can get just his jaw to respond to you for just a second, let go. That gives you a "yes answer" you can build on. Get it again, and again, and pretty soon you'll have the feet, the mind, the emotions — all following your thought. But get at least that one little piece every time you pick up the rein.

You don't have to ride with a clicker and treats to have the principles of operant conditioning working for you. However, if you don't understand them, they'll almost certainly work against you. You can say you don't believe in gravity, but if you throw an apple straight up, it's still going to come down and hit you on the head. The same is true with the principles of operant conditioning. These are real phenomena that all good trainers are aware of and use to create superior performance. The use of the clicker gives you an additional tool for marking behavior and rewarding your horse. It can accelerate the learning process for both of you.

WHY USE A CLICKER

So what does the does the clicker add to this process? After all, every time you let go of the rein you're giving your horse "yes-answer" information. You're also giving him something he wants — your hand out of his mouth. So why do you need the clicker?

That was the question I had as I was exploring both single-rein riding and clicker training. Other people could ride without their pockets bulging with treats. Why did I need this "crutch"?

Thank goodness for horses and the answers they give. It was my own Peregrine who explained this to me. We were just back from a John Lyons' clinic and I was schooling him in the arena, dutifully working through the work we'd just covered.

I had picked up the rein and released it — picked up the rein and released it — I don't know how many times. I really wasn't sure what I was looking for, but I trusted the process. It had always worked for us before. Only now I could sense Peregrine wondering how much longer this was going to go on. He was getting tired of this endless nagging at the rein. And then it happened. . . . I picked up the rein, and Peregrine didn't just release his jaw, he aligned his spine so he flexed at the poll.

It was a dramatic, definite feel that was so much more than anything I had felt from him on that ride. Click! I pulled a peppermint out of my pocket. Peregrine's ears airplaned back and forth. He crunched down the peppermint and focused right back on the task. I could tell he was working away at the puzzle. His interest was right back in the game.

Three releases later and he again had his balance organized enough for him to flex at the poll, only this time he *knew* what he'd done. He could repeat it over and over again, and then, suddenly, there was a new release that lifted out of the base of his neck. That was definitely peppermint-worthy.

After that ride I never again thought of the clicker

as a crutch. Peregrine knew what he had done, and he could repeat it. Out of all those oceans of gives that I had asked for, the click highlighted the important ones. It gave us both something to latch on to, landmarks to follow through this unknown territory we were exploring.

BUILDING LANDMARKS

So how do you use the clicker? Suppose you're riding a very stiff horse. Every time you pick up the rein you feel his jaw like iron resisting against you. You're after one single piece of behavior: tip your nose slightly to the side.

At first he just walks a small circle, following his nose without actually bending. But then he tips his nose slightly to the side. Click, release the rein, and give him a treat. He's just found the first right answer in the "Why would you leave me?" game.

Continue on: picking up the rein and releasing for those tiny gives of the jaw. What you want is so simple it's hard. This stage of single-rein riding reminds me of the treasure hunts we had when I was little. The most frustrating clues to figure out were always the obvious ones: the things that were hidden out in plain sight were always the hardest to find. That's the kind of puzzle you're asking your horse to solve. You're asking your horse to repeat something so simple that he may not even notice that he's doing it. That's where the clicker comes in.

You're going to pick up the rein and release it every time you feel him soften his jaw just a tiny bit. Eventually he'll figure out what you want, and you'll feel him move his jaw very deliberately to the side. But he won't be just tilting his muzzle to the side. He'll actually be relaxing his jaw. Click! That's another milestone to mark with the clicker.

Pick up the rein and release, pick up the rein and release until you get three of these clickable moments. Change rein and repeat the process on the right.

As his jaw relaxes more and more consistently the next milestone will appear. You won't make it happen. It will just evolve: he'll drop his head slightly. You won't notice it at first. Your focus will be so much on the jaw and rein mechanics that you won't notice this next layer until it is already happening consistently. And then you'll see it: the best feel on the rein comes not just when he softens his jaw, but when he drops his head ever so slightly. That's your new clickable moment. Now you're piggy-backing a very powerful differential schedule of reinforcement (Ch. 9) onto the underlying horse-training system of pressure and release.

"I KNOW AN OLD LADY..."

Pick up the rein and continue the process. You're still releasing him each time he softens his jaw, but you will only click if he softens his jaw and tips his ear slightly downward. Get three of these clickable moments and change rein.

As you work on each successive sequence of three clicks, the next milestone will appear. Again you don't make it happen—it evolves. Now he will soften his jaw, tip his ear slightly downward *and* flex at the poll. Click and jackpot.

You're no longer dealing with a simple system of one behavior (release the jaw) and one reward (release the rein). You're creating a sequence of linked behaviors: release your jaw, drop your head sightly, soften your poll, and — bingo! — now you also get a click and a treat.

You'll continue to click and treat your horse each time he gives you this additional piece of the sequence. As he begins to recognize the subtle differences that get him clicked, he'll get himself organized more efficiently. At this point, each time you touch the rein, you'll feel him soften his jaw, tip his ear and flex at the poll. You'll also see a change in his neck. He'll be flexed around to the side and his head will be more level with his withers. His nose won't be stuck up in the clouds anymore, and overall he'll be more relaxed.

So now you'll begin to withhold the click. You'll continue to release the rein each time you feel him soften his jaw. That's still the single criterion he needs to meet to get you out of his mouth, but now he has to do even more to get clicked. He has to tip his ear, release his poll *and* soften the long muscle of his neck.

Remember the analogy of the statue coming to life? This whole transformation into a soft horse really does feel like granite melting. You won't feel the neck soften until the poll softens, and you won't feel the poll soften until the jaw softens. It's a little like the children's song: "I know an old lady who swallowed a fly . . ." One thing just follows after the other.

> I know an old lady who swallowed a fly,
> I don't know why she swallowed a fly.
> I guess she'll die.
>
> I know an old lady who swallowed a spider.
> That wriggled and wriggled and tickled
>   inside her.
> She swallowed the spider to catch the fly,
> But I don't know why she swallowed the fly.
> I guess she'll die.

The Click That Teaches: Riding With The Clicker

I know an old lady who swallowed a bird.
She swallowed the bird to catch the spider,
That wriggled and wriggled and tickled inside her.
She swallowed the spider to catch the fly,
But I don't know why she swallowed the fly.
I guess she'll die."

And so on to the end of the song until the old lady finally swallows a horse. (She dies, of course.) Our little venture is going to have a happier ending, but we're going to follow the song's example of adding element after element to build a "softening" chain reaction.

BUILDING LONGER CHAINS

After the poll, softening the long muscle of the neck is the next element in that chain. You'll start to see the muscle flex and bounce, and the head drop level with the withers. The horse will flex easily to the side with no pull or resistance in his neck. As he does, click, he's released another layer of his body that you're going to mark with a treat.

You'll do the same thing you did to get your horse consistently softening his poll. You'll click him each time he successfully organizes his body and softens his neck along with the other elements.

But note: each element in the chain *must* be present and in the proper sequence for him to earn a click. If he simply bends his neck without first softening his jaw and lining up his poll, you'll use the skills you learned in the head-lowering exercise to straighten out his neck so he can begin again (Ch. 20).

As you work, you'll see his neck begin to have a smooth arc to it, stretching from his withers to his ears, and you'll feel changes happening under the saddle as well. His shoulders will begin to soften and his back will start to come up. The next layer of the statue is coming to life. Again, you'll withhold your click. You're going to wait for your horse to soften even deeper into the base of his neck. As he does, he'll be able to bend his head even further around to the side. You'll see wrinkles appearing in the base of his neck and you'll feel his withers lift and his shoulders soften (pg. 113). He's learning to release and lift from the root of his neck in preparation for collection and the engagement of the hindquarters.

So how are you doing all this? You could simply forget about geography and focus just on getting the jaw to soften, but I know many riders when they do this lose the connection to the feet. They end up with a soft, but extremely wiggly horse. Another way to do this is to begin with the basic "Why-would-you-leave-me?" exercise and perfect it with another pattern called three-flip-three. Three-flip-three will be explained in the next chapter. The beauty of this pattern is it connects both the jaw and the hip to the rider's hand. In three-flip-three the jaw opens the door to the hip, and the hip opens the door to the jaw. The more you connect with one, the more you can connect with the other. Combined they let you line up the "drill team" of hips and shoulders to produce beautiful lateral work.

THE EVOLUTION OF SOFTNESS

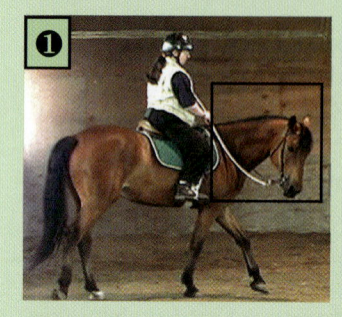

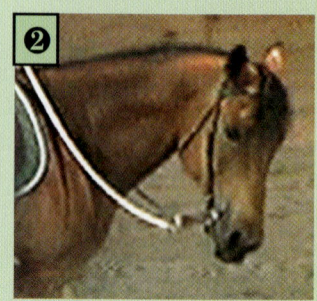

1. and 2.) As Robin softens his jaw and his poll, his neck muscles begin to relax. This isn't something the rider "makes" happen. It simply evolves with the softening of the jaw. Photo 2 shows the area in the box enlarged.

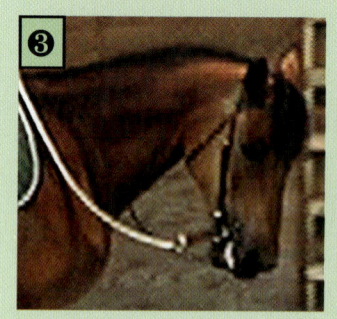

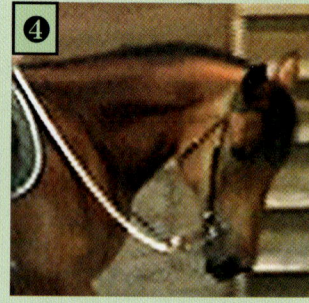

3. and 4.) As the process continues, the long muscle of his neck becomes more clearly defined, and you can see a definite triangle appearing as he lifts through the base of his neck. It's hard to see in these photos, but wrinkles are appearing along the shelf of his shoulder as he lefts the base of his neck.

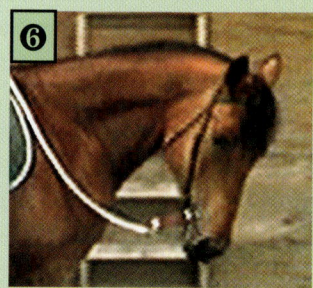

5. and 6.) You could do an anatomy lesson with these photos, the muscles are so well defined. Note the beautiful arch that has evolved as Robin's neck muscles relax, and he lifts from the base of his neck.

CHAPTER 26
Connecting the Feet: Three-Flip-Three

In this chapter you're going to combine the softening of the front end with the hip-flips of Chapter 21 to create lateral flexions. To do this you'll ride a pattern called "three-flip-three". The result will be a horse who is connected to the rein from the tip of his nose all the way through to his hind end.

CONNECTING THE FEET AND THE MIND

Our "Nervous Nelly" from the previous chapters is ready for a name change. He no longer jumps at every little sound he hears. The "calm down" cue took care of that (Ch. 20). Now that you know how to disengage his hips (Ch. 21), you can ride with other horses. He isn't dragging you off to visit with them, nor is he trying to get back to the barn. And thanks to all those softenings of the jaw (Ch. 25) that stiff-like-an-iron-bar resistance you used to encounter isn't there anymore, either. He's not as heavy on his forehand, and in fact, now that you think about it, he's not as crooked. Remember how you always had to keep shifting the saddle back into center of his back? Well now it's staying put where it belongs.

"Nervous Nelly" just doesn't fit him anymore. He's really gotten to be a lot of fun to ride. You used to worry all the time about having his attention. You never knew when he was going to spook and run off into the next county. Now that he's softening to the rein, his attention is with you. He's out of reform school and ready to begin his real education. You've got the calm, consistent horse you've always dreamed of, and all it took were a few simple exercises to create the change. Now it's time to go beyond basics and create the kind of performance horse many people never even imagine they can have.

DREAMS INTO REALITY

Years ago I was having a lunge line lesson on one of my trainer's Andalusians. I was bouncing all over the place trying to find my seat. I can only imagine how frustrated she must have been watching me unsettling all her fine-tuned training, but the extra spring in this horse's gaits sent me bouncing out of the saddle.

Finally, something clicked for me (no pun intended). My seat settled into the horse's rhythm. His gaits steadied and became even more suspended, and I felt heaven. That's the only way I know to describe it. I've talked about this many times with my clients. How do you describe these incredible sensations, especially to someone who has never experienced them? All I know is that I could have ridden an entire lifetime and never realized that a horse could move like this. And it isn't just the Andalusians and Lusitanos who can offer you this incredible freedom and lift in their gaits. I've since discovered that (unless they are very unsound) ALL horses can feel like this. So, my ultimate goal in riding is not centered any more around *where* my horse goes, but *how* he feels. I want this "died-and-gone-to-heaven" feel all the time. Now that you've got a safe horse to ride, the rest of this book will be focused on creating just that. The way you get there is through an exercise I call "three-flip-three".

THREE-FLIP-THREE

You'll be using the jaw softenings from the previous chapter.

(1.) The first "three" in "three-flip-three" means you will get three gives of the jaw in a row. You'll release the rein after each give.

2.) "Flip" means you'll focus on the inside hip and ask your horse to step more deeply under his body. Note: by the time you are ready to ask for the hip, your horse will already be balanced and yielding his hip to your hand. *The give of the hip is a little thing.*

3.) The second "three" means you'll ask for three more softenings of the jaw. The drill team balance of the horse that's developed will let you move his shoulders over laterally.

The Click That Teaches: Riding With The Clicker

STAYING ON THE BALANCE BEAM

Once you have your horse softening to you through the "Why would you leave me?" game, it becomes very easy to connect up the feet. As I said in the last chapter, the jaw delivers the hip, and the hip delivers the jaw. You still aren't concerned with *where* your horse goes. The pattern you'll be riding is not connected to any particular geography in your riding space. *How* your horse carries himself is still your primary focus.

In the previous chapter I had you focus just on the jaw. I wanted you to discover how much you could get when you stayed with one small element. As a result of the "Why would you leave me?" game your horse is now wonderfully soft, but he may also be meandering all over the arena. Yes, he's bending his neck, but sometimes he's also over-flexing and falling out through his outside shoulder. Other times he brings his head around too low and ends up leaning down onto his shoulder. This is all a natural part of the learning process for both of you. Horses do one of two things with their shoulders. They fall in on the inside, and they pop out over the outside. Everyone who rides has experienced both. The horse who leans in is the horse who cuts his corners, who falls in on his circles, and who canters counter-bent so you feel as though you have to hold him up through his turns.

The horse who pops out through his outside shoulder is the horse who drags you the entire length of the arena instead of turning when you ask. He's the trail horse who bows out his body spooking past the big rock, and drags you onto the path he knows heads back home.

One of the goals of single-rein riding is teaching your horse how to carry his shoulders in a balanced upright position. You want to get him so he is neither running out through the outside, nor falling in on the inside. An image I use that helps to visualize and feel this is that of a balance beam. As you study the photos of the horses in this book, you'll see the balance-beam balance that I am talking about—when it is present, and when it is not.

You want your horse to feel as though his whole body is balanced on the beam. When a horse falls through his shoulders, it feels as though he's fallen off the balance beam. You won't expect your horse to have perfect balance all the time — even Olympic gymnasts fall off the beam. But you do want him to know how to get back on the beam quickly. That's what you're teaching him layer by layer through this process with the clicker and single-rein riding.

And note: a horse doesn't have to be traveling on a straight path to be on a balance beam. Remember when you were little, and you used to walk along the raised curb of a sidewalk? The curb could arc around a bend, and you could still follow it. The same is true with the horse. Being straight refers to his balance, not his path. He can be straight on a circle which simply means his shoulders and hips are neither falling in nor out relative to track he's on.

RIDING THE PERFECT HORSE

When you ride, you are always sitting on two horses, the real, physical horse, and an imagined, perfect horse. You want to ride the perfect horse, otherwise you'll be so distracted by what the actual horse is doing, you'll fall off your own balance beam.

That's really what position work is all about, trying to get you to line up with your perfect horse. When you do, your real horse will often come into balance underneath you. It's like two photographic images that become superimposed one over the other until they become one image. The question is will the physical horse merge and become balanced with the imagined horse, or will the imagined horse deteriorate and become identical to the physical horse?

This is where the rider's concentration becomes important. If you imagine your horse tensing and spooking at every little sound, that's what you'll get. To change your horse, you have to change your image of him. You can begin by imagining that you are riding a trained, balanced horse. But suppose you don't know what that feels like. Suppose you've never ridden any horses besides your own, and they've all been greener than green. How can you picture something you've never experienced?

My image of the perfect horse is an ever-evolving one. As I ride and learn, I feel layers I've never experienced before. My image becomes more refined. I become aware of nuances in responses that seem obvious to me now, but were only vague, barely understood concepts before. A novice rider might not feel any of this. She may never have felt the way a horse can float through the shoulders, or engage and lift through his back. That won't be part of her image of the perfect horse. A more advanced rider than myself will be feeling things I haven't even begun to imagine.

The perfect horse for a barrel racer or a cutting horse trainer will be very different from the horse I'm imagining. None of that matters. We can each ride our own perfect horse. We can make up our images out of our life experiences. Even if you're a novice rider you've still experienced moments when your horse felt better than usual. Maybe your horse was more relaxed, or he turned better than he did the

Chapter Twenty-Six: Connecting the Feet: Three-Flip-Three

day before. Those rides go into a state of excellence that describes your perfect horse. You have other, non-riding images you can draw on. Maybe you remember pretending to be a tight rope walker as a little kid as you balanced along a fallen tree trunk. You know what good balance feels like. You can add new images to the mix. You can get off your horse and walk through circles and turns. When you lean out or fall in, you'll feel within yourself what happens to your balance. In contrast you can line your shoulders up over your hips and feel the ease with which you can move. You can take dance classes or study t'ai chi. You can work with an Alexander or Feldenkrais Practitioner. You can learn to move with ease and grace in your own body.

You can use all these images and experiences to imagine the balance of the perfect horse. When your real horse falls off the balance beam, you'll feel it as a lean against your leg, a pull against your hand, a lack of stability under your seat. You'll respond by stabilizing your hand, and putting more muscle tone (as opposed to tension) into your body. If your horse leans out, he'll encounter your leg like a barrier saying: "This door is closed. Don't even think about going this way." You'll wait for your horse to regroup and get back on the balance beam. Click!

You won't start by asking the entire horse to join you on the balance beam. That would be too much to expect in one step. Instead, you'll do it in pieces, lining up first the nose, then the poll, then the long muscle of the neck, then the base of the neck, then the withers, and finally the hips and shoulders. As you line up the head and neck, you'll discover that it's easy to get the rest of the horse on the balance beam. And the beauty of this process is that you'll know when you're ready to move on and focus on the next step because it will already be happening.

THREE-FLIP-THREE
Once the jaw is consistently softening to you in the "Why would you leave me?" game, you're ready to combine the jaw with the hip-flip exercise of Chapter 21 to expand the pattern into a new sequence called "three-flip-three". Here's the process:

Step One: Good, Better, Best.
Pick up the left rein using your single-rein technique. Release the rein when your horse softens his jaw. Get three releases in a row. Each time you slide down the rein, you'll be connecting with your horse a little deeper into his body. The first give is "good": he'll soften his jaw to you. The second give is "better": he'll tip his ear towards you. The third give is the "best": he'll flex at the poll. And with each give, he'll be lining up more of his body on the "balance beam". On the third give his inside hind leg will be stepping more deeply under his body, bringing him into a correct bend. He's ready for the next step.

One thing to note here: you are counting gives, not strides. At first your horse may have to walk several steps before he can get himself untangled enough to release his jaw. Eventually gives will match strides. This is what you are aiming for. When you've reached this level of perfection, his hips and shoulders will line up beautifully with his front end. For now you'll be playing a waiting game as your horse finds his way onto the "balance beam". Stay focused on your count. If you lose track of your pattern, you will make it harder you both of you to learn. Each time you let go of the rein, even if you're not sure you picked the right moment, that's a give, so count and *keep track*. (See pg. 164 for illustrations.)

Step Two: Flip the hips.
For the fourth give slide a little further down the rein, and instead of stabilizing your hand on the saddle for a give of the jaw, lift it up, as you look back at his inside hip. (See Chapter 21.) Don't twist and lean; turn only as far as you can look without dropping your shoulder and collapsing your ribs. On a stiff horse this won't be very far, but as you and your horse become more limber you'll be able to turn more easily.

Depending upon how much slack you took out of the rein, you'll get anything from a slight shift to a full turn. In this exercise we want to keep his feet in motion, so you don't want to take so much rein that you stall out the feet. With each of the previous gives, he was already bringing his hips onto the "balance beam" so you're not looking for a big change. The give of the hip is a small shift in balance. As you feel him step up more underneath himself, release the rein. (See pg. 165 for illustrations.)

Step Three: Connect the feet.
After the fourth release, immediately, without any delay, pick up the rein again and ask him to soften his front end three more times, but this time you're going to be thinking about your horse stepping laterally to the side. This is the piece that really connects the feet to the softening of the rein. You've already got your horse correctly bent, with his hocks underneath him and his weight off his shoulders. Now as you ask him to soften his jaw, it's easy to get him to take a step to the side. All you have to do is send your energy in that direction, and you've got your first step of lateral work. Click!

163

The Click That Teaches: Riding With The Clicker

THREE-FLIP-THREE

Step One: three baby gives of the jaw.   Step Two: yield the hips.

Step Four: Send the horse forward.
The third softening in Step Three completes a sequence but not the exercise. Next ask your horse to go forward by holding the reins in one hand right at the buckle, so they're even on both sides. Lift your hand and take it forward towards your horse's ears. As you do, ride him actively forward with your seat and legs. If you need to, cluck or bump him with your legs or reach back with your free hand to encourage him to move on.

Riding the horse forward is a critical step in this whole process. It's natural for a horse to lose energy as you ask him to flex and turn. If you don't include a step that puts energy back into the system, you'll end up with a horse who just drags along. You need to bump him forward until you feel a definite response. Keep working at this until your horse is moving along freely, and he no longer feels as though he's pulling his feet out of wet cement.

Once you've got your horse re-energized, change rein. If you were working on the left rein in the previous sequence, switch to the right. Don't grab the rein and pull your horse's head around. That's a mistake many riders make. If you pull him around to the new direction, you're missing an opportunity to experience how light and responsive he's becoming. Reach down slowly. Pick the rein up with fine motor control. Stabilize it and wait for your horse to respond to you.

That's the first give of a new set of three-flip-three. Just as before, ask for three softenings of the jaw, then the hip, then three more softenings of the jaw. That completes another sequence. Pick up the buckle, and ask your horse to walk on with energy.

Teaching a "go forward" cue is just as important as getting your horse to soften, but many riders forget to work on this piece of training because they ride out on trails and their horses move right along without having to be asked. Trails channel horses forward. A rider might not realize she hasn't really taught a "go forward" cue until the first time she gets to an obstacle her horse won't cross. It's not until her horse starts balking and throwing a fit that the rider realizes she's neglected something important.

What she has just learned is that the trail has more influence on her horse than she does, and that's a bad deal. If the horse in front of her canters off, her horse is going to follow whether she wants him to or not. If it's a windy fall day, he has lots of energy, but if it's hot out he just plods along.

That kind of going forward is not what I want from my horse. I want to be in charge of his leg speed. I don't want the horse in front of us, or the weather, or some unexpected goblin controlling my horse. "Three-flip-three" helps to tune up both a horse's gas pedal and his brakes. That's what makes it such a valuable lesson: the balancing behavior for each request is built into the overall exercise. (Remember the principle: **For every behavior you teach there is an opposite behavior you must teach to keep things in balance** (pg. 26)).

When do you add in the clicker to the three-flip-three pattern? At any point where you want to highlight a particular response. Initially you might be clicking for every softening of the jaw. Then you'd ask for two softenings in a row, click. Then three, click. Then three softenings and the hip, click. The first time he steps over laterally, you'll certainly click and make a big fuss. Each time you click you'll begin the pattern over from the beginning. This is just like the "I know an old lady who swallowed a fly" process. You'll be building it slowly, layer by layer.

Chapter Twenty-Six: Connecting the Feet: Three-Flip-Three

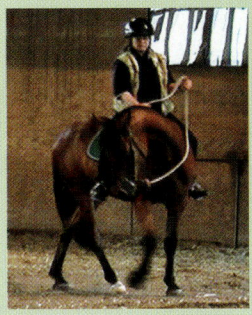

THREE-FLIP-THREE

Step Two, continued: yield the hips.

Step Three: three baby gives of the jaw: connecting the shoulders to the rein.

CLOCK DANCING AND LIGHTNESS FOR THE RIDER

To understand this pattern better here's a ground exercise I learned from John Lyons. For this one your horse gets to stay in his stall. Imagine that you're standing at the center of a large clock. Use your t'ai chi balance (Chapter 24) to put yourself into a right bend, meaning, if you were riding, you'd be picking up your right rein and your horse would be bent around your right inside leg. If you were to step forward onto twelve o'clock, you'd be walking straight ahead. Step back onto six and you'd be backing up. That's obvious. Now what happens if you step over onto eleven o'clock with your left foot? You'd be going both forward and sideways. If you were a horse, you'd be in a lateral flexion. If you stepped onto nine o'clock and then from there onto another nine o'clock, you'd be doing a western sidepass. If you were to step sequentially onto two one o'clocks with your left foot, you'd be walking the pattern for a half-pass in dressage.

Under saddle you can ask your horse to step with you on all these points of the clock. That's what you're doing in three-flip-three. All that, plus you're also expecting him to carry himself like Fred Astaire! You're asking him both to soften to you and connect his feet to the direction you're riding.

This is very important. You've probably all ridden horses you could steer but who were stiff and uncomfortable to ride. Conversely you can have a horse that's very light in its mouth but wiggles all over the place. It's easy in this work to get your horse really light in front and have absolutely no steering wheel. *How* and *where* must be connected to produce a functional performance horse. You're going to get there by learning how to "clock dance" with your horse.

How are you going to do this? For starters you're going to go dancing with a friend. Tell him you'll be the one who's leading and hold his left hand in your right. Now ask him to walk forward by simply stepping forward yourself. He'll follow the suggestion he feels from your hand. You can get him to step over onto one o'clock by stepping in that direction yourself and shifting your hand over. Get one step, then go forward again. Walk a couple of steps straight, then ask for another step onto one o'clock. Repeat this several times, then ask for one step onto two o'clock.

Continue to "dance" with your partner until you can get him to step on all the numbers between twelve and six. Six o'clock will give you a rein-back. Now see if you can figure out how to get him to step towards you on eleven through seven. If your partner is stiff, or if he's used to being the leader, you're going to experience a lot of resistance.

Step 4: Riding the horse actively forward. It doesn't take much to ride Robin actively forward, just a slight lift of the buckle and he balances beautifully between the reins.

The Click That Teaches: Riding With The Clicker

You may need to spend a few minutes getting him to shake out some of the tension he has in his joints. You want your human partner to be as light as your horse. If you feel resistance, the dance will be stiff. Notice the difference as your partner learns to relax his wrist and flow with you in the dance. If your horse learned to relax in the same way, imagine how this would feel under saddle. Remember the expression: if you think different, you are different. Next time you're riding three-flip-three imagine you're dancing with your partner. You'll be amazed at how easily your horse glides over with you.

TURNING THE RIDING RING INTO A DANCE HALL

Now that you've gone dancing with a human partner, you're ready to get back on your horse and take him dancing in the arena. Ask for three-flip-three. Begin by walking him forward a couple of steps on a loose rein. Then pick up the left rein, and ask for three softenings in a row, releasing the rein after each one. On the fourth request, ask for his hips, release the rein, then pick up and ask him to soften his jaw and step over onto one o'clock. He'll be so responsive and light he'll follow the suggestion he feels from your body and your hand. Click and give him a treat.

Riding from your center helps with this★. Your center is your powerhouse. To find it rest one hand behind you in the small of your back, and the other on your abdomen with your thumb in your navel. The area between your two hands is your center. To feel its power try this exercise: stand up and pivot your body, turning from your center. Contrast this with twisting through your rib cage. When you turn from your center, you'll be grounded, the turn is reflected in your whole body. It's much easier for your horse to read your intent and to follow your movement when you turn in this way.

As you're learning the feel of lateral movement, you may find that it helps to point in the direction you want to go. Use the index finger of your inside hand as your pointer as you stabilize your hand against the saddle. You'll be amazed at how easily your horse steps in the direction you're indicating!

Change rein so you can get the same response from the right, stepping toward eleven o'clock in your second set of three gives. Keep repeating this process until you can ask for two or three steps over at a time before you click. When he's good at this, ask for a little more of a sideways step so he reaches over to two and ten o'clock with his outside shoulder.

If at any point his hips 'fall off the balance beam", momentarily shift your focus and ask them to line back up with the rest of his body. Remember, when you think different, you are different. If you want his hips to move, put your focus on them.

When do you click in this process? Anytime you need to clarify, motivate, or appreciate. If you think it will help your horse to understand that the step he just gave was exactly what you wanted, then click and give him a treat. When you're asking for something new and challenging, the extra motivation the clicker provides will help keep him interested and working harder. And when he gives you a wonderful effort that feels great, click and give him a jackpot to let him know how much you appreciate him.

FLEXIBILITY AND "DRILL TEAMS"

The "dance floor" exercises in this chapter create lateral flexions. They in turn will make your horse more supple and flexible. What else they do depends on how you ride them. Initially, while you're first learning lateral bends, you'll probably lose control of your steering wheel. You'll be so intent on having your horse step over with his front foot that you'll completely forget he has a rear end. You'll get him over-bent and popping out with his outside shoulder. That's all right. Training is like swinging a pendulum. First your horse is too stiff, then he's too wiggly. Eventually you'll find the happy medium where he's perfect.

The key to good lateral work is getting the front and back ends of the horse to line up in sync with each other. Think of it as a drill team. When your horse is going around a corner in a lateral bend, his outside hind leg has a greater distance to travel than his inside front leg. It's easy to get the two ends of the horse out of rhythm. The challenge in good lateral work is to keep all four corners of the horse united. You need to be able to tell the hindquarters to speed up or slow down. You need to be able to tell the shoulders to get back on the balance beam. Single-rein riding gives you the tools to do just that.

If you're feeling a little woolly-headed at this stage, it means you need to stop reading, take a break, and go ride your horse. Ask him what he thinks about all of this. When you come back in, reread the last couple of sections. Remember this is a book made up of many layers. Each time you revisit a lesson, you'll see things you didn't understand before. And every time you revisit a lesson with your horse, you'll discover more of the good things it can give you. You have all the keys now to open all the doors in your training "house" (pg. 153). It's up to you to use them.

LIGHTNESS

The more you practice the routine of three-flip-

★ *Centered Riding*, by Sally Swift; Trafalgar Square, VT

Chapter Twenty-Six: Connecting the Feet: Three-Flip-Three

three, the more responsive your horse will become. To get an idea what this can feel like, clasp your hands together. Now let your left hand take your right hand for a "walk". Move your hands in a fluid circular motion, forward and back, left and right. Clasping your hands together like this gives you a good sense of what a light horse feels like. There's no pull, no resistance. Both hands flow fluidly together as you move them around. That's like picking up a lead rope or your rein and using it to guide a light horse. There's a physical connection between the two of you, but you're partners moving together. There's no drag or stiffness in the rein.

Did I say a light horse? Actually, it's all relative. Light depends upon what you're used to. That's heavy compared with what you can experience by doing another little exercise. Hold your left hand over but not touching your right hand. Imagine you're holding a small ball in your hands. Now move the ball in a circular motion, forward, back, up, down, left, right. Feel how light that is. Your hands are connected, but there's no weight. Go back and clasp your hands together. Move them through the same pattern. What felt light before will now feel heavy. It's all relative.

Is the goal always this much lightness? No. It depends very much upon what you enjoy riding. Light sounds good, and it is a heavenly feel, but many people feel more secure having a little weight in their hands. They need to know the horse is physically connected to the other end of the line. Somewhere between the two extremes of the old "twenty pounds of pressure in both hands" and no weight at all is where most riders and horses feel comfortable.

SELF-CARRIAGE

At this point some of you may be saying to yourselves, "This sounds like a lot to go through, all this picking up of the rein and releasing it. It sounds as though it takes a long time, and I'll have to learn a whole new way to ride. Why should I bother?" Here's an analogy that may help answer this question:

Suppose you're going to visit someone at their farm, and instead of giving you directions they arrange to meet you at a familiar location part way there. On the drive to their farm you're busy keeping track of your friend's car in front of you. You aren't watching for landmarks or counting lights. You do indeed get to the farm, but do you know the route? Could you get there by yourself next time? If you're like me, the answer is no. But give me a clear set of directions to follow, and, once I've figured them out, I can get there again on my own.

The parallel with horse training is obvious. If you are dependent on contact and molding a horse into position, that's all he's going to know. He'll follow the mold without really thinking about what he's doing. He won't be internalizing the changes you want. Take away the constant guidance and he's lost. But when you train with the clicker, the horse becomes a much more active learner. Ultimately it is up to him to organize his own body and create the balance you're looking for.

Here's another story: When I was little, we used to have treasure hunts. My father would hide a present somewhere in the house and we kids would have to find it. He'd give us the first clue. Sometimes it was a riddle we'd have to solve or a set of cryptic directions to decipher. The first clue would lead us to the next, a slip of paper tucked under the corner of a rug or hidden in the pages of a book. That clue would lead us to another and another until finally we would find the actual present. Finding each clue reinforced our efforts and kept us in the game. The present was the ultimate reward.

I remember the frustration we felt when we couldn't instantly solve the puzzle. We'd start demanding more clues. Sometimes, if we were really stuck, my father would give us a tiny hint that would get us jump-started again. Sometimes he'd just smile, rock back on his heels, and say nothing. The message was clear. If we wanted that present, we had to keep trying. And of course we always did. We'd work away at it until the puzzle was solved. We never had a clue we couldn't eventually find.

When we were really little, the clues were simple. As we got older they became fiendishly difficult. Those were the best. I don't remember any of the presents, but I still remember some of those clues. The treasure hunt itself was even more fun than the jackpot at the end.

I think this is why clicker training appeals to me so. It's like those treasure hunts. I've put my horse in a puzzle box. I'm holding up a cone or I'm taking the slack out of his inside rein. I've given him a puzzle, but I don't want to solve it for him. I don't mold him into the correct response, or micromanage his every move. I want my horse to succeed and build confidence. I set a puzzle for him, but I make sure it is one he can solve. A little frustration is okay, but not more than he can handle. I want the game to be fun for both of us. My horse learns that figuring out the puzzle gets him treats. And when he figures out a whole series of clues (read correct responses to the pick up of the rein) he gets a jackpot. For the final jackpot I jump off his back and start emptying my treat-filled pockets. I don't have bad rides anymore.

The Click That Teaches: Riding With The Clicker

I might have moments in a ride where my horse isn't getting the right answer, but I can't remember the last time I had a riding session that didn't end with me vaulting out of the saddle in delight after my horse has given me something special in response to my requests.

FIRST TROT

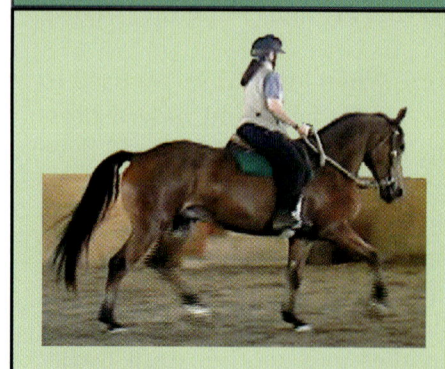

Robin's first trot under saddle showing the beautiful carriage that evolves out of three-flip-three and the clicker.

OLIVER

If I train on contact, all my horse learns is to allow *me* to mold his body. If I train on a release, my horse learns to mold *his own* body. That's a huge difference. If ever there was a horse who clearly demonstrated what this means, it's Oliver. Oliver was an Anglo-Arab in his late teens who lived in the same barn as Peregrine. He'd been ridden for years in a standing martingale. When I first met him he was a stiff, arthritic, nose-in-the-air, skittish horse. At some point in his life he'd had laminitis, a potentially crippling inflammation of the feet. He was sound now, but his left front foot was permanently deformed. His jaw had also been broken by a kick from another horse.

When I first started working with him, his owner was nursing his jaw back to health. She couldn't ride him, but she wanted to keep him active, so we started working together on basic ground work. The first step was, as always, introducing Oliver to clicker training via targeting. Oliver was one of those horses who really didn't seem to catch on to the significance of the clicker. There was no sudden "light bulb" moment when he realized that he could turn his person into a vending machine. He would touch the cone sometimes, but never with any real enthusiasm. He was in fact a very emotionally shut-down horse.

I've found that with some horses if you move on to using the clicker for other things, they begin to catch on, so I set his owner to work on basic leading exercises. His owner was a diligent worker. She wanted her horse to be happy, and she could see that he wasn't. He was like Eeyore in *Winnie the Pooh*. He had a good life. People loved him and took good care of him, but he continued to be depressed.

His owner persisted. Carrots didn't seem to hold his interest, so she brought breakfast cereal from home. We filled our pockets with Apple Jacks and Corn Pops. Oliver perked up. "Ooh," he finally said. "I get it! I can get treats!" The light had finally gone on!

When I first started riding Oliver, there was no understanding of softness. He was sweet, he was obedient, but riding him truly was like sitting on a two-by-four. When I first asked for a bend, he didn't have a clue what I wanted. He just stiffened and looked puzzled. I didn't want to do anything that would aggravate the arthritis in his eighteen-year-old joints. Getting him to soften in his body was a long, slow process. What made it work was the clicker. When Oliver gave even a little, he got clicked. He didn't slam on the brakes like other horses. He meandered slowly into a halt. That was all right. We let him do it his own way. Slowly Oliver caught on to the process. He could get carrots just for bending his neck! He was liking this game!

I didn't realize just how much Oliver had learned until I started free lunging him in the fall. We'd been focusing so much on the riding that we hadn't worked him at liberty since sometime early in the summer. On this particular day his owner couldn't come to the barn, and I had promised her I would get Oliver out of his stall. It was one of those raw November days when the cold really goes through you. I felt too frozen to ride, so instead I turned Oliver loose in the indoor arena and asked him to trot around me on a circle.

Oliver buzzed around with his nose up in the air and his back all inverted. Typical Oliver, I thought. I asked him for a couple of inside turns to get him more focused on his job. All of a sudden everything changed. He climbed up on the "balance beam". He got his hocks underneath him. He stretched out his neck and floated around the circle as though he was in a full lunging rig. It was a beautiful demonstration of a horse who had clearly understood the criteria for getting clicked. What's more, this wasn't a fluke. When I sent him off after giving him a treat, Oliver picked himself up again in the same glorious trot.

After that, Oliver became very consistent in his carriage. He was a beautiful horse to watch and—even with his arthritis and bad feet—a wonderfully soft horse to ride. But what I appreciated most was seeing the life coming back into his eyes. His owner had worked hard to give her horse a better life, and it was paying off in a very loving relationship.

Sadly, at age nineteen Oliver colicked and died. He is one of the many equine friends I have known to whom this book is dedicated.

CHAPTER 27
Soundness, Expectations, and Problem-Solving

If your horse is still at the "Nervous Nelly" stage, the last couple of chapters may have you thinking: "This is all too much work. Sure it makes sense. It's all right for a horse like Oliver, but I'll never get my horse that far." It can seem as though the work I'm describing in these chapters is light years away from the issues you're struggling with. Just remember these lessons are built upon many layers. If you make a start today — if you find one thing you can get your horse to do, and you keep working away at it — a year from now your horse *will be* different. Trust the process. It works.

However, if you do nothing, if you feel too stuck to make even a small change, a year from now you'll still be mired down in the same unwanted behavior. It doesn't take much to make a start, just the desire for things to be different.

EXPECTATIONS

I never expect anything when I train. I know what's normal because I've watched a lot of horses. That means I know it's normal for some horses to take a long time to release to pressure. I don't make any judgments about the horse based on that. A horse who leans against the bit isn't a good horse, or a bad horse, he's just a horse. I can change his behavior by changing the consequences of his behavior. If I keep pressure on the reins when he leans and release the pressure when he gives, my horse will stop leaning. If he doesn't, then I need to think about the five reasons why a horse might not respond the way the rider wants (see side panel).

REASON #1: SOUNDNESS

Most of us blame ourselves when an exercise isn't working right. "If we were only a better rider," we lament, "our horse could do what we're asking." Riding technique could indeed be the source of your problem. It may be that your seat is so unstable that you're not giving consistent messages, or maybe you're stiff or crooked, so the messages you think you're giving aren't what your horse feels. (Reason #5) If your horse is continuing to pull, it may be that you aren't anchoring your hand, or that the timing of your release is off. Videotaping a training session will help you spot problems in your technique, but before you take all the blame for your horse's crookedness, you need to make sure that he's physically sound enough to do what you're asking.

A horse who is very heavy on his front end may be trying to relieve pressure in his hindquarters. Some hind end lamenesses can be really hard to spot. It's all too easy to fall into the trap of thinking, "Oh, that's just the way he goes." Sometimes it requires the detective skills of a Sherlock Holmes to unearth the real reason for his stiff, reluctant movement.

Most of the school horses I learned to ride on were ex-racehorses. Today I would say that there wasn't a sound horse in the whole bunch, but at the time nobody questioned how they moved. Any irregularities in gait were explained away with a casual: "Oh, that's just the way he goes." At that time most of the horses at the local

---

FIVE REASONS FOR A LACK OF RESPONSE

Suppose you've been working diligently with your horse, following the exercises in this book, but you just aren't seeing the progress you thought you should be making. You need to examine the five reasons horses fail to respond the way the rider expects:

REASON #1: SOUNDNESS: The horse can't physically do what you're asking him to do.

REASON #2: PHYSICAL COMPETENCE: The horse doesn't know *how* to do what you want. He hasn't yet built the muscle patterning for the task.

REASON #3: UNDERSTANDING: The horse doesn't understand *what* you want. He's physically able, he just doesn't understand your request.

REASON #4: MOTIVATION: The horse does not want to do what you want. The issue is emotional.

REASON #5: COMMUNICATION The horse thinks he's already doing what you're asking for. The problem here is communication.

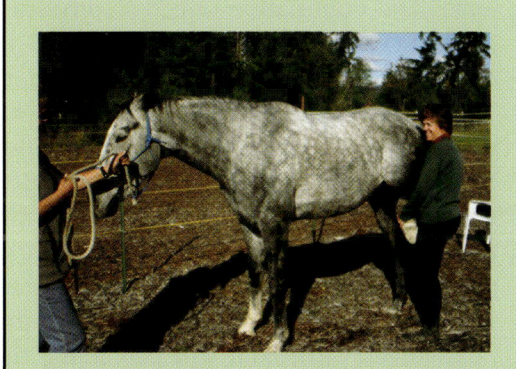

A flexion test is one of the many tools you can use to determine if your horse is physically able to work. Here the horse's leg is being held up in a cramped position. If he's sore in the joints that are being stressed, he'll trot off lame after the leg is released.

shows were just as stiff, so this was what I saw as normal. Then I had the opportunity to watch and to ride truly well-balanced, sound horses. The contrast was stunning. I can't look at these stiff, unbalanced horses in the same way anymore. I know how horses are supposed to move, and it's not like a shopping cart with two flat tires and rusted wheels.

I'm returning to this topic at this point in the book because I see a lot of horses with very real physical problems which their owners are not aware of. They've been told by others that an irregular gait is "just the way he goes," or that the reason he's resisting is because "he's just being stubborn" or "he's lazy." Words like "stubborn," "stupid," and "lazy" do not belong around horses. Do not let other people put these labels on your horse. They will not help you in your training.

In clicker training your horse is your partner. He wants to work with you and for you. If he's being "stubborn," it's probably because he doesn't understand what you want. If he's being "lazy," maybe you have inadvertently reinforced "stand still" instead of "go forward". Or perhaps he simply hurts too much to move out. In any case you want to look beyond the words to find the real reason.

The good news is a great many of these stiff, unsound horses can be helped by simply teaching them how to give softly and come into balance in their bodies. Resistance and stiffness are major contributors to joint damage. When you transform tension into softness, you can extend the working life of your horse by years.

But some horses will have reached a point where they need more than training to solve their problems. The cumulative effect of physical resistance, poor shoeing, badly fitting tack, hard ground, and demanding work will have damaged their joints. They need more than simply teaching them to give to the bit. They need medical intervention and maybe even a change in their job description. So why isn't this done? Why are we working lame horses? It certainly isn't because people don't care. Most people are not deliberately cruel to the horses they ride. If they didn't love and admire horses, they wouldn't be involved with them. The problem is that lameness issues can sometimes be very hard to spot.

If your horse doesn't seem right, be persistent about asking why. Give him the benefit of the doubt. If your horse is balky and refuses to move; if he's a grump and pins his ears every time you bring out the saddle, listen to him. Remember, his means of communicating with you are very limited, and as a species WE are notorious for not being very perceptive. It's all too easy to accept your horse's stiff, short-strided, ears-back, reluctant manner as normal—"Oh, that's just the way he is"—and not even realize that it indicates there's something wrong.

If your training seems stuck, listen to your horse. He may be trying to tell you that he simply cannot do what you are asking. And be persistent with your vets and farriers. Many times even a novice rider will see things that the professionals miss. You know your horse better than anyone. Trust the experts to do their job, but remember that you have valuable information to offer as well.

REASON #2: PHYSICAL COMPETENCE

Years ago I had a wonderful client who was an Alexander practitioner. We traded skills—I helped her with her horse, and she shared her expertise with me. The Alexander work is all about aligning your skeleton so you can move with optimal ease. I remember we were working one day on the way my hip, knee, and foot lined up while I walked. At that time I had a major twist down my right side. You had only to look at my riding boots to see the problem: my left boot looked reasonably normal, but the right one was completely broken down in the ankle and its sole was skewed off to the left.

My Alexander teacher began by getting me to realign the way I normally stood. Then she asked me to take a step forward. To my utter astonishment I couldn't do it—I could not lift my foot off the ground to take a step. From this new, beautifully aligned, wonderfully comfortable position, I could not step forward. Every time I thought about lifting my foot I felt as though I was going to fall flat on my face.

The experience gave me tremendous insight into what our horses must go through when we start rearranging their bodies. They must at times feel totally disoriented. It's no wonder you see so much underlying tension in many of the horses that are put into martingales and head sets. Here they are, in a totally unfamiliar position, being asked to move forward when they're feeling like I did, completely disoriented.

It's especially worth considering this point when you have a horse who's very heavy on his front end. He really may not know how to shift his weight and do what you're asking, especially at the trot and canter. He may think that if he shifts his balance he's going to fall flat on his nose. That's why the single-rein process is so useful. The small, non-habitual movements you ask for in each step are very similar to those used in the Alexander and Feldenkrais techniques. If you want to bring your horse into optimal

Chapter Twenty-Seven: Soundness, Expectations, and Problem-Solving

balance for performance, single-rein riding combined with the clicker is a superb way to do it. The gradual changes involved won't overwhelm your horse's ability to adjust.

REASON #3: UNDERSTANDING

If your horse is struggling with a lesson, he may not be ready for it. He may have only half understood an earlier lesson, and now that you've added another layer he's totally confused.

Whenever you're having trouble with an exercise, the solution is usually to be found in an underlying step. When you encounter resistance, go back to a point in the training where you can ask for something and get a "yes answer" back. Review the ten principles of training described in the first section of this book (Chapter 5). A review of basics will usually reveal the solution.

REASON #4: MOTIVATION

In single-rein riding the primary motivator is the release of the rein. The timing of your release is critical to your success. Your horse is going to give you more of whatever he was doing at the moment of the release. If he was pulling, you'll get more pull. But that's okay. Like clicker training, this is a very forgiving system. If you didn't notice that little pull you inadvertently reinforced, don't worry — it will get bigger. That's what reinforcement does. It strengthens the behavior.

"What!" you're exclaiming. "And you're saying that's a good thing? I don't want my horse to pull."

Of course you don't, but good feel and timing develop with experience and practice. You learn by contrast. By the time you've picked up and released the reins a hundred times, you're going to have experienced a wide range of responses. You'll have felt hard pulls, softer pulls, and maybe even a few true gives.

Suppose when you first started the "Why would you leave me?" game (Ch. 25), you kept track of all your horse's responses to the pick up of the rein. If you graphed those responses you'd probably end up with something that looked like a bell-shaped curve. At one end of the curve would be hard pulls. Even the most inexperienced rider among us would be able to recognize those and not release at that moment. As you move to the right along your graph, the pulls would get softer. Now it would be hard to tell: was that still a soft pull or did you feel a slight give? To the very right of your graph would be clear, definite gives. These may have happened at first simply because your horse turned his head to look at his buddy, but at least that let you experience the feel.

When you first ride this exercise, you're going to pick a point somewhere along this continuum from hard pull to soft give and say to yourself, "I'm going to click and release if I feel anything softer than this, and I'm going to hold on if I feel anything heavier."

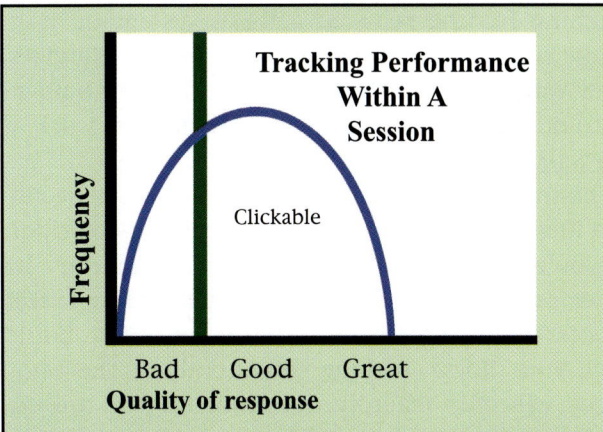

Tracking Performance Within A Session

[Graph: bell-shaped curve with Frequency on y-axis and Quality of response (Bad, Good, Great) on x-axis, with a green vertical line marking the "Clickable" threshold]

If you were to graph your horse's responses to one hundred requests for a give, you'd find that some of his responses would be stiff and resistant, most would be acceptable, and a few would be outstanding. You might decide that everything to the right of the green line is clickable. Over time that will cause a shift to the right of your bell-shaped curve.

If you're inconsistent and you release on pulls that are below your standard, you'll begin to notice that your horse's pulls are getting harder and more numerous. Perfect. Since you're now more aware of the difference, you can make a change for the better. You'll hold on when you can clearly feel a pull, and you'll click and release when the pull softens. As you do, your bell-shaped curve will shift to the right. You'll feel fewer hard pulls and more soft gives.

As you experience more gives, you'll be able to recognize them sooner. You'll become more particular about what a give really is. You won't release on a soft pull any more. You'll wait for that moment when your horse organizes his body and offers you a true give. Both you and your horse are learning this together, so your sense of feel and his responses will evolve together.

One of the things that can really help with this is counting. Count out each set of one hundred gives. Note how long each set takes, and what changes you observe during each set. You may be surprised at how much change occurs even within one set, and how quickly you can ask for a hundred gives from your horse. Counting may sound tedious, but it is actually very reinforcing.

As you work on this, your movements will become very fluid. This is a great way to build consistency and focus. You'll become much harder to distract. I have my clients pick up the reins and ask for a give so many times that it becomes an unconscious movement. This means that if a horse jumps underneath them, their hands will respond by automatically reaching for the reins in a fluid, systematic way. Many riders rush through these riding exercises. They want to get to the exciting stuff. They want to trot and canter. All this repetition and slow work at the walk sounds boring.

The single-rein exercises I've described can be ridden in all gaits, but if you're an inexperienced rider, or you're having trouble with your horse, don't let other people's expectations rush you through this process. Before you work the faster gaits, you should have your horse working consistently at the walk. Speed will only magnify the problems you are encountering.

"The walk is the mother of all gaits." You don't need to be in a hurry to go fast. If you do your walk work well, the other gaits will automatically improve. You can save a lot of wear and tear on your horse by working out his balance issues first at the walk. When you do go back to the trot and the canter, you'll be amazed at how much better they'll be.

One more point about resistance and the bell-shaped curve. If you were to chart your horse's responses to a hundred gives today, a month from now, two months, six months, you would notice that the curve keeps shifting to the right. What you consider a soft give now will be counted as a mediocre response in the future. Six months from now the two graphs may not even overlap. At it's very worst, your horse's performance will be better than anything you're experiencing today, and the other end of the spectrum will be so good it's off your previous charts.

REASON #5: COMMUNICATION

Have you ever found yourself saying: "This horse is so stupid (or so stubborn, etc.): he knows what I want—he's just not doing it."

As you experiment with these single-rein exercises you may well find yourself thinking exactly that. Your horse will be stuck in a pattern, offering you something that was the right answer a few minutes ago but isn't what you want now. You want him to walk forward, but he's stuck in back-up mode because that's what you've been working on for the last half hour.

Your horse is probably thinking, "My person is so dumb. Can't she see I'm doing exactly what she's asking? Why doesn't she just get off my case and let me do my job!"

You may be thinking, "Not me, I won't get into this situation." But I know you will. You're going to teach your horse lateral flexions with the single rein. You'll start out on the ground teaching the "Why would you leave me?" game and three-flip-three to your horse. As your horse glides over sideways, you'll click and reinforce him, telling him he's the smartest horse that ever was. Your horse is going to love going sideways. You'll end the session on cloud nine, wanting to tell everybody in sight how wonderfully clever your horse is.

The next day you'll bring your horse back into the arena. You're all set to have another great ride, but before you can get on, you want to recheck your girth. You'll pick up your inside rein the way you always do, and you'll turn towards the saddle. Your horse knows exactly what this means. You want him to walk sideways!

Before you start calling him names, remember, this is what you taught him the day before. You reinforced him for lateral work, and lateral work is what you're going to get. The solution is to play a game of move, counter-move. This is a game you want to learn to play well. You're going to need it.

Use your three-flip-three skills to counter his wiggling. If he rubbernecks off to the right, ask him to move laterally to the left. If he backs up, have him come forward. If he goes forward, ask for a hip-shoulder-shoulder reinback. In between left, right, forward and back is a halt. When his feet come to a stand still, click and treat.

Get on and ride, this time picking out a target to ride to. It can be anything from a clump of weeds, a rock, a marker you've set out. If he walks past the marker, think about the figure-eight pattern (Ch. 16). Ask him to soften to the rein through a tight hair-pin turn.

If he wiggles off to the side, use three-flip-three to send him back in the opposite direction. Whichever way he goes, use a single-rein counter move until he is standing on his target. Click and treat. Now pick out another target and ride move, counter-move to it. This makes a great review lesson for the single-rein skills you've built so far.

Always remember that you get what you reinforce. If you reinforce energy, you'll get energy. If you reinforce slow, you'll get slow. It's just that simple. Future behavior is shaped by present consequences. That's what operant conditioning is all about. We can expect a lot from our horses, and what's more, if we follow the principles of good training, we can get it.

CHAPTER 28
Collection: Hip-Shoulder-Shoulder

In Chapters 25 and 26 I gave you the keys to unlock many doors. In this chapter I'll show you how to use them to shift from the on-the-forehand balance of a green horse to the hind end balance of a performance horse.

RIDING THE HIND END

In three-flip-three (Ch. 26) you learned how to line up the "drill team". Your horse is now relaxed and settled in his work. You've got the beginnings of lateral flexions, but your horse is probably leading with his front end, walking over his outside shoulder, as he steps sideways. In a young, inexperienced horse the steering wheel is in the front end, along with most of his weight. You turn via the nose, directing him with opening reins. Horses can spend their entire lives in this balance. They may be highly capable and experienced at their jobs, but their balance is still be that of a "green" horse.

In this chapter your horse is going to learn how to shift his balance back onto his hind end. You'll still be asking him to soften his front end every time you pick up the rein, but the power steering will be back in his hindquarters. Now that his emotions are under control and you're working together, it's safe to put the power back into the system.

MATCHING STRIDES AND GIVES: STEP ONE: THE HIP

The pattern you'll be adding—hip-shoulder-shoulder—develops out of the three-flip-three exercise. Begin by asking your horse to walk forward as if in preparation for a three-flip-three sequence. He'll be so familiar with this pattern that as you pick up the rein for the first give of the jaw, he'll automatically connect his hip to his front end. The upward lift (mobilization) of his stifle joint will be in perfect sync with the release of his jaw.

You'll feel an even more definite give of the hip on the second and third steps your horse takes, and on the fourth stride, as you shift your focus directly to his hip, he'll be so well balanced it will be easy to get him to stop the forward motion of his front end, rock back onto his haunches, and pivot 180 degrees around.

That's a progression that results from something I call "good, better, best, bestest." In other words, the give of the hip doesn't just happen on that last pick up of the rein. It's happening in each stride of the sequence, building towards a stronger and stronger connection. That's what you want. A green horse is engaged only occasionally and only for brief moments. You may not at first be able to string three consecutive gives together without any intervening stiff steps. A highly trained horse is engaged one hundred percent of the time, even when he's walking out on a loose rein. His hips are always connected to the "marionette strings" of the reins. When you ask for three-flip-three, each stride he takes corresponds to a give.

Hip-shoulder-shoulder begins with a yielding of the hips that stops forward motion. That's step one. Click. Ride your "good, better, best, bestest" pick up of the reins until the yielding of the

YIELDING THE HIPS

This horse is connecting the rein to a 180 degree turn of the hips.

Yielding the hips creates great brakes, and prepares the horse for collection.

hips is smooth and consistent.

"RESET BUTTONS"

Suppose instead of yielding his hips, your horse simply bends his neck further around and over-flexes. If he thinks the correct answer is bend his nose to the rider's knee and bow out through his outside shoulder, you're going to counter by lifting the inside rein up and forward enough so that it presses against his neck right behind his ears. This will straighten him out so he can begin again. If he tries to walk forward, he'll encounter your stabilized hand acting as a "t'ai chi wall" (pgs. 37, 124-126). This will ricochet his energy into a step back. Instead of dragging your horse back with the reins as so many riders do, you'll just lift your hand, and your horse will slide his hips underneath him. It's a glorious feel when the elevation of the buckle is directly connected to the hips. That's what the hip-shoulder-shoulder exercise creates.

STEP TWO: HIP-SHOULDER

Once he's easily swinging his hips over and coming to a halt, you're ready to extend the sequence and put him back into motion. The set-up is still the same. You'll be riding three softenings of the front end into a flip of the hips, just as you have been. Begin by walking forward at an energetic pace. As you pick up the rein in that first set of three gives, you'll feel your horse soften first his jaw and then his entire neck to you. If you look down at the base of his neck, you'll see a series of wrinkles appear. This tells you that the muscles at the base of his neck are beginning to release. That's going to free up his shoulders and allow him to lift his withers.

On the third give you'll feel a definite softening of the withers as he yields his shoulders to you. As your focus shifts to his hips, you'll feel his inside shoulder stop its forward movement. He'll rock his weight back and pivot almost one hundred and eighty degrees around on his haunches. You'll now be facing in the opposite direction. Before your horse can walk forward again, pick up the rein and ask him to soften his inside shoulder and take a step back. You'll be using a skill you learned in the head-lowering exercise. You'll be asking him to straighten out his neck without walking forward.

If you've done your preparation well, this should be easy for your horse. He's already accustomed to softening his jaw after he swings his hip over. His feet have a "marionette" connection to the rein. Your job is to switch your focus quickly enough to be able to ask for this new dance step before he's changed his momentum and is walking forward again. This is easy to do. Simply remember how you danced with your human partner in the clock-dancing exercise (pg. 165). You'll get your horse to step back by thinking that's the direction you want him to move his feet. C/R.

You now have the first two elements in our new sequence: hip-shoulder. You want this segment to be very consistent before you add the third step and get hip-shoulder-shoulder. Repeat your preparation. Get your horse to walk forward at a steady pace. Ask for three softenings to the rein.

Get the hip to yield, then ask your horse to take a step back. C/R. Change rein and repeat. As you do this, your horse will soften his inside shoulder and glide it back. If you were watching from the ground, you'd see the inside shoulder drop down and back, so it actually lifts the withers and the outside shoulder up. It's a very distinctive feel that I refer to as the "Gene Kelly glide." Watch the famous dance scene from *Singing in the Rain*, and you'll know what I mean. There's a moment where Gene Kelly glides across the stage that reminds me of this shoulder movement. If you ever wanted to know what it would feel like to dance with Gene Kelly or Fred Astaire, teach your horse hip-shoulder-shoulder. You'll feel in them what it must be like to be partnered by a truly great dancer.

STEP THREE: HIP-SHOULDER-SHOULDER

Once you're consistently feeling your horse lifting his outside shoulder, you're ready for the next step in the dance. Instead of ending on the softening and step back of the inside shoulder, pick up the rein again and add the next element, another step back, this time of the outside shoulder. C/R.

Congratulations! You have just ridden your first segment of hip-shoulder-shoulder, and you're well on your way to developing an upper-level performance horse. As you perfect this over the next fifty thousand trials or so, you'll feel some remarkable changes in your horse. Oh, and don't be scared off by the number of repetitions. Remember, we aren't talking about a cookie-cutter assembly line but rather the progressive, almost magical, transformation of your horse.

COLLECTED STOPS

So what does hip-shoulder-shoulder do for your horse? For starters, it gives you collected stops. Back in the dark ages, when I first learned to ride, I was told three things. To get my horse to move I needed to kick him in his sides. To get him to turn to the left or the right, I was to pull his head to the

Chapter Twenty-Eight: Collection: Hip-Shoulder-Shoulder

HIP-SHOULDER-SHOULDER

This pair is practicing hip-shoulder-shoulder. 1–3.) The rider begins by asking for three softenings of the jaw, just as she would for three-flip-three. She was paying particular attention to the placement of her inside hand, keeping it low so her horse shifted his withers over as he softened his jaw. 4.) He is in a beautiful bend, ready for the next step. 5.) She lifts her inside rein to ask for his hip. Note how his jaw and inside leg are softening in perfect sync.

6.) As he steps across with his inside hind and yields his hips over, she'll release the rein. 7-8.) She'll immediately pick it up again in preparation for asking for his inside shoulder to step back. 9-10.) She completes the sequence by asking for his outside shoulder to step back. Click and treat. Each correct response in the sequence is reinforced with a release of the rein. Note the rider never pulls her horse back. It is his own momentum, magnified by the yielding of his hips, that keeps his feet moving seamlessly into a reinback.

side. And to get him to stop, I was to haul back on the reins. Over the years I've heard that set of instructions given to hundreds of beginners. That may be what you first learned, as well. It works, but it's crude, and it's why most of our horses end up in leverage bits. We're trying to stop our horses front to back, but that's not how a horse's brakes work.

Horses have two sets of brakes, one on the right side of their body and one on the left. Every time a horse stops via hip-shoulder-shoulder, you're tuning up his brakes. Practice hip-shoulder-shoulder to the left, and you're tuning up the left side brakes. Practice it to the right, and the right brakes will soon respond to feather-light pressure.

"Straightness is the perfection of left and right" has become one of my favorite expressions. It's something you'll understand better as you work through this hip-shoulder-shoulder exercise. As your horse perfects this exercise, he'll begin to anticipate each part of the sequence. He'll know he's going to soften his shoulder and step back as soon as he yields his hindquarters. As you touch the rein to begin a new sequence, he's ready for you. The initial cue now triggers the entire sequence, and instead of taking a large step to the side that rotates his entire body, he'll simply soften his hip and step back in a straight line. He's included all the elements of the sequence. Nothing is missing or skipped over. He's simply doing them so fluidly that each movement has become smaller and more subtle.

This is why it's important for you to teach these exercises to your own horse instead of letting somebody else do it for you. If you haven't experienced each layer of the training, you won't recognize these subtle shifts. They'll happen so fast that you'll miss them, and you won't realize that your horse has responded to you correctly. But if you've built these sequences yourself, you and your horse will be learning lightness together. You'll feel when he's right, and you'll also feel when he's skipping over things and leaving out pieces of the sequence. When he does, call him on it. Keep your hand on the rein and ask for the missing element. Remember, consistency in your horse begins with consistency from you. By the way, this is another one of those sections you want to highlight. It's critically important, but you probably won't understand it until you have ridden hip-shoulder-shoulder many times.

The Click That Teaches: Riding With The Clicker

COLLECTION AND ENGAGEMENT

The hip-shoulder-shoulder exercise refined my idea of collection. I had always understood that collection meant that the horse was to move forward from behind. I knew that engagement meant that he had to shift his weight off of his forehand. Working on the go-forward and backing cues gave me a way to shift his weight, but that's only part of the picture. Engagement means the horse is also elevating his front end. When you ride on two reins and a steady contact, it's easy for the horse to get over-bent and pull down on his shoulders.

If you're not sure what this means, look at the point of a horse's shoulder while he's being ridden. Is the angle of the humerus being pulled down, or is it lifting up? An over-bent horse will be pulling down through his shoulders and his hindquarters will not be engaging underneath him. The rider won't feel that wonderful magic-carpet ride when the hips lift you up on an engaged and collected horse.

When a horse is correctly engaged, the base of his neck lifts his withers. His neck elevates and he rounds his poll. This is what gives a well-trained dressage horse that truly elegant, regal look. You don't have to go to Europe and spend thousands of dollars to achieve this. You can turn any horse into a "king's mount" simply by teaching him to carry himself well.

LIFT

This filly working at liberty shows how much she's already learned to lift and collect via three-flip-three and hip-shoulder-shoulder.

Why is this important? Compare how she carries herself just moments into her first ride, and how she supports herself just a few short rides later. The lift through her topline helps her support the rider's weight with greater ease.

REVIEW TIME

You began this process because "Nervous Nelly" was more interested in everything else going on in the arena than he was in you. You played the "Why would you leave me?" game, first on the ground and then under saddle. You slid down the inside rein and asked his nose to tip slightly to the inside. Each time it did, you released the rein. When you also felt him unclench his teeth and relax his jaw, click, you stopped and gave him a treat.

After you had clicked him three times on one rein, you changed sides and repeated the process. Pretty soon he wasn't watching the "movie" going on around him. He was locked onto you. You barely needed to touch the rein to keep him with you.

You could have stopped there. Your horse was connected to you, safe to ride, paying attention to what you wanted. But you kept working. You wanted to see what I meant when I said the longer you stay with an exercise the more good things it will give you.

You started to ride the three-flip-three pattern. You asked for a good-better-best softening of the rein. It wasn't long before you saw this pattern emerging:

- On the first pick up of the rein your horse softened his jaw.
- On the second he tipped his ear to the inside.
- On the third he flexed at the poll.
- On the fourth it was easy to ask for his hip.

As he stepped more deeply under his body, you felt him lifting up through his shoulder. Now when you picked up the rein it was easy to direct his energy into a sideways step.

The more you worked on the gives of the jaw, the more readily he stepped under with his hips. The more he stepped under with his hips, the softer his front end became and the easier it was to take him sideways into lateral work.

You could see the "I-know-an-old-lady-who-swallowed-a-fly" progression of releases developing in him (pg 159-160). Every time you touched the rein, he softened his jaw, adjusted his head elevation, flexed at the poll, and softened the long muscle of his neck. The more you worked, the deeper these releases were. You could feel the changes in his spine as he learned to use his abdominal muscles to lift his front end.

Three-flip-three gave you lateral work, but at this point he wasn't always staying on the "balance beam". You often found that his shoulders would be leading. Yes, he was going sideways, but his energy was falling out through his outside shoulder. He was over-flexed and wiggly. You could get his inside hind to step over, but he never seemed to be able

Chapter Twenty-Eight: Collection: Hip-Shoulder-Shoulder

to catch up with himself. You still didn't feel both hips solidly supporting you. You needed to connect more with his outside hind leg, to create for him the substantial-leg stability that you know from your t'ai chi exercises (Ch. 24). And you needed to get better control of the shoulders so the whole "drill team" of front end and back end could stay together.

To do this you evolved three-flip-three into hip-shoulder-shoulder. You began by asking for the same three releases of the jaw that are part of three-flip-three. The pattern of gives was the same, but the intent was different. As you picked up the rein for the fourth give, instead of asking for a small shift in balance in the hind end, you now asked for a big step. You had him well prepared. As you picked up the inside rein and asked him to pivot around, it was easy for him to step more deeply up with his inside hind leg. He could then step over with his outside hind leg, rock his weight back onto that leg to stop his forward momentum, and take a step back with his inside hind leg. You had the "hip" of hip-shoulder-shoulder. In other words you could disengage, and then engage his hind end. Very neat!

Now you could take all the energy from his forward momentum, and rebound it into a rein back. Instead of dragging him back from your hand as so many riders do, you used the lift of your hand into the t'ai chi wall position and his own momentum to ricochet him into a beautiful step back. Now all you had to do was release the rein slightly and then ask for a second, then a third step, and you had all four legs freed up; your horse in balance; correctly bent and engaged underneath you; ready for the next request. That's hip-shoulder-shoulder. You've just created a collected stop. In the next chapter, I'll show you how to create a collected start, and a collected middle to create gorgeous collected gaits.

RELEASING THE BASE OF THE NECK.
One of the key elements that evolves through this process is the release of the base of the neck and the lifting of the withers.

To help you recognize these changes as they occur try this experiment: If you're sitting up in a chair reading this book, look back behind you. Most of you will turn in your rib cage to do this, but if you've had ballet training or studied t'ai chi, you may do it differently. Instead of turning your torso, which drops your inside shoulder down, you'll lift your "withers" as you turn, which elevates your shoulders and gives you a very elegant look.

If you aren't sure where your withers are, reach behind you and feel the muscles and vertebrae at the

> **BEND**
>
> Bending to the left and bending to the right: this horse shows the beautiful balance and calm attitude created by hip-shoulder-shoulder.

base of your neck. (In older people with osteoporosis this is where you'll see the "widow's hump" develop as the spine collapses.) Put your fingers on this withers area so you can feel it move. Turn letting yourself collapse through your rib cage. Feel what that does to your withers. You'll feel the turn, but you won't feel any lift.

Now glance down and to the side at your collar as though you were checking for a spot on your shoulder. When you do, you'll feel your withers rounding up under your fingers. Continue to look down at your collar, but turn slightly. You'll feel your withers lifting your shoulder through the turn. Now take your hand down and repeat the turn. Begin by lifting your withers. Feel the lift through your collarbones as you turn. Feel how easy it is to look behind you now that you aren't dragging down through your shoulders. Notice how graceful and elegant you feel.

Now reach up and place your index fingers at the base of your ears, just behind your ear lobes. Your fingers are lined up with the top of your spine. In other words they are pointing at your poll. Nod your head gently up and down to feel yourself give at the poll. How small can you make the nod? Can you just think it? Become familiar with the subtlety of this feel. Go back to your turning exercise. Raise your withers and look behind you. Do you feel that subtle, soft release of the poll as you do? You didn't have to actively think about it. As you lifted your withers, your poll automatically gave. The same thing happens in the horse.

As you continue this I-know-an-old-lady-who-swallowed-a-fly process under saddle, the base of your horse's neck will start to function like a giant hinge. Instead of leaning down and around to bend his neck, he'll lift his withers and his shoulders.

When you get to this stage, place two duct tape markers on your horse. They will help you spot the changes as they occur. Place a long strip of duct tape down the long muscle of his neck, and another where the wrinkles are appearing at the base of his neck. They'll intersect in a T.

LOOKING FOR WRINKLES

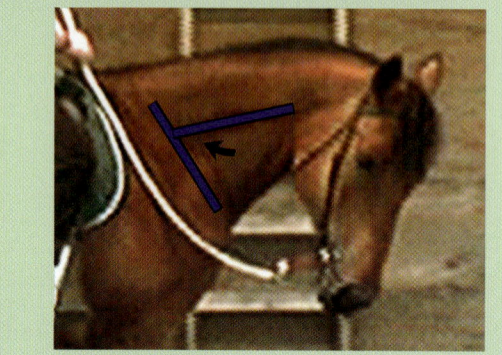

The duct tape markers: note the divot indicated by the arrow that develops at the intersection of these two lines.

As your horse learns to lift his withers, you'll see a large divot the size of your fist appear just below this intersection. C/R. Your horse is starting to elevate his neck. You'll feel his withers and shoulders lifting up underneath you. His shoulders will soften and become increasingly mobile and connected to your rein.

It's an intoxicating feel, but be warned. This kind of collection is addicting. Once you've experienced it, you'll never again be content with riding a heavy horse. This is one of those world-divides experiences. Other people won't know what you're talking about as you exclaim over the pleasures of riding a horse that's soft and deeply engaged. That's all right, your horse will appreciate the difference. I truly believe that horses love the way their bodies feel when they move with engagement. This kind of work is just as reinforcing to them as it is to you. It's a little like climbing a mountain. It can be hard work getting there, but once you've reached the summit the view is spectacular.

Keep watching your horse's neck. You're going to see even more wonderful changes. Think about how his neck used to look. The bottom of his neck was probably thicker than the top, but as he learns to elevate the base of his neck his crest will seem to swell, giving him a powerful, elegant look. Your horse's neck muscles are going to develop and take on beautiful definition. Go get your camera. You're going to want to take pictures!

The elevation of the withers is a key piece in the development of an upper-level performance horse, but you don't have to have lofty goals in the competition world to teach your horse to carry himself in this liberating equilibrium. When I first started riding Peregrine, my trainer said to me that even though he lacked the back strength to perform all the movements of a high-school dressage horse, he could still carry himself in a high-school equilibrium. She didn't mean years down the road, either. She meant that right from the start he could learn to carry his own weight, to lift through his body instead of pulling down onto it. That's been the guiding principle in all my training. Peregrine is a horse who was born with many physical problems, but today, at twenty, even after years of riding, he is sound, and he feels like heaven to ride. You don't have to be aiming for the Olympics to want that for your horse — and for yourself.

A SUMMING UP

So if your head wasn't spinning before from all these descriptions of single-rein flexions, it probably is now. Relax, don't worry about it. I don't expect all this to make sense right away. If these concepts are new to you, you're probably going to have reread these chapters many times before they will all begin to sink in.

To really use this book you have to put it aside and go out to the barn. You have to try this work—and that's what I hope you'll do. The more you experiment with these exercises, the more you'll get from them. Start with the first simple exercises, and see where they take you. Then come back and read through the text again. Once you've actually tried the work, you'll see things you missed the first time through that will make sense now.

This is a book that I want you to wear out. I want you to take it out to the barn with you. I want you to share it with your friends. I want you to refer to it over and over again as you train your horse. I want you to underline and highlight it. I expect to meet you at a clinic some day and have you hand me a copy that's all dog-eared and smudged. When I see that, I'll know that I've succeeded in writing the book my clients have been asking for.

CHAPTER 29
Gait Development

In the previous chapter you used a set pattern, hip-shoulder-shoulder, to create collected stops. Once you have collected stops, you can get collected starts. With collected starts and collected stops in place, you can develop longer and longer collected middles. That's gait development, and that's what you'll learn in this chapter. But first I'll explain why all this is important for the soundness both of your horse's joints and your back!

SOFT JOINTS – SOUND HORSES

Gait development is one of the primary reasons I became interested in clicker training. The clicker is a high-speed "yes answer" signal that lets you mark split-second moments of improvement in a horse's stride. A clicker-wise horse becomes very adept at figuring out exactly which element of a sequence is being highlighted. Clicker-trained horses know the game, and they'll very quickly begin to reproduce on their own more and more of the specific movements that earn them reinforcement.

With single-rein riding and the clicker we can teach a horse to be softer in his joints. This in turn will translate into smoother, easier-to-ride gaits. Here's a simple way to experience this directly in your own body. Hold your arm out in front of you with your elbow bent. Now make a tight fist. Really squeeze hard, so you can feel your elbow, your shoulder, even your jaw lock up. Now try moving your arm up and down. Feel how restricted your movement is.

Release your fist. Shake out your arm, and let go of all that tension. Now move your arm up and down. You'll discover that you have a much greater range of motion. Not only that, but your joints will feel much freer and softer.

If this represented two horses, which one would you rather ride? The first horse is going to have a short, jarring stride. The second horse is going to be much smoother and softer to ride. Furthermore, the second horse is going to stay sounder longer. That first horse, with its tight joints, is going to be pounding over the ground like a car with no shock absorbers, and his joints are going to wear out a whole lot sooner than those of the horse that travels softly and lightly.

When I was first learning to ride, I remember people saying things like "Oh, that horse has a rough trot. He can't help it; it's just the way he's built." Today I know that conformation is just one factor that determines the quality of a horse's gaits. What's just as important is the way the horse has been trained and ridden. Unless you have a major soundness issue, ALL horses have smooth, feels-like-heaven-to-ride gaits. It just takes training to bring them out consistently under saddle.

Many horses have naturally good balance that's not disrupted by a rider's weight; you can get on them and ride their "natural" pasture gaits and have a good time doing it. Other horses are more "ticklish", or they have weaker backs. They stiffen when weight is added. It's hard not to meet resistance with resistance, so the horse's stiffness creates stiffness in the rider. The horse locks up his jaw, tightens his shoulders, and learns to brace to

STIFF VERSUS SOFT

Same horse: very different look

Which horse would you rather ride? The one who is stiff and inverted, or the one who is round and soft?

It isn't just a matter of looking pretty. This twenty year old morgan mare has had seven foals. Her rider uses this work to strengthen her mare's back and keep her sound.

protect himself from the jarring bounce of his rider. The rider counters by doing the same. Both end up with sore backs and a sour attitude towards riding.

What's the solution? Put the trot on the back burner and focus instead on teaching your horse lateral flexions. There's a wonderful expression: *the walk is the mother of all gaits.* If the trot is jarring under saddle, going back to the walk not only makes good training sense. It also saves a lot of wear and tear on your horse's legs. Pounding along on stiff joints is a great recipe for lameness.

My own clients don't go out of the walk until they understand and really "own" the principles of single-rein riding. I want them to have picked up the reins so many times that their hands automatically know what to do. When they start working the trot or canter again, instead of stiffening and bracing, which is the old pattern, their body is already programmed to pick up the rein and ask for a give. They can relax and enjoy the wonderful new balance that all the preparation at the walk has created.

A REMINDER ABOUT TRANSITIONS

You may understand all this intellectually. Lateral flexions make sense to you. You can see how they would reduce the tension in your horse's body, but you're still puzzling over how to use them in conjunction with the clicker to develop a consistent, smooth trot or canter. The click ends a unit of behavior, so it would seem as though it would disrupt the very gaits you are trying to develop.

This is something that trips people up until they become familiar with the learning process the clicker represents. Yes, the horse does stop when he hears the click, but that's exactly what we want. Remember what I said in Chapter 9 about variable reinforcement, shaping, and duration, and in Chapter 16 under "Why Stopping Isn't a Problem"? Once you've used the clicker to teach a behavior, you can also use it to build duration through variable reinforcement.

When most of us first learned how to ride, we were probably taught the horse wasn't supposed to break gait — we had to keep him going no matter what. But we may have also been taught how important transitions are. What the clicker gives us is the opportunity to practice literally thousands of transitions. As you've seen in the previous chapters that's what you need to create a safe horse, and it's also what you need to produce a performance horse.

THE ONE–REIN STOP AND BRUSHING UP THE "GO FORWARD" CUE

So how does all this work in the context of gait development? Remember the discussion on the importance of teaching your horse to go forward in the three-flip-three exercise (pg. 165)? Each time you bring your horse to a stop, whether it's through a one-rein stop or the clicker, that gives you an opportunity to work on your "go-forward" cue.

This is very important because every time you pick up the rein and ask your horse to soften and yield some part of his body to you, you're bleeding off energy. If you're asking for changes of direction at the same time, pretty soon your horse will be slowing down to a standstill. If you don't know how to put energy back into your horse, you're going to be in for some very quiet rides—as in your high-energy horse is now the one standing with his feet stuck in cement. So strengthening the "go-forward" cue goes hand-in-hand with teaching your horse a one-rein stop.

Here's the process. Your horse is moving along in an easy-going walk. You prepare him for hip-shoulder-shoulder by first sliding down the rein and asking for three, "good, better, best" softenings of the jaw (pg. 173-174). Then you'll pick up the rein and ask for the hip to yield over. The instant that you see even a little movement, you'll click your horse and release the rein. He'll stop for his treat, which gives you another opportunity to work on your "go-forward" cue.

Going forward from no movement at the halt into a walk represents a much greater change than simply increasing speed within a gait. That means that every time you get your horse started again, you're making it very clear what your "go-forward" cue means.

Once he's in the walk, your horse is going to want to reproduce the behavior that just got him clicked. So the next time you pick up the rein, he'll be trying to figure out what he did before so he can repeat it.

Just as you built backing on the ground from a simple weight shift into multiple steps, you can build a tiny shift in his hip into the definite step that creates a halt. Click! Your horse is going to get a jackpot for stopping.

Each time your horse stops after you click him, you get to practice your "go-forward" cue again to initiate movement. As this sequence builds, you'll let your horse go a short distance, then you'll pick up the rein and have him to do a hip-shoulder-shoulder stop into a rein-back. Click and treat.

As this cycle becomes consistent, you'll add a new element to the sequence. Instead of clicking after the soft rein-back, you'll organize your outside rein (Ch. 32) and shift your seat to ask for forward movement. Your horse will probably ignore you at first. He'll be so focused on the pattern that he won't notice the change in the cue. Backing was the right

Chapter Twenty-Nine: Gait Development

COLLECTED STOPS AND STARTS

1.) This rider is teaching her horse collected stops. She has prepared for the halt by asking for three softenings of the jaw in a row. 2.) She releases the rein and then (3.-4.) asks for the hip. 5.) As she comes through the corner her horse stiffens and goes above the bit. As they work on more hip-shoulder-shoulder stops, her horse will soften into this step instead of stiffening against the pivot point into a rein back. (See text, pg. 183.)

6.) Her mare is still stiff, but she's stopped and yielded her hip as she takes a step back. 7.) As her horse softens her topline, her rider could click and treat, or, as she is here, she's accepted the softening by organizing the outside rein. (See Ch. 32 for an explanation of this step in the process.) 8.) Her horse continues to back engaging more deeply behind in preparation for a trot (9-10.).

answer before, so it must be the right answer now. People do exactly the same thing when they play the training game (pg. 17). Getting stuck in a pattern is part of the learning process.

You'll let your horse keep backing until he notices that this isn't working, that he hasn't gotten clicked and your seat is still asking for something. The instant he changes direction and steps forward — click! — he gets his treat. You'll keep working on this sequence until your horse responds by going forward the instant your seat changes.

At this point in the description of the lesson, people usually ask what it is they should be doing with their seat. Even if I tried to answer that here, the words probably wouldn't mean very much. The real answer comes from riding through the steps of this process. That's the brilliance of all these chunked-down, single-rein exercises. These steps are doing more than just training the horse. They train the rider, as well. If you don't know the feel you're looking for, go ride a thousand single-rein stops, or better yet, five thousand. That's what it takes to answer that question — the actual doing of it.

COLLECTED STARTS

So now you have a horse that stops on a very light rein, shifts his weight back, rocks his hocks underneath him into a collected stop. He then shifts his momentum forward again when you pivot your seat and ask him to walk on. That's the beginning of a collected start.

The next step is to ask him to continue on in the walk. You want him to carry all that beautiful engagement and connectedness forward. As he gives you that extra step or two that retains the elements that the stop and start have created — click! — give him a treat. You'll gradually build duration by withholding the click. If he falls out of balance before you can click, you'll use hip-shoulder-shoulder and your go-forward cue to reset his balance for another try. If he wants his click, he'll have to maintain that beautiful balance just a tiny bit longer.

Once the walk is solid, you'll follow the same procedure to refine his gaits at the trot and canter. And, yes, your horse will be stopping, but he'll also be learning which elements of his balance earn reinforcement. Just as you did with every other stage of his training, you'll build this work slowly until he's giving you a beautiful collected start followed by a collected middle of whatever length you want, topped off with a collected stop. If you want to highlight and reinforce any part of this cycle, you can do so easily with the clicker.

The Click That Teaches: Riding With The Clicker

COLLECTED START, MIDDLE AND END

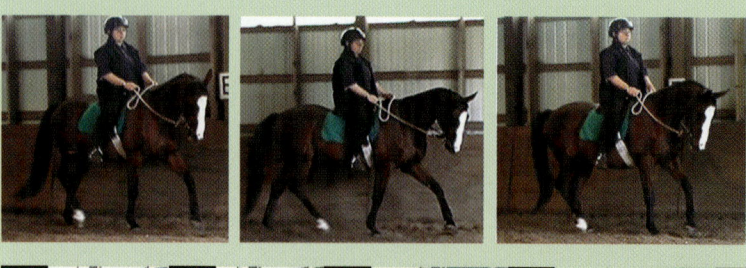

So here is what evolves out of all the bending and flexing: a collected start, middle and end, with beautiful balance throughout.

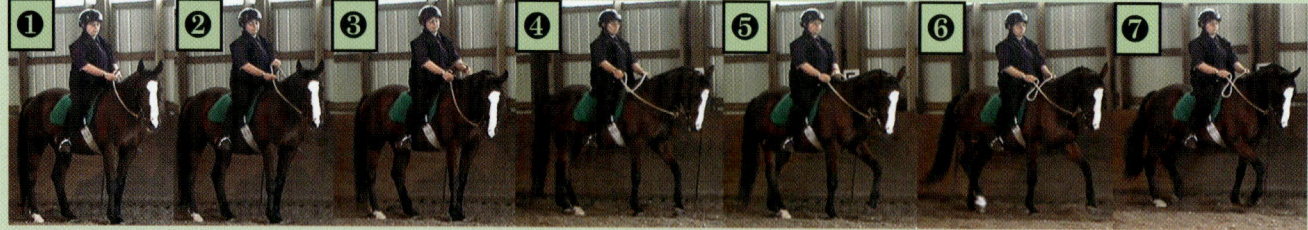

The collected start: 1.) Peregrine is standing at ease, but you can tell from the position of his right ear that he's attentive to my initial pick up of the buckle. 2.) As I slide down the inside rein, he shifts his weight into a right bend. Look closely at my leg position, and you'll see the subtle change in his rib cage. 3.) As I activate the outside rein, he softens at the poll. (See Chapter 32 for a detailed description of the pick up of the reins.) 4.) His hips are not level, so I've asked him to take a step back. This engages his hindquarters which will allow him to pick up into a trot more easily. Note the slight shift back in my torso. It's a subtle change in balance, but one that Peregrine responds to by backing. 5.) His hindquarters are coiled like a spring underneath me, and he feels relaxed and balanced. He's ready for the transfer of potential energy into kinetic energy, i.e. the transition into trot. 6.–7.) He's making a beautiful transition up into trot. Note in particular the activity of his hocks.

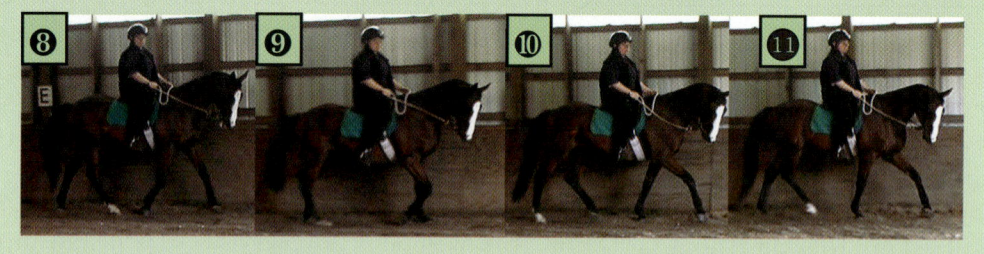

A collected middle: 8–11.) Note again the activity of his hocks, and the lift and reach through his shoulders. This is a trot that feels like heaven to ride!

A collected stop.

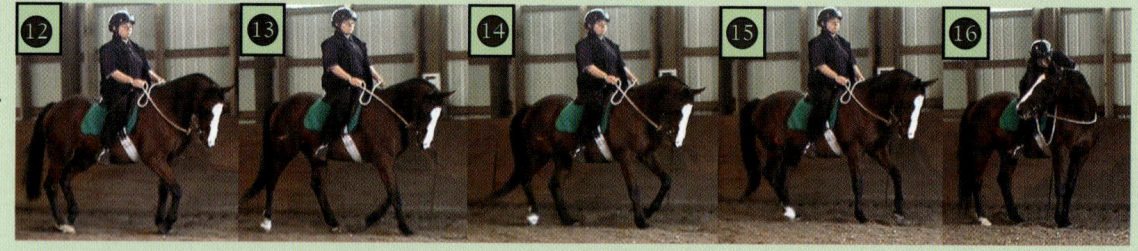

12–13.) I'm using the t'ai chi connections that have evolved through all the single-rein riding to signal my intent to stop. 14.) Within one stride he's lowered his hips, and (15.) come to a stop. 16.) Click and treat.

The beauty of this whole process is you began with very simple, but powerful lessons that helped your horse settle emotionally. (See Chapters 16 through 21.) Those same lessons evolved into the building blocks that you are now using to perfect his balance. The single-rein stop you learned that kept your horse from bolting and spooking, perfected, is the same tool you're now using to create smooth, spectacular gaits.

CHANGING NATURAL ORDERS

Through this work you have been changing several natural responses in your horse. It is natural for a

Chapter Twenty-Nine: Gait Development

horse to pull back against pressure. The head-lowering lesson reversed this (Ch. 20). As you worked, you added pressure to the rein, and instead of rearing up — the natural response —, your horse dropped his head — the trained response.

Hip-shoulder-shoulder reverses another natural order. It is natural for a horse to change leg speed before he flexes at the poll. (See pg. 82-83 for a review of this important concept.) In the sequence of photos on page 181, the horse has not yet made this switch. When she changes leg speed through the halt, she stiffens and goes above the bit. During the critical transfer point of energy her body is stiff.

In the photos of Peregrine on page 182, you'll see that he stays round and engaged throughout the process. He has made the transition. He has learned to give at the poll before he changes leg speed. The result is reflected in his beautiful balance, but to get to this point took thousands of repetitions of hip-shoulder-shoulder.

THE POWER OF REPETITION

As you can see from the size of this book, single-rein riding with the clicker breaks training down into many more steps than most of us were ever taught to see. It also relies very much on something most of us hate the sound of: repetition.

I am showing you how to be a good splitter instead of a lumper of behavior. In the previous chapters you've seen how the repetition of a set pattern can create some remarkable changes in a horse. Most riders never stay with these exercises long enough to see all the good things they can do for them. They think a couple hundred repetitions sounds like a couple hundred times too many. So when I say to them that after 50,000 repetitions of hip-shoulder-shoulder Peregrine was totally transformed as a riding horse, they look at me as though I'm from another planet. At this point you may be thinking the same thing! So this next section is going to explain in detail what I mean by repetition, and why I see it as such a valuable asset.

One further comment before I get into the heart of this discussion. After working Peregrine through the hip-shoulder-shoulder exercise I thought it was one of the power exercises, along with head lowering and a couple other key lessons that I saw could transform a horse. Now I've come to understand these lessons a little differently. *Any* exercise can be a power exercise provided you stay with it long enough. Everything is related to everything else. As you let repetition do its job, even the simplest of exercises has the power to transform your horse.

REPETITION AND CHANGE

When I talk about repetition, I'm not visualizing an assembly line where exact replicas of the behavior are churned out time after time. Instead I see a system where one element of a behavior is focused on for an extended period of time, and in doing so the entire behavior evolves and becomes much more complex.

Let's use head lowering as an example, an exercise you're already familiar with. Under saddle you can teach your horse to lower his head by taking all the slack out of one rein and then releasing it the instant your horse even thinks about dropping his head. If you're starting out with a very high-headed, stiff-backed horse, repeating this request more than once makes perfect sense: it will take more than one or two pick-up and releases of the rein to get that horse's head down out of the rafters. So most people would have no problem repeating this exercise as many times as it takes to get the horse to relax enough to drop his head below the level of his withers.

But there's more going on during all those repetitions than just that obvious layer. As you repeat the request for head lowering over and over again, you'll begin to observe several secondary changes in your horse's behavior. You'll see that it takes less time for him to drop his head. His jaw will feel softer when you pick up the rein. His back will no longer feel as stiff and hollow. He'll feel more relaxed both mentally and physically.

All of these changes will encourage you to continue with the exercise, and they're also reinforcing to the horse. He enjoys the feeling of softness and relaxation that comes with each release. Dropping his head is a much more comfortable and safe response for him than the high-headed, nervous state he started out in. So instead of the repetition being boring, so far it's reinforcing for both you and your horse.

As the process continues, your horse's head will drop lower and lower, and stay down longer until eventually he'll be consistently leaving his nose down around his ankles. This is where most people end the exercise, but that's because they've learned to see only the relatively major changes in their horse's behavior. When you start with a stiff stargazer, it's easy to observe these big changes. Now it's time to start noticing the smaller, more subtle, but often more important, changes that happen when you keep working on this — or any other exercise.

BOREDOM VERSUS TUNING IN

I've learned to value repetition because I've experienced where it can take me. So at the point

The Click That Teaches: Riding With The Clicker

BEFORE AND AFTER

Same horse, same rider, same day, just a half hour difference in time separated these two photos.

Repetition created this significant change. In this lesson the rider was working on three-flip-three.

where other riders think they're done, I'm going to continue working with my horse on the head-lowering exercise. I'm going to pick up that rein and release it a couple hundred more times.

I can focus this attention all in one or two sessions, or I can spread it out over many weeks of training, accumulating thousands of repetitions in the process. (How long a session lasts depends very much on where my horse is in his training, but generally horses have much longer attention spans than their human handlers.)

Is this boring? Not in the least. In fact, for me this is when riding becomes the most interesting. As I repeat this exercise, I'm going to feel some amazing changes in my horse's spine. I'm going to feel him release his back vertebrae by vertebrae.

I'm going to feel him align his skeleton so that any twists he might have in his spine disappear. I'm going to feel his shoulders straighten and his hips align themselves, so that he feels square and level underneath me. I'm going to feel him stretch even further until his nose is actually touching the ground. I'm going to feel his weight shift more onto his hindquarters. I'm going to feel his hind legs reaching up more under his body, and I'm going to feel his back lift.

As I learn to "listen" kinesthetically for these changes, I will feel even more things. I will feel energy coming into the rein each time I touch it. I will feel him relax deeper and deeper into his body, even as I feel him walking forward with more energy. And I'll feel him paying more and more attention to me as he integrates the internal changes he's experiencing.

As we continue to practice head lowering, the repetition will further refine the responses my horse is giving me. This process is reinforcing for both of us, and I can make it more so by adding in the clicker to highlight new changes as I feel them occurring. When I see my horse align his skull on his spine for the first time, click, I'll reinforce him. What I'm doing is drawing attention to that subtle change so we can both become more aware of it.

This is a wonderful process and one that can become quite addicting. Think about a child scratching out his first few notes on the violin versus that same child who with dedicated practice has become an accomplished musician. That's the difference in the level of response we can get from our horses through repetition. Many riders never go beyond asking for gross responses. One reason for this is that they simply don't know how much more their horses can give them. They become satisfied too soon, and they associate repetition with an assembly-line stamping out of exact replicas of a behavior until the response becomes mindless, automatic, and yes, very boring. With that kind of expectation, these riders often miss all the wonderful but often subtle changes that are occurring in their horses. They've never been trained to expect and watch for them. They don't know how important each little release under the saddle is, so they fail to notice it.

CLICKER TRAINING AND REFINING PERFORMANCE

All of this highlights one of the major advantages of the clicker. It helps us focus our attention on small steps and subtle changes in behavior. A clicker trainer is actively looking for things to reinforce. We don't just want to release the rein. We want to click and give our horse a treat. When we feel the horse lift his back so that he can stretch his neck down a little further, we notice it and we mark it with a click and a treat. Repetition is not boring. It's the

Chapter Twenty-Nine: Gait Development

foundation of this kind of training. The horse offers us a tiny piece of a behavior, and by focusing our attention on that piece we can cause it to grow and become much more complex in its form.

Our belief systems are important. We very much create our own realities. If your experience of repetition has been endless drilling without any seeming purpose, of course you would be put off by someone suggesting to you that you repeat an exercise not four or five times, but many hundreds. But I've always found that if I continue to be interested in an exercise, then my horse will be too. The moment I lose interest, so does he. What holds my interest are all the wonderful changes that I feel in my horse. Through clicker training you can learn how to tune in to — and make use of — subtle variations in your horse's gait and carriage. Once you do, you'll find that repetition is the foundation for new levels of excellence.

MEASURING PROGRESS

You'll be able to see this more clearly if you keep training records. It's easy to forget where you've been and to get frustrated because you don't think you're making progress fast enough. Horses do not train by clocks, and they don't have any final goal in mind. Success, goals, outcomes, ribbons, these are all human conceits. Goals are good things, but not if they become your only measure of success. Remember, one of the fundamental principles of good training is to put as many steps between you and your goal as you can, so if you're measuring your progress only by the major goals you achieve, you will become frustrated.

I was talking with a client just the other day. She's seventy-two, and she's just learning to ride. She rides a trusty old school horse at a nearby stable and takes some ground work lessons from me. She started out our most recent session feeling frustrated with herself.

"I should be able to post!" she declared when I asked how her rides during the week had gone. "Should"—what a terrible word. Listen to the vibration of it. It's full of judgment and implied failure. "I should be able to do this." It's a word that separates you from where you are and where you want to be. She wants to be able to post without bouncing and jarring on her horse's back, but the more she thinks about how she "should" be able to do that, the more frustrated she becomes and the further away from her goal she gets.

Pay attention to the words you use. They matter. Words like "should" and "trying" carry with them the implication of failure. Avoid them. Instead, learn to think like a clicker trainer. Acknowledge the small steps you and your horse are making. Keep track of them and appreciate them. This client started to

THE PRODUCT OF REPETITION

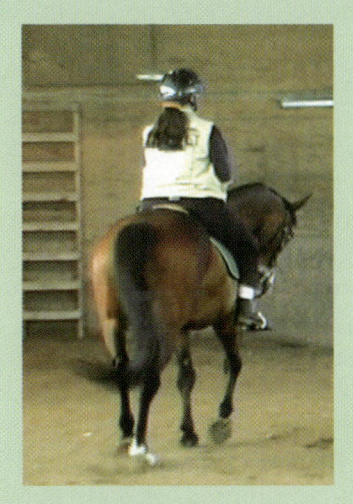

Repetition is a recipe for excellence. As you stay focused on one exercise, you begin to discover all that it has to offer. In this case, focusing on hip-shoulder-shoulder has helped build beautiful balance in my thoroughbred, Peregrine.

relax when I reminded her that just a few short weeks before her heart was pounding in her throat just getting up on top of such a large animal. Now she's trotting! That's monumental progress. She just needed to take a moment to remember.

It's important to do the same with your horse. And it's not just your horse who's learning a whole new way of riding. You are as well. I keep my horses at a stable that specializes in beginner lessons for children, so every day I see reminders of how long it takes to develop a capable rider. If you've been riding for a long time, you've probably forgotten those early, awkward days. Do you remember trying to get your horse to walk down the rail when all he wanted to do was veer into the center of the ring? I do. One of my clearest early riding memories was having to be rescued by an adult every time my horse put his head down to graze. As a three year old I didn't have the strength to pull his head back up again. How frustrating was that! As you go through the exercises in this book, be patient with yourself, and be patient with your horse. That patience will be rewarded

PECKING PIGEONS UNDER SADDLE

To learn more about repetition we're going to revisit the "pecking pigeon" lesson (Ch. 14). I first used this lesson when Robin and I were suffering from cabin fever, and he was exhibiting an excess of energy. Now you're going use it under saddle.

Remember the basic format of the lesson: you're going to pick a simple behavior — in this case walking

The Click That Teaches: Riding With The Clicker

forward on the buckle.
* Walk your horse forward one stride. Click and treat. Wait one second. Pick up the buckle and ask your horse to walk forward.
* After every click increase your count by one. So now walk your horse forward two strides. Click and treat. Wait two seconds. Pick up the buckle and ask your horse to walk forward.
* Increase your count by one. Walk your horse forward three strides. Click and treat. Wait three seconds. Pick up the buckle and ask your horse to walk forward.
* Keep repeating this basic pattern until you can walk your horse on the buckle for three hundred strides before you click. And note: standing still can be hard on a horse's back. You might not want him wait a full three hundred seconds between trials, but you can certainly have him wait for whatever length count you choose.

Sound simple? It is, except there are a few basic rules attached to this game. First your horse must not start to walk until you ask him to. There is no unrequested forward in this lesson. If he walks off before you ask, slide down your inside rein and take his hips around into a stop. (See Chapters 20, 21, and 28.) When he can keep his feet still for the same number of seconds that matches the number of strides you're working towards, ask him to walk off.

In other words, if you're about to head off for a count of four strides, but your horse starts off before you're ready, pick up the rein and take his hips around into a halt. Count to four. If he again walks off before you can finish your count, bring him back to a halt. Keep repeating this until he can stand still for four seconds.

It's actually an advantage to have a horse that walks off in the early stages of this game. Much better to be teaching this at four seconds than to be beginning it at fifty. If you should find yourself in that situation, drop your count down to a level where he can be successful.

This is a great lesson for over-eager foot movers. For some of these horses stopping to get a treat can be a distraction. They want to be moving! So you're going to reinforce them for standing still by allowing them to move. You're using the Premack principle (pg. 64) to reward a less desirable activity by allowing these horses to do somethiing they enjoy more.

At the other end of the spectrum this lesson helps the horses who would rather play statues than run races. You're saying to these stuck-in-cement horses that all they have to do is walk forward one stride—one tiny little stride—and, click, you will let them stop and stand still, plus you will give them a treat!

In both cases the horse gets what is most rewarding to him, either the chance to move, or the chance to stand still. And both horses will end up as 300-peck-pigeon horses.

Here's another rule only this one is for you: no steering. You're going to follow your horse wherever he wanders in your arena. If he meanders around in a tiny little circle, that's okay. If he wanders down into the far end, or hangs out by the gait, that's okay. Your only criterion is that he walks the set number of strides that you're working on. Which brings me to another rule:

Your horse cannot change leg speed once he's in motion. If he stalls out, lift up the buckle and bump him forward with your legs. If he rushes forward or breaks into a trot, pick up the reins and take his hips around.

How does this translate into the real world? Suppose your horse heads over to the gate and stalls out. Pick up the rein and bump, bump, bump with your legs until he walks forward. But remember: no steering. It's not up to you to pick the direction he turns.

Stalling out means you have to reset your count back to zero, so, if you were heading for seven steps on the buckle, but he stalled out at the gate at five, bump him forward into motion and count: one, two, three strides, etc. to seven. However many times he stalls out turning a small circle to get back to the gate, you're going to get him restarted and begin your count back at one. Eventually he will make it seven steps in a row. Click and treat. Let him stand still for seven seconds. If he's just been turning a lot of tight circles to get back to the gate, he'll appreciate the chance to rest.

Now suppose as you head off to eight steps, he decides to go visit the horse that's working at the far end of the arena. He leaves the gate and breaks into a trot. That's an unrequested change of leg speed. Before he's even one step into the trot, slide down the rein and take his hips around into a halt. If he walks off before you ask, take his hips around again. He must wait until you signal him before he walks off. Begin your count over at zero heading for eight steps.

The last rule is safety always comes first. So if you feel unsafe heading into any part of the arena your horse is choosing, slide down the rein and take his hips around. If you don't want to visit the goblins at the far end, you don't have to. You can decide that the 300-peck-pigeon game is going to be played in the near end of the arena. Your horse must stay within the boundaries you set. Any time he heads out of bounds, slide down the rein, take his hips around and head off in the other direction. As long as he doesn't change leg speed, you can stay with your count.

I won't tell you what you'll create with this lesson. I will leave it up to you to discover all the good things you'll create when you stay with it long enough to create a 300-peck-pigeon horse.

CHAPTER 30
The Transition to Where: Posts, Hotwalkers, and Riding in Circles

This is a short chapter, but it's another critically important one. You're going to take the lessons and the tools you've been learning — all those beautiful lateral flexions, those wonderful floating gaits, and that ability to ride your horse on the buckle — you're going to take all that and combine them with some simple rein mechanics in a lesson I refer to as "the hotwalker lesson". The result will be perfect circles. In other words, you're going to connect *how* your horse carries himself, with *where* he goes.

TAKING CHARGE

I remember watching a riding clinic at a local arena years ago. The participants were all focused on their position. They were working on staying soft and relaxed. The idea was that as they came into balance, so, too, would their horses. Their horses did indeed move more freely as the lessons progressed. There was only one problem. Not one of the riders could get her horse down into the far end of the arena without the horse spooking.

During the lunch break, one of the boarders at the stable rode a young thoroughbred that he was legging up for the track. You could tear apart this rider's position. His feet were too far out in front of him, his back was roached, his hands were horrendous. And yet his horse cantered calmly around the entire arena. There was no spooking, no sucking back, no leaping sideways off the track, just an obedient young horse doing his job.

This rider might not have had picture-perfect form, but he did know how to be effective. He knew how to give clear directions to his horse, and how to insist that his horse obey them. Those words probably sound out of keeping with the rest of this book. In clicker training we think of two willing partners working together, not of one being the director and the other the one who's directed. But the bottom line in riding is that somebody has to decide what the program is. The end result can look and feel like an elegant dance, but only if your horse has agreed to let you lead while he follows.

Riders need to learn how to become leaders. Your horse may want to go back down to the safe end of the arena, but you don't have to go there with him. And that doesn't mean you have to fall off either! It simply means you don't have to passively give in and go with your horse just because you're sitting on him.

That's a hard concept for novice riders to grasp. If the horse you're on top of decides to barge off into the bushes, you're along for the ride — isn't that right?

No. You are in charge. You set the course and the horse follows, not vice versa. It took me a long time to learn this with Peregrine. One of the many problems I had with him under saddle was turning, especially to the right. It sounds so silly. Most horses turn fairly easily, but not Peregrine. His locking stifles made turning seem next to impossible at times.

I remember so clearly the ride where I learned to take charge. I was spending the winter at my trainer's. On this particular day I was schooling Peregrine by myself in the indoor arena, practicing

---

CONVERTING "HOW" TO "WHERE"

When these photos were taken, Robin was just learning about circles.

He's turning in too soon. I've lifted my rein to straighten him out.

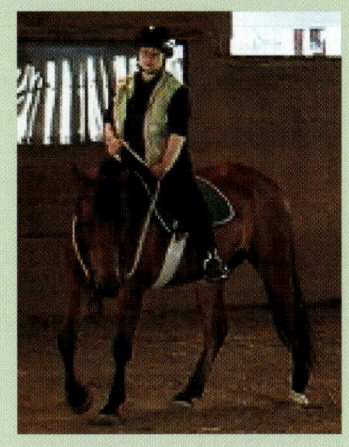

Now he's falling through his outside shoulder. I've slid down my rein to create an opening rein effect. That's all the help he needs to regain his balance on the "balance beam."

The result: beautiful balance.

the lessons we had been working on. All I wanted was a simple turn and I couldn't get it. I suppose I could have dragged him off the rail, but I was trying hard not to compromise the lessons I was working on. The general theory was that if I could just straighten out the twist in my own right side and get my body organized, the turn would flow easily. That was the theory: in practice it wasn't happening.

I finally got so frustrated with both of us that I started yelling at Peregrine. "Peregrine!" I snapped. "I don't care how wrong I am, you can figure this out. I don't care how twisted or lopsided I am, *this* is how I ask for a turn. This is how I always ask for a turn. I'm turning! You can turn with me!"

That's the day I learned that the horse goes with the rider, not the other way around. It's also the day I stopped being a passenger and became an active rider. I understood that position follows function, and that good riding can be boiled down to nothing more than a series of conditioned responses that the rider sets up and teaches to the horse.

So what was I doing? I was establishing a consistent series of events that indicated I wanted a turn. And I was right. Peregrine could learn what my signals meant. I just had to learn to be a post before he would listen to me.

That isn't to say form isn't important—it is. Mechanics do matter — a lot, but form follows function through these lessons. The more you and your horse come into balance, the more correct your position will be.

LESSONS FROM A POST

It's easy to imagine yourself as a post when your horse is standing still. It's even easy to imagine it when he's moving, so long as you don't care where he's going. In Chapter 25 I talked about making your hand firm and steady like a post to get him to soften into the bend. You didn't care where he went just so long as he gave you the response you were asking for. You were working on "how". Now it's time to complete the process and get "where" as well. To do this you have to become even better at being a post.

If you want a lesson in how a post can train your horse, tie a fidgety horse to a stout post. Do *not* try this with a horse that pulls back—he's not a suitable candidate for this experiment. Instead pick a horse who never stands still when you're holding him. The one who fusses and circles around you when you're trying to groom him but is otherwise a sensible fellow is the perfect candidate for this experiment. Tie him to the post and watch what happens.

Your horse will swing back and forth on the lead. He'll pace to the end of the rope, then swing back and pace to the other end. He may keep this up for quite a while. Be patient. The post has all the time in the world to train your horse. It doesn't have anywhere to go, and it doesn't watch clocks.

Your horse will try other tactics. He'll try to pull his head down to get at the few wisps of hay on the ground, or he'll paw in impatience. Ignore him. The post will.

He may get increasingly fussy. This is when you need to remind yourself about extinction bursts. Just before your horse is about to quit, he'll try his hardest to get the post to let go, but eventually he will stand quietly.

Posts are good teachers. They give clear, consistent signals, and they don't get frustrated, angry, or impatient.

People are better teachers, but only if they first learn how to be good posts.

Why are posts such good models for training? Simply because the horse can feel that the post is not going to budge. Try it yourself. Pull on a rope that's tied to a solid post, and you'll discover that it's a pointless effort. But tie that same rope to a tree branch or a post that's got some give to it, and the pulling becomes interesting. That's a lesson you want to remember next time you feel your horse pulling on the rein. If he's pulling, it's because your hands aren't stable.

HOTWALKERS

Being a post is a great image, but posts are rooted in the ground. What happens when your horse is in motion? How can you both be a post and move at the same time? Think about a mechanical hotwalker. The hotwalker is a post that moves along a set track. And unlike many riders, the hotwalker has no trouble getting horses to walk on perfect circles.

Suppose your horse tends to meander all over when you ride him. In your lessons your instructor is always making comments about the shape of your circles. You can manage egg shapes and watermelons, pears and cucumbers, but round like an orange eludes you. You work hard at it. Both you and your horse get sweaty with the effort, but you just can't keep him on a consistent pattern.

Now let's suppose that after one of these lessons you decide to put him on a hotwalker to cool him out. He's never been on one before, so let's see who can get a better circle — you or the hotwalker.

The hotwalker won't have any problem getting your horse to walk forward. The force of that mechanical arm is irresistible. Your horse can start out

Chapter Thirty: The Transition to Where

pulling on his lead and doing all the things he did to you under saddle, but just wait. That hotwalker is going to get him trained. Your horse may barge forward and try to head off to the barn. That's always been a major problem for you, but not for the hotwalker. The mechanical arm of the hotwalker isn't going to be dragged anywhere. It solidly adheres to the track of the circle. The lead becomes like an inside opening rein drawing your horse back onto the circle. The more your horse barges off the circle, the more the lead opens until finally your horse has no choice but to yield his hips and return to the track.

But when he does, he overshoots his mark and falls to the inside of the circle. The hotwalker still stays firmly connected to the track. As your horse passes under the arm of the hotwalker, the lead is drawn up so that it presses against your horse's neck, straightening him out and setting him back on course. Bowing out, falling in are both dealt with over and over again until your horse settles on the path of the circle. The hotwalker is neither patient nor frustrated. It just is, and it gets the job done.

You can be a human hotwalker by keeping a clear sense of the pattern you're riding and putting these two rein effects to work for you.

SELF-CARRIAGE

Riding on a single rein is similar to lunging. You don't have the outside rein helping to channel your horse onto a track. He's much more likely to fall through his shoulders and meander off course. So why not simply pick up your outside rein and hold him onto the circle?

The key word here is "hold". If you never let your horse make mistakes, he'll have a much harder time learning what you want him to do. Riding on a single rein will at first exaggerate your horse's faults. Oddly enough, that's good news. By magnifying what he does, single-rein riding makes the problem easier to fix.

Think about what happens to many teenagers who have lived under very rigid rules. When they first go off to college, they don't know how to create their own boundaries. They've always had control imposed from outside. Now they're living in a dorm with no one but themselves to enforce the rules. All-night parties and skipped classes become the norm. The lesson here is that you have to have some freedom to make mistakes in order to learn self-discipline.

If you never let go of your horse, he'll never learn self-carriage. He'll always be dependent on you to hold him in position. That's not what upper-level performance is about. It requires freedom to be truly beautiful. So instead of holding on and falling into the contact trap (pg. 155-156), you're going to be persistent, but you're also going to let go each time your horse finds the right answer.

RIDING THE CIRCLE

The more precise you are in this, the easier it will be for your horse, so set out cones or other markers to help you visualize the path you want to ride.

Take the time to make a nice round circle. Pace the edges of your circle off from a central marker, or, better yet, use a length of baling twine. Tie one end of the twine to a weighted object—a curry comb or brush will do the job. Place that end at the center of your circle, then walk a straight line out to the end of the rope. That's twelve o'clock. Place a marker there, and then walk the circle marked by the outer end of the rope, and place another marker at three o'clock, one at six, and one at nine. Once you have the feel of a circle in your body, you won't need visible guides, but for now taking the time to make a perfect circle will make a huge difference in the quality of your training.

Begin by asking your horse to adhere to the track of your circle. The cones will tell you if he's off course. Start with your horse tracking to the right. At first you aren't trying to keep his entire body on the circle. That would be too hard for both of you. Instead focus on just keeping his nose on the track.

Suppose he starts to leave the circle. Remember what would happen on a hotwalker. As your horse veers off from the circle, lift the buckle of the reins with your outside hand as you slide down the inside rein. Slide all the way down the rein until you feel the corner of his mouth, but keep your hand oriented over the track of the circle. The more your horse wanders off the circle, the more you will find yourself in an "opening rein" position. Your inside hand will be well out away from his neck while your torso remains upright, anchored in its carousel horse alignment (pg. 130).

Make sure your inside hand stays anchored over the track of the circle, just as the mechanical arm of the hotwalker would be. That means that as your horse bows out your arm will open further and further away from his neck. The more determined he is to leave, the more extended your arm will be. You want him to feel an increased muscle tone (as opposed to tension) in your body that says, "I'm staying here on the track." If you just passively extend your arm without putting any "t'ai chi wall" energy into your body, he'll still drag you off the track.

As he hits the end of the "hotwalker", your hand

will be out and down away from his neck with your arm fully extended. It will not be back behind your thigh. You aren't pulling on him. You aren't trying to drag him back to the circle. You're just solidly adhering to the track you are on. Nor will you be leaning over. Stay centered and upright. You're grounded in the saddle the same way the mechanical hotwalker is grounded in the center of its circle.

The pressure from your extended hand should bring your horse's nose back to the circle. If he ignores you and is determined to leave, lift your hand up and flip his hips. That will bring his nose back onto the circle. But be ready. This is a balancing act. Your horse is probably going to overshoot the mark and fall into the center of the circle.

Think about what this would look like if you were sitting on top of the mechanical arm of the hotwalker looking down at your horse. As your horse walks towards the center of the circle, he's going to pass underneath you. The more he falls in, the more the lead is going to press against his neck. The added pressure will straighten out his neck and get him to step back onto the track of the circle.

How does this translate into riding? As your horse falls in toward the center of the circle, you're going to lift your hand straight up. You're adhering to the track of the circle. As your hand goes up, his neck will run into the rein, and, just as it did for the hotwalker, the added pressure will send him back again. This is the same "reset button" skill you learned in Chapters 20 and 21. You're just applying it now in a different context.

A common mistake many riders make is that they anticipate their horse's actions. Instead of lifting their hand straight up, they drag it sideways over the top of the horse's neck. Now they're the one pulling on the horse, not the other way around. This may seem like just a matter of semantics, but it makes a difference in the quality of your horse's performance. When you take your hand across the neck, you're teaching him to allow himself to be dragged.

When you lift your hand straight up, you're creating an opportunity for him to give to pressure. There's a huge difference. In both cases, if I were to take a snapshot of the rider's hand position, it would look the same. The hand would be up and over on the far side of the horse's neck. But how it got there would be very different. One rider lifted her hand to a stable point of contact and waited for her horse to give to her; the horse walked under the "hotwalker" and ended up pulling on the rider's hand. The other rider didn't wait for the horse; she anticipated his pull and in doing so ended up being the one who was doing the pulling. Learning to set up stable contact points—to be a post or a hotwalker—is an important skill. It takes discipline and focus, but it results in incredibly light and responsive horses.

Another direction many people drag their hand is back behind their thigh. They are trying to keep the horse on the circle by dragging his nose back to the track. If the rider fully extended her arm, the point of contact would remain out in front of the horse. Instead with her hand on her hip the rider is creating backwards traction which over time will have a negative impact on her horse's gaits.

RIDING "HOTWALKER" CIRCLES

So now you have two rein effects you can play with. If your horse bows out on the track, you can open the rein to draw him back onto the circle. And if he falls in on the circle, you can lift the rein to send him out. You're going to ride around the circle using these two corrections. The more particular you are, the more effective this exercise will be, but if you're on a very wiggly or unbalanced horse, you might at first decide that the path you're aiming for is a wide one. The track you're trying to stay on is the width of a sidewalk. As long as his nose is over the "sidewalk", you'll leave him alone and ride him on the buckle — click. But the instant he veers off, you'll slide down the rein and ask for a course correction.

At first every time you let go of the rein, he'll wander off again, but as you keep working, using your rein effects to ask him to move his nose back onto the imaginary circle, the track you're on will become more consistent, and your "sidewalk" will get narrower. It won't be just his nose that's on the circle. As you feel his shoulders line up with his nose so he stays on the circle longer, mark that with a click and a treat. Once you've got his shoulders, his hips will begin to follow. As the wiggle in your horse begins to straighten out, you'll become more particular. Your "sidewalk" will be getting narrower and narrower until it is just a few inches wide.

Focus your attention down to a rope-thin line, and your training will become even more precise. Now any little deviation in your horse's balance will be important. But by this time, instead of making large, visible corrections, the movements of your hand will be minute. By the time you're riding a precise circle, your horse will be so responsive that just a tiny shift of your hand will move his withers over. Unless someone watching is very tuned in to your cues, he won't be able to see what you are doing. That's when riding becomes really fun, but it takes work and perseverance to get there.

CHAPTER 31
Putting Humpty Dumpty Together Again: The Three Training Turns

Circles are just the beginning of mastering geography. In this chapter I'll introduce you to three very useful training turns. These are basic patterns every rider learns for maneuvering in a ring. I was introduced to them first as a hunter rider. As a dressage rider I learned to refine them. But it was only as a single-rein trainer that I learned their true power. Once you have these turns, you'll be ready for diagonals, broken lines and reverse-arc circles.

HUMPTY DUMPTY IN PIECES

Learning the mechanics of single-rein riding is a little like taking apart a jig saw puzzle, or rebuilding a house piece by piece. Imagine you want to move an old farm house to a new site and restore it. You'd reach a point where you'd have the entire house spread out on an acre of lawn. You'd have the bricks for the chimney all labeled and piled over there, the beams from the kitchen here, the foundations stones there. Some of the bricks and beams and stones would be too cracked and crumbling to be used again. You want to preserve as much of the old house as you can, but you also want to rebuild it so it's stronger and better than it was before. You'd have to replace those pieces that are unsound.

That's what you're doing with single-rein riding. You're taking your horse's training apart layer by layer and building it back stronger and better than it was. The first time you go through this process, you're going to look at all the separate pieces without knowing how they all fit back together. It's as though you're looking at those pieces of a house strewn across your lawn, but without any labels attached to them. If you've never rebuilt a house, all you would see would be a jumble of bricks and lumber.

If you've been practicing each of the exercises I've described so far in this book, you may feel the same way about your horse's training. True, your horse has become incredibly responsive. His jaw is soft, and you've never had a more connected feel. You can think "I want his right front foot to step over onto two o'clock," and that's exactly what happens. It's fun, it's exciting, but at times it has also been incredibly frustrating.

You've gone weeks at a time when you couldn't get your horse to walk a straight line. He could bend, he could circle, he could go sideways, but straight eluded you. When he was a stiff, tense horse you could steer him just fine. Now he feels wonderful to ride, but you have no navigational controls.

You thought you understood what I said about straightness being the perfection of left and right, so to solve the problem you focused on the hip-shoulder-shoulder exercise. Your horse got so good at it that he didn't want to do anything else. He'd go forward a step or two, and then he'd swing into a beautiful rein-back. It felt great, but it's not what you were asking for.

I know exactly what you're going through. Been there, done that. You work on tuning up your horse's brakes and you lose forward motion. So then you work on transitions and now that's all your

ALL THE KING'S HORSES

Single-rein riding is very much like taking apart a jig saw puzzle and then putting it back together again.

You're taking your horse's training apart piece by piece.

Only instead of reassembling the original picture, you're building it back stronger and better than it was.

In this chapter, you'll be reassembling more of the finished picture.

horse wants to do. This is a natural part of the learning curve. Remember: for every exercise you teach there is an opposite exercise you must teach to keep things in balance.

So here's where you are in this process. You've dismantled the "house" and at this point you may be feeling as though you'll never get it rebuilt, but you're actually much farther along in the process than you realize. You've got all the pieces. They're solid and strong. You know what each piece does individually. Now it's time to see how they all fit together. It's time to rebuild the house.

To switch metaphors for the moment, you may feel as though your horse's training is like Humpty Dumpty—all in pieces. But take heart, the old nursery rhyme notwithstanding, you can put these pieces back together again.

PUTTING HUMPTY DUMPTY TOGETHER AGAIN

The three training turns—rollbacks, half-turns, and half-turns-in-reverse—will take you a long way toward reintegrating the pieces of your horse's training, and now's the time to introduce them.

Please note that the order in which I describe these turns is not necessarily the order in which you'll teach them to your horse. If I had a horse with arthritic hocks, for instance, I would not begin with rollbacks. I'd start with half-turns and half-turns-in-reverse, and only gradually ease my way into rollbacks. For a horse who leans in around all his corners, I might begin with half-turns-in-reverse, and for a twisted horse who's badly counter-bent I might start with rollbacks. If I wasn't sure where to begin, I'd pick whichever turn felt the easiest, and then I'd gradually add in the others.

ROLLBACKS

A rollback is an easy turn to visualize. It's a tight turn executed into a fenceline. The horse exits the turn in whichever gait he entered it. For example, if you're trotting into a rollback, you'll trot off after the turn. Rollbacks are another way to build superb brakes. If I'm on a nervous, high-strung horse who thinks the only speed is fast-forward, I'll use rollbacks to bleed off energy. In the process I'll also be working on his steering wheel.

Rollbacks can also do the complete opposite. They can add energy and create more engagement. As you perfect this turn, your horse will become much lighter on his front end. You'll be able to ride your horse forward with energy and then use the turn to ricochet that energy into the opposite direction. It's like throwing a ball hard and fast against a wall and letting the energy bounce back to you. When your horse is light, you can add energy and still have him turn on a dime.

You can also use rollbacks to get a sluggish or stuck horse in motion. A green horse that's just being backed for the first time very often just stands still. Remember Robin? That was his reaction when I first got on him (pg. 80-81). I got him to move by asking for rollbacks. That is, I picked up the rein and asked him to bend his nose around to the side. Eventually he took a step onto a tight turn. C/R. Out of those turns, I was able to create forward movement.

The photos on page 193 show Robin tracking to the right along the arena wall. If you begin in this direction, you'll start off on the right rein, tracking right.

• Pick out a spot on the rail where you'd like your horse to turn. You're going to be riding a 180 degree turn. What with all the hip-flips you've done, your horse is set up to be light, but the first time you ride this turn you may be so focused on the geography that you'll forget about all your previous training, get heavy-handed, and just drag him through it. You can do it that way once or twice just to get a feel for the pattern, but after that you'll set up the turn with the "good, better, best" preparation that you learned in the hip-shoulder-shoulder exercise (Ch. 28).

• Several strides out from the point where you'd like him to turn, release the reins down to his withers.

• Pick up the buckle to signal that you want something, but this time change rein to change the bend. If you were asking your horse to bend to the right as he walked down the track, you'll now be bending him to the left. He'll still be walking in the same direction. He'll just be bending toward the wall. (Frame 1.)

Note: your left rein is now your inside rein even though it's to the outside of the ring. Be certain you understand this: inside and outside are relative to the bend you're asking for—not the direction you're traveling.)

• Ask for three more softenings of the jaw: "good, better, best." (Frame 1-3.)

• Pick up the rein a fourth time, expecting to feel your horse soften his jaw and step more deeply up into the bend. As he does, lift your hand, look back over your horse's left hip and ask for the turn. He understands hip-flips, so he'll disengage his inside (to the wall) hind leg and begin to pivot into a turn. Release the rein. Do not hold on all the way through the turn. (Frames 4-10.)

Chapter Thirty-One: Putting Humpty Dumpty Together Again

ROLLBACKS

A Rollback: frame by frame.

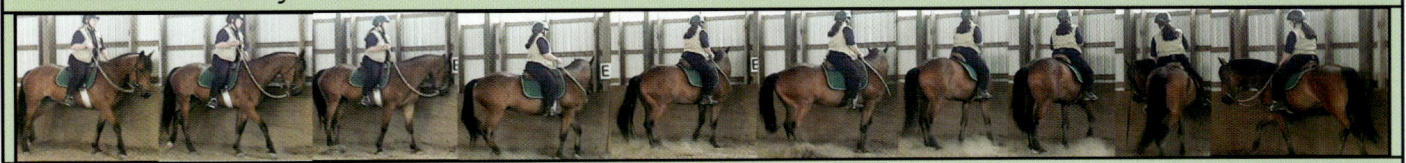

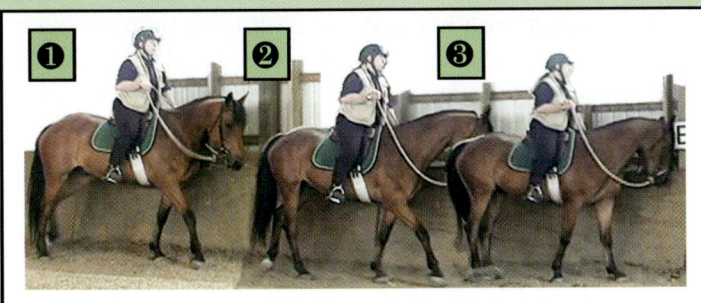

Robin has good form going into the rollback. The preparation begins several strides away from the turn. 1.) I've asked Robin to continue to track right but to soften his jaw to the left rein. 2.) Robin is more fully committed to the left bend. Note a deepening arc in his body as he connects his hip and jaw to the left rein. 3.) Asking him for a "good, better, best" change of rein has prepared him beautifully for a turn.

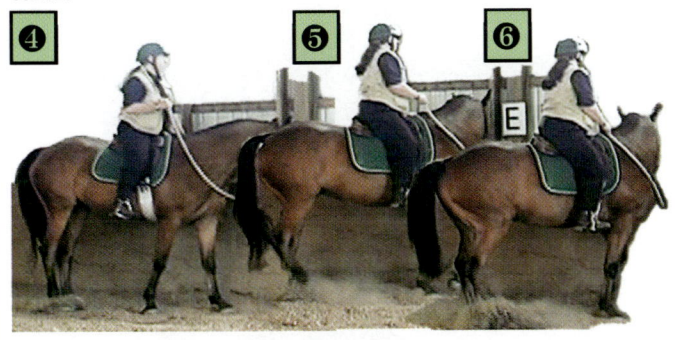

4.-6.) As Robin begins to turn, I release the rein, touching down to his withers with my right, buckle hand. A common mistake people make is to hold onto the rein through the entire turn. Here, I'm releasing Robin into the turn which will make him light and responsive in his balance. Note how Robin lowers his hindquarters as he goes into the turn.

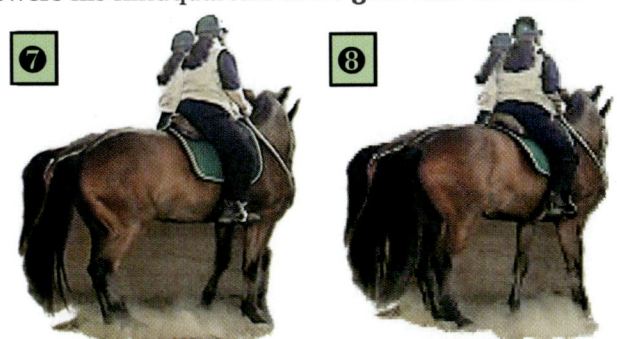

7.-8.) **Frame by frame you** can see the turn unfold. I've released the rein down to his withers as I feel him commit to the turn.

If your horse hesitates in the turn, you can always pick the rein up again, but you want him to complete the turn on his own.

9.-10.) Robin's balance is **committed to the turn.** I don't need to hold onto the rein to drag him through the turn.

11.) As Robin exits the turn, I'll activate the new inside **rein and ask him to step up in**to a left bend.

12.) The last frame shows one of the benefits of rollbacks: they help create beautifully balanced halts like this one.

193

There's a balance point in a rollback where the horse becomes committed to the turn. That's when he pivots around his hind end. If this doesn't make sense, walk a couple of rollbacks yourself. Use your t'ai chi walk (pg. 148) to find the pivot point in your balance. It's a little like jumping off the edge of a diving board; if you lean out far enough, eventually you'll get to a point of no return.

In a rollback there's a point where the horse is committed to the turn, and he doesn't need you pulling him around to ensure that he finishes the motion. You want to release the rein at that point, so you'll be ready to receive him on the far side of the turn. As you come out of the turn you'll be on the left rein, tracking left. The problem is that your horse is probably going to over-rotate and come off the track.

The first few times you ride a rollback you and your horse will probably miss the timing of the exit. He'll come out of the turn, and you'll remember too late that you have to be ready for the over-rotation. His front end will be walking off the track before you can respond to it.

To correct for this, use the skill you learned in the "hotwalker" exercise in Chapter 30. Adhere to the track by lifting your inside rein. Wait for him to respond to the added pressure. As he steps back onto the track, click, he gets a treat.

The click is there to clarify, motivate, and appreciate. If your horse is having difficulty with any aspect of the rollback, chunk down the process by clicking and reinforcing each phase of the turn.

Once he's completed his rollback, walk him off down the rail. You're now on the left rein, tracking left. Pick a spot where you'd like him to turn and repeat the process, this time changing the bend to the right in preparation.

One caution: if you have a horse who's afraid of a particular spot in your arena, be careful where you place your turns. If you keep walking him down toward the goblins and then repeatedly turn him away just before he gets to them, he may start thinking you're afraid of them too.

That's not a message you want to be sending. Set up the rollbacks so your horse turns to face the goblins, ride all the way past them, then ask for another turn. Click and reinforce him after each turn. He'll be learning that turning to face the goblins is a good thing. It earns him treats.

As the rollback becomes perfected, when you pick up the rein that's to the wall, it will feel as though you're literally picking up your horse's inside hind leg. Think of it like a puppeteer picking up a leg on his marionette horse. As you lift your rein, you'll bring his inside hind to a stop so he can pivot around that leg. That will rock him back onto his haunches (frame 6, pg. 193). He could stiffen and go above the bit, but you're going to use good single-rein technique to prepare him for his turns so he stays soft throughout.

If you let your horse slow down as he approaches the turn, or you hold onto the rein throughout, your horse may end up sucking back from your hand and getting sticky to your leg. You'll have a hard time getting him to engage his hip to create active, forward gaits. This is one of the reasons that many horses who are ridden on contact lack impulsion.

In contrast, if you ride your horse forward into the turn, releasing the rein as he commits his energy into the pivot, he'll become more engaged. You're connecting a deep reaching up and under of his inside hind leg to a softening of the jaw. The result will be an ability to both collect and energize, leading ultimately to piaffe.

A beautifully executed rollback.

HALF-TURNS

The easiest way to think of a half-turn is to visualize a giant ice cream cone. Ride your horse down the length of the long side of your arena. To change directions turn off the rail, ride a large semi-circle, then take a diagonal line back to the track. That's a half-turn.

Sounds easy? It is. You're just riding a simple change of direction, but embedded within that figure is a powerful training exercise. Let's chunk it down to see all the details and small steps that are involved. You're going to ride this turn as a single-rein exercise.

Why one rein? We want to dance with our horses. You may be able to turn just fine on two reins. Your

Chapter Thirty-One: Putting Humpty Dumpty Together Again

horse can follow your directions because he has learned to stay within the boundaries set by the two reins, but is he really following your body? On a single rein he has more choices. He can make more mistakes. When you drop down to one rein, you'll find out just how connected the two of you really are.

The illustration to the right begins with the horse tracking right. Your horse will be bent to the right, traveling to the right. You want to start your half-turn at the far end of the long side, so that your horse has plenty of room to return to the track. If you were to begin it just as you were exiting from a corner, you'd run out of space before you could complete your turn.

HALF TURNS

RIDING A HALF TURN

1.) You'll begin your preparation for the turn approximately two-thirds of the way down the long side. You'll start sooner on a stiff horse; later on one that is light and responsive.

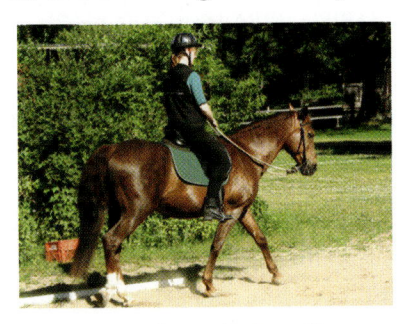

This horse is on the rail, bending to the right on the inside right rein.

2.) Use an opening inside rein to ask your horse to leave the track and follow you on a half-circle.

Use the skills you learned in the hotwalker exercise in Chapter 30 to guide your horse off the track. He should follow the suggestion of your opening rein and leave the rail. As he circles off the track, if he falls in over his inside shoulder, lift the rein to move him back onto your half-turn; if he bows out, use an opening rein to bring him back onto the arc of the turn.

3.) Once you've completed the semi-circular turn off the rail, you'll change rein and change the bend.

You want to feel his hips lining up with the path you're about to take. Release the rein. When the buckle rests on his withers, the reins are even. You want him to line himself up in balance between the two reins. This is very important. If you leave this step out, you'll have a hard time building straightness later on. As soon as you release, pick up the rein again and ask for the change of rein.

195

The Click That Teaches: Riding With The Clicker

4.) Your horse will now be bent left, but moving to the right back to the same track he just left.

How you set up and ride the diagonal return to the track is the key to this exercise. You could simply point your horse's nose at the wall and ride straight to it. That would give you simple navigation, but we want to create more than that, so you're going to add lateral flexion to the exercise.

5.) You'll be asking your horse to step forward and over keeping his hips and his shoulders lined up like a drill team as he returns to the track.

As you reunite with the track, continue to the left. If your horse is carrying himself well, you can organize the outside rein and ride with two reins. Otherwise continue down the track on the left inside rein. Set up another turn as the opportunity presents.

To get back to the track your horse has to keep stepping up underneath himself with his hind end. As he comes back to the track, he'll be using this added engagement to lift his outside shoulder. Look for this response. As you become more aware of it, you can click and reinforce it. As you do, you'll get an increased energy and lift in his gaits that is heavenly to ride.

The most common problem with half-turns is one of simple navigation. On a single rein you may not be able to get your horse to leave the track. If he's stuck on the rail, go back and review the hotwalker exercise. Work on circles and simple changes of direction across the center of the circle. Now return to the track. Again ask your horse to follow your opening inside rein. He should respond to the suggestion from your body and follow the feel of the rein onto a turn. As he responds, click and give him a treat to let him know that was the right answer.

After you click, if you're lucky, your horse may stop on the track you were riding. Give him his treat, and continue on. In all likelihood, however, he'll end up out of position. Circle him back to the rail, and look for another opportunity to set up a turn. Click him again for correctly turning off the rail.

As this becomes smoother and easier, have your horse walk a few more steps before you click and give him a treat. You'll now have a horse who follows your suggestions and will circle off the rail.

When you change rein to head back to the track, your horse may not understand that he's to move in the opposite direction to which he's bent. He may try to follow his nose across the center of the arena. Instead of ending up at the track back on the same side he just left, he'll turn towards the opposite wall. This is often caused just as much by the rider losing her bearings as the horse not understanding the signals. These are simple turns, but it's easy to get lost. To avoid confusion, before you get on your horse, walk the pattern. Feel out the flow of the turns and the changes of bend. The more you walk them, and the more you ride them, the more subtleties you'll discover. These are exercises you'll be using throughout your horse's training to keep him supple and engaged.

If your horse keeps getting confused when you change rein and heads off in the wrong direction, the hotwalker exercise can again come to your rescue. You used the opening, guiding rein earlier to let him know you wanted him to leave the track. Now you're going to lift the rein to ask him to move his shoulders over and bring them back in line with his hips. Your outside hand lifting the buckle will assist you with this. Lift it up and out to the side adhering to the track your horse would be on if he were perfect. That will create a limit to how far he can swing his

Chapter Thirty-One: Putting Humpty Dumpty Together Again

head to the right. The reins will form a triangle with your horse's nose as the point.

You want him to feel the point of contact of your lifted, outside hand. He should step over – into your receiving outside rein. This is an important step toward learning how to use an outside rein for engagement. After riding for so long on a single rein, many riders forget how to integrate the outside rein back into the program. It's important to stay alive with energy in this hand and use it as part of the communication system.

This is another one of those sections you want to highlight. It's easy to skip over something like this and not realize how important it is. The lift of the outside rein with your horse stepping up into it is a major part of these exercises. If you don't understand this section, ride the turns, then come back in and review this lesson. Your horse will show you how important it is.

FIRE HOSES, MARCHING BANDS, AND MOTOR BOATS

Your horse is very much like a fire hose. If he doesn't have enough energy, his walk will be flat and hard to steer. He'll be wiggly through his shoulders. He needs to send enough energy forward from his hindquarters to keep the momentum of the walk going. One of the major problems many riders have with these turns is they simply don't have the horse marching along from behind. They turn off the rail by dragging the horse's nose around with an opening rein. The horse over-bends his neck to relieve the pressure on his mouth. His shoulders bow out, and his hind end gets left behind. Been there, done that. This is all part of the learning process. You can't ride smooth turns on a horse that's not moving energetically from behind.

Imagine your horse as a drill team made up of five members marching along. The members of the team are the hips, shoulders, and nose. You'd think the nose would lead the team because it's out in front, but this isn't the case. It's the hips that initiate the movement and drive everything else forward. Think about a motor boat that has the engine and the rudder in the back.

This is the difference between a green horse and an upper-level performance horse. A green, just-been-started-under-saddle horse follows its nose. To bring this horse off the rail you'll use an opening, guiding rein. A horse that's further along in its training has shifted its equilibrium into its hindquarters. This horse is guided from behind, and it's the rider's hips in perfect unison with the horse's that create the turn.

If this sounds confusing, it's because people do not naturally turn this way. People follow their noses just as an untrained horse does. If you tend to walk tipped forward, curling your shoulders forward and down, you may not have any kinesthetic references for riding from the hind end. For you these will be just words on the page. You may understand them intellectually, but once you're on the horse you'll see the turn as something that happens in front of you, not something that's guided from behind. As much as you may want to shift your horse's balance, that won't happen until you shift your thinking and internal references. Here's an exercise that will help.

Set two water glasses one in front of the other on a smooth, flat surface. One represents the horse's front end, the other his hind end. If you take the front glass and move it around the table, the back glass will be left behind. But if you move the back glass, you can push the front one forward. At first you may be navigating a wiggly course, but with a little practice you'll be able to steer your two glasses through half-turns. You'll feel how you have to shift the position of the "hindquarters" glass to keep the front glass oriented in the pattern, just as the driver of a motorboat adjusts the angle of the outboard to steer the boat anywhere he wants to go.

If falling on the forehand is a problem for you, borrow a lesson from the old-fashioned finishing schools for girls and walk with a book on your head. That will balance you on your "carousel horse" central axis (pg. 130). When you ride, think of that balance and your horse will turn with more balance as well.

The first few times you ride this pattern, you'll probably change rein either too early or too late. Too early will result in an awkward shift onto the diagonal. Your horse's hips won't be lined up with the new bend, which will make the change harder for him, and he'll end up angling straight at the wall with no lateral flexion.

When you're late with the change, you'll cut your diagonal off; you'll come too far around on your semicircular turn off the wall, so the diagonal return will be short and steep. For smooth, beautiful turns and symmetrical figures, it's important to get the timing right. Walk the exercise, again using your "t'ai chi" walk (pg. 148-150) to find the balance. You'll feel how far your horse has to come around the turn to line up his hips and commit to the diagonal return to the rail.

Once again, the clicker can help you and your horse get correctly balanced and aligned. Suppose your horse has been following his nose after the

The Click That Teaches: Riding With The Clicker

change of rein so he heads off across the arena to the opposite wall. To correct this, you'll lift your inside hand. As he heads off in the wrong direction, the added pressure on his neck will ricochet him back to the left. As he reunites with the track and shifts into a lateral flexion, click, stop, and give him a treat. Let him know that's exactly what you want. It may not have occurred to him that he can walk in the opposite direction to which he's bent.

You'll gradually extend the number of steps you'll ask him to walk, until you can ride the entire pattern fluidly. By clicking and reinforcing the internal steps you'll help him to integrate the changes of balance you're asking him to make.

HALF-TURNS-IN-REVERSE

A half-turn-in-reverse is literally what the words suggest: it's a turn off the rail ridden in reverse order from a half-turn. Look at the diagram on this page. Turn the horse around, and you have a half-turn. The difference is in where you start the turn. Look at the orientation of the "ice cream cone". In the half-turn-in-reverse, you begin at the bottom of the "cone", where all the melting ice cream dribbles out. A half-turn begins at the opposite end with the scoop of ice cream.

HALF-TURN-IN-REVERSE

RIDING A HALF–TURN–IN–REVERSE

1.) Ride all the way through the corner as though you were going to be staying on the track.

Correct

The rider is using the inside, right rein to guide her horse through the corner.

Incorrect

This time the rider demonstrates what happens when you anticipate the turn and fail to ride all the way through the corner. Note how her horse is both counter-bending through the turn and inverting her topline.

2.) Begin your half-turn-in-reverse close to the corner so you have plenty of room to move off the wall and complete your turn.

2a.) As the rider comes out of the corner heading down the long side of the track, she releases the rein as a preparation for changing to the other rein.

2b.) She picks up the buckle and slides down her left rein. The first rein you pick up is by definition your inside rein. So even though she is still tracking right down the long side and the left rein is to the wall, this is now her inside rein.

198

Chapter Thirty-One: Putting Humpty Dumpty Together Again

3.) Once your horse is bending to the left ask him to move off the wall.

The rider is using her "three-flip-three" and "hotwalker" skills to ask her horse to bend left, but move off the rail to the right.

You asked for this same movement in the half-turn; the only thing that's different is the geography. In the half-turn you were returning to the track using a lateral flexion. Here you're leaving the track.

You're using skills you learned first in the three-flip-three exercise (Ch. 26). You're asking your horse to walk forward in the opposite direction to which he is bent.

Leaving a wall is often harder for horses than returning to it. That's why we talked about the half-turn first. The first few times you ask your horse for this new turn, he may not leave the wall at all. He'll counter-bend for you, but his feet won't leave the track. But by now you know several exercises that you can use to help him understand what you want.

You can use the "hotwalker" exercise (Ch. 30) and ask him to move his shoulders over. If he steps even one foot off the rail, click and reinforce him. You want to let him know that this really is what you want him to do.

You could also go back and review half-turns. The smoother and more responsive he becomes when you ask him to return to the track along a diagonal, the more likely it is that he'll be able to leave the wall along a diagonal.

A third alternative would be to turn your request for a half-turn-in-reverse into a rollback. In a sense, a rollback is a condensed version of the turn you're trying to ride.

Set up another turn as the opportunity presents. As your horse bends towards the wall, ask for a rollback turn. As you repeat this, gradually widen out the rollback. Take it further and further off the rail until you're riding a smooth half-turn-in-reverse. Click and reinforce each small measure of improvement.

4.) Once you're far enough off the track to make a smooth, balanced arc, turn to the left and return to the track.

5.) Continue to ride down the track. You are now tracking left, bending around your new inside, left rein.

TELEPHONES AND CONTACT POINTS

These turns are preparing you for the transition back to riding on two reins. As you ride through the three turns, you will find that your lifted buckle hand is playing a greater and greater role. It's controlling the overflexing and bowing out of the outside shoulder, and it's receiving the engagement of the hind end. Pay attention to these changes. They will become increasingly important.

If this doesn't make sense as you read these words, it may just mean that you and your horse haven't yet worked far enough through these lessons for this layer to reveal itself.

Training is so very much like peeling the layers of an onion. You have to peel the outer layers first to see the underlying ones.

For now be aware that you want to pay attention to the feel in your buckle hand. When you lift the rein, you want your horse to follow the rein and pick up his topline.

One of the images I think of as I ride these turns

is that of a telephone. When you first begin on a single rein, you lift up the buckle and then slide down the inside rein to your point of contact. It's as though you have picked up a telephone and called your horse.

When he responds with a give, he's answered the phone. When you release the rein, setting the buckle down on his withers, you've hung up the phone on your end. In the early stages your horse also hangs up his end. His attention goes back to the "movies" going on around him, but after a while, he will stay on the line even after you've hung up. In other words, even though the rein is loose, your horse is still connected to you, still paying attention to your signals.

The training turns reconnect you to geography. You're riding patterns that include changes of rein and direction. As you release one rein and change to the other, your horse not going to be "hanging up the phone". As you pick up the buckle, you'll feel a weight shift down both reins. Be watching for this. It's an important step towards engagement.

Engagement occurs when your horse rebalances his weight over onto his outside hind leg so his inside hind leg can step more deeply under his body. This in turn will lift his outside shoulder. Think back to the "t'ai chi walk" exercises (pg. 148-150) to understand this balance. An over-flexed horse won't be engaging in this way. Instead, his outside shoulder will be bowing out. He may be going sideways, but he won't be able to elevate his front end.

When your horse is correct, you'll both see and feel his outside shoulder lift up as he steps forward. You want to position your outside hand so you can receive this lifting of the shoulder. Think of your horse as a dance partner. If you aren't there to receive him, he can't join up with you.

Finding the right contact point is a problem for many riders. They're so used to riding horses that are on their forehand that they think they have to follow the outside shoulder. They think they have to make extra room for the shoulder to get through the turn, so they let their hand move forward toward their horse's ears. This lets the horse pop his shoulder out even more instead of lifting it. He's trying to follow his dance partner, but the more the rider moves his hand forward, the harder it is for his horse to engage his hips.

You need to receive your horse's outside shoulder but keep your hand stable relative to your hip. The direction your hand should move is up and *out*, not up and forward. Think about lifting a heavy bag of grain. You want to be able to get underneath the weight of the bag so you can lift it with your thighs instead of your lower back. Your horse needs to do the same thing. If his shoulder is popping to the outside, he won't be able to get his hips underneath him to elevate his front end.

The three training turns teach you how to connect all five members of the "drill team": head, shoulders and hips. As you perfect them, your horse will become truly straight and engaged. The "telephone" is never disconnected. Even when the rein is slack, your horse remains connected and balanced. It's a glorious feel. It will be tempting at this stage to pick up both reins and take your "new horse" through his paces, but you have a few more patterns to learn first. You're going to add some new geometry to the mix, beginning with a change of direction across the diagonal. The end result will be a horse you can ride through patterns that are far more complex than many dressage tests. He'll be balanced, engaged and ready to return to riding on two reins.

DIAGONALS

Think about how a drill team maneuvers through turns and changes of direction. Different members must speed up or slow down to keep the whole team marching together. The same thing holds true with your horse. When he goes around a turn, his outside hip and shoulder have a longer distance to travel than his inside hip and shoulder. It's easy for the drill team to get out of balance, especially when you add in lateral flexions. The geometry you're about to ride will test your ability to keep your horse's hips and shoulders aligned. The first challenge is a diagonal.

A diagonal is a simple change of direction across the arena. It should always be ridden out of the second short corner, not the first. Picture your ring as a rectangle that you're cutting in half to form two identical triangles. Remember your high school geometry. The hypotenuse of a triangle—the diagonal across your ring—is the longest side. You're going to use its full length to create a clean change of bend as you change direction.

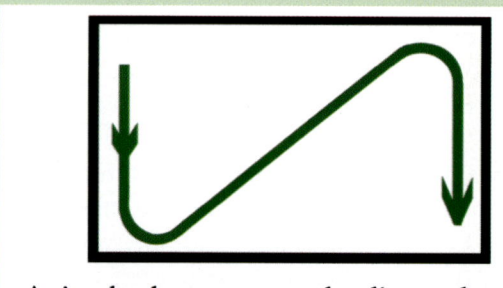

A simple change across the diagonal can be an interesting challenge when ridden as a single-rein exercise.

Chapter Thirty-One: Putting Humpty Dumpty Together Again

DIAGONALS

In simplest terms, riding a diagonal is just that:

You're riding from one end of the arena . . .

. . . across the center of the arena . . .

. . . to the opposite corner.

A diagonal can be treated as a simple change of direction. However, ridden as a single–rein exercise it becomes a challenging and powerful test of your horse's balance.

Sound easy? It is, especially with all the preparation you've done riding the three training turns. But your first few attempts riding a diagonal as a single–rein exercise may still run into problems. You may go through stages where you can't get your horse off the track. You ask for a diagonal, and all he does is bend his neck around to your knee and continue down the long side. Or you might find you can leave the track just fine, but you can't get back to it. Aaargh! It would be so easy if you could just drag him over with the outside rein.

Keep reminding yourself that this is the whole point of riding on a single rein. You want to bring these problems to light so you can solve them. Sure, you could drag your horse across the diagonal using two reins, but that's not the point. You're trying to fine tune the connections, not "bandaid" over them. All the exercises you've done to this point will help you ride perfect diagonals. you'll be using three–flip–three (Ch. 26), the "hotwalker" lesson (Ch. 30) and the skills gained in the three training turns (Ch. 31, pgs. 192-200).

RIDINING A DIAGONAL

2. Your horse needs to remain committed to the original bend until he has completed the corner and turned off the rail. It's easy for your horse to anticipate the turn and cut in on his corner. Be certain to ride a complete corner before heading off the rail.

One of the most common problems riders encounter when they first ride a diagonal is they simply can't get their horse to leave the rail. This is especially true if they've been doing a lot of lateral work.

Suppose you've been working on lateral flexions to soften your horse's jaw and neck and make him more responsive. You've done a great job, only now your horse is stuck in a pattern. He thinks you want him to step sideways in the three–flip–three exercise of stepping onto the numbers of a clock (pg. 165). As he tries to show you how well he understands, you'll get some great sideways steps. In

The Click That Teaches: Riding With The Clicker

another context stepping sideways down the track would be the right answer. It's just not the answer here. You want your horse to read all of your body's signals, not just some of them. However, you never want to get mad at your horse for offering you something you've taught him to do.

So what do you do? Nothing. The first time this happens you'll probably get all bollixed up with the reins. You'll have the horse's head over-bent to the side. His shoulder will be popping out; you'll be disorganized. It's a mess. So throw the whole, tangled thing away and start again.

Next time think about the figures you've already ridden. How did you get your horse to circle off the rail in the "hotwalker" exercise? How did you get him to change direction through the three training turns? Use what you've learned to break down this exercise into smaller steps. If the diagonal is truly stuck, go back to those earlier exercises and focus on the elements that will help your horse understand the very first step of what you're asking for now. As he takes that first solid step off the rail, click and reinforce him.

This is really important to understand from your horse's point of view. He thinks stepping sideways down the track is the right answer. He's not trying to ignore you. He just hasn't listened to the entire message. Think about these two requests: "Pass the cup of tea." And "Pass the cup of tea over your head." By adding that second phrase I change completely the action I'm looking for.

That's what happens in riding. As you ask for more complex combinations it's easy for your horse to get confused. He may not have noticed the one new element you've added. You're setting up a turn onto the diagonal, but your horse thinks you want something else. If you reprimand him for the "mistake", you're going to create a frustrated, confused horse. He was trying to please. He was sure he was doing exactly what you wanted, only you're telling him he's wrong. If it's frustrating for you, it's ten times more frustrating for him.

This is very important to understand. You don't want to poison your cues (pg. 102). Your horse is not being bad, or stubborn. He just hasn't sorted out the newest layer you've added to the puzzle. The clicker will help him. Go back to an earlier place in the training, review your cues, and then, when he takes that first step onto the diagonal, click, tell him he's right, and give him a treat!

BEHAVIOR CHAINS

Once your horse figures out that you want him to leave the rail, he may start cutting the corner and beginning the diagonal too soon. Many riders will scold their horses for anticipating a signal when really what they should be doing is appreciating such a willingness to perform. In a diagonal you're chaining several behaviors together which is going to create a lot of enthusiasm on your horse's part.

In a behavior chain, the trainee—be it a horse or a human—performs a series of behaviors one right after the other, all for one final reward at the end. Think of this simple chain: walk forward, halt, back up, C/R. Each element in the chain is first taught separately. Each element has a cue that triggers the behavior. When you teach these behaviors without poisoning your cues, you can string them together into a chain that becomes self-reinforcing. That is, you can reinforce the correct performance of the first behavior not by giving a reward but by presenting the cue for the next. The second cue predicts another opportunity for reinforcement so it can reinforce the preceding behavior.

The strongest chains are built with the most familiar, most highly reinforced behaviors coming at the end of the chain. The animal works from the newest, less certain behavior towards the most familiar so its confidence grows as it progresses through the chain. The reward is given at the end of the chain.

Reining patterns, jump courses, and dressage tests all represent complex behavior chains. The question is, has the trainer understood the nature of chains and built them well?

You can practice building behavior chains by breaking the diagonal down into its component parts and training it as a chain. I'll show you the segments that go into a diagonal, and some of the pitfalls you may encounter. I will leave it up to you to train it according to the needs of your horse

One of the cautions in working behavior chains is to be certain to keep your internal cues distinct. If you get sloppy about having cues for each separate step, your chain will fall apart. Karen Pryor gives a wonderful demonstration of this on one of her early videos, *Slap, Clap, Furbish*★. In the beginning she teaches a person to execute a simple two-part chain: on cue, clap your hands; then, on cue, turn in small circles. The video shows that as long as the internal cues are maintained, the chain persists—that is, the trainee keeps clapping her hands until she's given the cue to turn, and then the turning leads to a click and a reinforcement. When Karen deliberately drops the cues from the chain, the trainee rushes through the chain to the turning behavior. The hand clapping very quickly fades down to a single quick clap that

★ *Slap, Clap, Furbish*, by Karen Pryor; Sunshine Books, MA

Chapter Thirty-One: Putting Humpty Dumpty Together Again

LINKS IN A CHAIN

Here's one of the links in the chain. The horse has left the corner and is moving across the center of the ring. You want him to leave the track bent in this case to the left, and in the center of the arena pass through a moment of straightness before changing rein in preparation for the approaching corner.

merges into the first turn.

If your horse's performance is not as precise as you would like it to be, first make sure *you're* not anticipating the next step in the sequence and letting the internal cues of the chain fall apart.

For example, on the diagonal, you have to keep riding all the way through your corner. If your horse starts to cut the corner, use your "hotwalker" skills to lift the inside rein and move him back out to the rail until *you* are ready to turn. You don't want your horse cutting corners in the arena. And you don't want to cut corners in your attention to details. The more precise and focused you are here, the better his work will be later.

When your horse leaves the rail, he may change the bend prematurely. Riding a diagonal is a lesson in riding "balance beams". Your goal is to improve your horse's balance. You don't want him falling through his inside shoulder as he leaves the rail. You want him to stay committed to the rein you're on.

Use your "hotwalker" skills again to ask him to complete the turn off the rail. Do not change rein until you feel him lining up underneath you in the bend you are riding. On some horses this can mean that you'll go across the entire length of the diagonal without changing rein. You'll enter the far corner still asking your horse to line his body up with the original bend. For example, you might enter the corner tracking to the right after a change across the diagonal, but you'd still be asking him to bend left. That's okay. The important thing is that you get the response you are looking for not just the geography.

CHANGING REIN

Okay, you've solved the previous problems. You're able to ride good, clean corners without your horse cutting in. You can make a smooth entry onto the diagonal, and your horse stays committed to the bend you're in. The next piece in the puzzle is changing rein. You want to make a smooth transition from one bend to the next.

This is more a matter of the rider's focus and dexterity than it is a problem for the horse. Remember, you want a moment of straightness as you change from one bend to the next. You'll set this up initially by releasing the rein and touching the buckle down to the horse's neck. Then pick up the opposite rein, ask your horse to bend around your inside leg, and at the same time step laterally over to the track. This is the same skill you developed riding the diagonal line back to the track in the half-turn. If you have problems completing the diagonal, spend time reviewing that turn.

Perfecting the change of rein so your diagonal becomes a symmetrical figure is one of the challenges of this exercise. Whether your horse changes bend prematurely and over-rotates past the line you are on, or persists in holding onto the original bend all the way across the diagonal, you want to ride for response not just geography. To create excellence in performance, that's a skill you need to learn.

Diagonals are a place where many riders let the geography dictate what they're asking for. The horse crosses the diagonal trying to fall over his inside shoulder. The rider does a good job sticking with the "hotwalker" lifted rein to ask her horse to move his shoulders back in line with the rest of the drill team until she gets to the corner. That's when she gives up asking for the original bend because they're past the geographical landmarks for it.

What does her horse learn from this? That whatever his person is doing, he can just ignore it. The rider may have taken all the slack out of the rein, but the pressure will go away soon. From the horse's perspective he doesn't have to change anything. This

The Click That Teaches: Riding With The Clicker

pressure is just more "static on the line". With each failed attempt the rider is teaching her horse to ignore her even longer.

That's why on some horses you may have to ride all the way across the arena and through the next corner before the horse will finally becomes convinced that you really do want him to move his shoulder over and stay committed to the bend he carried out of the very first corner of the diagonal. You really do want him to wait until you signal him to change bend. You have a variable reinforcement schedule working against you, and it may take quite a bit of convincing before your horse stays with you on the diagonal.

This may sound like a problem, but it's really not. Each time you ride your horse through the far corner counter-bent, you're actually preparing for another wonderful training tool: reverse-arc circles.

CHANGING BEND

The change of bend is an important part of riding a diagonal. The transition from one rein to the next should include a moment of straightness.

You want to feel your horse lining up the "drill team" so he isn't simply falling through his outside shoulder as he heads to the rail.

The change of rein sets your horse up for the final link in the diagonal. He returns to the track correctly bent and stepping deeply into the far corner. Lessons learned from riding half-turns and half-turns-in-reverse will help create perfect diagonals and beautiful carriage. Note how round this horse is as he steps into the corner.

Chapter Thirty-One: Putting Humpty Dumpty Together Again

REVERSE–ARC CIRCLES AND REVERSE–ARC DIAGONALS

If you want to increase your horse's maneuverability and create a sport car-like ride, this is the way to do it. In a reverse-arc circle the horse is bent in the opposite direction to which he is traveling.

Reverse-arc circles free up the hips and help the horse to lift his outside shoulder. They are also a great way to energize and lengthen the stride. Once your horse is comfortable holding the reverse arc bend through the far corner of a diagonal, you can expand the figure into a full circle.

An easy way to learn to ride reverse arc circles is to teach them using diagonals.

1.) Instead of changing rein as you cross the arena, stay on the same rein you were on at the beginning of the diagonal. In the photo below that's the left rein.

SETTING UP A REVERSE–ARC CIRCLE

2.) That will mean you'll approach the far corner bending to the outside of the arena.

3.) Ask your horse to go through the corner bending to the outside. Click and treat if he gets even a step or two through the corner maintaining the bend.

4.) Gradually extend the number of steps until your horse is walking an entire circle bent to the outside.

As you can see from the photos, as you cross the arena and head towards the far corner, the left rein is still functioning as your inside rein. It is still asking your horse to bend around your left inside leg, but now the left rein is to the *outside* of the arena: hence the name: reverse-arc circle.

Once you can ride reverse-arc circles, you can play with them to create complex patterns. For example, you can ride reverse-arc diagonals.

Begin by tracking to the left, bending to the left. Ride across the diagonal of the arena without changing rein. Enter the far corner in a reverse-arc circle. You'll be tracking right but still bending left. Go through the second short corner in a reverse arc and come off the rail as though you were going to continue onto a circle.

Instead straighten out onto the diagonal. You are now tracking left, bending left. Return to the track. You've done two complete changes of direction without ever changing rein. Congratulations. You haven't been out of the walk yet, and you've just taught your horse how to counter-canter!

BROKEN LINES

A broken line is like a shallow serpentine off the track. An easy way to think of it is to pretend that you're passing another horse on the rail. Broken lines are a test of your horse's responsiveness and maneuverability.

By now your horse should understand your request to leave the track, but if he's still sticky, go back and review your training turns. You may discover that he's simply not limber enough yet to execute a smooth, symmetrical broken line. The solution here is a simple one: give him more room. Let the figure overlap the end corners at first.

As your horse becomes more flexible, he'll be able to make smoother transitions from rein to rein. Everyone who rides knows what "good side" and "bad side" means. Your horse picks up one canter lead better than the other. He turns better, his jaw is softer, everything feels better and responds faster on his good side. He seems stiffer all around on the other. The problem is, his good side keeps switching Last week you were sure he was stiffer to the right, but now it seems as though it's the other way around. That's normal. The "bad side" is going to be the side that gets the least attention. As you school that side, it will get better in relation to the other, and it will become the "good side".

As you ride these school figures, you may find

The Click That Teaches: Riding With The Clicker

BROKEN LINES

Begin as usual by tracking to the left. As you enter the long side of the arena, change rein to the right.

Ask your horse to bend to the right but move to the left, off the wall.

If he understands half-turns-in-reverse, he should have no trouble with this.

Come at least a horse's width off the track.

Change rein back to the left and return to the track.

Continue on along the track.

that your horse responds well in one direction but is sticky in the opposite bend. The broken line exercise will help your horse become more even in his body and more responsive to quick changes of direction.

REMEMBER: HAVE FUN!

You've done your homework. You've perfected the three training turns. You can ride broken lines, diagonals, and reverse-arc circles. You taught these first in the walk and then in the trot. You started out with a stiff horse and turned him into a sports car. It's time to take him out to the "test track" and enjoy the ride!

You're going to mix and match, using the different figures and training turns to create a complex mosaic of movements. You won't be stuck on the rail any more. You and your horse will be using the entire dance floor.

Pick up an active trot and let the maneuvers flow one into the other. As you become familiar with the bends and turns, you'll be able to thread them together so that your horse can execute a seamless series of movements that builds balance, energy, and straightness. The result will be a trot that "knocks your socks off". When it gets truly wonderful, click and give both of you a treat for a job well done. You've earned it!

And while you're jackpotting your horse for a super ride, pause a moment and notice how much work he just did all for that one click. You began by reinforcing tiny units of behavior. If he got stuck in a turn, you marked the first step off the rail. Now you've just ridden an improvised pattern that's more complex than many dressage tests. You've built your horse's confidence. He knows he's connected to you. He understands what you want, and the turns are as much fun for him as they are for you. The freedom of movement he's experiencing is self-reinforcing, and furthermore he knows that there's a jackpot at the end of the chain.

The other thing you may notice is that your horse hasn't broken into a sweat the way he used to. Resistance and tension are what created the sweat before. That's gone now. You'll be able to ask much more from your horse without tiring him out. If you want to keep your horse fresh and energized, clicker train him!

PART 6
RIDING FOR PERFORMANCE

In the previous sections I divided riding into two separate criteria: *how* your horse carried himself and *where* he went. I turned chunking down behavior into a fine art and created many more steps in this process than many of you would have thought possible.

The result is a very rideable, very beautiful horse. You could easily continue on at this point and spend the rest of your riding career happily exploring single-rein concepts, but you'd be missing out on some glorious layers. The outside rein has a very real function in riding, and it's time to bring it back into active use.

You've already begun that process with the training turns. In this section I'll define the role of the outside rein, and I'll give you a simple exercise for connecting it back into the system. I'll show you how to use this work out on the trail, and how to develop it into shoulder-in and piaffe. Finally, I'll share with you some stories to show you how all the pieces fit together.

MAIN LESSONS COVERED:

1.) Adding the Outside Rein: Reviews how to organize both reins and connect the softening of the front end to the powerhouse engagement of the hindquarters.

2.) Shoulder-In: Converts the lateral flexions of Part 5 into the engagement of shoulder-in.

3.) Riding in the Real World: Shows you how to use the tool box you've been collecting throughout this book to help your horse handle the challenges of riding out.

4.) Collection: Piaffe made possible.: Shows you how to assemble the layers to create advanced performance.

This final section shows you how to connect all the training steps to create a "one in ten million" horse. Enjoy the ride!

RIDING FOR PERFORMANCE

I wish I could share with you all the stories behind all the horses featured in this book, but there just isn't room. I will tell you just about these two: Magic, the Tennessee walker in the upper left photo, is owned by Debra Olson-Daniels. In the winter of 2002 I got a phone call from Debra. She was at her wits end with her horse. He was bolting with her under saddle, spooking at his own shadow, and attacking her on the ground. Debra was a novice horse owner trying her best to follow the instructions from traditional force-based training. The result: Magic was becoming increasingly confused, frustrated and aggressive. That's when she contacted me and started experimenting with clicker training. Through the clinics, books and videos Debra gained the skills she needed to transform her horse.

Early on she questioned her ability to spot the "clickable" moment. I told her if she liked what Magic was doing, if it looked pleasing to her, she should click and reinforce it. Her artist's eye led her to the beautiful horse you see here. She told me she would go out to the barn to train. When she got to something she didn't understand, she'd go back in the house and review the videos and books. Exactly right!

The other horse pictured here is Aimee, a ten year old Arabian. I introduced you to Aimee earlier (pg. 142). You cannot appreciate how far this mare has come without seeing her "before" picture. Aimee's previous owners beat and starved her. When her current owner, Julie Jacobs, rescued her, Aimee's back was covered with sores from an ill-fitting saddle. Julie had had horses all her life. She was an experienced rider, but prior to clicker training she had never had any formal training. Step by step clicker training helped her reach past Aimee's fears to create the beautiful horse you see here.

Aimee, two months after she was rescued.

Both these horses teach a powerful lesson: Trust the process. It works.

**CHAPTER 32
Riding on Two Reins:
Engagement and the 300 Peck Pigeons**

The outside rein has a very real role to play besides simply limiting how far the outside shoulder can bend. It receives the engagement of the hind end. In this chapter I'll define the functions of both the inside and outside reins, and I'll give you a simple exercise for connecting the outside rein back into the system.

REINS

Your reins have four jobs. They control: 1.) head elevation; 2.) bend; 3.) engagement; and 4.) leg speed.

When you are riding on two reins, the job of the inside rein is to monitor head elevation and bend. The job of the outside rein is engagement and leg speed. This puzzled me for the longest time. I could understand the first three things easily enough, but the last confused me. Surely we could control leg speed with just one rein? We do that all the time using one-rein stops and tight turns. That's true, but those gross changes in leg speed are not what is meant here. What we are creating is cadence. Cadence is rhythm (the number of steps taken per unit of time) plus suspension. In terms of gait development this is where the horse transforms into the wonder of our dreams. We are riding Pegasus, the winged horse whose feet never touch the ground. Does this sound too fanciful? Just wait. As you explore the role of the outside rein, this may well be what you experience. But for starters, it might help to go back and review the discussion of stuck accelerator pedals in Chapter 15. Robin's experience has a direct bearing on what follows.

DORSO-VENTRAL FLEXIONS

When you first ask your horse to give at the poll in response to pressure from two reins, he will be confused. He's used to processing information from one side at a time. If you pick up the left rein, he responds to the pressure by bending left. If you pick up the right rein, he bends right.

So what happens now if you pick up both reins? Your horse is a good sport. He's going to try to figure you out. He'll feel you organize your inside left rein first, so he'll start to look left, but then he'll feel you add the right rein, so he'll try to look right. But—you silly human!—you're still holding on to the left rein.

Your horse is left wondering how can he possibly soften to the right. He's trying to do what you've been teaching him all this time, and now you're in the way, blocking him by keeping contact on both reins.

Your horse will probably get confused, and he may even get a little frustrated. You'll feel the reins tighten as he tries to find the release. For the moment all that lovely softness you've been working so hard to create will disappear. He'll pull up against your hands, which just creates more pressure, but wait—it also reminds him of his very first single-rein lesson. "Down" was the answer then. Maybe "down" is the answer now.

He's willing to try, but he's got a problem. With pressure on both

---

ADDING THE OUTSIDE REIN

This series of photos shows this team's first experience with this lesson.

1.) This Arabian has learned to soften to the right and to the left via three-flip-three lateral flexions. 2.) However, when his rider activates both reins by lifting the buckle up and stabilizing her hand against her body, he's not sure what to do.

3.) She waits patiently while her horse experiments.

4.) When he gives at the poll, he discovers that all the pressure he feels from the bit goes away. He'll earn a click and a treat for rounding his topline, plus she'll release the rein.

209

corners of his mouth he can't simply drop his head. He has to get his body organized first. He has to lift his back and give at the poll in order to lower his nose. Congratulations! He just engaged his body dorso-ventrally instead of side to side. Click! Give your horse a treat and give yourself a huge pat on the back. You've just ridden your first truly engaged step on your new performance horse!

REMEMBERING TO LET GO
When a horse is first learning this exercise, he's going to be using his muscles in unaccustomed ways. He's going to get tired fast, and that's what causes problems in conventional training. The horse needs short breaks from this exercise, but that's not how most people are in the habit of riding.

Instead, as I mentioned earlier (pg. 155), what's normal and natural for most people is to hold on to what they've created. They've been diligently following their trainer's instructions to get their horse "on the bit". They've been driving the horse's hindquarters up underneath him and fixing their hands. Their horse has finally rounded through his back and given at the poll. They aren't going to let go of something that was so hard to get in the first place. Instead of releasing after the first instant that they feel the horse organize his body the way they want, they hold on. They've fallen into the contact trap.

The horse may be fine with this for a stride or two, but then his neck will begin to ache. If you want to experience the ache the horse feels through his back and neck when he first goes on the bit, try looking down at your navel. Unless you've been doing a lot of sit-ups and you've got strong abdominal muscles, your neck and shoulder muscles will start to hurt pretty fast.

If the horse's neck hurts more that his mouth, he'll start to pull against the rider's hands to try to stretch out and relieve his muscles. The rider normally counters by fixing her hands harder, or in the classic form of this downward spiral, getting a stronger bit. Now the pressure the horse feels in his mouth is greater than the ache in his neck. He has to find another solution, so he learns to lean on the rider's hands.

As one set of muscles begins to ache, the horse wiggles and shifts around to find other positions that feel comfortable, but this just compounds the problem—what the rider now has is a crooked horse who's using the steady contact of both reins like a prop to lean against. So what's the solution? Letting go, then building duration slowly just as you have with every other exercise in this book.

PECKING PIGEONS AND BUILDING DURATION IN ENGAGEMENT
A well-trained Western horse knows how to work on a slack rein, but most English-trained jumpers and dressage horses work on contact. This means all the slack has been taken out of the reins and the rider has a direct feel of the horse's mouth. The problem with riding on steady contact is that after a while the horse will start to use it for support. Instead of feeling nice and light in the rider's hands, the horse will feel like dead weight. He'll lean on the rider's hands, just as we lean against a wall for support.

I certainly don't want my horse to lean on me, and I don't want to be leaning on him, either. But the other extreme is abandoning the reins altogether. Light doesn't mean disconnected, anymore than contact means the horse is using the reins for support. Connected might be a better term to use.

I want my horse to learn to carry himself in balance, and that's why I'm asking him to "go on the bit". A horse naturally carries 70 percent of his weight on his front end, but his power house is in the back. By teaching him to shift his weight, I can get him to bring his hind legs more underneath him. This lets him use the power of his hindquarters to lift his front end.

He has to use his abdominal muscles to engage his hind end. When done correctly, the horse rounds his topline: his back lifts, his neck elevates and lengthens, he flexes at the poll, his jaw releases into the rider's receiving hand. Instead of being strung out and looking like a sausage, he looks round like an orange. His hind end is underneath him and the plane of his face is perpendicular to the ground. Think of the classic European statues, or a stallion displaying proudly to his rivals, and you'll have the right image.

It's a wonderful look, but it's also much more than that. With his back elevated, the horse is supporting the rider's weight in a way that's healthier for his spine. It takes some conditioning before the muscles involved are strong enough that he can hold himself in this posture comfortably for many strides.

AN EXERCISE FOR ADDING IN THE SECOND REIN
So how is this done in actual practice? When I first started teaching this work, I'd get to this point with a team, and I'd tell the rider to organize the outside rein. These were riders who had ridden for years in traditional ways, but who had devoted an extended period of time learning single-rein flexions. When I asked them to organize their outside rein, they were clueless. They had forgotten how to hold two reins! Now that their horses were so responsive to the

Chapter Thirty-Two: Riding on Two Reins

STEP ONE: PICKING UP THE BUCKLE

1.) The rider has lifted the reins up with her outside hand and anchored them firmly against her body. 2. When her horse stops pulling against them and softens at the poll, 3.) she releases the reins down to his withers..

Note how solidly the rider's hand is anchored against her body. She's using both hands to keep the reins steady. If your hand bounces even a little, your horse will continue to pull.

nuances of balance that could be transmitted down the reins, their old habits felt amazingly awkward.

To help with the mechanics I developed a three step process for picking up the reins. As it adds the engagement of the outside rein, it retains all the good connections that the single-rein flexions created. To prepare for this exercise your horse should already be familiar with the lessons in the previous sections. He should be working well in lateral flexions and understand the single-rein training turns.

Step One: Lift the buckle of the reins to your sternum with your outside hand. If you were wearing a button-down shirt, you'd place your hand about three buttons down from the top. The exact position will depend on the length of your reins and the height of your torso. Anchor your hand solidly against your body.

Your horse is going to feel an even tension on both corners of his mouth. As you cue him with your legs to go forward, his initial response to this will probably be to raise his head and pull against the rein. That's normal, and it's all part of teaching your horse that he can still move actively forward from behind even though he feels even contact from both reins. To counter any pulling, be certain to anchor your hand solidly against your sternum.

The instant that you feel any softening, release the reins and let them drop back down to your horse's neck.

Anchoring your hand is an important part of the exercise. A lack of stability will just encourage your horse to keep on pulling. I have some riders grab hold of their shirt to give them a clearer feel of how much their hand is moving. Even a little movement in your hand will just encourage your horse to go on pulling. If need be, use both hands to anchor the reins against your body.

As your horse settles into the exercise, you won't need to anchor your hand. He'll soften to just a lift of the buckle. (If your horse has trouble doing this and persists in pulling through his topline even after many repetitions, check for soundness. All that pulling may signal more than a lack of understanding. If you determine that nothing is bothering him physically, go back and review the basics of single-rein riding.)

Lifting the buckle of the rein all the way to your sternum lets you experience a wider range of motion than you may be accustomed to. This is important for both safety and training reasons. Lifting the buckle draws the reins up to you so you don't have to lean forward and unbalance your seat every time you pick up the inside rein (Pg. 119).

If you don't draw the buckle up far enough, you'll end up with too much rein between your inside hand and your horse's mouth.

If your horse is feeling anxious, that extra length can be a real hazard. Your horse can scoot out from under you before you have a chance to connect with his hips and disengage them. As you practice lifting the buckle to your sternum not once or twice, but many hundreds of times, you're programming a muscle pattern into your hands that will let you

The Click That Teaches: Riding With The Clicker

automatically find the right height that instantly connects with your horse's mouth in an emergency.

With the reins anchored on your torso and your seat sending your horse actively forward, your horse will probably discover that bringing his hocks more underneath his body and softening his poll releases the pressure he feels in his mouth. This is the beginning of going on the bit.

If instead your horse swings his nose to the inside or leans into his outside shoulder, just wait. Continue to keep your reins anchored on your sternum. Since your horse has done a lot of lateral flexions, he may think you want him to bend. When bending to the side isn't rewarded with a release, he'll try other options. He'll bring his nose back in line with the rest of his body, and he'll discover that softening his poll gets you out of his mouth. Click! Once this is happening consistently, your horse is ready for Step Two.

Step Two: Pick up the buckle and lift it to your sternum. As your horse follows your hand and softens at the poll, instead of releasing the rein as you have been doing, gently slide down the inside rein with your inside hand. You'll feel a contact point where your horse softens his jaw into the feel of the rein. Release the rein.

This is an important step. There's a major

STEP TWO: ASKING THE HORSE TO GIVE LATERALLY

1.) Slide down the inside rein as you lift the buckle.

This rider doesn't have to force a give. Her horse is already stepping deeply under his body and softening his jaw just to the lift of the buckle. With the slide down of her inside hand she's simply accepting something he's already giving her.

STEP TWO: WHAT TO LOOK FOR

2.) Instead of pulling against the rider's hand as she lifts the rein up, this horse is yielding softly to pressure. Note how his entire topline has rounded. His hocks are underneath him, there's beautiful muscle definition in his neck, he's flexing at the poll, and he's stepping up softly into the bend. All the elements are there for the rider to proceed to the Step Three.

difference between forcing a give and receiving a give. Lightness comes from preparation. By the time you're asking for this step, your horse will already be offering a give of the jaw. You won't need to lock down the inside rein to force a give. Instead you'll be receiving something you recognize is already happening.

Again, you'll repeat this segment many times until both you and your horse are comfortable with it.

Step Three: When your horse is consistently softening into the inside rein, you're ready to add the outside rein. Begin with Steps One and Two. Pick up the buckle with your outside hand and bring it to your sternum, then slide your inside hand down to receive a give on the inside rein. At the point where you would normally click and release the rein, instead, steady your inside hand on the rein.

You're ready to pick up the outside rein. At this point many people have to remind themselves how to do this. This may sound silly to you now. You've been riding for years. Picking up both reins is an automatic response. But after you've been riding on a single rein for a while, you may need a refresher

Chapter Thirty-Two: Riding on Two Reins

STEP THREE: ORGANIZING YOUR OUTSIDE REIN.

1.) The rider has stabilized her inside hand in preparation for picking up the outside rein. She's ready for the next step: hooking the outside rein with the little finger of her right hand.

2.) Once she has both reins anchored in her inside hand, she can reach down with her outside hand and pick up the outside rein. Note: she *does not* release the reins through this step. The relationship to her horse's mouth remains steady.

3.) Her inside hand keeps a stable point of contact. Her outside hand opens and lifts. By picking up two reins, in a sense she's still riding on the buckle. She has just shortened the buckle so her hands can be in a more comfortable position in front of her body.

course when it comes to using both reins at once. (If you need to, use a saddle stand and practice off the horse until the movements described below are fluid.)

To pick up the outside rein, keep the feel on the inside rein steady. This is now your stable point of contact. Your inside hand will not be anchored against anything solid, but because your horse is no longer pulling, you can keep a stable feel with ease. Keep your outside lifted hand at the height it's been, but shift it to the inside across your chest so that you can hook the index finger of your inside hand around the outside rein. You'll now have both reins anchored in your inside hand.

Reach down with your outside hand and pick up the outside rein. Keep your inside hand steady, but move your outside hand into a comfortable position. Your horse will follow the feel of that rein, and because of what he's already experienced in Steps One and Two of this exercise, he'll organize the outside of his body so that he softens and connects even more through his topline. The instant he does click and release the reins.

This is where the pigeons we met in Chapter 14 come back into the equation. Remember the pigeon study in which a behavioral scientist used a variable reinforcement schedule to increase the number of times the pigeons in the experiment had to peck a bar before they earned the reward of a few kernels of corn. She gradually increased the amount of

This lovely Arabian has learned to go from this . . .

. . . to this, in the space of one session. As his rider becomes more familiar with the process, she'll lengthen and engage her own spine. Her upper arm will drop in a vertical line from shoulder to elbow, and her hands will follow her horse's hips instead of his mouth, as they are here. These comments are to help train your eye. For a first go at this lesson, she's doing great!

The Click That Teaches: Riding With The Clicker

behavior they had to give her until they were on a variable reinforcement schedule of 300. Remember also that this is how I taught Robin to walk quietly on a lead during a long stretch of bad winter weather (pgs. 75-78).

Riders can learn from these pigeons. If you and your horse were on a VR schedule of three hundred, that would mean you could pick up the reins and float on a point of contact without releasing the rein for three hundred strides, and your horse would stay on the bit throughout. That's a tremendous amount of work for one release. This is what dressage riders want, but the problem is they usually don't build their variable reinforcement schedules slowly enough. They pick up the rein and hold on well past the point where their horse needs them to release. The result is a stiff horse and a frustrated rider.

An alternative is to use the three steps outlined above to build a long VR schedule. At first you're going to release on a fixed rate of reinforcement. As you organize your outside rein, as soon as your horse softens his poll, you'll release both reins. That's a one-to-one schedule.

Begin a new sequence: pick up the buckle — slide down your inside rein — feel your horse respond by softening into the bend — organize your outside rein, and wait for the release through his whole topline. Click and reinforce. Begin again.

Be careful. At this point many riders begin to rush through the process. Step two gets lost in their hurry to pick up the outside rein. Be certain that your horse gives you the response that is associated with each step before moving on. By building the steps the way you have, you'll be able to recognize when your horse has responded correctly. If he stiffens, your hand will automatically hesitate and wait for the give to happen before moving on to the next step in the sequence.

And note, if things get disorganized, you can always slide back along the reins to an earlier step. If you're asking your horse to release his topline in step three, but something distracts him and you feel him tensing up, don't wait for trouble. Instead, slide your outside hand back up to the lifted buckle position. If you need to disengage his hips and bring him to a halt, you'll be able to do so from this position. Practice sliding back and forth between rein positions so this option is fluid and available to you.

As soon as your horse is consistently organizing his body and softening his poll as you pick up the outside rein, switch to a VR schedule of two or three. Instead of releasing the instant he softens his poll, wait another stride or two. Remember that the VR schedule is an average. If on the second stride your horse stiffens slightly, continue to hold the reins until you feel him soften on the third or the fourth stride.

Since you're riding a clicker-trained horse, you have an additional option besides simply releasing the rein and beginning a new sequence. You can also click your horse and give him a treat. This is a great advantage and really helps him to integrate the responses you want him to make. Suppose you've stretched your horse out to a VR schedule of four. Your horse stays soft on the first three gives, but stiffens just slightly on the fourth, so you hold on until you feel a softening coming back on the fifth stride, and you release on a soft give of the sixth stride.

You pick up both reins again going consistently through each of the three steps to do so. Your horse gives beautifully through each of the steps, and now you feel a little extra lift coming up through his shoulders. Click, you're going to mark that extra effort with a release and a nice treat.

By using the pigeon model of variable reinforcement schedules, you're not only helping your horse to internalize the criteria you want, you're giving him time to build the physical strength he needs to carry himself comfortably. He won't have to choose between relieving neck and back muscles that ache versus easing the pressure from the reins. Long before his muscles begin to scream out their protests, you'll be releasing the rein and giving him the little breaks he needs.

He'll also learn that it's safe to go on the bit. When a horse gives at the poll and drops the plane of his face onto a perpendicular line to the ground, he can't see the horizon line clearly. You're blocking his ability to scan for predators, and that can make some horses very nervous. If your horse tenses up when you ask for engagement, he may not be protesting because of physical discomfort. He may simply feel vulnerable.

The solution is to ask him to give for just an instant. It's a little like teaching young children how to swim: instead of insisting that they stay under water for a long time, you let them bob up and down until they discover that being under water isn't so scary. As they learn to hold their breath longer and longer, they'll soon be comfortable swimming under water all the way across the pool. The horse learns in the same way. Each time you release, you're letting him "come up for air". He can check for predators. As he learns that it's safe to go on the bit, he'll be able to stay there longer. Pretty soon going on the bit will seem like the most natural thing in the world to him. He'll be a 300-peck pigeon.

Chapter Thirty-Three: Lateral Work: Shoulder-In

CHAPTER 33
Lateral Work: Shoulder-In

In this chapter you'll be putting more of the "humpty-dumpty" pieces together again. You'll be using the hip-shoulder-shoulder exercise to develop half halts and a "reset" button. And don't worry, if you aren't sure what those are, I'll be defining them. I'll add in a ground exercise to ease the claustrophobic feeling many horses have when they work in close to arena walls, and then I'll show you how to use the clicker to set up beautiful lateral work. In case all of this sounds overwhelming, I'll also share with you an "ugly duckling" story of Sahib, a horse who started out as a lesson-program drop out and became one of our clicker superstars.

SHOULDER–IN AND HAUNCHES–IN
You're riding an engaged horse on two reins. Now it's time to turn your lateral flexions into the perfection of shoulder-in. Shoulder-in is an elegant movement in which the horse lifts his outside shoulder IN off the track and travels on three (or alternatively four) tracks. He moves AWAY FROM the direction to which he is bent.

Haunches-in, by contrast, has the horse moving his hips to the INSIDE of the track and bending IN the direction to which he is traveling. Both are very beautiful movements and very useful in the development of a horse's gaits and upper-level performance.

What you have been riding to this point are lateral flexions. A flexion is designed to make your horse more supple and responsive. Shoulder-in and haunches-in add engagement. In other words, both halves of the drill team are lined up and in balance.

LATERAL FLEXIONS REVISITED
You can think of shoulder-in as the perfection of the lateral flexions you've been riding so far. When you first experimented with teaching your horse to move sideways in three-flip-three (see "Clock Dancing", Ch. 26: pg. 165), you got pieces of his body to respond to you for a step or two. He stepped onto two o'clock with his right front foot and the rest of him followed. This is a lateral flexion. You've used it to create more softness and flexibility in your horse. It's important to recognize, however, that you can have a horse flexing laterally without necessarily having him engaged. We want both. The end result will be shoulder-in.

When you went "clock dancing" with your horse, sometimes he had his hips underneath him as he moved sideways and sometimes he didn't. You could probably feel the difference. When the "drill team" was lined up, he felt smooth and organized, and when it wasn't he felt rushed and out of balance. You might not have been able to verbalize what the difference was, but you could certainly feel it. When his body felt balanced and organized, click!, you gave him a treat.

Your horse liked his treats, so he started figuring out what he was doing to get clicked. He began offering those lined up, organized moments more and more consistently. As you became more familiar with the feel, you could help him out. You were both in this together, and pretty soon people in your barn started commenting

---

SHOULDER-IN AND HAUNCHES-IN

Lucky, a Connemara cross, demonstrates the difference between shoulder-in and haunches-in.

Shoulder–In: Lucky is bending to the right, but he is traveling down the arena rail, moving away from the direction to which he is bent. His outside shoulder comes IN off the track. His handler walks into him, and he yields out of her space.

Haunches–In: Now Lucky is in a haunches-in bend. He is still bending right, but now he's swung his hips to the inside of the track and he's stepping towards his handler as he moves down the rail. In other words, he is bent IN the direction to which he is traveling. As he moves down the rail, his handler will step back to make room for him.

215

on how good your horse was looking. A couple people even asked where you were taking dressage lessons! You're well on your way to turning those lateral flexions into the perfected movement known as shoulder-in.

HIP–SHOULDER–SHOULDER AND THE HALF–HALT

The "clock dancing" of three-flip-three (pg. 165) evolved into hip-shoulder-shoulder. This is one of the essential precursors of shoulder-in. You've done hip-shoulder-shoulder to the left and the right. You can ask your horse to walk forward, then you can pick up either rein and ask him to stop and back up. (If you need a review, see Chapter 28.)

Your horse is ready for a new suppling exercise, one which will engage him even more deeply and connect him solidly to both reins. This is a set-up for yet another exercise which leads directly to shoulder-in.

- Walk your horse forward.

- Pick up the left rein, and ask for hip-shoulder-shoulder, bending to the left.

- Back him several strides.

- At the point you would normally click him to end the behavior, change rein instead.

- Keep him backing, but ask him to change the orientation of his body so he's backing and bending to the right. Click and reinforce.

- Repeat this until he can change rein easily while he continues to back.

- Walk him forward. Pick up the rein and ask for hip-shoulder-shoulder. Back him several strides, change rein and continue to ask him to back. But now instead of clicking him, ask him to go forward out of the rein-back. Click and reinforce.

As you read this, you may be wondering what your "go forward" cue is. I could start a long discussion about rotating your pelvis and adding energy, but I don't need to. By the time you've ridden all the underlying layers that prepare your horse for this exercise, you will have a "go forward" cue beautifully programmed into your body. When you change your thought, you'll automatically change your seat. It's up to your horse to notice this change and respond to it.

Remember the discussion in Chapter 17 about horses getting stuck in patterns? Your horse will probably continue to back even after you've changed your seat to give him the "go forward" cue. You aren't doing anything wrong. Even if he continues to back the length of your arena, be persistent. Continue to present your cue to go forward. Backing is hard work. Eventually he's going to realize that it isn't getting him anything. He'll notice your cue. It may take him another step or two to process all this, but eventually he'll stop backing and take a step forward. C/R and repeat until your horse is walking forward promptly each time you ask, when you ask.

You're now ready to add in your outside rein, just as you did in the exercise described in the previous chapter.

- Walk your horse forward, pick up the left rein, and ask for a hip-shoulder-shoulder rein-back.

- At the point where you would now change rein, continue instead to back up on your left rein.

- Add your outside rein by moving your right hand over so you can hook the right rein with your left hand.

- Slide your right hand down and pick up the outside rein. That will give you a good point of contact to ask him to engage both his hips in a dorso-ventral flexion. C/R.

- Expand this until he's backing several steps, then rock him forward with your seat and walk off.

Congratulations! You just rode a collected, fully engaged start! It's going to feel grand! You have also created the "reset button" you're going to need to teach your horse shoulder-in. You want your horse to become very fluid in this exercise. This "reset button" is an important element not only for lateral work, but also for further gait development. (Review the chapter on Gait Development.)

CLAUSTROPHOBIA

Horses do not like narrow, trappy spaces. Think about what a nervous horse does when you ask him to trot between two obstacles that are set up close together. He'll either balk or race through like water rushing through a narrow channel. Lunge a horse close to a wall and you'll see the same thing. He'll speed up if he feels trapped between your body and the wall.

You have to resolve your horse's natural claustrophobia before you can ask for shoulder-in down the fenceline of your arena. He's going to feel crowded by the barrier. You have to show him that he has all the room in the world to do what you want.

Here's a ground exercise that will help prepare your horse for shoulder-in under saddle:

Chapter Thirty-Three: Lateral Work: Shoulder-In

CIRCLES TO THE WALL: A GROUND LESSON TO PREPARE FOR SHOULDER-IN

- Using a regular halter and a nine to twelve foot lead, lunge your horse on a small circle to the left. Get him moving consistently around you.

- Imagine that there is a straight line running from the wall (12 o'clock on a circle) out to the outer rim of your lunging circle (six o'clock on the circle.) As your horse approaches six o'clock, take a step or two back along that line towards twelve o'clock. At the same time let the rope slide through your left hand so you end up holding the tail of the rope in your left hand.

You're going to be asking your horse to change direction. You'll do this by sliding up the rope with your right hand and extending your arm out to the side. I always think of a maitre d' at a restaurant leading you to your table. "Your table is this way," your hand says with a flourish, indicating the direction you want him to go. Your left hand is now holding the end of the rope. Swing this gently in a circular motion toward your horse to indicate to him that you would like him to add energy and step forward into the change of direction.

- The repeated changes of direction will bring you closer to the wall. If your horse feels trapped by tight spaces, he'll speed up as he passes between you and the wall. Take your time closing up this space. If your horse seems nervous, move your circle further out from the wall. Work on perfecting the change of direction before you bring him in closer to the wall. As you ask for turn after turn, you'll gradually be able to close the space between you and the wall.

- Eventually you will be standing against the wall. As he bends through a change of direction, he'll stop as he comes around to face you. C/R.

If being close to the wall still worries him, instead of stopping, he might change direction on his own and head back the other way. Use the change of direction skills you both learned out away from the wall to send him back the way he came. Keep asking for changes of direction until he can stop on his own roughly parallel to the wall. If need be, take him back out away from the wall and repeat the entire process until being close to the wall no longer concerns him.

- Now it's time to perfect the exercise. Keep asking for changes of directions. As he steps through the semi-circle, click when his inside hind leg flexes up and his jaw softens into the bend. The more comfortable he is with this response, the more parallel he will come to the fence, so put it on a high rate of reinforcement out away from the fence where it is easiest for him.

217

The Click That Teaches: Riding With The Clicker

- Gradually extend the number of steps you ask for around the semi-circle until he is stopping parallel to the fence and facing you. C/R. If he's still feeling claustrophobic about the fence, he'll stop with his hips angled slightly in off the wall. Your final goal is to have him parallel to the wall facing you. Without moving your own feet off the track, you'll be able to swing him around a half circle, and he'll end up on the other side, again parallel to the wall and facing you from the opposite direction. Remember to click when his inside hind flexes up into a softening of his jaw.

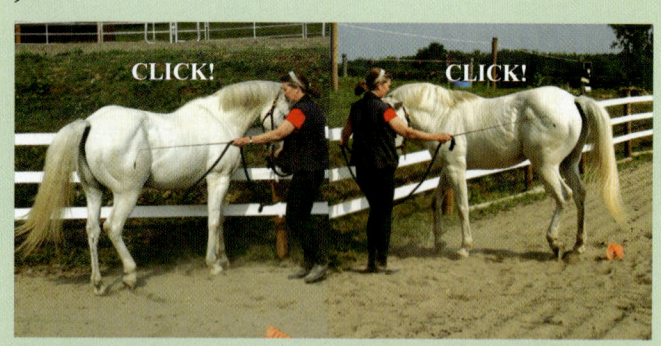

- Keep repeating this pattern until he stops with his body parallel to the wall.

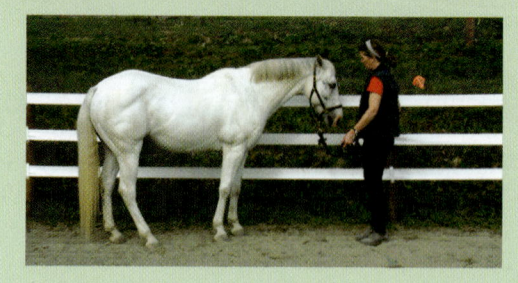

He will gradually be willing to step closer and closer to the fence.

In this sequence the horse first stepped from right to left into the fence. His handler rotated around her right leg so she was in position to send him back around her to face her in the opposite direction. This is a great prep for any exercise where you will be working in close to the rail.

This is a complicated exercise, so you'll build this sequence slowly. Don't expect your horse to step completely over to the wall right away. A very claustrophobic horse will get part way around, feel crowded, and bounce back in the opposite direction. If your horse does this, spend plenty of time working him from side to side in the center section of the arc. Don't try to get him up against the wall all in one session.

As you're working, watch what your horse does with his inside hind leg. As you ask him to step over away from your rope, you'll see his inside hind leg step across the line of his body. C/R.

That's the response you want to highlight. It's easiest for him to do this away from the wall, where he has plenty of room. Watch his inside hind leg as he steps sideways away from the wall. You'll see him take one, two, three crossover steps to swing around to your other side. Get in rhythm with this. This is where timing is everything. You want to click on the upward lift of the leg as he steps across. That's when the stifle is releasing and you'll be reinforcing the active mobilization of his hind leg.

If you're late in your timing, you'll be reinforcing your horse for locking his joints into their standing still position. (If you can, have someone videotape you in this exercise so you can develop a visual image to match these words. To get collection without compression you need to have a good feel for this step.)

You should probably dog-ear this page. This is another one of those sections that's critically important. The first time through you may not catch all the layers in this seemingly simple exercise.

It's easiest for your horse to step across when he's out away from the wall. You'll refine your timing out here, until a gentle swing of the rope causes him to bend the joints of his hind leg and engage his hips.

As he gets in closer to the wall, he's going to feel crowded. You'll be swinging the tail of the rope, asking him to step over, and he'll be thinking, "You stupid human, can't you see there's a wall there? I

218

Chapter Thirty-Three: Lateral Work: Shoulder-In

can't go any further."

He knows what the signal means. He just doesn't think he can do what you're asking.

If he ricochets off the wall into the swing of your rope, stay with your original request to step over. As soon as he's far enough off the wall that he doesn't feel crowded, he'll step back over away from your rope, click and treat. Eventually, instead of ricocheting off the wall, he'll answer each request of your rope by stepping over until he is where you want him, parallel to the fence.

Once he's no longer feeling crowded, he's ready for the next challenge. Instead of sending him back the other way, ask him to take another step towards the wall. Of course he can't. The wall is right next to him. There isn't room for him to move any closer, but he understands that the swing of the rope means he's to release his hip. You may not be able to see his hip from your position in front of him, but you'll feel his weight shift even through a slack rein. Click and jackpot. Your horse is learning how to mobilize his hindquarters in preparation for shoulder-in and piaffe.

Of course, your horse may not guess right the first time you try this. He knows the swinging rope means he's supposed to move something. If he can't figure out how to release his hip so close to the wall, he may try stepping forward. Counter by asking him to step back, then try again. It's move, counter-move. The shifts in weight will help him to find the right answer. When he releases his hip, it's jackpot time.

By the way, if you have a horse who tends to spook out of corners, this is a great exercise. Start well down the long side of the arena away from the spooky area. Take plenty of time getting him comfortable lining up and facing you against the wall. Then gradually start to inch your way down the wall as you ask him to change directions through a half circle. It may take you a long time to inch your way around the entire arena, but think of the number of times he'll be facing the goblins, then turning and putting his back to them. It's a great way to help horses who feel trapped in the corners of your arena.

RIDING THE SHOULDER-IN EXERCISE

You've done your ground-work preparation. Now it's time to ride. After you've warmed your horse up by working lateral flexions and hip-shoulder-shoulder collected stops and starts out in the middle of your arena, ask him to walk along the track. Use the technique described in the previous chapter to engage him on two reins. At this point he should be walking forward on two parallel tracks. That means that his right hind leg is stepping on the same track as his right front, and his left hind is stepping on the same track as his left front. Think of a railroad track and you'll have the right idea.

You're going to ask your horse to bring his outside shoulder in off the track, hence the name shoulder-in. In shoulder-in, your horse will be on three tracks, or if he's more steeply angled off the wall, on four. There is some controversy about whether a correct shoulder-in is a three or a four-track exercise. Whichever way you want to ride the movement, you can teach it with the clicker.

The first step of shoulder-in is very much like the first step of a diagonal. In fact your horse may misinterpret your request, thinking you want him to leave the rail. This is where you'll use your hip-shoulder-shoulder reset button (Pg. 174). Immediately stop your horse and ask him to take a step back so he lines up parallel to the wall again.

As he rocks back, you'll feel his hips lower and mobilize. This is the perfect moment to ask him to rotate into shoulder-in. Think of doing wheelies on a bicycle. If you've got all the weight shifted off the front end, it's easy to spin the bicycle around. In shoulder-in we want the horse to rotate his shoulders onto the inner track, but to do this, he has to unweight his front end.

He'll probably over-rotate again and start to walk forward off the track. Activate the "reset" button. Stop him and ask him to back up. Back him as many steps as needed until he is parallel to the wall and evenly engaged in both hips. As you feel his hips mobilize, ask again for shoulder-in. Repeat this sequence until you feel him rotate his shoulders in off the track and take a sideways step with his inside hind leg. Click, give him a jackpot, and make a huge fuss!

Repeat this sequence. For now you're working on the set up for shoulder-in; you aren't trying to get multiple steps yet. Take your time building this. The hardest part of lateral work is initiating it. Once your horse has his hips underneath him and understands how to step sideways, staying in shoulder-in is easy. If he should lose his balance, it's a simple matter to ask him to start over again.

With the clicker you're giving shoulder-in a premium value. Lateral work may require extra physical effort, but it will become one of your horse's favorite games. The clicker makes it easy for you both to learn the correct feel. You aren't trying to force your horse into contorted positions. Instead, you're both working together to find those feels-like-heaven moments that come from true shoulder-in.

The Click That Teaches: Riding With The Clicker

MORE CLOCK IMAGES

If you're puzzling over how you should be riding the shoulder-in, here's an image from Mary Wanless' *Ride With Your Mind*★. As you ride, imagine that you are sitting at the center of a clock. If you were riding absolutely straight, you'd be looking at twelve o'clock and your inside and outside hips would be lined up even with three and nine o'clock.

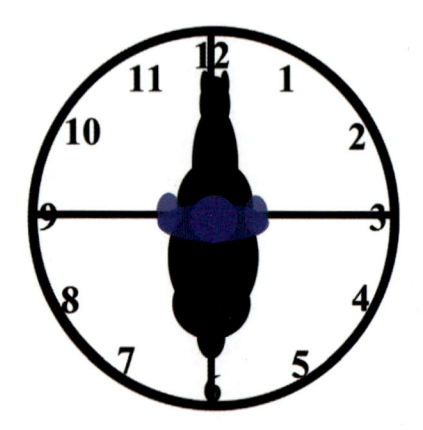

In shoulder-in, your body rotates around your central core axis. When I ride, I imagine a carousel-horse pole that runs from my head straight down through my torso (pg 130). You might think this would make me stiff. It doesn't. Instead it reminds me to stay upright through my ribs and to turn from my center. Instead of twisting my shoulders to try to generate shoulder-in, I keep them aligned with my hips. That in turn keeps me aligned with my horse.

For shoulder-in imagine rotating your hips and shoulders around your own carousel-horse pole. Your inside hip and shoulder move back as your outside hip and shoulder move forward. If you are tracking right asking for shoulder-in, that would mean that you are now sitting on a ten-and-four-o'clock line.

In other words your inside hip and shoulder would be lined up with four o'clock and your outside hip and shoulder would be on ten o'clock.

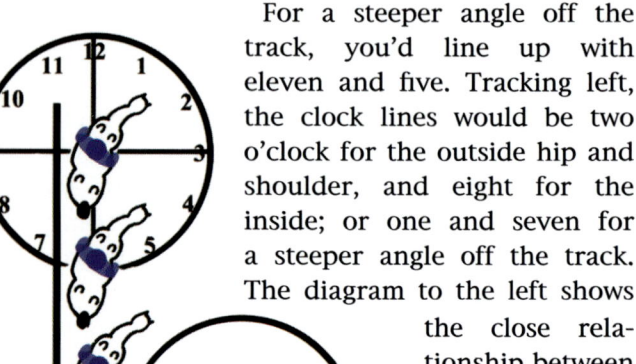

★ *Ride With Your Mind,* by Mary Wanless; Trafalgar Square, VT

For a steeper angle off the track, you'd line up with eleven and five. Tracking left, the clock lines would be two o'clock for the outside hip and shoulder, and eight for the inside; or one and seven for a steeper angle off the track. The diagram to the left shows the close relationship between circles and shoulder-in.

For haunches-in tracking right, you would bring your inside hip and shoulder forward, and your outside hip and shoulder back, so you'd be on a two-and-eight-o'clock line. To make this clearer walk the patterns on the ground as you think about the clock images. That will help you sort out the differences between shoulder-in and haunches-in bends.

A HORSE SCHOOL DROP-OUT

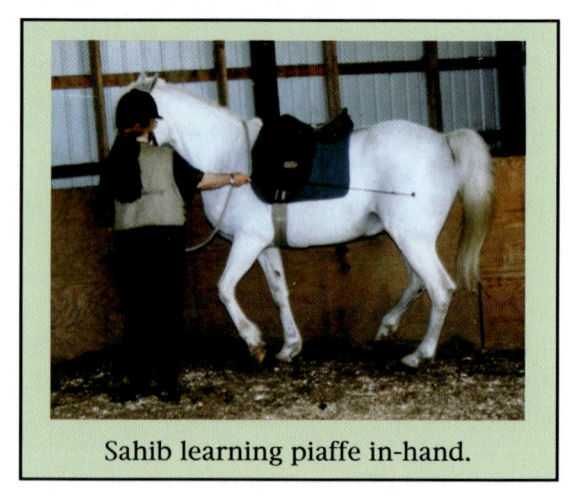

Sahib learning piaffe in-hand.

If you're reading straight through this book, this may be another point where you say, "This sounds like an awful lot of work just to get a few steps of fanciness. I don't have time to go through all of this. I just want to ride."

The reality is that all of these exercises flow easily one into another. By the time you get to shoulder-in it will be the natural next step in the process. At the stage where your horse is acting like a "Nervous Nelly" you aren't going to be worrying about the niceties of shoulder-in. You're going to be focused on prying him down out of the rafters. If you're sitting on a stiff-as-a-board horse, nothing I've written

Chapter Thirty-Three: Lateral Work: Shoulder-In

in the last few chapters will mean a thing to you. Until you've taken your horse through the "I-know-an-old-lady-who-swallowed-a-fly" exercises of Chapter 25, the nuances of feel and response that you need for shoulder-in simply won't be there. But once they are, they'll open up connections that very quickly lead to true shoulder-in.

Is all this work worth it? "Go to people for opinions and horses for answers." That's an expression I very much believe in, so let's go ask one of the horses who has experienced this process. His name is Sahib, a beautiful Anglo-Arab, who for several years worked with me as my lesson horse. Sahib began by flunking out of school. We might as well call a spade a spade. That's what happened.

In the spring of 1995, when Sahib was eleven, he was purchased as a school horse by the owner of the stable where I keep my horses. He came from a summer camp up in Vermont where he'd been used mostly out on trails and occasionally in beginner riding lessons. Sahib seemed like a wonderful horse, the kind of sweet-natured fellow teenage girls fall in love with. He had big Arab eyes and a kind, expressive face. He was a perfect size, sixteen hands, with the smoothest gaits you're ever likely to sit on. The girls in the lesson program loved riding him. The only problem was the feeling wasn't mutual.

It takes a very special horse to work in a lesson line. Beginner riders can't help but grip and grab. They lose their balance. They bounce at the trot. They hang onto the reins. A horse who can safely and happily take young riders through the early stages of the learning process is a very special individual. Not all horses have the temperament to be school horses, and Sahib, unfortunately, was one of those. What he particularly didn't like were stiff riders. They made him tense. When they bounced on his back, he'd stick his nose up in the air and clack his teeth. He went around. He did his job, but he clearly wasn't happy.

The real problems began in the winter. Sahib started bucking. He didn't do it often, but you could see it coming. A rider would pick up the canter and start to do the "beginner clutch". Sahib would tense up, the rider would clutch harder, and he'd start to pitch. The owner of the stable didn't wait for someone to fall off. She pulled him off the school line. She wasn't going to use a horse she couldn't trust in her program. The problem now was what to do with him? What was causing the bucking? Did he need more turnout? Was his back sore? Or did he just not like beginner riders? If she gave him a rest, would she be able to use him again?

Sahib had one rider who got along well with him, one of the few adult riders in a program geared mainly for the after-school crowd. With Sahib out of the main school line, they were both turned over to me. Naturally, the first thing I did was introduce Sahib to the clicker, and from there we moved on to single-rein riding.

In our first lesson together I gave my new student a "pony ride". I'm sure that's not what Laura was expecting. She was an experienced rider. She wasn't used to being on a tether, but that's what Sahib needed. I started him out in-hand while Laura sat on his back. I sent Sahib around me on a small circle by stabilizing the inside rein against his neck. Sahib's first reaction was to stiffen against the pressure.

I kept his feet in motion and my hand steady. When he softened his jaw and gave to the pressure on the rein, I instantly released my hand and clicked.

As I clicked Sahib for softening his jaw, his whole world shifted. Riding had never been like this! He started talking, nickering excitedly every time I clicked. His jaw became soft as butter. He was figuring out fast what made this vending machine work!

Laura could feel Sahib's balance changing under her. He was becoming more level, so riding him was less like sitting on a chair with one leg shorter than the rest. And the clicker helped her follow what I was doing. She could associate each change in Sahib with the exact moment that I clicked. They were both enjoying the benefits of clicker training.

As our sessions together proceeded, Laura learned the techniques of single-rein riding. Sahib turned out to be a superb teacher. For my purposes he was turning out to be the perfect school horse. I started putting other riders up on him. My students ranged from beginners with no training experience to very capable riders. Sahib adapted to each of them. He could go very quietly for the beginners, or he could collect and add energy for the more advanced riders.

Sahib spent the winter learning the early stages of single-rein riding. With each of his riders we focused on the three-flip-three exercise (Ch. 26). He repeated that pattern so many times that he probably dreamt about flipping his hips! But it certainly created the entry point into lateral work.

For lateral work I started him in-hand with a rider up. That let his riders feel the correct balance shifts before they had to ask for them on their own. The clicker proved its worth yet again. Lateral flexions got a premium reward of peppermints and extra grain, so Sahib very quickly learned to love going sideways. In fact, for many of his beginner riders the real issue was getting him to walk straight. He would start offering lateral flexions the moment he walked into the ring!

I never get mad at a horse for offering behavior I've taught him. Instead I appreciate his eagerness to work. I love it when a horse starts offering me behavior. That tells me that he understands the lesson.

It also tells me it's time to work on stimulus control. With Sahib, that meant initiating a move, counter-move response. If he started walking sideways while we were still adjusting the girth, I simply asked him to shift his weight forward and back, forward and back, until he stood still again. C/R. As his riders progressed in their skills, they were able to do the same thing under saddle.

All of Sahib's training occurred during these lessons, and yet his training kept advancing. We progressed from simple flexions to the beginning stages of shoulder-in. The first time Laura asked for it on her own, Sahib answered her with perfect positioning.

As we continued to develop his shoulder-in, I began to think about piaffe. Mobilizing Sahib was easy. We did it with novice riders teaching him. What made that possible was the clicker. Now I know that there will be people who will read this with a great deal of skepticism. They'll say you can't do that. You can't possibly teach something as complex as piaffe this way. Sahib will tell them they're wrong.

If I can recognize the first baby steps of piaffe, I can mark them with the clicker. If I then follow that with a major jackpot, the horse will do the rest. He'll try to find that jackpot moment again.

That's all I did with Sahib. We positioned him for piaffe. When he gave me even the most awkward step or two, I pounced on him with handfuls of treats. The first time we worked on piaffe I carried a bucket of freshly picked spring grass. Is it any wonder that he caught on fast? For Sahib, piaffe has forever become linked to that bucket of grass. It's one of his favorite games.

My point in sharing Sahib's story with you is not to teach you how to train piaffe, or even shoulder-in. The real message is something much more important. It goes back to something I have emphasized throughout this book: we very much create our own realities. If you believe something is impossible, then that's what it will become. But if you follow the principles of good training, you never know where they will take you. The first principle for me says go to a place in the training, no matter how simple and basic it may seem, where you can ask for something and get a "yes" answer back. That's your starting place. Then, for every goal you have, again, no matter how simple it may seem, put in lots of small steps.

Sahib began as a school-line drop-out. Today he has a person of his own who loves him very much. She began as a timid, first-time rider who gripped and grabbed like any other beginner. Sahib took care of her through this vulnerable, early stage. They survived snow slides off the arena roof, windy days, and wild teenagers. With the clicker we built Sahib's confidence, so he could build hers. They've become partners in a process that brings me great joy to watch.

This book is based on my experience of average, everyday horses going beyond normal expectations. With each of these horses we simply went back far enough in their training until we found a place where we could make a change. From that simple little step the rest emerged. That is the true essence not only of clicker training, but of all good training.

SAHIB

Sahib enjoying a relaxed ride with his owner.

CHAPTER 34
Using Your Training Tools in the Real World: Riding Out with a Horse Named Fig

If you're a trail rider, you may have been thinking over the last couple of chapters that you've been reading the wrong book. Arena riding isn't what you're interested in. You want to be out in the real world, not trotting around doing endless school figures in the safe confines of an arena. In this chapter you're going to see how all these lessons can be used to solve real-world challenges. Especially, if you have a difficult horse, you'll be glad you have these "tools" in your kit as you head out to the trails.

NIGHTMARES

What would you do if your dream horse turned into a nightmare? That's the situation many people find themselves in when they go horse shopping. They pick out what appears to be a sweet, even-tempered horse, only to find, once they get it home, that it's anything but. Many of you reading this would know exactly what you'd do in this situation. You'd get rid of that horse. But what if the horse is dangerous? Would you still be able to sell it, knowing that it might injure or even kill someone? If it's a healthy, young horse, would you be able to give the order to have it "put down"? Or would you feel stuck, not knowing what to do?

An aggressive horse can become a "hot potato" passed from one owner to another, but eventually somebody is going to be left holding onto it with some difficult decisions to make. That's exactly what happened to my client, Megan Roy, when she bought a thoroughbred mare named Fig.

FIG REVISITED

If you have my first book, you've already met Fig and read about her "reform school" experiences. Since *Clicker Training for Your Horse*★ came out, I've been asked many times about Fig—and since handling aggressive horse is an important topic—I thought I'd include an update on her training here. For those who haven't yet read about Fig, here's a brief review of her history.

Some horses posture and make ugly faces. My own horse, Peregrine, does. When people bother him in his stall, he pins his ears and grumps at them. Fig did more than just grump. When I first met her, she would attack anyone who came near her. That wasn't the kind of horse Megan thought she was getting. She thought she'd found a sweet-natured, easy-going horse. She wasn't prepared for Fig's unprovoked and violent attacks.

The traditional training approaches Megan tried just made things worse. A professional trainer who was used to dealing with rank thoroughbreds might have been able to show Fig "who was the boss," but any time Megan tried to get tough, Fig just got tougher. When she tried to ride her new horse, Megan discovered that Fig was just as dangerous under saddle as she was on the ground. Fig knew how to intimidate riders. Clearly spooking, bucking, rearing, and bolting were tactics that had worked well for her in the past. Riding a horse like this was simply too dangerous. If you

FIG

With the help of the clicker, Fig changed from being an angry horse, dangerous horse ...

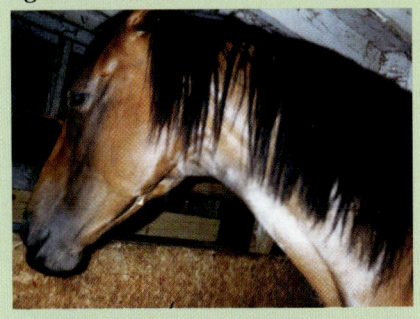

to a loving pet, ...

and a wonderful riding horse.

★ *Clicker Training For Your Horse,* by Alexandra Kurland; Sunshine Books, US and Ringpress books, UK

accidentally fall off sweet old Nell who never does anything wrong, you might end up with a few bumps and bruises, but if you fall off a horse like Fig you aren't going to be so lucky. I've seen horses like her deliberately spin and kick at a fallen rider. This was the horse I was invited in to train.

TRAIN WHERE YOU CAN
Clicker Training for Your Horse★ describes in detail the story of Fig's clicker transformation (see Chapter 21 of that book, "Crossing the Line into Aggression"). Step by step we gave her an understanding of her world and the tools she needed to cope with her rage. She became what Megan had always intended her to be, a family pet.

We began with Fig where I begin with most horses, in a stall, teaching her to touch a target. Without leaving the security of that stall, we taught her the skills she would need to be a safe riding horse: head lowering, rein-backs, hip flips, even hip-shoulder-shoulder.

From the stall we literally inched our way into a small paddock that served as a round pen. Megan learned how to work Fig at liberty, how to ask for inside and outside turns, and how to balance her into a steady, quiet trot. She taught her horse lateral flexions, and she learned how to use them to interrupt spooks. Finally, when Fig was ready, Megan got on for short rides at the walk. Preparation had changed Fig from a dangerous, not-to-be-trusted horse into a safe, reliable ride, at least within the confines of a small paddock. That's basically where we were at the time I finished my first book and winter footing closed down the riding season.

In the spring we moved from the round pen into a larger paddock next to the barn. This is where Megan learned how to become an active, in-charge rider. At that time, Fig's idea of a ride was to glue herself by the gate. This will be familiar situation to many of you riding green horses. Kicking, jerking on the reins, getting angry, and yelling are all tactics I've seen used by riders in response. They often result either in the horse planting itself even more firmly by the gate or blowing up in frustration. Megan learned to employ a different tactic, one that used patience instead of force to connect Fig's mind to her feet. The result was willing, forward movement. The principle she used is the one I introduced way back in Chapter 5 of this book: eventually everybody will sit down.

BE PATIENT AND PERSISTENT
Remember the basic concept? If you stand long enough, eventually you're going to want to sit down and rest; if you sit long enough, you're going to need to get up and move around. Whatever you're doing, eventually you're going to need to do something else (pg. 25). So if you're on a horse who's stalled out, patience is the answer. Pick up the rein, take the slack out, and wait.

Your horse can't stand still forever in one spot, especially if his head is bent around to the side. Eventually he's going to have to move, even if it's just to shift from one hip to the other. If you release the rein at that exact moment, you'll be reinforcing movement. Pick up the rein again and wait.

At some point your horse will make a decision. That's what Fig did. Standing by the gate wasn't a great option. It meant there was always pressure on the corner of her mouth. Moving seemed like a better choice. Fig pulled her feet out of the "cement" she was standing in and left the gate. But she still wasn't prepared to go very far. She'd walk a small circle and then the "magnetic attraction" of the gate would suck her in again, and the process would begin all over.

You might be thinking, "This is nonsense. Megan just needed to get tough and show her who's boss." Fig, I am sure, had had that approach tried on her many times before, and in her case all it had done was create an even more aggressive and unridable horse. In the end, whatever method we used, it had to be Fig's choice to work with us. I know there are riders who could have gotten Fig going much faster than we did, using pain and punishment to make it clear that they weren't accepting any of her "nonsense". We chose patience and persistence instead.

Eventually everybody will sit down, and eventually Fig walked away from the gate and kept going.

USE THE SKILLS YOU'VE LEARNED
Megan spent the early part of the spring riding in the paddock, and on days when that was too muddy, up and down her driveway near the barn. The driveway presented new challenges—trail obstacles. She learned how to use three-flip-three (Ch. 26) so she could keep Fig soft and under control, and still be able to get around parked cars, lamp posts, sleeping dogs, and that greatest of all challenges, fresh spring grass. Megan was learning how to use hip-shoulder-shoulder to create a physical and emotional 'reset button" for Fig.

This was a critical tool. A horse that is rushing is anxious either to get to somewhere or away from something. Either one is a bad deal. Suppose you're out on the trail and your horse starts pulling to get home. You shorten up the reins to get him to walk

★ *Clicker Training For Your Horse,* by Alexandra Kurland; The Clicker Center, NY

Chapter Thirty-Four: Using Your Training Tools in the Real World

flat-footed, and the next thing you know he's coiled tight, ready to explode. Every time you check his forward movement you just coil the spring tighter. With Fig's history, we couldn't afford to let that happen.

A horse who understands "reset buttons" can stop, shift back, reorganize, and calmly continue forward again. He doesn't get anxious because he isn't being held back. Instead his energy is simply redirected.

Megan struggled with this concept at first. It was more than just the mechanics that tripped her up—she was simply too nice. Learning to use lateral work effectively is all about learning to be assertive. You have to be able to say: "This is my space, stay out of it."; "This is the direction we're walking, walk with me."; "This is the pace we're going, stay with me." We spent a long time at this stage, both in-hand and under saddle, while Megan learned to become a post (Ch. 30).

When the pastures dried up enough for riding, we moved from the driveway to a large field. We set out cones as visual markers and created a "riding ring" to work in. Fig had other ideas. She wanted to go back to the barn.

If you've ridden out on a young horse, you've probably had this experience. Riding outside of fenced areas on a horse that wants to be back with the herd means convincing him that he can't drag you back home. I wanted Megan to ride within the large rectangle marked out by the cones, but each time they turned towards the barn, Fig would bow out through her outside shoulder and the two of them would end up down by the pond on a narrow path leading back to the other horses.

Megan got lots of practice disengaging Fig's hips (Ch. 21). She also got lots of practice using another mechanical skill: sliding her hands from one rein position to another. In single-rein riding, people often get stuck with their hands glued to one position on the rein. It's as if the rein has suddenly become a hot electrical wire, and they can't let go. Their horse is heading into the bushes. They need to flip his hip around, but the reins are too long. The hand that's on the buckle is up past their ears, doing no good at all. Their horse is popping further and further out of position. Nothing feels right. Their riding instructor is shouting directions which they are only half hearing in the wind: something about letting go of the rein, and they're thinking, "You've got to be crazy! That's the last thing that feels safe to do!"

It's in situations like this that you learn to be a functional rider. You don't learn it sitting on a sweet horse who never puts a foot wrong. You may be able to ask for a beautiful hip flip on that horse, but you won't really understand the full power and function of it until you're on a horse that's dragging you off into a briar patch. Mind you, this doesn't mean that you should take chances with your safety, or that you have to get on dangerous horses to learn to ride well. *Good training should be boring to watch* is my motto. With Fig, we started in a ring where her desire to leave was small. As Megan's skills grew, we were ready to move out onto the driveway, where that desire was stronger but could still be managed. By the time we moved to the field, both Megan and her horse were ready for the added challenge.

EXPLOIT EVERY OPPORTUNITY TO ADVANCE YOUR TRAINING

It took Megan a couple of sessions to learn how to keep Fig within the rectangle we'd marked out, but then it became a non-issue. Our next challenge was grass. How do you deal with grass?

Most people actively try to stop their horses from grazing while they are riding. With Fig we exploited her love of fresh, green grass. She'd do a nice set of work for us; Megan would click her and let her eat for a minute or two. Grazing helped her relax by dividing the overall training session up into small segments. Fig knew she'd get to graze again, so she never made a fuss about leaving the grass, nor did she try to reach down to it while she was working. Once we allowed Fig to have grazing time within her work sessions, grass never again became an issue.

We spent the late spring and early summer schooling in the field, working on fundamentals. Then an injury interrupted our training program. Fig stepped on a sharp piece of slate and sliced open her hind foot. Megan spent the next couple of months soaking and wrapping the wound. The old Fig would never have let Megan anywhere near her hind feet, even for routine cleaning. The new, clicker-trained Fig cooperated beautifully through the whole procedure.

We resumed riding in the fall, but we were interrupted once again, this time by icy footing. Over the next winter Megan worked on lateral flexions and added "Robin's pose" (pg 45, 72) to the repertoire. Fig loved it. You'd groom her, she'd pose. Saddle her, she'd pose. Ground drive her, give her baths, etc., she'd pose.

TEACH NEW SKILLS TO COUNTER OLD HABITS

Ground driving was a great confidence builder for Fig. We began teaching her to drive in early March, before the ground had thawed enough for riding.

I followed the procedure I described earlier with Robin (Chapter 15). We used the ground driving to help Fig become more comfortable leaving the security of the barn. At first we helped her out by having Megan walk beside her while I handled the drive lines. As we headed up the driveway, I used the lines to ask Fig to yield laterally from one side of the roadway to the other. Lateral flexions engaged her mind. They kept her busy and gave us something positive to click and reinforce. Fig stopped worrying about leaving the barn and instead became eager to play this new game.

Megan's driveway is a long one. We walked Fig past the house and the gardens, past the field where we had ridden the summer before, and up into a small woodlot, where the driveway forks into a small turn-around.

The only place where Fig was truly afraid was in the turnaround. There every little sound made her stop and stare. Instead of letting her stand transfixed with her nose in the air, we asked her for head lowering (Chapters 3, 8, and 20).

Once Fig could drop her head and stand relaxed, we asked her to go on. When she rushed, we used hip-shoulder-shoulder into head down to redirect her energy (pg. 175).

I don't know how many times we walked up and down the driveway during that first session. We wanted to show Fig that it was safe to leave the barn. It wasn't forever. She only had to go a little way up the drive, and then we'd head back and let her check in before turning around for another circuit. By the second session she was noticeably more relaxed, and by the third she was settled. In the past, when Megan had tried walking her this far up the drive, Fig would pull away from her and go bolting off back to the barn. Now she was walking calmly along even in blustery March weather that used to send her bucking across the fields.

When Megan got back on Fig in the early spring, it was as though she had never taken so much as a day off. Fig picked up exactly where they had left off back in December. Only now all the issues they'd been working on in the previous year seemed to have melted away. The ground work they had done over the winter had paid off.

Just as aggression comes from a place of fear; patience, confidence, authority, and ultimately the respect every one wants so much from their horses comes from a place of knowledge. The more you learn about good training principles and the methods that accompany them, the more these qualities will be there.

PERFECT YOUR PRACTICE

As Fig's walk improved, we began to reintroduce the trot. I can almost see some of you doing a double take as you read that last sentence. "Wait a minute!" you exclaim. "Are you saying you worked all this time and you never trotted!?"

Yes. Exactly. "The walk is the mother of all gaits." In their first summer of riding neither Fig nor Megan were ready for the faster gaits. It would have served no useful purpose letting Fig trot around with her nose in the air all out of balance and counter-bent. Good training takes the time it takes. Megan needed to stay in the walk while she learned the mechanical skills that would help keep Fig emotionally settled. We weren't in a hurry. Trying to rush things just creates resistance, and in the end it slows training down. If you think you have to walk, trot, and canter in every riding session, ask yourself what you're really practicing. Are you practicing good quality, balanced gaits, or is your horse just getting better at racing around out of control?

Practicing what you don't want makes no training sense at all. At some point you have to break the cycle by going to a layer in your training where what you practice is what you actually want, even if that means working on the smallest of small steps. Many of the exercises I've described in this book may seem very basic to you, almost too trivial to do, but the question is: Can your horse do them? Can he do them consistently, without resistance, and in any and all of the environments that you want to ride him in? If the answer to that is yes, then you'll be able move very quickly through these exercises and cover in a matter of days what somebody else might take months or even years to learn.

But if the answer is no—your horse doesn't lower his head on request, or soften easily to the bit, or know how to stop without bracing—then you'll want to take whatever time it takes to perfect these exercises. I don't need to tell you to work them through first in the walk before you move on to the trot and canter. You know you're not ready for speed. You may even be feeling a huge sense of relief because I'm telling you that you don't have to.

But what if you're an experienced rider who just wants to get on with it? My advice is to go right ahead. Work your horse the way you want. Forget about all these baby steps and just enjoy your rides. If your horse's behavior deteriorates, well, that's the neat thing about resistance. If something doesn't bother you enough to fix it now, that's fine. When your horse reaches a point where you can't stand the stiffness, or the barging through, or whatever else that he's

Chapter Thirty-Four: Using Your Training Tools in the Real World

doing, you'll take the time it takes to solve the problem. You'll identify the point where he can no longer do what you're asking, and you'll work through the steps needed to resolve the block. And something else will happen: you'll discover that training is fun!

Suppose you understand all this. You like the philosophy behind the training, but you're thinking you just don't have time to do all these lessons. You work all day, and you've got your kids to take care of at night. The only time you get to ride is on weekends, and sometimes not even then. In the real world there are rainy days, muddy fields, and hectic schedules that get in the way of your riding.

If you're feeling guilty because you can't work your horse every day, relax. Megan and Fig had many interruptions in their training, including long stretches when they couldn't work at all, but they still made steady progress. Clicker-trained horses do not forget their lessons. So begin where you need to begin and enjoy the process. Forget about how long things take, or what your neighbor can do with his horse. None of that matters. What matters is that you and your horse are staying safe, making progress, and enjoying the process.

HELP YOUR HORSE CONQUER THE GOBLINS

By the time Megan asked Fig to trot, they were both ready, but that didn't mean she wasn't still a little nervous. She'd had enough bad rides on the old Fig to be afraid of what might happen. Fear is just common sense in disguise. There's nothing wrong with being afraid—the key in riding is not to let it take over your body. That's why Megan had spent all that time in the walk programming in the mechanics. I wanted Megan to know the work so thoroughly that no matter what Fig did, Megan would automatically respond correctly.

The first trot lasted only a couple of steps. Fig felt Megan's tension. Her back stiffened, and her nose shot up in the air, but she trotted. Click! Fig came to an abrupt stop and waited for Megan to hand her a treat.

Megan took a deep breath, got her horse reorganized, and asked again. Fig went a couple of steps, and then - click! - she was back at a standstill. It didn't matter at this point that her trot was far from ideal. Our first goal was simply to get the behavior. What we were reinforcing was a successful transition. Before the trot could get out of control and become dangerous, click, it was over. With each stop Fig's confidence inched up another notch. The wild rides of the past had scared her just as much as they'd scared Megan.

With the clicker Fig was learning that she only had to go a couple of steps and then the trot would be over. She began to relax and offer smoother transitions.

As Fig relaxed, so, too, did Megan. She began to stretch the trot out. Instead of going just a couple of steps, Megan kept Fig trotting for a full circle. The field she was riding in had a gentle slope to it. Fig kept her balance well on the up side of the hill, but going down was harder for her. The trot got quick, she bowed out under the branches of a large maple tree, and Megan got a little "trail ride" practice ducking under the overhanging leaves.

On the uphill section of the circle, Fig relaxed and softened her topline. Click! She got a jackpot reward of a peppermint. Megan's confidence was building. The added energy of the trot wasn't winding Fig up into a tense knot the way it used to. She wasn't spooking and bucking off back to the barn. She was relaxed and calm, clearly enjoying this newest stage in the riding.

The next trot was glorious. Fig softened into the transition. She was round, on the bit, and absolutely beautiful. I heard Megan's surprised exclamation at the feel. She had never ridden anything like this before! That's why you wait, stay patient, and do your homework. The rewards are these heavenly rides!

Over the next few months, Megan expanded Fig's world even more. She started trail riding with another horse along for company. Fig's confidence soared. As long as she had a companion, she could go for miles and be calm and collected. What a difference from the previous riding season, when any unexpected sound made her jump.

Riding in company, Fig was perfect. Alone was a different matter. Out by herself, her courage failed her. During one of these rides I became the other "horse" in Fig's herd. I walked along beside them as an interim step to build Fig's confidence.

Our first challenge were several small storage sheds on a neighbor's property. Fig must have thought I was a very stupid horse, because I didn't seem to know about the goblins hiding inside them. She certainly did, and she wasn't going anywhere near those buildings! As we came abreast of them, she jumped sideways and spun back toward home. If I wanted to be eaten alive, that was my business, but she wasn't hanging around to let the goblins get her!

Megan stopped Fig in her tracks with a well-timed single-rein stop (Ch. 21). The hip flip spun her around to face the shed. That was okay. Fig could stand her ground as long as she didn't have to go any closer. Here was a perfect opportunity for Megan to practice the skills she had used so many times at home.

She set up a figure-eight pattern (Ch. 16). She began about twenty feet back from the shed and asked Fig to walk a circle to the left, then a circle to the right, with a straight line between them facing the sheds. They were far enough away from the buildings that Fig felt safe. She could walk toward the sheds, and she could turn her back on them and walk away without getting upset. If she got too close and tried to bolt off, Megan countered with a single-rein flip of the hip that put them right back on the pattern they were riding. Fig began to settle. She walked in a straight line toward the sheds. Click! She got a treat and was allowed to graze for a couple of seconds.

Over the next few minutes the figure eights brought Fig closer and closer to the sheds until finally she just walked right past them. The goblins had vanished and the sheds had become just part of the landscape.

Our next challenge was a low-hanging grape arbor at the back of the sheds. Fig balked at the entrance.

No problem, we just went back to figure eights, only this time with an added element: I stood a couple of horse lengths out in front of the arbor and became the target she was to ride to. When Fig walked a straight line toward me, click, I gave her a treat. As Fig's confidence grew, I gradually inched my way back under the arbor. Fig finally walked up to me and then just kept going—under the arbor, past a swimming pool, and on through an overgrown hay field to the woods beyond.

Our next great challenge was a shallow stream. Fig balked at the edge of it. She wasn't crossing this monster-sized ditch! She was going home where it was safe. A quick hip-flip brought her back to the edge of the stream, where she planted her feet. Here was another opportunity to practice figure eights and straight approaches to obstacles. The trail was wide enough to give Megan some maneuvering room, and the streambed was fairly shallow with just a trickle of water running though it. The opposite bank rose up onto a small hill, making it the perfect place for a crossing. Megan worked her figure-eight pattern until she could walk Fig straight toward the stream without her spooking to either side. At this point she picked a spot where she wanted Fig to cross and asked her to go forward.

Fig took a tentative step toward the stream. C/R.

She dropped her head to sniff the rocks. C/R.

She jumped over the ditch. Megan brought her around on a single rein so she was facing the ditch again and rather belatedly clicked her and gave her a treat.

Megan asked Fig to walk forward, whereupon Fig angled sideways to the ditch. Megan countered with a move, counter-move dance (pg. 172). She had Fig step laterally left and right until she was again lined up straight facing the ditch. C/R. Megan asked Fig to go forward again. Fig dropped her head. C/R. Now it was a waiting game while Fig decided what to do next. The hill on the opposite bank made our work easier. Standing with her hips higher than her front end wasn't very comfortable. Fig stepped across to the shallow side. C/R.

Crossing streams is just like going in a trailer. It isn't enough to load your horse once. You want to take him on and off the trailer many times until he's totally at ease with it. That's what we did with this streambed. Megan took Fig over it a dozen times or more. Our requirements became more complex. I wanted Megan to be able to walk Fig into the stream from any angle she chose, turn her sideways, walk along the streambed, and then choose an exit point and have Fig walk calmly out. Click and jackpot!

PREPARATION IS THE KEY

Megan was learning how to apply the lessons she had worked on at home to real-world conditions. To ride out in safety you need to understand the basics so well that they stay with you even in an emergency. If your horse spooks at a sudden noise in the underbrush, your hand is on the rein asking him to yield his hips over before you even know it. You don't have to think. You just do it. That's how automatic you want your response to be.

That's only half the process. The other half is remembering to bring your whole training toolbox along with you. If your horse becomes emotionally unglued out on the trail, your job is to remember what you did on those first rides back at the barn, when he was every bit as anxious about getting back to the gate. You need to remember the hip-flip lesson where you discovered that you didn't have to let your horse drag you off. You need to remember the "calm down cue" to ask your horse to drop his head. You also need to know how to keep him from overflexing and disconnecting his feet from your reins. You need to know how to be a post and a hotwalker. You need to remember what you're supposed to do, and you will because you've practiced these exercises hundreds of times at home. Out on the trail when your horse is beginning to feel like a wound up coil about to explode, you'll know how to diffuse the situation. Your tools will work because you've laid a good foundation and you've remembered to use them.

Preparation: that's the key to every step of the training. Once you understand that, it's easy to ride in the real world.

CHAPTER 35
Piaffe

In this summing-up chapter I'll show you how all the lessons in this book build towards piaffe, one of the movements of advanced collection. To illustrate this lesson I'll share with you the story of Magnat, a "one in ten million" horse.

PIAFFE

Bob Bailey, one of the great pioneers of clicker training, has described the clicker as both the most forgiving and the least forgiving of training methods. How can it be both?

In the hands of a recreational pet owner clicker training offers flexibility and kindness. And for a professional trainer it offers all that plus pin-point precision. By the time you are ready to train piaffe, you will understand what that laser-fine accuracy gives you. You will know that at this level if you are sloppy in your timing, your training will suffer. You will appreciate the sharpening of your eye and the quickening of your timing that clicker training creates. You will have learned to chunk down lessons, and you will have also learned to see the next step as it emerges.

As of this writing I have mobilized a handful of horses into piaffe, not a great number, and certainly not enough to make me anything more than a beginner at this level of training. For people not familiar with dressage, piaffe is a movement of advanced collection where the horse appears to trot in place. That sounds simple enough. Lots of horses "piaffe"—that is, they jig in place—when they're excited, but getting them to do it on cue, as a controlled, focused movement can take years of training.

Piaffe is more than simply getting a horse to pick up his feet in sequence, though that's a good beginning. In a true piaffe the horse mobilizes his hind quarters through a lowering of his hip angle. This allows his front end to elevate as he releases his back into a cadenced, energetic, and very vibrant movement; the horse should be deeply relaxed, but highly energized.

To piaffe correctly you need to teach your horse to engage his hindquarters, to soften and release his jaw, and to raise the base of his neck so his whole spine can release into the movement. The first horses I taught all understood how to work in-hand through the lateral movements of shoulder-in and haunches-in. In those pre-clicker days I crashed and bashed my way through these lessons and eventually managed to produce something resembling piaffe.

To teach piaffe these days I begin with the lessons of single-rein riding and, of course, the clicker. I use all the exercises described in this book to teach the horse to be light and to work on the release of the rein. When I pick up the reins, I want to feel no weight through them at all, just energy. It's a lovely sensation. The horse is mobilizing underneath you. You feel his power and energy, but at the same time every joint in his body is soft and relaxed, and his mind is totally focused on you.

This a great way to ride, but it's not natural (pg 105). What's natural for both the horse and the rider is to lean and to pull. When you

MAGNAT

Magnat at age twenty-seven: still a clicker superstar.

As I looked through all the photos I have of Magnat, this one seemed the most fitting for this last chapter. It's not a photo of piaffe, but one of enduring partnership. It illustrates one of the central themes of this book — that clicker training helps us keep our horses sound and working well for decades. Magnat came to me at age fourteen with a serious heart condition, but with good riding he has continued to be a clicker superstar well into his late twenties.

This photo was taken on New Year's Day, 2005. It celebrates the beginning of Magnat's tenth year with his owner Ann Edie. At the age of twenty-seven he still shows the beautiful carriage that makes him a "one in ten million" horse.

pick up the reins on "normal" horses, you feel the weight of their bodies dragging against you. Resistance creates wear and tear on joints. Over time it creates pain which is the root cause of most riding issues. So it doesn't matter whether your goal is to just ride down the trail or to strut your stuff in a show ring, learning "unnatural riding" makes good horse sense (Ch. 18, 29).

The beginning place for all horses is the same. You start by teaching your horse to give and soften through one side of his body at a time (Ch. 19, 25). Safety always comes first. If your horse has soundness or behavioral problems, you deal with those (Ch. 27). After that, whatever your performance goals are, single-rein riding will help you get there.

If your goal is collection, it becomes especially important that you work your horse very systematically. You are only ever asking your horse (and the rider) to learn one thing at a time. You start by teaching your horse to soften and move his jaw in the direction you want. The more times you ask your horse to give in his jaw, the deeper into his body he is going to release (pg. 159). It's a really wonderful approach to riding. Dressage in particular can become very technical and complicated. With single-rein riding and the clicker you can chunk the training down into very small, manageable steps that become the building blocks for all kinds of advanced work.

How do these building blocks create upper-level performance? The answer lies in understanding that the most important difference between a young horse just starting out and a trained horse is that the later understands the basics better. Think of a Lego set: you only need a few basic shapes to put together an endless array of exciting structures. That's how training works as well.

INTRODUCING MAGNAT

Magnat is a beautiful gray Arabian, a true story-book horse. He was fourteen when I first met him in 1992. He belonged to clients of mine who wanted to do recreational trail riding. They found him out west on a business trip and fell in love.

The first time I sat on Magnat, he felt like a dream horse. His original trainer had given him an excellent foundation. He was soft; he was light; he had beautiful gaits: he was the perfect dressage horse. The trouble was he was a disaster out on trails.

My clients wanted Magnat for their weekend guests, many of whom were non-riders. When the lead horses galloped off without him, Magnat had emotional meltdowns of nuclear proportions. I began to hear Magnat horror stories whenever I visited. Even the more experienced riders were beginning to shy away from him.

On top of his behavioral problems, Magnat's physical condition began to deteriorate. Over the summer he lost weight and his coat turned dull. He had a stark, drawn look to him. He wasn't the same beautiful horse who had come off the trailer just a few short months before. My clients were beginning to question whether he was the right horse for them. They could see that their needs didn't match his, but they weren't exactly sure what was best for him.

That's when I stepped in and asked that he be sent to me for a month of training and evaluation. I was assuming that this was simply a case of a nice horse in the wrong job. I had ridden Magnat. He was a super horse, but he was also the proverbial square peg being forced into a round hole. The stories I kept hearing just didn't match up with the horse I knew he could be.

During the first week he was with me, I kept thinking, "there's something wrong with this horse." When I rode him, his back end just didn't feel right. I knew he had fallen a few weeks before out on the trails. His rider had taken a wrong turn up a slope that turned into nothing but sheer rock. Mag had lost his footing and gone down hard. I also knew that he'd been badly kicked by another horse out in the pasture. I was beginning to wonder if some of Magnat's overall problems weren't due to lameness.

I had my vet check him. We started with a routine exam. His back end felt so draggy to me, I was sure that's where the problem was. We went through all the standard flexion tests. We found nothing. We lunged him, we circled him, we jogged him up and down. Nothing.

As a final thought my vet brought out his stethoscope and listened to Magnat's heart. Bingo! That was it. Mag had a heart murmur, and not just the little run-of-the-mill murmur many horses have. Mag had the kind that brings vet students running to listen with own their stethoscopes. No wonder he was washing out and falling on the trail rides. No wonder he looked so terrible and had no energy. Magnat's heart simply couldn't pump enough oxygen to his muscles to sustain that kind of strenuous exercise.

I called his owners and gave them the news. The murmur had apparently been caused by an upper respiratory infection, and the virus had lodged in his heart. We did an ultrasound, and it showed growths that looked like little cauliflowers blocking his valves. Magnat's owners were in a terrible position. It was clear they couldn't ask him to be a trail horse, but they also didn't feel comfortable selling a

Chapter Thirty-Five: Piaffe

horse with this kind of physical handicap. Mag could probably do light ring work, mostly at the walk, but they weren't interested in that kind of riding. And who else would want a horse with a bad heart? The answer was that I would. I needed a school horse, and most of the lessons I would use him for could be done in the walk. Mag and I were a perfect match for each other.

A CHANGE OF CAREERS
So Magnat became my lesson horse, but first we had a little reschooling to do. The first time I rode Mag in the indoor arena he balked halfway down the long side and spun 180 degrees around. He whirled so fast that I wondered if he had any cutting-horse training in his ranch background. When I turned him back, he threatened to rear, so we rode a long series of "squashed road kill" figure eights (Ch. 16).

As I recall it took about two hours, but by the end of the session Magnat was taking me straight down the center line to stand by the back door. Within another session or two, the balkiness had diminished to a slight hesitation as he approached the far corner of the arena. If I rode him forward through the corner, he would relax and be fine for the rest of the ride.

After about two weeks of reschooling, I could put anyone up on him and know he'd take care of them. Mag might have been over-faced by beginners out on the trails, but in the ring he was a perfect gentleman. The work agreed with him. He put on weight. He lost the scruffy look to his coat. His eyes brightened. I was fast discovering that he was an enormously gifted horse and a wonderful teacher. Magnat had found his niche.

The following spring I took on a new client, Ann Edie. Ann brought a new challenge into my life: teaching a blind rider. When we started together I had no idea what would be possible, or how far we could go, but as always the principles of good training helped me out. Safety is always my number one concern, so I started with Ann where I start all new riders—I put her on a lead line. After a couple of introductory position lessons, we started in on the foundations of single-rein riding.

This was a learning process as much for me as it was for her. I knew I relied heavily on visual cues to tell me when to release the rein, so one of my first questions was how would Ann know when Magnat had done something right. Would a drop of the head feel different to her than a give to the side? Apparently the answer was yes, because Ann consistently released the rein at just the right moment.

We started with head lowering and gradually added in other lessons. We went through the I-know-an-old-lady-who-swallowed-a-fly jaw softenings (pg. 159) and the three training turns (Chapter 31). In that early stage we had two major training issues. The first was Magnat's lingering tendency to spook out of the far corner of the arena. This behavior had all but disappeared after his first week or two with me, but with the more tentative lesson students it would resurface at the start of a ride. It was an unpleasant hole in his otherwise exemplary behavior.

Our other issue was Ann's extreme stiffness on her left side. Her left arm was the arm she used to hold her guide dog. Guide dogs are taught to pull, so for Ann lightness on that side had become a foreign concept. I wanted her to let go, but she wanted to hold on tight. When Magnat tensed up in the far end, the last thing she wanted to do was release the rein. Her tension naturally made him more nervous, which, of course, just made her hold on even tighter.

If you want to unlock stiffness in either a horse or a rider, single-rein riding is the way to go. I know that at times Ann wondered why I was putting her on what seemed to her like such a nervous horse, but they were actually a good match for each other. As Ann released the tension in her body, Mag relaxed and gave up the tension in his.

Once or twice a week I'd get on and have some fun with Magnat. It was a pleasure to ride such a gifted athlete. Magnat breezed through things other horses struggled with. If only he didn't have a heart condition, I kept saying to myself, there'd be no limit to what he could do. I didn't know yet about the power of clicker training.

Magnat was my only full-time school horse, but because of his heart murmur I always tried to limit the number of riders who used him. I soon found myself reserving him primarily for Ann. They had become such a solid team that I wanted to be sure he was always fresh for her rides.

With the basics mastered, we started in on lateral work. Ann learned how to ask him to connect each foot to the reins (pg. 165). She could pick up either rein and ask each individual foot to step in any direction she wanted—left, right, front, back. She learned how to take Magnat sideways into a shoulder-in or haunches-in bend (Ch. 33) using just a single rein, and then she started to ask him to engage fully through his body onto two reins (Ch. 32).

MAGNAT MEETS PIAFFE
Magnat taught himself to piaffe, or at least that's how it seemed. I was giving an introductory lesson

to a young rider. As usual with a new rider, I started on a lead line. Mag was feeling crooked to me, so I positioned him against the wall and asked him to bring his hocks more underneath his body. I was asking for straightness and engagement. Mag gave me what I wanted plus a little bit more. He started to mobilize behind.

Magnat was absolutely correct. I had lined him up in the position a trained horse would be in if you were going to ask for piaffe. He had all the pieces, had learned all the subroutines. What he did now was combine them to give me the next layer in the training—piaffe. They weren't clean steps of piaffe, but they were a clear attempt to mobilize both hips.

I clicked and gave him a huge jackpot. His young rider didn't have a clue what was going on. I was emptying handfuls of grain into Mag's mouth, and as far as this rider was concerned, the horse had just taken a couple of rabbitty, not very comfortable steps forward—what was all the fuss about? I tried to explain what was going on as I set Magnat up for another request. He mobilized again. Now his rider was interested. This was a neat feel, and being told that he was riding advanced training got his attention.

REWIRING BASIC INSTINCTS

Horses will naturally do a version of piaffe when they're excited or feeling stressed. You see it in horses jigging down the trail or prancing at the in-gate before a competition. In many ways a piaffe is nothing more than a controlled explosion. The difference is that we want it to feel relaxed. That's where the clicker comes in. The challenge in training is to have the brain say "I'm relaxed" even though the body is saying "I'm excited." Piaffe isn't just about getting the legs to move in the right sequence. It's really a reprogramming of the horse's basic flight instinct. I can say to a horse: "Lower your head and relax." That's easy. Head lowering is a direct trigger for the mental state of relaxation. On his own a horse is only going to drop his head when he feels safe. All the time he's grazing with his head down, feelings of pleasure and relaxation are being linked to that body position. When you get a horse to drop his head in training, you're tapping into a strongly conditioned emotional response.

Piaffe is different. Now I'm saying, "Stay in this posture that normally triggers a surge of nervous energy, only stay relaxed." That's the challenge this highly collected movement presents.

Magnat normally shows tremendous self-control when he's carrying a rider. He knows he's supposed to be calm when he works. He doesn't spook at strange sounds or fly around the arena snorting and flagging his tail the way he would if he were loose. So when he started to piaffe, it worried him. He was sure he was doing something wrong. He would start to mobilize, and then he'd tense up. I could almost feel him thinking, "I'm not supposed to be doing this." But before he could work himself into a tizzy, I would click even the smallest suggestion of a piaffe. That stopped him in his tracks. "You wanted that!!?" he seemed to be asking.

I answered his question by positioning him again. He mobilized—I clicked: big handout and lots of praise. Three clicks later I was getting consistent steps of piaffe. Magnat was catching on at lightening speed.

The key to triggering piaffe with Magnat was being able to reward specific criteria clearly and precisely. As he lowered his hip angle and released his hind leg up into the mobilization of his joints, I clicked. The clicker gave us two things: it let me mark the exact moment in his stride that I wanted to reinforce, and it gave Magnat a reason to reproduce that moment over and over again.

ONE IN TEN MILLION

It is because I want to work at this high level of collection that I'm so interested in clicker training. For me this is what the click is really all about. Yes, you can solve basic behavioral problems and safety issues with it, but where it really shines is teaching the precision work of upper-level performance.

Magnat showed me this so clearly. I got him when I was first experimenting with clicker training. I was using the clicker with my own horse, Peregrine, and with most of my clients' horses, but initially I didn't teach it to my own school horse! A standard riding exercise had solved his far-end-itis arena problems. And other than that, Mag was so good that I really didn't think he needed clicker training. That only shows how wrong I can be! But Magnat was working well, and I was busy. My training time was limited: in other words, I had all the standard excuses.

It finally got to the point where Magnat was the only horse I was working with who wasn't clicker trained. That just didn't seem right, so I set aside some time and taught him to touch a target. That was one of the best training decisions I have ever made. Magnat has shown me more about the value of clicker training than just about any other horse I've worked with.

I didn't need the clicker to teach Magnat the basics of good riding. He came knowing these, but he didn't know the *perfection* of the basics. That's where the clicker came in. I used to say that Magnat was a one in a million horse. Now I say that he's one in ten million. That's the difference that clicker training has made.

SIMPLE MATH
In a very real sense, Magnat taught himself piaffe. I wasn't asking for it. I was looking for straightness and engagement. He combined my requests and made the leap himself. With a few single-rein riding exercises he had learned to engage both his left and his right side. It's as though he had learned to do simple addition. Soften to the left rein: two plus two equals four. Soften to the right rein: two plus two equals four on that side as well. What Mag discovered on his own was the times sign. Now four times four equaled sixteen, and we had something much greater than a simple sum of the two halves—we had full mobilization of the hindquarters. And Magnat hadn't just found the times sign. Without any direct instruction from me, he'd also figured out what to do with it.

The clicker let us complete the equation. The instant I recognized what was happening I was able to capture the moment. Those first tentative steps of mobilization didn't look like much of anything. I could have dismissed them entirely as simply a ragged attempt to engage. Instead I pounced on them with a jackpot and shaped them into something special. Where did we go from there? I worked him in-hand with Ann aboard, and over the next few sessions we stabilized the piaffe into an organized movement. By working small segments and clicking good moments, we helped Mag internalize the criteria we were after and link them to a rider's cues. His piaffe became very elevated and exceptionally beautiful.

THE CANTER CLICKER–STYLE
Why would we bother teaching piaffe to an older horse, and especially a horse with a heart condition? To some extent the answer is the same mountain climbers give—because it's there. Magnat has a beautiful piaffe. He really lowers his hip and gets very elevated in his hock action. He's a joy to watch in the movement. The piaffe opened the door to the canter. Once he was mobilized in-hand, I found I could also canter him in-hand. I could position him for a canter depart and walk next to him while he gave me a beautifully round and collected canter.

As a school horse, Magnat is worth his weight in gold simply because he can canter in-hand. Watching a novice rider learn to canter, even on the best of school horses, can be a nerve-jangling process for an instructor. The rider doesn't yet have the feel of the canter in her body. She may be giving the gross signals for the canter, but all the subtleties are missing. The horse doesn't really know what's wanted, so he rushes forward into a fast trot. The rider starts bouncing and grabbing at the reins. If the horse does manage to break into the canter, it's a rag-tag affair that scares many riders so they clutch even harder. At this point the solid-citizen school horses will fall out of the canter into a bone jarring trot, and the not-so-steady horses will blast forward with their eyes bugging out. It's a close call at that point who's more tense—the horse, the rider, or the instructor watching all this.

I wanted to avoid that scenario with Ann and Magnat. I didn't need them scaring each other and developing bad habits, so I started them out in-hand. Magnat's soft-as-butter canter helped Ann relax into the motion of his back. Because they skipped over the carnival-ride stage of an unbalanced horse, Ann was able to develop a superb seat at the canter.

EVERYTHING IS EVERYTHING ELSE
So how do you teach the canter in-hand and other advanced work to a horse? You come at it like a crab—sideways. You build the layers one by one, knowing that all the time you're working on these simple exercises you're really schooling advanced training. There isn't an exercise in this book that I haven't used with Magnat many times over. The result is an extraordinary horse with extraordinary talent.

If you're thinking I haven't told you the specific steps for teaching piaffe or the canter in-hand, go back and reread that last paragraph. The training steps are simple and can be summed up in one short phrase: perfect the basics. That's really all there is to training.

RIDING MAGNAT
In October of 1996 I gave Magnat to Ann. It is now 2005. Magnat is twenty-seven, and he is still in full work. Because he works without fear or tension, his heart condition has become a non-issue. His piaffe has matured into a beautiful movement, and his gaits are simply breathtaking to watch. He is truly a one in ten million horse.

One of my desires in writing this book was to share with you what it is like to ride a clicker-trained horse, so I asked Ann to write about her experience with Magnat. What she has written expresses perfectly what it is like to ride these horses. It is my hope that you will find as much joy in your horses as we have found in ours.

RIDING MAGNAT

While contemplating the question – what is it like to ride Magnat? – I happened to be listening to a group of musicians on the radio discussing the question: what makes a melody great? The answers they came up with contained some technical elements, but they soon resorted to metaphorical phrases and intangible comparisons, such as the great melody "fits the breath," and the great melody "resonates with the heart."

I find myself in much the same dilemma as these musicians in trying to describe the experience of riding a truly extraordinary horse who has had the benefit of several years of clicker training. Although many technical components go into the production of a really memorable ride, the irrepressible smile, feeling of wonder, and expression of "WOW!!" that arises so regularly these days when I ride Magnat simply cannot be described in anything but poetic terms.

Yes, athletic talent and neuromuscular conditioning are part of what makes the ride so special; and yes, many hours of repetition and drill over many months have gone into it; and yes, there is extraordinary lightness and balance. But this is still far from the sum total of the experience.

One of the musicians described the great melody as "a journey which has many familiar passages, and which also contains some wonderful surprises which cause you to look at the world in a completely fresh way and gives new meaning to life." This is the best description I can find of what it is like to ride Magnat.

Magnat comes out into the arena every night feeling relaxed and eager to work. He knows he will be appreciated and rewarded for his performance. He knows that he is a respected dance partner and member of the team, not a mere subject of training. This awareness and active participation on the part of the horse is one of the benefits bestowed by clicker training.

Our rides begin with simple warm-up exercises. In the course of executing figures or doing some softening and balancing work, I will pick up the reins and suddenly feel the most indescribable lightness!!!

We may be in a super-buoyant, floating trot, a deliberate, balanced, ballet-like piaffe, or a heavenly rocking-horse canter. Whatever it is, it will feel as though I am floating on a magic carpet. He is so responsive in these moments. It's as if there are clear filaments of two-way communication from my finger tips to each of Magnat's feet. The slightest breath of a touch on one of those lines will be answered by an immediate floating response.

The musicians described music as a journey which "contains some wonderful surprises." That's how I feel about riding Magnat. Each ride contains surprises and special pleasures we have not experienced before. It is like coming around a bend in the road and seeing a spectacular sunset, or a grove of awe-inspiring redwood trees, or the grandeur of an ancient castle, or the peace and cool of a Buddhist temple. It truly takes the breath away! It creates the deepest joy and aliveness in my heart! It causes a persistent smile and an expression of "AH!" to arise.

These moments have totally changed the way I think about riding. I feel such awe for Magnat and for what we create together. In this moment I know, without the slightest doubt, exactly what I ride for— it is just this amazing feeling of total balance, effortlessness, lightness, and energy. Magnat seems to feel the same excitement and joy, for he literally beams with pride, and recently he has begun uttering deep chortles in his throat at these moments.

I let the magic moment go on for as long as I dare, wanting it to continue forever, but knowing I must capture it with a click, before it disappears like a soap bubble or a delicious dream.

The click creates a pause in the music. Magnat comes to a halt; I throw my arms around his neck in a huge hug, shower him with lavish praise, and empty my pockets of the most desirable treats!

The "WOW" feeling is definitely addictive. The glow of the experience lingers and stays with me long after the ride. Our whole human-horse relationship is one of appreciation, respect, and awe.

This is, for me, the great gift of clicker training. When taken to the high-performance level, it creates transcendent moments of great joy.

—Ann Edie

ASSEMBLING THE CENTAUR

These pages are packed. I don't expect you to be able to process all the material in this book the first time through. As you reread the book, some phrase that didn't mean anything to you before will suddenly jump off the page. You'll see an exercise that seemed almost too trivial to bother with and realize it's the key to unlocking the next big layer in your horse's training.

One of the advantages of teaching is that I get to go over the same basic exercises many, many times. Each new client gives me a chance to review what's in my toolbox. I may be teaching the same beginning step I was teaching six months before, but I always learn something new each time I revisit a lesson. As I've said many times, all you really have in training are a few basic building blocks. Putting them together into advanced work is easy once you understand the pieces. When you work with only one or two horses, you sometimes forget how important it is to go back and review the foundation exercises. So what follows are a few final thoughts to summarize where we've been.

CLICKING YOURSELF

Before I ride, I fill my pockets full of appreciation. That's what the treats I feed my horse represent. Each time I click, I'm providing him with information: "That step you just took was a good one" or "I liked the extra lift I just felt in your back."

Appreciation is information, and it turns into love. With the clicker I'm not just telling Peregrine and Robin that they did something that will get reinforced, I'm also thanking them for a job well done. Peregrine has no natural lifting power in his back. He has bad stifles and damaged feet, and yet he gives me the most extraordinary work. A pat on the neck just isn't enough to thank him. Appreciation. That's what the peppermints and the carrots represent. Appreciation and a thank-you for being such a great teacher.

The clicker is also appreciation for me. It's not just Peregrine who's getting it right. Each time I click it means I've also figured something out. I got my balance right so Peregrine could respond with his. You need to remember that. The clicker is not a one-way line of communication. Your horse is your partner. Each click is for both of you. Your horse may get the peppermint, but you both get the appreciation.

DR. DOOLITTLE

Beginning with the very basic steps outlined in this book, I've tried to explain how to talk to your horse. No, I don't mean like Dr. Doolittle, through a spoken language, but kinesthetically, through your body.

Peregrine understands this kinesthetic language. He answers me not with words, but with behavior. We carry on conversations that are rich and wonderful. People watching see the outward show of our conversation. They see soft canter departs or a seamless transition into half-pass. They see piaffe or a perfect square halt.

What I experience is the delicious give and take of an intimate and intense conversation with a partner I have come to know and trust deeply.

Both Peregrine and Robin have learned to listen and respond to me not because they are afraid of the painful consequences of disobedience, but because they are anticipating the pleasure of their rewards. The click and the reinforcement that follows are like exclamation marks bringing attention to a job well done. They love their treats, but what they really work for is the conversation itself. I feel that in everything we do together.

My hope with this book is that clicker training will bring you to a similar place of trust and understanding with your own horses. Remember there are no limits. As you explore the many layers of clicker training, you will understand the true meaning of those words.

Have fun on your journey!

APPRECIATION

Before I ride, I fill my pockets full of appreciation. That's what the treats I feed my horse represent. Each time I click, I'm providing my horse with information: "That step you just took was a good one" or "I liked the extra lift I just felt in your back."

Appreciation is information, and it turns into love. With the clicker I'm not just telling Peregrine he did something that will get reinforced, I'm also thanking him for a job well done.

The Click That Teaches: Riding With The Clicker

BOOKS AND VIDEOS:

Clicker Training For Your Horse, by Alexandra Kurland; Sunshine Books, US and Ringpress books, UK

The Click That Teaches: A Step–By–Step Guide in Pictures, by Alexandra Kurland; The Clicker Center, NY

The Click That Teaches: Video Lesson Series:
  An Introduction to Clicker Training
  Lesson 1: Getting Started with the Clicker
  Lesson 2: Ground Manners
  Lesson 3: Head–Lowering: Your Calm–Down Cue
  Lesson 4: Stimulus Control: Putting Behavior on Cue

All the books and videos are available from:

The Clicker Center
110 Salisbury Rd.
Delmar, NY 12054

theclickercenter.com

ABOUT THE AUTHOR:

Alexandra Kurland earned her degree from Cornell University where she specialized in animal behavior. She has been teaching and training horses since the mid-1980's. A pioneer in the development of humane training methods, Kurland began clicker training in the early 1990's. She very quickly recognized the power of clicker training for improving performance, for enhancing the relationship people have with their horses, and for just plain putting fun back into training. Today through her books, videos, clinics, and many articles, she has become a leading voice in the development of clicker training in the horse community.

ACKNOWLEDGEMENTS

My special thanks to all the people and horses whose photos appear in this book: Bob Viviano and Crackers, Tam Mrose and Mariah, Debra Olson Daniels and June Bug, Katie Bartlett and Willie, Julie Varley and Allie, Amy Lacy and Pal, Julie Varley with Ann Edie's Icelandic stallion Sindri, Kathy Santola and her Friesians, Barbara Melville and Brittany, Kate Graham and Lucky, Val Pape, Elaine Bates and Ceasar, Sandy Atchinson and Nikita, Leslie Peeples and Bri's, Monique Hammerslag and Trixie, Donna Garlock, Alicia Recore and Sahib, Patti Sanborn and Eli, Becky Jarvis and Mac, Debra Olson Daniels and Magic, Julie Jacobs and Aimee, Lucia Coleman and Sun, Janet Carruthers and Cody, Ilse DeWit and Sindra, Kelly Hotaling and Fred, Marla Foreman and Dublin, Lisanne Pearcy, Sidney Manzanita, Mary Arena and Tibra, Sharon Kallaji and MissFire, Lin Sweeney and Scotch, Megan Roy and Fig, Ann Edie and Magnat.

My thanks also to all of you who I have met at clinics and in lessons. Thank you for your willingness to explore with me this style of training. It is out of our work together that this road map has evolved. Thank you to my local clients for your patience while I worked on this book. I know how tired you are of hearing that things have to wait until after the riding book is finished. Well, here it is, finally!!!

My thanks also to Bettina Drummond who showed me how beautiful horses can be, and to John Lyons. Many of the lessons in this book are derived from his training. And a special thank you to Karen Pryor who gave us all clicker training.

My thanks to everyone who helped with the photographs: Julie Varley, Debra Olson Daniels, Julie Jacobs, Ann Edie, Bob Viviano, Melissa Alexander, Kathy Santola. and all the others who participated in the seemingly endless number of photo sessions.

Many of the photos in this book were created from digital video. Still photos were extracted from the video using Final Cut Pro and Adobe Photoshop. When you pull photos in this manner from digital video, you lose a little in the quality of the image. What you gain hopefully is well worth the trade off. Working from video, I was able to capture the important details of each lesson and to show precisely the exact moment of the "click". This process represents many hundreds of hours of work. I wish to thank my family, my horses, and my friends for tolerating my disappearance into the computer over the past several years.

And as always my special thanks go to my clicker superstars, Peregrine and Robin, and to my beloved Pippin who taught me the core of all this work and for whom this book is dedicated.